The City in Literature

The City in Literature

An Intellectual and Cultural History

Richard Lehan

UNIVERSITY OF CALIFORNIA PRESS

Berkeley / Los Angeles / London

University of California Press
Berkeley and Los Angeles, California

University of California Press, Ltd.
London, England

© 1998 by
The Regents of the University of California

Library of Congress Cataloging-in-Publication Data
Lehan, Richard Daniel, 1930–
    The city in literature : an intellectual and cultural history /
Richard Lehan.
        p.   cm.
    Includes bibliographic references and index.
    ISBN 0-520–21042–5 (hardcover : alk. paper). —
ISBN 0-520-21256-8 (pbk. — alk. paper)
        1. Cities and towns in literature.   2. Literature, Modern—
        History and criticism.   I. Title.
    PN56.C55L44   1998
        809'93321732—dc21   97–3443

Printed in the United States of America
9 8 7 6 5 4 3 2 1

The paper used in this publication meets the minimum requirements of
American National Standard for Information Sciences—Permanence of
Paper for Printed Library Materials, ANSI Z39.48–1984.

In memory of
Edward Scott Lehan

To
thE city he
loveD
anD the
citY
he never knew

Over the great bridge . . . with the city rising up across the river in white heaps and sugar lumps all built with a wish out of non-olfactory money. The city seen from the Queensboro Bridge is always the city seen for the first time, in its first wild promise of all the mystery and the beauty in the world.

A dead man passed us in a hearse heaped with blooms.

F. Scott Fitzgerald

When the stanger says: "What is the meaning of this city?

Do you huddle close together because you love each other?"

What will you answer? "We all dwell together

To make money from each other"?

T. S. Eliot

The police force would have to be doubled when the stars started to arrive. At the sight of their heroes and heroines, the crowd would turn demoniac. . . . New groups, whole families, kept arriving. He could see a change come over them as soon as they had become part of the crowd. . . . It was a mistake to think them harmless curiosity seekers. They were savage and bitter, especially the middle-aged and old, and had been made so by boredom and disappointment. . . . They realize that they've been tricked and burn with resentment. Every day of their lives they read the newspapers and went to the movies. Both fed them on lynchings, murder, sex crimes, explosions, wrecks, love nests, fires, miracles, revolutions, wars. . . . Nothing can ever be violent enough to make taut their slack minds and bodies.

Nathanael West

Lo! Death has reared himself a throne

In a strange city lying alone

Far down within the dim West[.]

Edgar Allan Poe

Contents

Illustrations

Preface and Acknowledgments

This study came about after I had completed books on F. Scott Fitzgerald and Theodore Dreiser and had become aware of how important the city was to the modernist imagination. At that time I encountered Lewis Mumford's *The City in History* and saw the usefulness of a sequel dealing with "the city in literature." Originally this book was to be a study of the modernist city—from Pound and Eliot and Joyce to Thomas Pynchon. But the more I learned about modernism, the more convinced I became that I could not separate the modern experience from the experience of antiquity that is often overlayed in modernist texts. And the more I studied modernism, the more I became aware of what it owed to romanticism, and in what ways both movements, along with postmodernism, were questioning Enlightenment assumptions.

This study has in part been written against the grain of prevailing critical theory. When I was in graduate school, the New Criticism competed with influence studies. I was never fully satisfied with either approach: I saw how limited was an approach that reduced one text to the influence of another, and I thought a lot was left out when texts were measured primarily by their supposed ambiguity and paradox. Even when critics like Lionel Trilling moved us toward cultural study, I felt that a strong bias toward Matthew Arnold and Henry James—toward an aesthetic reality and upper-class consciousness—excluded the reality of (say) Theodore Dreiser, never mind more popular forms of expression. I had no desire to reverse the hierarchy. What I wanted was a methodology that would account for the "reality" that the text itself had created.

Structuralism and poststructuralism seemed to take us even further away
from the material text, and phenomenology and the New Historicism
were hardly corrective movements. I found many texts being read in a
distorting context: Dreiser through Heidegger or naturalism through an
extended trope like the gold standard, which distorted a biological system by turning it into economics. Much of this theory—from structuralism to deconstructionism—was rooted in linguistic assumptions.
While we obviously cannot get into a literary text other than through its
language, I did not feel that a literary text should be reduced to only its
language, or be connected through language with some lost ideal (in
America usually Emersonian), or have its meaning manufactured solely
by the critic. When the text was not the product of classroom invention,
it was in a world elsewhere.[1]

My reservations were perhaps ungenerous, since I learned much from
the criticism that I resisted. But I often wondered what would happen if
texts were grounded in a theory of place—especially the three "kinds" of
places that dominate in literary study: the city, the estate, and the road.
And I further wondered what happened as these places changed under
the force of history. Thus, although this is not a book about literary or
other kinds of theory, it did emerge out of thoughts about critical in-
quiry. The desire to create a material text and to root such a text in an intellectual and cultural tradition—that is, in history—led to the way that
I first conceptualized the city.

At first I was satisfied to abstract an urban "reality" from different
texts. But soon I realized the problem was more complex than one that
suggested that Defoe believed "this," Melville "that." Each was working
with narrative conventions that pre-textualized a work and gave rise to
literary movements. When such conventions became trite, they were
often parodically dismissed, at which time more original devices (such as
those by Joyce and T. S. Eliot) came into play. Before he took us into his
narrative maze, Roland Barthes told us that there is no Realism—only
realisms, that each novel creates its own system of reality. If this were so
then the image of the city that emerged from these texts would also be
part of a larger narrative reality. How then to get at these divergent rep-
resentations, or what in this book I term "re-presentations"? Over a period of time I formulated a theory of narrative modes, which took me
from the rise of the novel to comic realism, romantic realism, natural-

---

1. See Stanley Fish, *Is There a Text in This Class?* (1980), and Richard Poirier, *A World
Elsewhere* (1966).

ism, modernism, and postmodernism—each mode offering a radically different view of reality, including a radically different view of the city. I came to see that literary elements were reconceptualized in the face of historical and cultural change, including the commercial, industrial, and postindustrial realms through which the city evolved. Thus, as literature gave imaginative reality to the city, urban changes in turn helped transform the literary text. This shared textuality—this symbiosis between literary and urban text—became the methodological basis for this book.

My interest in the city took me in a slightly different direction. The city had become such an impressive monument in Western civilization that it came as a surprise to see the intellectual resentment it had generated. In Europe, such resentment was embodied by Jean Jacques Rousseau; in America, by Jefferson. Even though Jefferson's vision of the city had long been eclipsed by that of Hamilton's, the Jeffersonian ideal still dominated the views of Pound, Fitzgerald, Faulkner, Dos Passos, and the Southern agrarians. Fitzgerald was wise enough to see that an ideal had been located in an exhausted past, and that an American like Gatsby was fated to play out this situation tragically. Others on both sides of the Atlantic saw the city give rise to a radical individualism that in turn gave way to mass man; they saw the dangers inherent in the crowd, which could quickly turn into a mob—each an unpredictable threat in an era when the nation-state fought against totalitarianism. The city, once an Enlightenment ideal, was being questioned in romantic, modern, and postmodern thought. A sense of being at home in the city was replaced by its opposite—the "unhomely," expressed as the uncanny and often embodied by the outsider, the Other, the mysterious stranger, or the lonely man in the crowd, all anticipated by the Dionysus figure. The wilderness may have given way to the city, but what was wild in nature was never fully repressed by the city, and this book became a study of what was both overt and hidden in the urban maze.

In the course of working on this book, I have incurred many debts and obligations: I should like to thank the Guggenheim Foundation for a fellowship in 1978–79 and the University of California for a President's Fellowship in 1988–89. I am grateful to all the libraries, literally around the Western world, that helped so generously with my reading needs, especially the staff at the UCLA University Research Library; my thanks also to the Frances Loeb Library, Graduate School of Design, Harvard

University, for help with illustrations. I am indebted to those who so generously read parts or all of this mansucript in its various stages: Edward Callahan, Robert Kruse, and Vincent Pecora. I am grateful to people whose conversations and correspondence helped more than they could have known, especially Denis Donoghue and Ray Ryan. And I am equally grateful to those who encouraged me to work through my ideas as papers for conferences or contributions to books and journals, particularly Donald Pizer. I should also like to thank those in the English Department at UCLA for their assistance, most notably Jeanette Gilkison—and those at the University of California Press for encouragement and help, especially James Clark and William Murphy. For help with editing and proofreading, my thanks to Robert Metzger, Alice Falk, and Erika Büky. Writing a book of this nature is a long process; it would have been a much more lonely experience without the love and companionship of my wife Ann.

PART I

Reading the City/
Reading the Text

CHAPTER I

The City and the Text

I

The city has determined our cultural fate for the last three hundred years—has become inseparable from our personal and national destiny. As the product of the Enlightenment, urbanism is at the very heart of Western culture, the source both of political order and of social chaos. As such, the city is also the source of intellectual excitement and challenge. That is what this book is about: the ways the city has been conceptualized from its origin to the present time. The emphasis is upon the rise of the modern city as an Enlightenment construct and the literary and cultural response to that idea—the dissenting paradigms—from the eighteenth century to the present.

I arrive at the city as an evolving construct by superimposing urban upon literary modes and vice versa. I see the modern city evolving through three stages of development—a commercial, industrial, and "world stage" city. I also see the rise of the city as inseparable from various kinds of literary movements—in particular the development of the novel and subsequent narrative modes: comic realism, romantic realism, naturalism, modernism, and postmodernism. These modes, in turn, contain subgenres like the utopian novel, the gothic novel, the detective story, the young-man-from-the-provinces novel, the novel of imperial adventure, the western, science fiction, and dystopian narratives. In charting the development of these literary currents, my account is largely, but not totally, chronological. It is also spatial, as I move from Europe (concentrating on London and Paris) to America (concentrating on New York) and then across the North American continent (ending with a discussion of Los Angeles).

The subject of the city is too complex to reduce to two or three themes; I have thus drawn many strands through this book, allowed loops of meaning to interconnect and interpenetrate. The annular structure of *The City in Literature* reflects the annular structure of cities themselves, involving a series of concentric circles. The inner circle traces the history of the city, especially the modern city; the outer circle concerns the way those cities have been represented; and the connecting circle involves literary and urban movements. Here we become familiar with literary concepts like modernism, in which the subject of the city becomes a defining issue.

When Christopher Wren drew up a plan (1666) for a new London with the Royal Exchange replacing St. Paul's cathedral as the new center, his idea only reflected what was happening in practice. Daniel Defoe gave us a portrait of this new city, an entity held together by commercial need. While Defoe welcomed the city as offering a new way of life to a new class of people, Dickens saw how this process had become so materialistic that it hardened the heart and diminished compassion, altering our sense of human scale, our sense of community. Dickens was a brilliant recorder of this urban transition; he reaffirmed a sense of community and tried to bring this world back to human scale through sentimental characters (who believe that the goodness of the heart can overcome the evil that it faces) and new urban observers like the detective. He also saw the need for new secular-holy places; home life became more unpredictable—the hearth was subject to the uncanny. Attempts to redeem the new city failed because anonymity had replaced community, sentiment evaporated within Chancery and the Circumlocution Office. Dickens, the last of the comic realists, believed in a world held together by a moral presence. As the world of the city became more complex, the Esther Summerson figure no longer functioned convincingly and comic realism was exhausted of meaning.

With the decline of the estate, the young sought their destiny in the city. There Balzac's aspiring heroes meet Vautrin, the new Napoleon, the man of power who becomes a law unto himself, anticipating Nietzsche's superman and Dostoyevsky's Raskolnikov. While Dickens treats the rise of the industrial city in *Hard Times,* that subject finds its most persuasive depiction in literary naturalism, especially that of Zola in Europe, Gissing and Moore in England, and Dreiser and Frank Norris in America. Zola captures the sweep of such change in his *Rougon-Macquart* novels, written between 1871 and 1893, but covering the period of the Second Empire (1851–71). While Zola treats the provinces, the center of these novels is Paris, to which his characters come in search of an essential self, and in search of power. Probably no modern writer better described the emergence of the new industrial city with its resulting proletariat. In America, Dreiser and Norris depicted the same forms of urban and industrial power, as the city moved toward empire.

While the romantics are often thought of as being unsympathetic to the city to the point of hostility, this is not completely true, as we see in romantic realism. Here a mythic construct is superimposed on the city to explain its meaning in symbolic, religious, or mystical terms. Modernism is the second stage of romanticism, the older view of the city transformed by new literary techniques. As the modernists move toward new forms of subjectivity, the meaning of the city becomes more dense, until we see the city through layers of historical meaning, or until it blurs into the opaque vision.

At the center of empire, demands were made on capital cities that weakened their center, as in the novels of Conan Doyle and Bram Stoker, driving other popular novelists like Rider Haggard back to primitive truths; this process was questioned by Joseph Conrad, who saw a thin line between the destructive element in both primitive and civilized societies, an element that the modern city tried to conceal. Both Conrad and T. S. Eliot saw the modern city in sepulchral terms, as a city of the dead, or at least in decline. Such a view was shared by social commentators like Max Nordau, Henry and Brooks Adams, Herman Hesse, and Oswald Spengler (and later Arnold Toynbee).

As the city became more materialistic, it engendered a hostility in the literary imagination—a hostility that went hand in hand with a distrust of Enlightenment values. From Ralph Waldo Emerson to Ralph Waldo Ellison, writers have depicted the material city cut off from a spiritual energy. Thomas Pynchon, however, entertained no such binary view: he emptied Eliot's past of mythical meaning, removed Defoe's transcendental signifiers, and set his characters in a perpetual present in which they were cut off from everything except the constant play of urban signifiers and cultural stimuli. A sense of the uncanny, a sense of mystery that the mind cannot fathom, is at work in Pynchon's city. Strange connections are made—perhaps the work of a paranoid mind, perhaps the work of urban conspiracy.

All of these urban visions suggest that beneath the surface of the modern city are forces at work as old as our origins. These forces have taken many shapes. Dionysus embodies the disruptive force in the city; his spirit is later embodied by the carnival, still later by the mysterious stranger and the man in the crowd, and again by Freud's theory of the uncanny as the return of the repressed. Natural disasters also threatened the city. And lastly, what the city cast off became another force that challenged it from within. The major writers and thinkers of the Western world have had to come to terms with the city, each era offering us an urban identity that reveals our secret cultural values. The urban drama played itself out against a Europe transformed by the Enlightenment, by an America that offered a New Jerusalem, and by a wilderness and a frontier against which the city assumed its meaning.

II

Urban history is a fairly recent discipline. One can find books that touch upon the idea of the city as early as Plato's *Republic* and Augustine's *City of God,* but these books are about the good life as it is affected by place. And one can find historical accounts of cities in texts like John Stow's portrayal of Renaissance London or Walter Besant's description of nineteenth-century London. But the first books that consider the city as a subject in and of itself were written by early sociologists like Max Weber, Emile Durkheim, and Georg Simmel.

The historians of the new city emphasized three ways of conceptualizing it. A number stressed the origins of the modern city. The most important of these commentators, Oswald Spengler and Lewis Mumford, see a short-circuiting process once the city becomes disconnected from the nourishing vitality of the land. Spengler took Simmel's description of the city and recast it as a form of agrarian mysticism. Contrasting country and city, he insisted that the roots of human life are in the soil. Cut off from a source of nourishment beyond itself, the city became a closed system, entropic, which led to the decline of civilization: instinct was sacrificed to reason, myth to scientific theories, barter and exchange to abstract theories of money. Other urban historians concentrated on what they believed were the physical laws of the modern city. Robert E. Park, for example, maintained that the city was externally organized in terms of laws of its own. His colleague Ernest W. Burgess illustrated this point when he insisted that the city grows in concentric rings. A third group of urban historians concentrated on the effect of the city on its inhabitants: what happens when the city becomes a state of mind. Spengler, as I have suggested, was interested in this problem, but he never gave it the systematic attention of Weber, Durkheim, and Simmel. Weber was primarily a social behaviorist. He saw the city in institutional terms and defined cities by their predominant function. Durkheim, on the other hand, believed that each city created a state of mind. Each culture, he insisted, established norms that regulated behavior; these norms were internalized as part of the individual's personality. He argued that the rise of Protestantism brought with it an emphasis upon individualism which, with the loss of the craftsman in the newly industrialized societies, led to a sense of alienation and of helplessness that increased the number of suicides. As the individual became more private, more autistic, modernism tried to find substitutes—through art, for example—for lost primitive impulses, especially for religious and communal beliefs. Simmel also created a typology of modern urban humanity that saw it subject to great nervous stimulation, which blunted feelings and created matter-of-fact ways of dealing with people. This in turn led to an emphasis upon roles in which human relations were secondary not primary, and a premium was put on utility and efficiency—that is, on an intelligence that could work the system at the expense of kinship or other ties. While Weber emphasized economic factors, Simmel emphasized the psychological. A shared belief among these emerging urbanists was that modern man, placed under great stress, feared becoming superfluous and anonymous.

As historians tried to explain the city through conceptual systems, writers of literature relied on imaginative systems. *The Waste Land* has an affinity to Spengler's conception of the modern city, and Dreiser's *Sister Carrie* has an affinity to Robert Park's model of the mechanical city. Eliot and Spengler concentrate on what happens to the city when it is cut off from a source of energy beyond itself, and Dreiser and Park concentrate on the physical laws that control this self-enclosed system. Simmel and Durkheim concentrate on the psychic effect of those laws when the city is seen more blindly from the inside out. In Pynchon's *The Crying of Lot 49* and *Gravity's Rainbow,* a sense of control gives way to the fear of the city as machine, its inhabitants becoming superfluous and anonymous, subject to great nervous tension as Strangelove technology adds rocketry to the bomb—they display a discontent that has its origins in what were once Enlightenment ideals.

As we move through the major writers who constitute this study, we see that the city and its literature share textuality—that the ways of reading literary texts are analogous to the ways urban historians read the city. Shared are constructs built on assumptions about the mechanistic, the organic, the historical, the indeterminate, and the discontinuous. From Defoe to Pynchon, reading the text has been a form of reading the city.

III

As the city becomes more complex as a physical structure, the ways of seeing it become more difficult and the individual more passive in relationship to it. The city came into being when a surplus of food allowed a diversity of tasks. Diversity is a key to urban beginnings and continuities, and diversity is also the snake in the urban garden, challenging systems of order and encouraging disorder and chaos. And as the city reached out into the hinterland and eventually beyond itself in the name of empire, more was demanded of the urban center. The industrial city brought with it urban pollution and slums: smokestacks became a way of life. The urban crowd, unstable and volatile, made city life increasingly unpredictable.

As the city was transformed according to its change of function, the center became more complex as both work and the population became diversified. Such diversity led inevitably to the "Other"—an urban element, usually a minority, deemed "outside" the community. But in mythic-symbolic terms, an embodiment of the Other is the mysterious stranger—the Dionysus figure in the early city, the mysterious man from nowhere, who disrupts the city from within. The cult or secret organization (like Pynchon's Tristero) has taken over that disruptive function in the postindustrial city. What the city casts off became another force that challenged it from within, as we see in T. S. Eliot's wasteland, F. Scott Fitzgerald's valley of ashes, and Thomas Pynchon's Tristero, as a sense of apocalypse gives way to entropy.

The city often presents itself metonymically, embodied by the crowd. We look through the crowd—whether Eliot's and Baudelaire's walking dead or the violent mob in Dickens, Zola, Dreiser, West, and Ellison—to the city. No matter how different the aggregate, the crowd dominates the urban fiction of both the nineteenth and twentieth centuries. In Sue's *The Mysteries of Paris,* Rodolph walks the street at night with his servant, follows a crowd, and ends up saving a young girl (who turns out to be his lost daughter) from harm. And in *The Crying of Lot 49,* Oedipa Maas picks the mail carrier out of the crowd and follows him through the streets of San Francisco until he takes her back to where her journey began, the zigzag duplicating the maze that makes up the postmodern city.

Each crowd offers a way of reading the city. In the scene from Sue, the observer is able to break through the anonymity of the crowd; in contrast, Oedipa finds the city unreadable, a system of signs that, self-reflexively, refer back to themselves, keeping the self within its own hermeneutic circle. From Defoe to Pynchon, the ways of reading the city offer clues to ways of reading the text, urban and literary theory complementing each other. Thus we can look to the city from its very origins to reveal a special meaning. The spectrum of such meanings—real and conjectured—is the subject of this book.

PART 2

Enlightenment Legacy

CHAPTER 2

From Myth to Mastery

I

The city is the place where man and nature meet. The city promises a way of regulating the environment, subduing the elements and allowing a certain control over nature. The earliest cities were established to meet the basic needs of their inhabitants—the need to worship, to feel protected, and to find solace in the community. At some point roughly five thousand years ago, wandering tribes felt the need to settle in a central place, perhaps a site where they could bury and worship their dead. Such a central location needed protection: thus the need for the fort. Most urban historians believe that the city could not have come into existence without a surplus of food, which enabled a diversification of work and social function. Such a surplus also led to trade with other communities. When oral transmission was inadequate or no longer within the powers of aged members, the city needed a recording system. The city thus emerged together with the development of writing, what Lewis Mumford calls "the permanent record" (*City in History,* 97).

The needs of the city gave rise to three primary institutions: the temple, the citadel or fort, and the market. In early hieroglyphics, the ideogram of the city consisted of a cross enclosed in a circle (Lopez, 27–28). The cross represented the convergence of roads; the circle, a wall or a moat, marked the space within which the citizens cohere and the space beyond which they need protection. The temple took its meaning from myths of the land that explain and purport to control the fertility of the earth, animals, and women. Even if the temple were controlled by a priest, its functions were connected with female processes of reproduction, and the temple was often inseparable from a goddess like Athena. The fort involved the world of men. Usually strategically located high on a hill (such as the acropolis in Athens) or at the entrance to a river or port, the fort presupposed a wall behind which the city could find protection. The crossroads, the place where the roads brought people together, revealed the human need to extend to others. It had sacred implications, clearly marked in literary works from Sophocles' *Oedipus Rex* to Dostoyevsky's *Crime and Punishment*. But eventually holy needs gave way to more mundane activity, and the crossroads became the marketplace or trade center within a trade route.

The crossroads were often the extension of riverways. Cities came into being in great river valleys: Euphrates and Tigris in Iraq, Nile in Egypt, Indus in Pakistan, and Hwang Ho (Yellow River) in China. Even in North America, where cities came late, this holds true: Montreal, New York, and San Francisco are at estuaries of major river systems, and each is the entrepot settlement from which a great valley—the St. Lawrence, Hudson, Central Valley—is tied to a larger economic world. The oldest cities in historical record are those located between the Euphrates and Tigris Rivers in Mesopotamia.

Wherever the river touched the land it brought life. Surrounded by farmland in river valleys, cities came about when masses of people settled to work fertile soil, and the earliest of mythologies acknowledge that the city takes its being from the flow of the river. Early Babylonian myths claim the city emerged out of water and chaos. In the beginning there was only Chaos and two kinds of water—freshwater (Apsu) and saltwater (Tiamat). Into this realm Lahmu and Lahamu are born and have children who comprise all of heaven and earth—a god of heaven (Anu), of air and earth (Enlil), and of water (Ea). Perhaps because they embody order, these gods attract the enmity of Apsu and Tiamat, which leads to a war in which Marduk (son of Ea) destroys Tiamat. This mythic story embodies the origins of the city. Once in place, the city is a power container, a source of material order and control. As in the story of Ea and Tiamat, however, chaos and order war with one another. Material institutions never quite contain the mythic; order never quite controls disorder.

From the earliest of times, the city contained both spiritual and material power. As a city became more powerful, it was often able to extend its power to its god, sometimes raising it to the top of a larger pantheon of gods; in turn the god gave authority to the king, who acted in its name. This is what happened in Babylon under Hammurabi (1792–1750 B.C.) when Marduk was raised to chief god. Like all shrewd rulers, Hammurabi claimed he ruled through the auspices of a god: the Code of Hammurabi was engraved on a black diorite stele, topped with a sculpture showing the king receiving the laws from Marduk. Marduk's supremacy was recognized by all the powers that eventually occupied Babylon—the Kassites, Assyrians, Chaldeans, Persians, and Macedonians. When Nebuchadnezzar brought the Jews captive to Babylon, Marduk, called Bel (Lord) in Aramaic and Baal in Hebrew, became a hated symbol, and he entered the Old Testament in the Ahab story, just as Marduk's ziggurat possibly became connected to the biblical Tower of Babel.

Babylon has most of the features of the Sumerian city. In its center (*libbi ali*) was the temple. Since the king was the high priest, he originally lived in the temple. In time, as his religious function was taken over by the high priest, he lived in the palace, first within the temple region and later just beneath it. Outside these sacred walls was the second area of the city, enclosed by another set of walls known as the gate or gates (*babtu*), which served as both citadel and administrative offices. Outside the gates, the city ran to the farmland, which provided food and raw material.

The Babylonian temple was a monument to dependency on the elements and ritualized the fertility myths that reveal the animistic relationship between man and the land. The citadel, which became a part of the wall it straddled, was entered through the lower city. The size and arrangement of the walls and the gates, with their display of lavish wealth, symbolized the status of the city. Eventually the king's palace was located in the gate and his soldiers were garrisoned there. The harbor or marketplace provided the crossroads of the city, not only because it brought people together but because ideas from different cultures were exchanged there, so that it energized and vitalized the city at the same time as it made it rich.

Each of these areas had its function and its ritual, but all functions and rituals were subsumed to the importance of the temple. The temple of Marduk, with its seven-story ziggurat, rose three hundred feet into the air and was topped by a blue-glazed building that housed the sanctuary. A processional or sacred way led from this temple through the Ishtar

Gate and outside the city walls to another sanctuary, called the New Year's Chapel (*bit akitu*). Once a year the king led the way to this sanctuary, where, stripped of all royal insignia and humiliated by slaps in the face and the pulling of ears, he knelt in prayer before the god of the city—in this case Marduk. It was on this day that, in accordance with this fertility rite, Marduk died and rose again, marking the end of one year and the beginning of the next, the end of the harvest and the anticipation of the new planting. Even as the city moved away from the land, it recognized its dependency on it, as well as on the rise and flow of the river, the turn and angle of the sun and moon. The city became a symbolic statement of this dependency—not only in its building of the temple but also in its naming the streets after gods. The symbolic imagination was clearly at work in the first cities, which took their meaning from religion and myth.

II

One tradition of the city came to us from the Near East, another from ancient Greece. Interestingly, the rise of cities in Greece follow a pattern similar to the rise of cities in Mesopotamia, Egypt, and Israel. Traces of this kind of city go back to the Minoan palace towns in Crete during the Bronze Age (roughly 2800–1000 B.C.). Here tribal chiefs became much richer than chiefs elsewhere in the Aegean, built larger houses (later termed "palaces"), and ruled from centers like Knossos. In 1876, the archaeologist Heinrich Schliemann discovered in Crete royal graves going back to the sixteenth century B.C., older than the world of Homer. In 1900, another archaeologist, Arthur Evans, uncovered the early palaces at Knossos, which revealed the largest Bronze Age center discovered up to that time.

The first of the great mainland settlements was at Mycenae. Homer described it in some detail, since at the time of the Trojan War it was the luxurious home of Agamemnon. Homer tells us that it was the most advanced of the independent palace kingdoms, which included Pylos on the west coast of Greece, Athens on the Acropolis, Thebes on the Grecian mainland, and Iolcos in Thessaly, the legendary home of Achilles. At its height, Mycenae seems to have waged war on Troy, which suggests it had reached an expansionist mode, thus providing a historical basis for Homer's epic. After 1300, Mycenean culture waned as tribes infiltrated Greece from the north. The Dorians overran the Peloponnesus and the Ionians overran the mainland.[1]

After the collapse of Mycenae, palace civilization was wiped out and culture reverted to the level of the old village, based on tribal principles of organization. Not much change took place until the beginning of the Iron Age. Bronze, made of copper and tin, was more difficult to produce; iron ushered in the rise of the self-sufficient, patriarchal village, based on kinship relationships that began with the family and moved out to the clan, the phratry, and the tribe. The center of these villages was usually a fortified hilltop (as in Athens) with settlements surrounding it at the bottom. The city-state would eventually take root here. Central to the city-state were two political institutions: the magistracy, which carried on the priestly, warrior, and judicial functions of the king or chief; and the assembly, which grew out of the tribal tradition of collectivism. As the landed aristocrats consolidated authority, the power of the king declined. The aristocrats became even more powerful during an era of expansion, as colonies were developed on the Black Sea and the Mediterranean. These colonies provided valuable raw material and new markets that stimulated economic expansion. But as the emphasis shifted from land to commerce, the aristocrats lost their greater power. This change ushered in new forms of democracy, including a constitution that limited state power, the election of magistrates, and the shift of power to the assembly. Athens became more and more powerful, reaching its high point of development with the defeat of Persia in a war that lasted from 499 to 479 B.C. But Athens became the victim of her success when a new imperial reach weakened the center. Unable to combat the attack from Sparta during the Peloponnesian War (431–404 B.C.), Athens never recovered its former status.

The history of Athens recapitulates the rise and fall of most cities. As the center of Attica, it cleared space for more democratic kinds of activity and the liberalization of laws: those not of noble birth, for example, were able to run for public office. The city and countryside had a sym-

---

1. Greece was divided into a number of geographical regions: Thessaly, in the north; Phocis, in the central region (principal city, Delphi); Boeotia, southwest of Phocis (principal city, Thebes); Attica, southeast Boeotia (principal city, Athens); the Isthmus of Corinth, west of Attica; the Peloponnesus, in southern Greece (principal city, Sparta; other important cities in the Peloponnesus were Mycenae in the northeast and Olympia in the west central part). Homer's epic heroes are tribal chiefs from these and other regions (Menelaus was king of Sparta; Agamemnon, king of Mycenae; Achilles, lord of Phthia and Hellas in Thessaly; and Ulysses, king of Ithaca).

biotic relationship and prospered politically, economically, and culturally. But there were problems at home between aristocrats, who owned the land, and the new traders, who were making claims to power. Eventually overpopulation led to colonization, especially by farmers who wanted to own their own land. Down to 500 B.C., Hellenic states had suppressed a powerful, urban bourgeoisie. From 800 to 500, economic activity had quickened based on a rural, agricultural economy that consolidated the wealth of the landed nobility. By 500 the agora, or marketplace, began to dominate, and there was a shift in class wealth, just as there was in England with the rise of the new merchant class during the Puritan revolution.

Each "revolution" was a "re-presentation" of the city. Babylon, Athens, and London supply historical experiences separate in time, each sharing elements of the same morphology. As the city moves through history, it moves through urban modes. The move from a landed to a commercial culture, for example, saw the gods become weaker as civil institutions became stronger. Aeschylus makes this process clear in his Oresteia trilogy, when the case the Eumenides bring against Orestes for killing his mother, Clytemnestra, and her lover, Aegisthus, is settled in a court of law rather than as a blood feud. Significantly, the idea of justice is defined by Solon at just the point in history when Athens moves from being a heightened aristocracy to a democracy.

Despite the urban desire for order, a primitive energy could not be suppressed; this idea was embodied in the Dionysus myth, as expressed especially by Euripides. In 406 B.C., Euripides died at the age of seventy-five in the kingdom of Macedon, having been exiled from Athens two years before. Among his papers was a play, *The Bacchae,* which means literally "women possessed by Bacchus." The play is a tale of a god who drives a whole city insane, entices its king to dress as a woman, and encourages the city's women to tear the king apart with their bare hands. Euripides' play is set in Thebes 2,400 years earlier, during a time of legendary Greek heroes. A stranger appears in the city (harbinger of the "mysterious stranger" plot) and claims to be a god. He insists that he is the son of Zeus by Semele, a mortal from Thebes. Dionysus leads Pentheus through the center of Thebes, beyond the city walls and into the untamed wilderness—always a threat to the city—where Pentheus is killed. There are two groups of women in the play: the first are Dionysus's loyal followers, who have come with him from Asia Minor in the East; the second are natives of Thebes, who participate in the killing of the king. Agave, the king's mother, completely deluded by Dionysus, leads the attack on Pentheus, thinking him a mountain lion. Dionysus's mother, Semele, can be traced back to the Stone Age, although she was imported to Greece from Asia Minor (western Turkey), where she was worshipped as the goddess Mother Earth.

Dionysus appears to have been a god known to the Minoans of Crete and later to the Mycenaens of mainland Greece, who were ruled by Agamemnon. God in the form of a bull-man existed in Crete, and Greek myth later identified him with Dionysus. Dionysus, god made flesh and animal made human, thus bridged the link between the divisions of being in nature. Several Greek myths suggest that human sacrifices may have been offered to Dionysus. Plutarch, for example, reports that in fear of the Persian invasion of Athens, the king was urged to offer up the young men to Dionysus Flesh-eater (Evans, 40, 46, 50). Euripides suggests to Arthur Evans a history of the worship of Dionysus: "It originated in Crete in the orgiastic worship of a young vegetation god, spread to Asia Minor in the form of the cult of Bacchus and Rhea, and finally entered Greece in the entourage of Dionysus and his satyrs. In all its habitats, the religion involved the same basic orgiastic rites and was centered on a divine pair: the ecstatic son and his old mother." Just as the mother appeared with various names, so the son took on different names—Dionysus, Bacchus, Sabazios, Cretan, Zeus (Evans, 65–66).

At some point in the sixth century B.C., Athens annexed the town of Eleusis with its cult of the black goat. In March of each year, a celebration was held in Dionysus's honor in a meeting place seating 17,000 people. During this celebration, the Dionysian chorus stepped forth and began a recitation. This activity became the basis of tragedy and comedy: the former came from *tragoidia,* meaning "goat song," and the latter from *kōmoidia,* meaning "revel song." With these events theater is born, even though the Greek celebration never lost its sense of being a religious event. Thus in the sixth century B.C. the worship of Dionysus gave birth to tragedy, comedy, and satyr plays—the satyr being a burlesque daimon whose lineage went back to ancient Minoan civilization. As Evans explains, "In his myths and rituals, Dionysus embodied both a feeling for the living continuities of nature and a concept of the human personality as an organism deeply rooted in the non-rational forces of the cosmos" (61, 80–81). As the city grew, its inhabitants became more and more cut off from nature, losing touch with the earth, the animals, and the cycles of the year. As a result, a reaction against Dionysus occurred, for he was the one who brought all of these realms together. The worship of Dionysus was eventually taken over by those on the margins of the city. (We find a contemporary remnant of this in Pynchon's Tristero, the underground cult in *The Crying of Lot 49*.) The god is driven underground, repressed by the forces of institutional authority, to console the marginalized and foreshadow urban revolt, whether the revolt of Christ on the outskirts or of the Christians in the center of the Roman Empire.

The attempt to impose order on nature worked within limits. The embodiment of those limits was Dionysus, who will reappear in many guises—among them the masked participant at the carnival or the masquerade, the mysterious stranger, and the man in the crowd. The vampire legend, though it stems from a different mythology, carries the same function: Dracula, supported by at least three women, stalks the night, disrupting the ordered Victorian London that he has mysteriously entered. Ancient myth gives way to mystery in the modern city.

III

As significant as the Greek city-state is to the history of the city, Rome involves another order of development. Geographically, Rome has all the elements that one looks for in an early city: it is centrally located on the west coast of Italy, fifteen miles up the Tiber River, where an island in midstream provides a convenient bridgehead. Seven hills, ranging from two hundred to three hundred feet above sea level, provide a natural defense. The tribes that eventually settled Italy came from different directions. In 3000 B.C., Neolithic farmers crossed the Adriatic and settled the southeastern shore. By 1800, immigrants from central Europe settled in the Po River Valley and introduced the Bronze Age to Italy. By 1700, migration from what is now Hungary to northern Italy brought advanced farming, breeding of animals, and bronze tools. From 1000 to 750, the Villanovan people provided the transition from the Bronze to the Iron Age. By 500 B.C., these prehistoric groups had in turn been transformed by newer settlers.

Originally the power in Rome was in the hands of kings, who ruled from about 750 to 500 B.C., but eventually a landed class became more powerful and gave rise to an aristocracy that usurped the power of the king. This power was increased further when Italian communities made alliances with Rome to protect them from attacks by the Gauls in the north and the Samnites in the south. After the victory of the Punic Wars (264 – 146 B.C.), Rome became a true urban center, attracted a rural population, expanded its productive base, and increased its overseas profits, soon dominating the whole Mediterranean region. As power consolidated in the new aristocratic class, there were unsuccessful or short-lived attempts (by Tiberius Gracchus and his brother Gaius, for example) at land reform. So powerful were the large landowners that they went unchallenged until 88 B.C. But the need for overseas forces allowed Roman generals to challenge that power; so Sulla, for example, enjoyed dictatorial rule (82 – 78 B.C.) that was a reign of terror. As a successful general and one of the largest landowners in the district of Picenum, Pompey consolidated both military and aristocratic powers — and extended them further when he formed a coalition (the First Triumvirate) with another successful general, Julius Caesar, and the aristocratic Crassus. Caesar was rewarded with the governorship of the Gallic provinces in the Po Valley and France. From there he conquered the rest of what would later become France, Belgium, Holland, Germany, and Switzerland, at which point he broke with Pompey, crossed the Rubicon, and returned to Rome in 47 B.C. His obsession to centralize power led to the conspiracy that took his life in 44 B.C. Thirteen years later, Augustus would triumph over Antony, initiating the two hundred and fifty years that constitute the greatness of Rome and its empire.

Augustus expanded the building of Rome: he constructed roads (60,000 miles) and aqueducts, engineering marvels made possible by the discovery of cement, which hardened (unlike lime mortar) under water. He introduced the Egyptian solar calendar of 365 days to replace the unreliable Roman lunar calendar. He disbanded a large part of the army, won control of the senate, and established communications between Rome and the provinces. He created a network of small cities (each with a population of roughly 50,000) throughout the empire. His greatest legacy was to provide the basis, despite periods of internal strife, for two hundred and fifty years of peace. The good life, however, led to complacency. When tribes threatened the boarders, the army was increased; but as Petronius revealed in his *Satyricon,* a decadence had set in by the time of Nero (A.D. 37 – 68). The great Rome fire of 64 Nero blamed on the Christians, initiating the persecutions, followed by a series of executions (including that of Seneca), which bred new revolts. The decay and the strife from within only increased the threat from without.

IV

When the Roman Empire fell in A.D. 410, contemporary historians had the natural inclination to blame Christianity; they could point out that one hundred years after Christianity became the national religion, the Roman Empire was no more. Augustine's *City of God* was his response to the charge that Christianity destroyed the Roman Empire. To the argument that Christian otherworldliness undermined the practical needs of the empire, Augustine (354–430) responded that moral decadence undid Rome. The *City of God* is one of the first attempts at a philosophy of history. Greek thought postulated history as cyclical—with no telos, or final goal, toward which history moved. Augustine argued that history was linear, moving from Creation through the Redemption of Christ and continuing, in the manifestation of the Spirit, toward the City of God. Adam's fall altered man's nature, altered human will, and led to man's seeing himself as his own center and history as cyclic: sinful ways were bound to be repeated. For Augustine, such cyclicality left out Christ's redeeming power of grace that led to a redirected love outside the self and to a linear history moving us toward eternal life. The city of man must relate to the City of God as the body relates to the soul. When the city of man promotes justice and peace, it is in harmony with the spiritual love of the City of God.

The City of God was an invisible city, to be acknowledged at the end of history (Augustine refused to equate the City of God with the church, or the city of man with fallen Rome). Through history those in the divine and invisible cities will know suffering inflicted by the human city, but being of the elect they will triumph in the end. Augustine's is the apocalyptic vision: the city becomes realizable only at the end of life. The two cities manifested themselves in human society with the birth of Cain, who belonged to the city of man, while his brother Abel belonged to the City of God. Augustine grafted the history of Greece and Rome onto the Bible. He saw Jewish and classical thought converging once the Old Testament was translated from Hebrew into Greek.

Augustine was thus "re-presenting" the mythic city in religious terms: myth had now become Christian doctrine, and as the doctrine changed so changed the idea of the city. Augustinian Christian belief in linear time took us from the act of creation to the Last Judgment as announced in the Apocalypse, or the Book of Revelation. The Bible established the two ends of time, the temporal spectrum through which humanity must pass. Augustine's theological frame of time became the basis for historiography, at least until Edward Gibbon. Many subsequent versions of the city come back to this re-presentation, and the quest through the secular city ends at, say, Balzac's Père Lachaise cemetery, or is projected into the future (Joyce's Bloomusalem), or is attacked as diversionary (as it was by Marx). Augustine thus seems to have made serious revisions in Cicero's idea of *res publica*—the belief that the community is defined by a common acknowledgment of law and interests. Augustine believed that fallen man was incapable of such urban harmony; he retained the Platonic ideal of the state but modified it toward Christian ends realizable at the end of time.

Following Augustine, the Renaissance also broke with the classical conception of cyclical time, substituting instead the idea of progress. The word *civilization* was an Enlightenment term that suggested the movement of history toward what ought to be: the belief that history had a purpose. Edward Gibbon reverted to a cyclical view of history, seeing Rome as the crowning of history's most splendid cycle and believing that the fall of Rome involved a highly civilized society, weakened by Christianity from within until it fell to external forces. Christian zeal and fanaticism, passions derived from the Jews, and the promise of an afterlife—such radical religious ideas brought about the decline of Rome by undermining the civic virtues of the Romans. Gibbon's argument is similar to the one that Pentheus uses in *The Bacchae:* that a fanaticism had brought the realm to a state of disorder, zealousness had led to chaos. As strange as it may seem, Gibbon's argument is a re-presentation of the Dionysian myth, with the Christians now playing the part of Dionysus.

The rise and fall of empires is one of the major themes in any history of the city. Whether there is a pattern that explains the rise and fall of Athens, Rome, Jerusalem, Alexandria, Vienna, and London is open to dispute. But any discussion of empire must begin with a sense of a city's origin, its connection to nature, and the way it relates to the land, until the agrarian process gives way to the production of commercial goods and the rise of an urban class, and until such power and wealth are played out in imperial reach. Such seems to be the destructive nature of empire. At some point, every major city has shifted emphasis from a landed economy to a commercial economy, and with that transformation has come the radical change we know in history as the Puritan revolution, the French Revolution, and the American Civil War. Such change is accompanied by the birth of a middle class, the rise of national banks and new money systems, and the shift toward parliament and more democratic forms of rule, often ending as centralized power—imperialism and more recently totalitarianism.

The literary imagination has treated such historical processes. Flaubert's *Salammbô,* Joyce's *Ulysses,* Eliot's *The Waste Land,* Pound's *Cantos* and "Homage to Sextus Propertius," William Carlos Williams's *Pagany* and *Kora in Hell*—all overlay the modern city with the city of antiquity, which undoes Augustine's linear time and explains history cyclically. The practice is consistent with Pound's "repeat" and Eliot's "falling towers" themes, consistent with modern memory and the paradigm of urban "re-presentation."

V

From the fifth to the fifteenth century, the city reached a low point in Western culture, despite the rise of the Carolingian dynasty in the seventh century. Charlemagne, the son of Pepin, was crowned emperor in 800 and brought the dynasty to its zenith. After the death of his son, Louis I, the Carolingian empire was split into three parts by the Treaty of Verdun (843) and never recovered its power. Unlike most empires, the Carolingians did not leave a memorable capital city: Aachen was never Athens or Rome.

Lewis Mumford believes that the sixth to the eleventh centuries were the era of the greatest medieval urban decline, especially when "the darkness thickened" during the Saracen and Viking invasions of the eighth to the eleventh centuries (*City in History,* 249). Several reasons are suggested for the decline of the city in the Middle Ages. The loss of the Roman Empire broke down the political unity necessary for urbanization. Feudalism depended on the lack of central power, as the liege lord offered the individual protection one could not get from higher authority. In addition, the church condemned commercial profits and usury. As a result, according to Henri Pirenne, from the beginning of the Carolingian era, the merchant class was primarily Jewish, "so much so that the words *Judaeus* and *mercator* appear almost synonymous" (Pirenne, 11)[2]

---

2. Pirenne's claim supports that of Max Weber, who connected Puritanism and the rise of capitalism and who argued that Puritanism gave capitalism a stability it did not have in church doctrine. Lewis Mumford, however, has questioned Pirenne's account of medieval urbanism because Pirenne "refused the title of city to an urban community that did not foster long-distance trade and harbor a large mercantile middle class—a quite arbitrary definition" (*City in History,* 255).

The Renaissance offered a model for a new kind of city that would change the medieval design. Mumford believes that Thomas More's *Utopia* (1518) is a harbinger of this transformation. More regretted the overspecialization of the guilds into hierarchic, often mutually hostile orders. Anticipating an eventual increase in the urban population, he saw the need for larger cities and the need for a standardization of building. He also saw the need for better cooperation between the urban and agricultural areas, realizing that the hostility between the two had slowed the process of urban growth by decreasing the amount of crops available. More anticipated Huizinga's argument in *The Waning of the Middle Ages* (1924). Huizinga also stressed the move from a religious to a humanistic culture. Poverty, for example, became a social evil rather than an apostolic virtue. There were marked changes in the ideas of chivalry, courtly and romantic love, and death. Love, for example, began to take on meaning in its own right instead of being a feudal agreement between families. The pastoral was reconfigured, and allegory gave way to symbolism, with a more mysterious connection between the symbolic elements (Huizinga, 162, 186). Many of these changes were reflected in the culture and absorbed into More's idea of utopia.

Though urban growth had slowed from the fall of Rome to the Renaissance, it quickened under the influence of humanism. As we shall see, it then changed drastically with the Enlightenment when a radically new concept of the city came into being.

CHAPTER 3

The City and the Estate

I

Medieval-Renaissance London ended at 2:00 A.M. on Sunday, September 2, 1666. A fire started in London's Pudding Lane and burned for five days; when it was over, the London of Chaucer and Shakespeare was no more. While the embers were still warm, Christopher Wren designed a new London, a plan that would have made the Royal Exchange the center of the city with magnificent boulevards radiating from it (see figure 1). Charles II liked the plan, but he found it impossible to implement because the real estate rights were prohibitively expensive. Although Wren's plan failed, it tells us a great deal about a shift in ideology: the old idea of the spiritual city, founded as a sacred burial place with the sanctuary in the center, had given way to the commercial city organized around the East India House, the Bank of England, the Royal Stock Exchange, and other trading firms and counting-houses. It was this new commercial London that gave rise to a new breed of men who became wealthy from trade and other investments—men who made money by handling money, men like Thomas Gresham, the founder of the Royal Exchange, and the banker Josiah Child.

These men were part of the cultural revolution that moved England from a feudal to a commercial society. Feudalism was a process outside market rules: the tenants were compelled to pay rent because of the force exercised by the landowner. Marx and Engels saw feudalism as an inter-

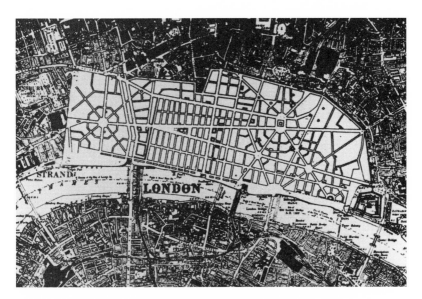

Figure 1. Wren's plan for rebuilding London after the fire of 1666, placed among the present surroundings of the city. Wren visually represented the spiritual aspects of the city giving way to the material. Courtesy of the Frances Loeb Library, Graduate School of Design, Harvard University.

mediate stage between the slave society of the ancient world and the capitalism of the modern. Capitalism began with merchant capital—the overseas trade and colonization that led to the rise of Spain, Portugal, Holland, England, and France. It came simultaneously with the rise of fast clipper ships that allowed trade of slaves, precious metals, and simple manufactures. Commerce led to a surplus of profit, and the surplus that brought capitalism into being was inseparable from the city. A landed world gave way to an urban world; wealth that previously came from the indentured land was superseded by wealth that came from urban trade and commerce. With this shift came a shift in social institutions: parliament contested the king's power, as national banks and the stock exchange revealed wealth to be part of a commercial process. The city, the center of such activity, shifted the balance of power away from the countryside.

Radical changes in social and cultural institutions were complemented by radical changes in philosophical assumptions, as we can see in Francis Bacon's *Advancement of Learning* (1605). Bacon felt the need to turn away from the domination of Greece and Rome. He wanted an empirical philosophy, a scientific methodology, and an emphasis on natural history (the basis for science)—a materially based system that would replace Platonic idealism and Aristotelian syllogistic reasoning. In the *Novum Organum* (1620), Bacon argued that nature can best be understood by an inductive, empirical methodology; his book was thus a direct response to Aristotle's *Organon,* a treatise on the nature of logic in which Aristotle argued that nature could best be understood through forms of deduction.[1] Bacon concluded that man must understand nature before he could control it: knowledge and power, epistemology and economics, meet in man. Once the empirical challenged the symbolic, it also challenged the supremacy of myth, and the religious and the commercial realms were bifurcated. Mechanistic philosophy and empiricism were the intellectual handmaidens of capitalism, and they came into being simultaneously with it.

Capitalism is a material process held together by money working in an investment-market system based on the tangibility of production, distribution, and consumption. The capitalist system is the economic equivalent of matter in motion. Both Adam Smith and David Ricardo believed that the system ran on principles as discoverable as the laws of nature—and that capitalism was equally autonomous. Smith (1723–90) believed that the market system of production—enclosed and self-energizing—was the key to economic progress. He distinguished between a system based on a surplus result (the profit motive) and one that merely provided subsistence—that is, between capitalism and feudalism. Ricardo (1772–1823) picked up where Smith left off. He also saw profit as the key to the capitalistic system, but he believed that as capitalism progressed the profits would fall. In fact, the discovery of new lands and the development of new techniques kept profits up. As risks decreased, profits did fall; but as the rate of loss also fell, the average was sustained.

Surplus profit led to the urban commercial world and brought such urban institutions as banking into being. Banking had begun in Italy with the rise of manufacturing and the distribution of goods along medieval trade routes. Goldsmiths lent out their gold as extended credit. This led to the practice of financing trade by credit—of discounting and rediscounting trade bills—and local businessmen suddenly found themselves in the banking business. Credit supplemented money, creating in effect a

---

1. In his epistemology and philosophy of nature, Aristotle is very much the empiricist, insisting that all knowledge starts with the senses. But he also believes that general truths can be abstracted from empirical data—the deduction that Bacon challenges.

larger supply of capital. The Bank of England was set up to manage the national debt, and the money supply was backed by gold and by regulated credit. By expanding and contracting credit, the Bank of England controlled the production-consumption-profit-credit circle of activity.

The system turned on gold. If gold flowed out, the bank contracted the credit base; if gold flowed in, it expanded the base. Gold flowing out was a sign that exports were falling short of imports. Contraction was a sign of unwanted expansion marked by full employment, rising prices and wages, and a bull market on the stock exchange. Contraction thus safeguarded gold and stabilized prices. This system worked, and the amount of money available increased, so long as the quantity of gold increased with finds in California, Russia, and South Africa. And as Britain acquired more gold, it could increase its line of international credit, fueling the world economy. Credit continued until the end of the nineteenth century when the amount of gold available stabilized because no new deposits were found. A limited gold supply put the brakes on an expanding international economy and, in part, explained the series of world depressions that occurred from 1893 to 1929. For this reason the gold standard had eventually to be abandoned. Credit and the process of production and trade were being held in check by the amount of gold available in the world. Once gold was abandoned and a "gross national product" was substituted as the basis for the amount of money available within the national market, world trade and credit once again took off, leading to even larger markets and new cycles of international capitalism.

Daniel Defoe is important to this discussion of economics and the new city because he witnessed the transition from an agrarian to an urban culture. In *The Complete English Tradesman* (1726), Defoe wrote of the new merchant class, "our merchants are princes, greater and higher, and more powerful than some sovereign princes," and he contrasted the "immense wealth" of this new commercial class with the declining fortunes of the landed aristocracy. It was this new class which in great part was responsible for the magnificent new townhouses that dominated such squares as Leicester, Bloomsbury, Soho, Red Lion, and St. James, built by such families as the Bedfords, Harleys, Portlands, Portmans, and Grosvenors. These houses were to the city what the estate was to the country.

This was also the London of the new coffeehouses that, along with other functions, served as clearinghouses for commercial business, as Lloyds was a clearinghouse for mercantile insurance. Each coffeehouse attracted a different clientele, but those that served the new commercial investor also supplied commercial information (regarding the arrival and departure of ships, stock listings, and so forth) and thus in effect acted as the first newspapers. More formal newspapers came into being soon after and became the voice of the city. This was the London that by 1700 had a population of 575,000; by 1750, 675,000; and by 1800, 900,000: over 10 percent of the combined population of England and Wales. Soon after the turn of the century, London became the first modern city in the Western world to exceed one million inhabitants.

Daniel Defoe perhaps most eloquently celebrated the origins of the modern city, and he depicted the religious and the secular as outside one another, independent realms that function well so long as one is not overlaid upon the other. Defoe's Crusoe has no difficulty compartmentalizing the two. On the one hand, he takes to the Bible and sees signs from God everywhere: God's hand is inseparable from the earthquake, from his illness, and from his good fortune when he thrives upon his deserted island. On the other hand, in order to thrive Crusoe must employ an empirical sense and learn when to plant corn, when to brave the ocean tides in order to fish, how to build a kiln, and when to bake the clay that will become his pottery. Crusoe's empiricism reinforced his scientific mind. He eventually comes to see nature as subject to laws that are repeatable and hence knowable by the human mind. These laws give him an insight into how nature works, and the means of controlling it. And out of this control comes Crusoe's sense of power and then—as he supervises the growth of commercial institutions—his claim to wealth. In *Robinson Crusoe* (1719), Defoe has anticipated the rise of the commercial city and recapitulated the history of preurban London—a city that employed money and technology in complex ways, a city that had become the center of a nation and would soon be the heart of an empire.

Defoe, in other words, moved very close to the Enlightenment mentality that became the basis for the modern city and that absorbed—and repressed—the mythic nature of the city. The Enlightenment rested upon the belief that life could best be understood and lived through the power of reason—that is, through the empirical process that allowed an understanding of how nature worked. Such an understanding eventually led to a system of laws that explained nature and was suited to the commercial and later an industrial exploitation that created new forms of wealth. The Enlightenment was a revolutionary movement, taking us from an agrarian to an urban world, from the realm of the estate to a new-moneyed order, from a belief in birthrights to an insistence upon natural rights, from the authority of the divine right of kings to parliamentary and democratic government, from landed wealth to commercial and later industrial wealth processed through such new institutions as the national bank and stock exchange. The Enlightenment was anticlerical, antiroyal, antiaristocratic; man now had the means to understand his physical and social world, to create a social equality through new forms of government, and to live more securely through new technology. In shifting emphasis from birth rights to natural rights, the Enlightenment gave a new importance to the individual and the right to create oneself. Yet it was not inconsistent with a belief in religion, because the priority of reason did not preempt a belief in a Maker whose rational universe was unfolding before us. But such a view sat uncomfortably with a secular discourse that gave priority to matters of empiricism, science, technology, and money and to the trust in a national mission that was soon inseparable from the dictates of imperialism. Moreover, Enlightenment leanings toward mechanistic beliefs such as those of Hobbes offered the most dangerous contradictions to the religious idea of the universe. If creation could be reduced to matter in motion, and if such matter instantiated a completely physical process inseparable from the descriptive laws of science, then there could be no miracles in nature—nothing supernatural that would interrupt the physical laws. And if this was true, what then could be the meaning of Christ the redeemer? And if all knowledge was materialistic, then all knowledge was also quantifiable. Behind the Enlightenment was an encyclopedic movement and an encyclopedic mentality—the belief that knowledge could be catalogued and accessed in a mechanical way.

Daniel Defoe wrestled with the early application of these ideas, especially as they related to how the commercial city worked. A novel like *Robinson Crusoe* recapitulates the historical process: we move in the novel from isolation to community, from individual authority to government by consent, and from a wilderness to a primitive agrarian realm to the beginnings of a commercial order. We move, that is, beyond the dictates of survival to a form of feudalism (where goods in a hierarchical society are produced for use and not for sale), and then to the beginnings of commercialism.

From the beginning to the end, *Robinson Crusoe* functions on two levels—spiritual and physical. Crusoe eventually begins to think of his two Fathers—a heavenly father and an earthly father; of two kinds of survival—heavenly and earthly; of two kinds of time—heavenly and seasonal; and of two kinds of observation—that which will record heavenly signs and a more empirical kind that will reveal the workings of nature and secondary causes. A spiritual agency demands that he be aware of signs from above, and indeed the storm, the earthquake, and his own illness take on special religious significance for him. But equally important, Crusoe becomes an expert observer of the physical world and develops a finely trained empirical eye. By observing how nature works—the rhythms of the seasons, the significance of the rise and fall of the tides—he learns when he can best plant his corn and when it is safest to fish and travel the ocean. Such understanding of nature makes possible a certain amount of control over it, and this control is extended when he brings to nature instruments and tools, which he finds on the boat and which he begins to make with his own hands (such as the pottery he makes in his own forge). No sooner does Crusoe begin to control physical nature than he takes on the task of taming the animals, especially the wild goats that run about the island. And once he has control over both the physical and the animal worlds, he moves to control other human beings—first Friday and later the sailors, who eventually sign what amounts to a Lockean contract of government, giving Crusoe authority over them. At that point, Crusoe leaves his island and returns to civilization. When he eventually returns to the island, this time to divide up the land, he allows some to be taken as community property but reserves to "my self the Property of the whole" with the right to sell it (*Robinson Crusoe*, 237).

Robinson Crusoe's story takes us to the doorstep of the modern Enlightenment. He has shown humanity moving toward the empirical mind that can conceive the new science, which in turn is necessary for technology, the end product of which is commerce and profit—that is, money. These influences transformed the medieval-Renaissance world, moved it from a feudal to an urban base, as the cities of Europe became the money capitals under the influence of the new middle-class merchants, traders, and speculators. As in Defoe's novel, birthrights are replaced by natural rights—the right to create oneself beyond a worldly father, even as one looks for signs of approval from a heavenly Father.

Yet even though Defoe reconciles the physical and the spiritual, his world is not typological. Crusoe never looks to the Bible for literal correspondences but seeks in it signs that must be evaluated and interpreted in the context of his own situation—that is, he looks to the Bible for broad meaning and general examples that can be applied to the physical world, which operates according to its own terms. Unlike Milton, Defoe moves us away from myth and legends of the past and creates his own narratives. The loss of the typological at this time helps explain the rise of the utopia; one must now create models based on the here and now rather than simply take them from the Bible.

In creating a narrative that relies heavily on a sense of place and of individual development, Defoe was consolidating various kinds of sub-genres, such as the tour book, the diary, and the memoir, as well as the biography and the autobiography in both their secular and spiritual manifestations. But what is most important to see is that this new sense of human and individual destiny was inextricably connected with the city and the new commercial order. In *Robinson Crusoe* Defoe anticipates the coming of London, but his work that analyzes that London in detail is *Tour of Great Britain: A tour thro' the whole island of Great Britain* (1724–27), one section of which describes London. This is the famous "Letter V," which appears in a two-volume collection of thirteen "letters" describing Great Britain. This discussion of London comes in the center of the book because London, for Defoe, was the center of the world: everything emanated from and was controlled by its institutions. Defoe's emphasis was upon commercial London as a marketplace and a trade center for the world. He estimated the size of London as seven and a half miles east to west, and five and three-quarter miles north to south, or slightly over forty-three square miles. Within this area he computed there to be 5,099 streets, lanes, and squares, encompassing 95,968 houses, with a population of 651,580. He described at some length London's expansion, incorporating the surrounding villages of Deptford, Islington, Miles End, Newington-butts, and Southwark, which in turn had incorporated Newington, Lambeth, and Borough.

Defoe argued that the power had been transferred from the court to the city, from a feudal to an urban realm. The court now envied the city's wealth; the city had outlived the attacks upon it by the court; and the court had to recognize that the city was "necessary" to its very being—providing both money and defense. Defoe also saw in his *Tour* that a large urban population made a division of labor necessary, as everyone became wage earners. The ability to earn good wages in turn advanced the commercial base of the society. More than any other document, Defoe's *Tour* showed how London had transformed not only its immediate environs but all of Great Britain, moving the population away from the land and away from the remains of a feudal society toward a commercial society that turned on money. Defoe was the first to see what has now become an axiom: in a premarket society, money follows power, but in a market society, power follows money. London was the source of this new money—a monument to the commercial self.

Defoe continued his discussion of London in a tract titled *Augusta Triumphans; or, the Way to Make London the Most Flourishing City in the Universe* (1729). Here the emphasis was on the social needs that London must serve. Aware that not everyone will succeed within the confines of the commercial city, Defoe called for institutions that would help or protect illegitimate children and for licensed mental hospitals to care for the genuinely mentally ill. He attacked gaming houses, which could distract the less industrious; bewailed the use of liquor for the same reason; and called on justices of the peace to punish the idle, the lewd, and the criminal. More positively, he called for establishing a London University to educate those who could not go to Oxford and Cambridge; his desire was directed toward the middle class and toward the City, which had to replenish itself in human terms. He also called for decent wages to encourage human industry and to keep the system going. Almost every item of concern involved the city as a commercial institution: Defoe encouraged the able to succeed within the new possibilities of the commercial city, and he offered assistance to those who had become the urban equivalent of the damned.

Defoe's sense of confidence in the new commercial city was, ironically, reinforced rather than questioned in *A Journal of the Plague Year* (1722). It would have been easy for Defoe to have discussed the infected city of London in mythical and biblical terms that questioned the very idea of the city. Cain had founded the first city in defiance of God's order; and cities like Babylon and Jerusalem were stricken by God for being corrupt. But Defoe did not use religion to reject the city. Although Defoe was only a child when the plague hit London, he tells the story from an immediate point of view—that of H.F., a London merchant—fashioning a character who can move beyond the physical realm. H.F. is an empiricist, concerned with physical data and the general laws or conclusions that can be drawn from such evidence. But he is also a reader of signs. Initially, those signs include the Bible, which he holds separate from the secular. The biblical and the empirical—divine and natural law—work side by side; they can reinforce each other but do not interpenetrate as they do in Renaissance typology or in the writings of Bunyan and Milton. H.F. stays in London during the plague because he has opened his Bible to a passage that indicates God will protect him: "Thou shalt not be able by the terror or night....A thousand fall at thy side, and ten thousand at thy right hand; but it shall not come nigh thee . . . there shall no evil befall thee, neither shall any plague come nigh thy dwelling" (*Journal*, 34).

But while he is capable of seeing connections between the state of infected London and besieged Jerusalem, while he believes God may have sent signs that the plague was coming such as the "blazing star or comet [that] appeared several months before the plague" (40), while he quotes Jeremiah on the need for a city to show humility and repentance in the face of such affliction (205), and while he is mindful that such signs cannot be discounted as indications of divine vengeance and displeasure, he is also wary of seeing the plague as a punishment directly sent from God. In a remarkable paragraph, he distinguishes between divine and natural agency and insists that the plague was "propagated by natural causes." While God can intervene in natural operations, He is ordinarily more likely to let life operate through natural causes: "Now 'tis evident that in the case of an infection there is no apparent extraordinary occasion for supernatural operation" (205). If God's will is being revealed, it is through natural rather than miraculous means. H.F. insists upon this distinction because, as he points out in a passage that immediately follows his discussion of causality, the plague was caused "by goods brought over from Holland, and brought thither from the Levant; the first breaking out in a house in Long Acre where those goods were carried and first opened" (206). Although he is a marvelous reader of signs, H.F. is reluctant to conclude that those signs indict the commercial meaning of the city; in fact, much of his remorse comes from the way the plague has so completely disrupted the commercial operations of the city. It is an unfortunate event that may have a totally natural sequence of causes.

With Defoe we lose a sense of allegory, of direct correspondence between the city of man and the City of God. God still speaks to us through signs, but now we must individually interpret them. Also, H.F. and seemingly the author himself are reluctant to interpret those signs as a condemnation of the new, commercial city. Defoe shared the Enlightenment optimism connected with the city, now built on the belief that it can control nature and be a monument to self. Such belief was inseparable from empiricism, science, technology, money, and a new nationalism—all seemingly in harmony, or at least not in disharmony, with the will of God. But Defoe's optimism was tenuous so long as the plague threatened the commercial order. Behind the desire for order was the reality of an intrusive chaos that could disrupt the urban process. Defoe stressed the greatness of the new commercial order at the same time that he turned a blind eye to the chaos working within it.

II

The prosperity that Defoe depicts in the city was not equally shared by those who stayed on the land. Some of the landed families—such as the dukes of Leeds, Devonshire, and Marlborough and the earls of Pembroke, Bradford, and Portland—maintained their wealth by investing in the new commerce or, like the Russells, in the new joint stock companies. Others maintained their positions by marrying into the new money, as did the duke of Bedford when he married his grandson to the granddaughter of Sir John Spencer, a London merchant, or as did Lord Acton of Shropshire, who himself married the daughter of a goldsmith from Leadenhall Street. But despite these examples, a quiet revolution was taking place, as the center of wealth shifted away from the landed class and toward a new, urban commercial class that was a moneyed rather than a landed aristocracy. Only 200 of today's peerage were created before 1800.

As a result, many country estates were taken over by such families of new wealth as the Clives, the Pitts, and the Grosvenors; and a number of old estates went into decline as the source of wealth shifted from the land to the city. This situation became even more pronounced with the spread of enclosure, the practice of fencing off lands formerly open to the public. Between 1760 and 1845, enclosure affected more than five million acres of common fields and forced the last of the tenant and yeoman farmers off the land and made them surplus farm labor, sending many to the cities. The enclosure movement brought new land under tillage and provided a needed increase in the food supply, but it was also a land grab influenced by commercial speculation and protected by a new legal and political system.

Almost every novel written in or near the last half of the eighteenth century touches on at least one of these matters. Samuel Richardson's *Clarissa* (1747–48) is the most revealing, since the Harlowes are intent on marrying Clarissa into another propertied family so that they can increase their holdings. Almost all of the events in this novel are set in the context of the estate as opposed to the city, as is Henry Fielding's *Tom Jones* (1748) and Oliver Goldsmith's *The Vicar of Wakefield* (1766)—novels that involve women who are kidnapped or flee from the estate and are brought into the city, where their experiences are unhappy ones. With some indulgence one can even think of *Tom Jones* as a *Clarissa*, if only the novel had been told from Sophia's point of view; or of *Tom Jones* and *Clarissa* as *The Vicar of Wakefield,* if only Squire Western or Mr. Harlowe had been capable of expressing the sense of the lost daughter as well as did Reverend Primrose.

Such speculation points to the curious fact that many of these novels treat the same kind of narrative situation, remaining within the framework of the estate as it is transformed by the city. In *Tom Jones,* Paradise Hall remains unchanged and, along with Squire Allworthy, is the moral frame of reference to which the novel constantly returns—just as the estate and the Mr. Knightley figure as a rule prevail later in the novels of Jane Austen. But in *Clarissa* something different was happening, and the story was played out in proto-gothic terms.

Many books deal with the rise of the gothic novel in this period, but I know of no critical discussion of how the rise of the new city, the decline of the landed estate, and the rise of the gothic interrelate. Yet many of these novels—Horace Walpole's *The Castle of Otranto* (1764), Ann Radcliffe's *The Mysteries of Udolpho* (1794), and William Godwin's *Caleb Williams* (1794) come to mind—connect the passing of the estate with an evil emanating in the city. The narrative patterns in these and other gothic novels are very similar: the story is set in the past, in a feudal castle or a landed estate that has been touched by the hand of death and is caught in the process of decay. The connection between the past and the present has been threatened by a fraudulent claim upon the estate, or the estate has come by new owners— often rich merchants or members of the new city's commercial class—or the estate has been intruded upon by the new city types such as the libertine, whose hardened heart and jaded virtues are the by-product of his city ways. The result is that the world of the old father has been disrupted by the ways of the new, and a curse has been put on the land, which disrupts the natural processes in a mysterious, uncanny, and sometimes supernatural way.

In Walpole's *The Castle of Otranto,* for example, Otranto has been usurped from Prince Alfonso by Manfred, who insists on his fraudulent legacy. The usurpation seems to violate the laws of nature and to start all the supernatural events that finally overthrow Manfred. In Radcliffe's *The Mysteries of Udolpho,* Montoni, the embodiment of the city libertine, makes fraudulent claims upon three estates—Udolpho, Villeroi, and La Vallée, the last the estate of Emily St. Aubert. In order to put his claims beyond question, Montoni tries to force Emily to marry Count Marano and later to sign papers that give him control of her estate. In Godwin's *Caleb Williams,* Ferdinando Falkland is an inverted Squire Allworthy figure: he eventually loses his power of sentiment in the city and becomes a moody, distempered man, who vents his rage by murdering his neighbor Tyrrel. Tyrrel has himself become a classic villain by imprisoning his cousin, Emily Melville, and trying to force her to marry Grimes, who, like Lovelace in *Clarissa,* helps her to escape so that he can rape her. As in *The Mysteries of Udolpho,* much of the action on the estate is counterpointed by the action in the city, especially scenes in which Caleb goes to London pursued by his enemy, who becomes a demonic extension between the city and the estate, much like Dickens's Orlick in *Great Expectations.*

The victim in this sequence of events is usually a woman who has been used as a pawn, either to acquire a claim to the estate or to strengthen it.[2] The villain attempts to get her to marry against her will; when she refuses, he imprisons her in his house or castle or, in the case of Clarissa, in a house of ill repute. In scenes typified in *Clarissa* and also in the masquerade episode of *Tom Jones* involving Lady Bellaston, she is tricked by men or women in disguise, as part of the plot to seduce her. The disguise embodies the concealed evils that work beneath the urban surface, and it once again connects the city with the carnivalesque. If the seduction fails, the heroine is raped—an event that always assures her death. If she is saved, it is by the man of sentiment, who often embodies the lost values of the estate in contrast to the libertine, who embodies the new secular values of the city. The man of sentiment—a kind of diminished Squire Allworthy or Mr. Knightley—tests his values against his sense of feeling. Through the power of kindness and a good heart, he is repelled by the ways of the libertine and comes to the heroine's rescue— as do Belford and Valancourt in *Udolpho.* In *The Castle of Otranto,* Theodore is a prefiguration of this character; in *Caleb Williams,* the role is played by Caleb himself and later by Falkland. These novels are resolved by repudiating the man of the city, who is the source and origin of the evil, and by reestablishing the man of sentiment, who is the last vestige of the world of the estate.

I have been discussing novels written in the last half of the eighteenth century to make connections among the city, the estate, and gothic fiction. But these elements also appear in such nongothic novels as Jane

---

2. In *The Contested Castle* (1989), Kate Ellis provides a feminist reading of gothic fiction. Ellis views the gothic as destroying the realm of the home, arguing that the woman is the victim of such a process. But she fails to see in what ways the threat to "women's space" comes from an urbanized masculinity.

Austen's *Mansfield Park* (1814), where the threat to the estate comes in the persons of Henry and Mary Crawford, spawned and bred by the city, and where the novel turns on a key scene—the playacting scene—in which the values of the city are explicitly contrasted to those of the estate. Austen, of course, preserved the integrity of the estate in her novels, including *Northanger Abbey* (1803/1818), where the elements of the gothic novel are themselves parodied.

Austen's attempt to preserve the estate intact by destroying the genre in which it is most severely transformed was clearly both feudal and futile, and the narrative structure persisted into the nineteenth and twentieth centuries in novels that depict an even greater division between the city and the country as a result of the industrial revolution. In Emily Brontë's *Wuthering Heights* (1847), for example, Mr. Earnshaw brings Heathcliff from Liverpool into the world of the estate, and Heathcliff eventually makes claim to both Wuthering Heights and Thrushcross Grange. He victimizes Hindley Earnshaw and Isabella Linton before he succumbs to the supernatural presence of Catherine, whose claim to the estate is embodied in her daughter, Catherine Linton, and her nephew, Hareton Earnshaw. The story is told by one of the last remnants of the estate, the servant Nelly Dean, to Mr. Lockwood, who has intruded upon this world (which he never comes to understand) from London.

This discussion hardly exhausts the manor novel, but the main argument should be clear: once the symbiotic relationship between the city and country turned parasitic, the world of the estate was transformed and took on a mutant quality. Its most radical transformation helped create the subgenre of gothic fiction, a representation rich in the cultural change of a historical moment in which institutional power was shifting from the land to the city.

III

Charles Dickens moved even further from Defoe's double frame of reference involving God and man and closer to the city of man. Dickens opens up the meaning of the Western city and its institutions, offering insight into the new commercialism, the world of banking and exchange, and institutions like Chancery, which hold it all together at the expense of great human suffering. Dickens's city was both lure and trap: a lure to those who are called to it as if by a magnet, because only the city offers the means of realizing a heightened conception of self; a trap in its workings, which lead to human destruction.

Dickens is among the last of the sentimental novelists—the last to use characters who test their sense of reality and moral value against their own feeling. His early novels express the belief that good can triumph over evil, and that all action can be evaluated by the motives behind it. A novel like *Oliver Twist* (1838) is close in its assumptions to those of Henry Fielding. When Oliver is sent into the London streets along with Fagin's gang of pickpockets, their first victim is Mr. Brownlow, who happens to be a close friend of Oliver's dead father, and whose good heart will make him the moral authority to which everything in the novel is referred. Although London at this time had a population of over one million, Dickens reduces its meaning to the realm of the estate: Mr. Brownlow functions almost exactly as did Squire Allworthy in *Tom Jones*. In fact, the ending of *Oliver Twist,* turning as it does on new information about the nature of Oliver's and Rose Maylie's birth, is almost exactly like the resolution of *Tom Jones*. Dickens goes beyond Fielding in revealing the depths of the city: he limns the world of Fagin, and especially of Bill Sikes, who is the first of his many Cain figures—a brutal murderer who is destined to wander the city alone, cut off from his fellow humans.

By the time of *Dombey and Son* (1848), the commercial city has become further transformed by the rise of new industries, which bring factories and urban slums, and by a change of emphasis from the human to the inhuman as forces of the new technology transform the landscape. In *Dombey and Son,* Dickens indicts the commercialism of London and moves his novel in a direction quite different from that of Defoe. Paul Dombey is Dickens's first detailed portrait of a man so obsessed with profit that it shapes his life and destroys his ability to love. He dismisses his daughter Florence as irrelevant to the masculine world of business, and he allows James Carker, his business manager, to embezzle large sums from the firm. This story is told against the backdrop of a London that is being transformed by the railroad, which is changing the scale within which the city works. But in this world of masculine forces, it is woman who finally triumphs—first in the person of Edith Granger, Dombey's second wife, who wreaks revenge on both Dombey and Carker by enticing Carker to elope with her so as to destroy both his and Dombey's reputation; and second in the person of Florence, who can now console her bankrupt father and elicit from him the love he had previously refused to give. Although Dickens had anticipated Dombey in some of his earlier minor characters, never before did he present such a clear portrait of a man whose life is ruined by commercial greed. And never before had Dickens so clearly focused on the way the new city had been taken over by commerce and technology—by the forces of money and industry—and so clearly shown how these influences can deaden the heart and create machines of human destruction.

In the center of Dickens's novels is often the shrewd lawyer, like Tulkinghorn or Jaggers, who links the world of the estate (Chesney Wold or Satis House) with the world of the city, and whose source of power is privileged information that he uses or withholds to suit his purposes. In *Bleak House* (1852–53), such information concerns the illegitimate birth of Esther Summerson and the fate of her mother, Lady Dedlock, whose secret past has not prevented her from marrying into one of the most powerful families in England; Esther's story also involves her father, the ill-fated Captain Hawdon, whose decline has taken him into the opium dens of London and to the very edge of both life and society, where he ekes out a living copying legal documents. This broken family moves from the top of the social scale (Lady Dedlock) to the bottom (Captain Hawdon, or Nemo—"no one"—as he is called), with Esther mediating the difference as she travels with John Jarndyce and at the same time observes and sympathizes with the poor and derelict. A bridge between these totally different worlds is also supplied by Tulkinghorn, who, suspicious of Lady Dedlock's past, launches an investigation that links almost every character in the novel: Snagsby, Kenge and Carboy, Guppy, Smallweed, George Rouncewell, Mr. Weevil, and finally Jo, the street sweep, whose poverty takes him literally to Nemo's door. Dickens's city, which sometimes gives the impression of being atomistic, is really connected on the human level both by the unscrupulous presence of men like Tulkinghorn and by the redeeming presence of Esther Summerson. Tulkinghorn's understanding of the secret past allows him control over the commercial city, which he exploits for power and wealth.

The end of this commercial process is misery, suffering, and death. John Locke was among the early observers to see the wilderness as a wasteland waiting to be reclaimed as property through individual work and effort. Reversing this view, Dickens saw the city as using up the land and creating a wasteland, a system of physical debris and human dereliction. An urban entropy is at work: chaos threatens order and urban forms of death intrude upon the commercial process. The wasteland effect is even stronger in *Our Mutual Friend* (1864–65), a novel in which people make their living by recovering bodies from the Thames—a novel that T. S. Eliot was reading when he wrote *The Waste Land*. In

Bleak House, waste as an end product to an urban process is physically embodied in Krook's junk shop, the equivalent of the famous Boffin's Bower or dust piles in *Our Mutual Friend,* as well as in human characters like Jo and Nemo.

But in *Bleak House,* Dickens's City of Death is not without the possibility of redemption, and the source of that redemption involves both Esther Summerson and Inspector Bucket of the new detective force. Esther is obviously the pure embodiment of the sentimental heroine whose sense of good, whose power of the human heart, can soften and allay the evil and misery that she sees around her. In a Henry Fielding or Jane Austen novel, the moral center is a Squire Allworthy or Mr. Knightley, who resolve the conflict by insisting upon the authority of the estate. In the city, no such authority exists: the John Jarndyces and Leiscester Dedlocks are moved aside to make room for persons of sentiment like Esther Summerson and Mr. Brownlow. (Can the summer sun burn away the enshrouding winter fog?)

Modern criticism has been unkind to Esther, which tells us a good deal about our lack of belief in the redeeming power of sentiment. Critics sympathetic to Esther impose upon her qualities that are drawn from modern novels; they see her as guilt-ridden by the circumstances of her birth, revealing a deeply troubled consciousness, as if we can be comfortable with our literary women only when they are neurotic. But Dickens was not embarrassed by Esther, and I believe that he allowed her to narrate half the novel so as to complement the authorial narrator who treats primarily the institutional problems of the novel. Esther, in contrast, draws our attention—and our pity—to the people who suffer because of those institutions. It is Esther who deeply sympathizes with Caddy Jellyby, Mr. Gridley, Miss Flite, Ada, Charley, and Jo; and it is Esther who has mixed feelings toward Richard Carstone and reinforces our moral indignation against Skimpole, Vholes, Guppy, and Smallweed. Esther embodies the power of the human heart to confront evil and suffering with a sense of compassion and to bring the city back to human scale.

But the city maze is better fathomed by Inspector Bucket than by Esther. Far more intuitive than she, Bucket can cut through the anonymity and the mysteries and secrets of the city and use this information for good, just as Tulkinghorn can use it for evil. It is surely no narrative accident that Esther accompanies Bucket on his famous trip through and beyond and back into the city in search of Lady Dedlock. Just as Dickens uses two narrators to come to terms with the city in both institutional and human terms, so he uses two characters to break through the mystery of the missing Lady Dedlock. Inspector Bucket breaks through the disguises, but he can do that only when hard or troubled hearts have been softened by Esther, who is able to get key information from the woman in the brickmaker's cottage and from the hysterical servant of Mr. Snagsby. As Esther kneels beside her, the woman "put her poor head upon my shoulder; whereupon she drew her arm around my neck, and burst into tears" (*Bleak House*, 865) before she reveals the final path Lady Dedlock took to Nemo's grave.

In *Bleak House*, the city is a tragic setting—a lonely place where the family is often left behind on the estate, a physically gigantic realm in which space is now manipulated by machines like the new locomotive, an amoral world that turns on money and on mystery and intrigue as personal knowledge gives way to anonymity. Dickens seems intent on humanizing this city, bringing it back to human proportions. Never before *Bleak House* did Dickens's plots turn so completely on secrets and undisclosed information. In *The Old Curiosity Shop* (1840–41), Dick Swiveller confronted the mysterious origins of the Marchioness, whom he named Sophronia Sphynx; and in *Martin Chuzzlewit* (1843), the detective Nadgett reveals the secret of Jonas having murdered Tigg. But these episodes appear trivial when compared to the use of revelation of secrets in *Bleak House*. In that novel, which indicts the process of law, it is not surprising that a lawyer, Mr. Tulkinghorn, and a lawyer's clerk, Mr. Guppy, uncover the secret of Lady Dedlock's past and attempt to use that information for their own selfish purposes. Their schemes are foiled by Inspector Bucket, perhaps the real hero of the novel, who undoes the mystery of the city to reveal that Lady Dedlock and Captain Hawdon are Esther's parents, and who discovers Lady Dedlock—after a frantic chase through the East End—dead at the cemetery in which Hawdon is buried. As in many city novels, one strand of the story ends with the grave, while another ends with a new life, as Esther and Allan Woodcourt start over. And although the original Bleak House has been lost in the tangles of Chancery, the novel also ends with the possibility of another Bleak House, to which Esther and Allan retreat—a house that also stands in opposition to Chesney Wold, the dying estate of the Dedlocks, which is giving way to gothic disorder, as Dedlock loses his power and influence to the world of the encroaching city.

Thus we move in *Bleak House* from power to mystery to waste and death. While the city is redeemable in *Bleak House*, it is just barely so, and its pernicious influence extends beyond itself. As that influence reaches the countryside, it transforms the estate, that last vestige of the feudal world, into the gothic. The world of the father becomes inverted, caught in the clutches of death, and is turned into a haunted realm. This is exactly what happens in *Great Expectations* (1861), when Pip is released from his indenture to Joe Gargery and the village world to go to London in search of his "great expectations," as Dickens contrasts the worlds of the city and the landed village. Pip's life is totally disrupted by his move to London; there he must create himself, subject to a new kind of personal destiny. The meaning of the landed life is embodied in Joe Gargery and Biddy. They are content with their lot and live in humble dignity. In contrast, Pip's call to the city starts a chain of events that leads to discontent and the desire for all that goes against the grain of his moral nature: he breaks with his family, feels embarrassed by their humbleness, ties his fate to the loneliness of the city, and desires its products—money and material success.

In Dickens's later novels, there is a sense of the uncanny. Between the country and the city is a strange, eerie, primitive world of the marshes— a world of water and mire with houses sinking into the mud, a world of sluice gates and mills. The narrative flash points in Dickens's fiction occur where water and land meet, or where the country and the city intersect, or where the past and the present converge. Here we find the return of the repressed: out of this world emerges a primitive evil, slinking in the form of various almost mutant outcasts. In *Oliver Twist,* Bill Sikes emerges from and goes to his death in such a region, as do Quilp in *The Old Curiosity Shop* and Bradley Headstone in *Our Mutual Friend.* In *Great Expectations,* Orlick slithers from such a realm with a primitive, uncanny evil clinging to him. This sense of evil exists prior to the city, as a natural condition to which humanity is subject, regardless of place. Such a setting is also connected with the cemetery: in *Great Expectations,* both Magwitch and Compeyson emerge from the marshes, flee across its bogs, and take sanctuary in the cemetery. Compeyson is the ultimate embodiment of evil, and his influence touches all the main characters of the novel—most directly Magwitch and Miss Havisham, and thus indirectly Pip and Estella. Dickens connects Satis House (with its obviously ironic name), the marshes, and the graveyard to the unweeded garden that surrounds the house, which reveals nature unreclaimed. That Pip's journey to the city begins and ends at this very place is central to the novel. Pip violates his sense of right and wrong, his sense of truth, both at Satis House and in the city; he violates all that he holds dear. The dead estate leads to the city, where he will deal with another consummate

Figure 2. London Bridge. Dickens contrasted the medieval stone with the modern iron bridge; T. S. Eliot's somnambulant crowd crossed the bridge to King William Street where they renewed their secular pursuits. Each vision charts the rise of a new materialism. Courtesy of the Frances Loeb Library, Graduate School of Design, Harvard University.

master of mystery and secrets—the lawyer Jaggers, who also bridges both worlds, and whose web of information entangles all the main characters of the novel and allows him to hold most of them in a grasp so soiled that his constant hand washing is to no avail. His clerk, Wemmick, compartmentalizes these two worlds of the novel: the world of the soiled city, where he looks for "portable property," and the world that parodies the estate, where he attends his aged father in a home modeled on a feudal castle (complete with drawbridge). In *Great Expectations,* Dickens was beginning to show the limitations both of a feudal past and of a materialistic present caught in the grip of death, making it impossible for Pip and Estella ever to be reconciled. After many of his readers complained about the novel's unhappy ending, he did revise it to offer a glimmer of romantic hope. But as the scale of the city increased, the human scale was diminished, and by the time he got to *Our Mutual Friend,* his last complete novel, Dickens had serious doubts about what the beneficent will can do against the forces of urban blight.

Our Mutual Friend picks up the theme of the landscape transformed. The novel's first paragraphs contrast the "Southwark Bridge which is iron, and London Bridge which is stone" (*Our Mutual Friend,* 43)—that is, contrasts the medieval and the Victorian (see figure 2). Later Charley Hexam is described as a boy "of uncompleted savagery, and uncompleted civilization" (60). Throughout this novel, we are between worlds. *Our Mutual Friend* is Dickens's most serious and severe indictment of the commercial city with its vast differences between the very rich and the very poor, with its derelict population living off offal and death. Dickens here connects the end product of the commercial city with waste and death, something he had been anticipating by connecting many of its custodians with the French word *merde*—Mr. Merdle and the Murdstones, for example, and the Turveydrops and the Tite Barnacles. As Eugene Wrayburn and Mortimer Lightwood travel through the city, their coach, Dickens tells us, "rolled down by the Monument and by the Tower, and by the Docks; down by Ratcliffe, and by Rotherhithe; down by where accumulated scum of humanity seemed to be washed from higher grounds, like so much moral sewage, and to be pausing until its own weight forced it over the bank and sunk it in the river" (63).

Out of the river come the dead bodies that Gaffer Hexam and Rogue Riderhood recover for money. And out of the river steps John Harmon, who is mistaken for dead, and who enters the city disguised as Julius Handford and later John Rokesmith. In *Great Expectations,* Pip changed his name to make it more elegant when he entered the city; Harmon changes his name as a disguise to play out the carnivalesque quality of the city. He becomes a mysterious stranger in a world of deception and pretense, spawned by the money that indelibly marks all of the city's inhabitants: the Veneering (the newly rich), Bella Wilfer (who must overcome her greed before she is worthy to marry Harmon), and Bradley Headstone (whose ambition and desire for status turn his jealousy of Wrayburn into psychotic rage).

In *Our Mutual Friend,* Dickens shows how London can no longer be redeemed in personal terms; he refers to it, in fact, as a hopeless city: "Such a black shrill city, combining the qualities of a smoky house and a scolding wife; such a gritty city; such a hopeless city, with no rent in the leaden canopy of its sky; such a beleaguered city, invested by the great Marsh Forces of Essex and Kent" (191). Here Dickens explicitly connects the city and the marshes; and at the end of the novel it is within such marshes that Bradley Headstone and Rogue Riderhood lock in mortal combat, grasp each other in an "iron ring" (874; Dickens uses the phrase three times in this passage), and fall to their deaths in the water and the mud from which the city—indeed life itself—emerged.

At the end of *Bleak House,* the principal lovers are reconciled; but Bella Wilfer and John Harmon, Eugene Wrayburn and Lizzie Hexam share a more uncertain future than do Esther Summerson and Allan Woodcourt, their fate more problematic. In almost every one of Dickens's novels, the transformation from a corrupt to a new life is marked by a period of illness in which a character is nursed back to health: Mrs. Nickelby and Kate, for example, nurse Madeline Bray back to health; the Marchioness nurses Dick Swiveller; Charley and Esther Summerson nurse Jo, the street sweep, before they succumb to smallpox and are nursed back to health themselves; Little Dorrit nurses Arthur Clennam; Joe Gargery, Pip; and Lizzie, Wrayburn. But in *Our Mutual Friend,* the city itself seems infected, even more so than in *Bleak House;* it has become a great dumping ground, bespotted with large mounds of offal and trash within which people scavenge for valuables—just as the lifeblood of the city, the Thames, has become a river of human debris. No longer is there a meaningful reader of urban signs; no one seems able to break through the uncanny maze, solve the mystery, and redeem the city. One wonders if this is why Dickens abandoned London in his next novel, the unfinished *The Mystery of Edwin Drood,* centering the action in Cloisterham, his fictional name for Rochester. Originally a medieval town, Rochester was also being transformed into a modern, industrial city, but it was still intelligible in a way that separated it from the unredeemable London of *Our Mutual Friend.*

PART 3

Modernism/Urbanism

CHAPTER 4

City of Limits

I

Dickens exhausted the possibilities of the sentimental novel, and comic realism gave way to literary naturalism. Literary naturalism derives mainly from a biological model, in which human life is grounded upon animality. Its origin owes much to Charles Darwin and his theory of evolution, which rests on his theory of natural selection. Darwin created a context that made naturalism—with its stress on theories of heredity and environment—a convincing way for those in the late nineteenth century to explain the nature of reality.

Darwinism was both a continuation of and a challenge to Enlightenment assumptions. As a theory of evolution, it put the emphasis on the physical process of the universe, on matter unfolding in time. But as a theory of natural selection—that is, the theory that all species change through a process of adaptation to their immediate environment—it put the emphasis on the accidental rather than on a necessary unfolding, thus seriously challenging the notion of design. Darwin's theory of evolution contained the idea of devolution and degeneration. Natural selection argues that the best in the species are attracted to and mate with each other. The worst in the species are left to mate and generate their own offspring. Literary naturalism gave far more attention to evolutionary throwbacks than to the forward progress of the species—as Zola reveals in his *Rougon-Macquart* novels.

Before Darwin's ideas were widely available for literary use, they had to be transformed by Émile Zola (1840–1902) in his *Le Roman expérimental* (1880). Zola in turn based his theories of heredity and environment on Prosper Lucas's *Traité...de l'hérédité naturelle* (1850) and especially on Claude Bernard's *Introduction á l'étude de la médecine expérimentale* (1865). Zola believed that the literary imagination could make use of the ideas in these books so long as the novelist functioned as a scientist—observing nature and social data, rejecting supernatural and transhistorical explanations of the physical world, rejecting absolute standards of morality and free will, and depicting nature and human experience as a deterministic and mechanistic process. All reality could be explained by a biological understanding of natural laws. "I wanted to study temperaments and not character," Zola wrote: "I chose beings powerfully dominated by their nerves and their blood, devoid of free will, carried away by the fatalities of their flesh" (quoted in Knapp, 21).

Zola gave his contemporaries a wholly new way of thinking about the novel. Temperament was more important than character; setting could not be separated from a naturalistic theory of environment, nor plot from theories of evolution. Man occupied a halfway house between the realm of the animals and some more-perfect realm of being that future development would reveal. While the naturalistic novel often deals with a static moment of time, it also presupposes an atavistic past or a futuristic ideal toward which characters can be drawn. The futuristic plots move toward forms of science fiction and utopian fantasy; the atavistic plots approach dystopia and the animalistic, often the monstrous, although in some naturalistic narratives (for example, those of Jack London) this pull away from civilization and decadence toward the more savage sometimes restores a lost vitality.

Thus, while these novels presume the reality of evolution, they often work in terms of devolution: degeneration and personal decline are embedded in most naturalistic fiction. And such degeneration finds its equivalent on the social level, where the fate of the individual is often inseparable from a declining family or the new, urbanized crowd. The crowd comes out of the masses, and the mob comes out of the crowd— all at the expense of community. Not just an aggregate of individuals, the crowd has a life of its own, becomes a kind of atavistic animal, and is capable of bestial and violent behavior, mindlessly following a leader. The leader's own fate at the hands of the mob is extremely precarious. Built into the problem of controlling the crowd is the problem of misused power—of fascism and other forms of totalitarianism. Misused power is at work in such Zola novels as *Nana* and *Germinal* and leads to social decline: the corruption of the family and the individual finds a natural correspondence in the corruption of the state. Everything is corrupt and capable of degeneration and debasement, from the highest orders of government and the salon to the workers in the mines to the people in the street.

And yet naturalism, while pessimistic, has an optimistic element built into it. This optimism stems from the usually unexpressed belief that while the fate of the individual is circumscribed, ending in sickness and death, the species is fated to move ever upward and onward in an evolutionary march toward greater perfection. While these ideas are only implicit in Darwin, they were made explicit by Herbert Spencer, one of Darwin's most influential interpreters. Literary naturalism thus had two concepts—the bright and dark side of progress—competing within it. A good many of the later naturalists projected a more highly evolved man in the future (H. G. Wells's *The Invisible Man,* 1897) at the same time that they showed how debased man could become if moved back in evolutionary time (Wells's *The Island of Dr. Moreau,* 1896).

One of the major *differences* between literary naturalism and the romance fiction which preceded it is that in naturalism the focus changed from the distant past to the more immediate present. Naturalistic authors foregrounded more contemporary problems. Zola, for example, whose writing career spanned the years 1870–90, concentrated on the years of the Second Empire (1851–70). All of his novels deal with some topical issue of these times: the greed of the peasantry for land, the movement of the peasantry from the land to the city, the fate of the urban worker, the corruption of the high-society prostitute, the rise of the department store, the function of the urban market, the fate of the new industrial worker, the rise of the steam engine and the railroad system, the fate of a degenerating France as it prepares for war with Germany.

II

Modern realism takes much of its meaning from the rise of the new city, and this is as true in France as it is in England. Medieval Paris lasted well into the nineteenth century, though in the seventeenth century the medieval walls were torn down and turned into boulevards lined with trees from the Madeleine almost to the Bastille. In 1797 under

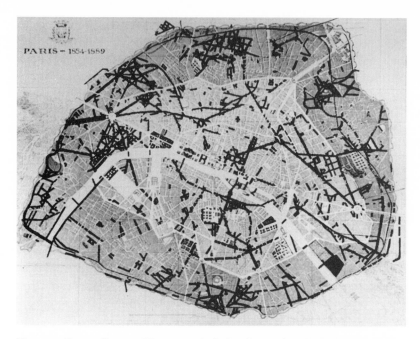

Figure 3. Baron Georges Haussmann's design for modern Paris. Haussmann destroyed medieval Paris in the name of the new empire. Courtesy of the Frances Loeb Library, Graduate School of Design, Harvard University.

Napoleon a far-sighted plan, known as the Artists' Plan, was drawn up and served in great part for the city that Haussmann would later build (see figure 3). This plan in turn owed much to Christopher Wren's plan for London. Wren's brilliant conception of a new city reflected its new commercial functions, with the Royal Exchange instead of St. Paul's occupying the physical center of the city.

As France moved from an agrarian to an urban base, the function of Paris changed just as London had changed in the seventeenth century. By 1824, the Bourse was as much a monument as Notre Dame or the Louvre. By the time of the July Revolution of 1830 and the reign of Louis Philippe, the seeds for a new Paris were already planted. Perhaps most instrumental in the change was the invention of new sources of power, especially the steam engine, which freed the factory from a rural source of water power and allowed it to come into the city, bringing with it the proletariat. These workers would make up a major source of the new urban population and would become the major concern of people like Eugène Sue and Victor Hugo, as well as Karl Marx and Friedrich Engels. It was also at this time that Louis Philippe tried to suppress the workers' movement, making little provision for absorbing their expanding numbers.

It is exactly this world that Eugène Sue (1804–57) addresses in his monumental novel *The Mysteries of Paris*. Sue's novel is ten volumes and over a thousand pages long. Published in the newspapers in serial form in 1842 to 1843, it became a sensation in its time. The time of the plot is 1838, eight years into the rule of Louis Philippe. The story involves Rodolph, grand duke of Gerolstein, a small German state, who is exiled when he has a child by the evil Lady Sarah Macgregor, who delivers the child to the even more evil lawyer, Jacques Ferrand, who sells her into white slavery, all the time letting Lady Sarah and Rodolph believe that the child is dead. These are traditional characteristics of the melodramatic plot from *Oedipus* to *Tom Jones*.

Sue creates a melodramatic world in which good and evil are entirely distinct. Rodolph, the exiled prince, embodies good; Ferrand, the lawyer, or the minister of the new commercial order, embodies evil. Strangely, the greatest influence on Sue was James Fenimore Cooper. Sue took the sequential plot structure of the Natty Bumppo novels and moved it to the city: the city replaced the forest, the underworld gang replaced the evil Indians, Rodolph sharing a skill for survival with Natty. As contrived as this plot may seem, the novel was immensely popular and influential in the nineteenth century. It received so much attention, in fact, that it attracted the interest of an unlikely reader, Karl Marx, whose discussion of it in *The Holy Family* (1845) is its most extended critique. Marx uses this novel, along with other works of the time, to attack the Young Hegelians, who, he felt, advocated too idealistic a notion of reality: he believed that Sue, in that tradition, debased the idea of mystery, turning character into caricature. Marx insisted that Sue established a transcendent rather than human basis for relationships, turning Fleur-de-Marie, Rodolph's daughter and the novel's heroine, into a grotesque form of life (K. Marx, 230–34).

What Marx is specifically analyzing in *The Holy Family,* subtitled *A Critique of Critical Critique,* is that form of idealized consciousness—here Christian in form and embodied by Rodolph—that positions itself within the social matrix. Marx's point is that although the social conditions of Paris under Louis Philippe have changed radically, the consciousness that informs the city is still medieval. As a result, instead of liberating Fleur-de-Marie, Sue only imprisons her more deeply within her environment. Sue not only holds on to the image of medieval Paris, he holds on to the consciousness—the very ideology—that keeps medieval Paris in place. Thus by failing to see that a new consciousness is necessary to account for such new economic evils as the slums of Paris, Sue only reifies the evil that he mistakenly thinks he is opposing. Despite the sympathy that Sue created for the Paris poor, Marx believed that he failed to come to terms with the new Paris.

Hugo's *Les Misérables* (1862) brings us a step closer to the world that Marx had in mind. This is not to say that Hugo is any less melodramatic than Sue: this novel also turns on a multitude of coincidences. Despite the number and variety of characters and the distances that often separate them, Hugo nevertheless brings all of his principal characters together in the compressed space of a Paris slum. Good and evil are as easily divided in Hugo's world as in Sue's, although by the end, a character like Javert can move from a simple to a complex understanding of this world—so complex, in fact, that it costs him his sense of identity and ultimately his life. The biggest difference between Hugo's and Sue's novels, however, is that *Les Misérables* is compellingly told against the unfolding of history. The novel covers the twenty years from 1815 to 1835—that is, from the defeat of Napoleon at Waterloo until after the Revolution of 1830 and the reign of Louis Philippe, ending shortly before the point where Sue began. Hugo was thus looking back on events that had occurred almost forty years earlier; and he was doing it from exile, having been forced out of France in 1852 by Louis Napoleon, whom Hugo had attacked for betraying the idea of the republic. He spent fourteen years reworking his novel, completing it in 1862.

As in most novels of romantic realism, Hugo superimposes an extended religious trope onto the city itself; *Les Misérables* describes a climb out of hell toward a secular kind of redemption. As part of this scheme, Jean Valjean becomes a secular Christ. At one point in the novel, he is literally buried alive and then resurrected from the grave. When he enters the gigantic Parisian sewer system, carrying the wounded Marius like a cross, he is entering a Dantean nether world.[1] And when he crosses a River Styx and is freed from this underworld by the gatekeeper Thenardier, the symbolism paralleling Christ's redemption is clear. The descent into the secular hell of the city is inseparable from the political resolution of the novel, which is in turn inseparable

---

1. In *The Politics and Poetics of Transgression* (1986), a book heavily influenced by Freud, Peter Stallybrass and Allon White connect the urban slum and the sewer (mediated by the rat), reading works like Henry Mayhew's *London Labour and the London Poor* (1861) in a cloacal context. They also examine Freud and the carnivalesque.

from the union of Cossette and Marius and from their reconciliation with Valjean—who, like Javert, his opposite, must die so that another form of reality can come into being.

Hugo takes us to the edge of the modern city—but only to the edge. We are still very much in a kind of Hegelian realm. Hegel believed that through logic we superimpose categories that give meaning to the chaos of reality. That reality in turn is part of a transcendent process, by which romantic history works through us. Those who are opposites in life—such as Jean Valjean and Javert—thus find their synthesis in the person of a Marius, and history moves idealistically onward. Waterloo, Hugo maintains, was a temporary deviation on the part of progress. But even Waterloo and a restored Louis XVIII could not recapture the past or hold back history, and a new spirit of liberalism worked its will, finally expressing itself in 1830. Hugo felt that his story of Jean Valjean, Javert, and Marius was inseparable from that historical process, that the contradictions that would end the lives of both Valjean and Javert were the contradictions of history, and that the spirit of a higher will was working through Marius. This spirit would redeem Paris, both as the capital of France and as the container of the poor. Hegel could not have expressed it any better.

III

Honoré de Balzac (1799–1850) wrote out of the belief that there was a connection between animality and humanity, nature and society—that an urban world created a social species analogous to the animal world of nature. *La Comédie humaine* contains ninety novels and stories written with this assumption in mind. The keystone of this fictional sequence was Balzac's belief that as aristocracy had been destroyed by the growth of capitalism, the transition from an agrarian to an urban world had created new social forces and, as a result, new human types.

Balzac's *Lost Illusions* (1837–43) and *The Splendors and Miseries of Courtesans* (1844–47), both a part of his famous *Human Comedy,* take us substantially beyond the political ideology of Sue and Hugo. Balzac deals roughly with the same narrative time span as Hugo; *Lost Illusions* begins after the defeat at Waterloo and ends around 1822, when the narrative is picked up in *Splendors and Miseries.* Beginning in 1824, that novel treats the last six years of the Restoration and concludes just before the July Revolution in 1830. After Lucien de Rubempré signs a Faustian pact with Vautrin, the two travel on to Paris, where Vautrin concocts a scheme to marry Lucien into royalty. This scheme eventually leads to Lucien's suicide, an event that moves Vautrin to perhaps the first genuine grief that he has ever experienced. Vautrin is one of Balzac's most memorable characters: he has red-brick hair concealed by a wig, a powerful physique, a resonant voice, piercing eyes, great intelligence, and an iron nature that allows him to triumph over his enemies. The rest of *Splendors and Miseries* is given over to the story of Vautrin, who becomes first a police collaborator and eventually a police magistrate. By the end of the novel, the archcriminal is running the police.

Vautrin is introduced in "Ferragus and the Thirteen" (1833–34); he next appears as the criminal Jacques Collin, also known as Trompe-la-Mort, in *Père Goriot* (1835), where he lives in the Pension Vauquer along with Eugène de Rastignac. Vautrin is modeled on an ex-convict named Vidocq, who was chief of the French *brigade de sûreté* from 1811 to 1827 and from 1831 to 1832; his memoirs of 1828–29 recounted his transition from criminal to police chief. Balzac met Vidocq in April of 1834 and saw in him the social complexity that Vautrin was to express: he symbolized the devil, the artist challenging God, the essence of capitalism, and finally the city itself. Vautrin makes no distinction between the pursuit of money inside and outside the system: criminality and respectability are merely different ways of engaging the capitalistic process, two sides of the same coin, as his move from criminal to policeman suggests. Capitalism functions within urban institutions, but the great capitalist is able to challenge institutional limits, just as the criminal challenges the limits of the law. Balzac takes us to the city of limits: we cannot have wealth without poverty, success without failure, the capitalist without the criminal. Vautrin assails limits, becomes at one and the same time the man of law and the criminal.

At that moment, Balzac moves beyond premodern Paris. No longer are we in a realm where good and evil are mechanically separate; we are not in the worlds of Sue and Hugo, in which a transcendent reason morally divides experience in two. Balzac creates two morally different urban prototypes in Vautrin and Daniel d'Arthez—one the man of power, the other the committed artist. Both see how far they can push their sense of self; both test their roles against urban limits. Much as Sue and Hugo can be conjoined to Hegel, so Balzac's Vautrin anticipates Nietzsche. Nietzsche begins by questioning the assumptions that often dominate the novels of Sue and Hugo: he attacks the Christian legacy that allows the Apollonian to suppress the Dionysian, and he attacks the Enlightenment legacy that privileges reason, science, and technology. Nietzsche instead emphasizes human consciousness testing the limits of conventions. As with Zola, physical limits establish the extremes between those who submit to limits and those who defy them. In Zola's novels, many succumb to the forces of Paris in the Second Empire, while others transform the new city. Balzac saw the material nature of the city, the city of physical limits; he focused on the city as a set of competing dualistic forces. He was the link between comic realism and literary naturalism. After Balzac the novel would never be the same, and Emile Zola was the most immediate inheritor of his literary legacy.

IV

The events in Zola's novels go back to 1830, ten years before his birth, when Louis Philippe took over the political reins of France in the name of the Second Republic. As one historian tells us, "it was not long before liberals came to see that their idealism was misplaced; the system of divine right and ultra-royalism had been driven out, only to be replaced by a regime of landlords and capitalists with a bourgeois monarch. There was not much to choose between the two" (Wolf, 71). Under Louis Philippe, France became a commercial, urban, industrial country. Industries like textile manufacturing were being taken over by machines. As we have noted, the invention of the steam engine freed such industries from relying on water power supplied by rural rivers and brought them to the city, creating a major shift in population. By 1840 over 672,000 men, 254,000 women, and 130,000 children were working in French factories, far outnumbering the older and more traditional urban trade workers—tanners, dyers, hatters, masons, and smiths (Wolf, 278). Much of this new industry was being financed by English investors—the Rothschilds, Barings, and Hopes—whose families had amassed fortunes supplying the money base for the industrial English revolution (Wolf, 278).

The change in December of 1848 from Louis Philippe to Louis Napoleon Bonaparte was not so abrupt as it first appeared. Three years after Louis Napoleon became president, on December 2, 1851, Paris was occupied by troops loyal to the new president. One year later, Louis

Figure 4. Avenue des Champs-Elysées, Paris. Haussmann's city accommodated the imperial center of empire and suggested a new scale that dwarfed the human. Courtesy of the Frances Loeb Library, Graduate School of Design, Harvard University.

Napoleon became Napoleon III, the emperor of the Second Empire; its new constitution of January 14, 1853, codified his powers. Once again a liberal revolution gave way to a conservative political reaction, the new power consolidated by the new emperor. Zola later saw these events as a betrayal of the liberal cause. But many historians have stressed the enlightened aspect of Napoleon III's regime. Canals and rivers were dug or widened, keeping open the best transportation systems in Europe. And Baron Georges Haussmann (1809–91) was hired to remove medieval Paris and build a modern city. Haussmann demolished almost 20,000 Parisian hovels and built 43,777 new homes; he lengthened rue de Rivoli from the Bastille to the place de la Concorde and built the Boulevards Saint-Michel, Sébastapol, Strasbourg, and Magneta (see figure 4). The Saint-Martin canal was covered and transformed into a boulevard. The Bois de Boulogne and Vincennes were made into public parks, and in a new spacious context such urban buildings as the Louvre, the Hotel de Ville, the Palais Royal, the National Library, Notre Dame, and the Paris Opera became monuments. Paris became the center of Europe with six railroads converging on the capital. In 1855 and in 1867, Paris hosted the World's Fair; in 1856, the Congress of Paris. Under

Napoleon III, new credit lines were established by two lending institutions—the Credit Mobilier, which handled primarily industrial loans, and the Credit Financier, which handled primarily agrarian loans. When Napoleon III came into power, 74.4 percent of France was rural; by the time he lost power in 1870, 68.9 percent of France was rural. In that time, Paris almost doubled in population, and there arose a number of urban centers: Lyon, Marseille, Bordeaux, and Lille.

Zola captures the sweep of these events in his *Rougon-Macquart* novels. Written between 1871 and 1893, a period slightly more than twenty years after the Second Empire, they cover the years from the eve of the Second Empire (1851) to the French defeat at the Sedan during the Franco-Prussian War (1870)—or, as Zola put it in his introduction, "from the perfidy of the coup d'état to the treason of the Sedan" (*La Fortune des Rougan*, vi).[2] Zola describes these years from the point of view both of the countryside, where a greedy peasant class begins to consolidate power, and of the city, where a new middle class rises to power under the auspices of Napoleon III.

To say that Zola believed that the life lived closest to nature was good, the life lived closest to society bad, oversimplifies, although at times this seems to be the case. Rather, Zola was suggesting something slightly different—namely, that modern man had been displaced from the natural environment, had lost contact with his instincts and a more rudimentary and basic sense of self, and had become more and more distanced from the rhythms of the natural life. Money and bureaucracy had replaced the workings of nature and natural feelings.

The center of the *Rougon-Macquart* novels is the center of France—Paris—to which many of the townspeople come in search of a heightened sense of self, in search of power at its functioning center. The Paris novels are *La Curée* (1872), *La Ventre de Paris* (1873), *Son Excellence Eugène Rougon* (1876), *L'Assommoir* (1877), *Nana* (1878), *Pot-Bouille* (1882), *Au Bonheur des dames* (1883), *La Joie de vivre* (1884), *L'Oeuvre* (1886), *La Bête humaine* (1890), and *L'Argent* (1891). While *Germinal* (1885), *La Terre* (1889), and *La Débâcle* (1892) are not city novels, they depict action that has its origins in the economy and politics of the city. Thus over half the novels in the series deal with the world of Paris, and the rest cannot be separated from its influence.

---

2. Unless otherwise noted, translations from the *Rougon-Macquart* series are from the E. Vizetelly edition (1886). Since this edition is unreliable, all translated passages have been checked against the original French.

La Curée is the first novel to establish the meaning of Paris as both the center of France and the center of Zola's narrative world. Aristide Rougon comes to Paris from the provincial town of Plassans to hunt *la curée* (the quarry). Early in the novel, Aristide—he will later change his name to Saccard—looks down over the entire city from a restaurant window on the Buttes Montmarte and sees Paris much as Eugène de Rastignac sees it at the end of *Père Goriot:* as a world to be plundered and conquered. This goal is realized when he makes a fortune out of Haussmann's rebuilding (that is, out of the ruins) of Paris. Zola continued the story of Saccard in *L'Argent,* another novel about the power of money, as the title indicates. A more ambitious novel than *La Curée,* it was based on a financial scandal in the Third Republic involving an engineer named Eugène Bantoux. He engaged in foreign speculation financed by L'Union Generale, a bank with close ties to the pope, which was attacked and defeated by the financial forces of James de Rothschild. Zola saw in this incident a modern paradigm: the bank as the center of the city, financing investments all over the world, is caught up in the forces of political and religious strife, its workings affecting directly or indirectly the lives of people all over the world. Saccard engages this world when he meets a young engineer, Hamelin, who needs help financing a silver mine in Palestine. Connected with this are spin-off investments in railroads, steamship lines, and foreign banks. Zola is here describing the beginnings of the world city—the visible tower of the financier with its invisible power, the beginning of the cartel-like financial deal, as capital moves and controls the underdeveloped lands around the globe. Money is a force greater than military or political power. Even when Saccard's plan is defeated and his scheme collapses, the money he generated has built new cities and brought remote lands into the grip of the modern world: "The village of five hundred inhabitants, born at first around the mine in process of exploitation, was now a city, several thousand souls, a complete civilization, roads, factories, schools, fertilizing this dead and savage corner" (*L'Argent,* 434).

What Zola showed so clearly in *L'Argent* is how power is transformed through the workings of the city—in this instance, through its financial institutions. The biological process of life and death has been transformed, moved from the realm of nature to the realm of the city. In *La Ventre de Paris* and *Au bonheur des dames,* he analyzes this idea in some detail, describing two kinds of marketplace—les Halles Centrales, supplying food, and the modern department store, supplying material goods. The city organizes the means of satisfying biological needs as long as one has money. It is in the getting of money that modern man reveals his basic nature, a combativeness that he did not leave in the jungle. In the *Rougon-Macquart* novels, Zola showed how modern urban institutions are really systems of control: control over the landscape, over natural and industrial resources, and finally over the people themselves. Zola's is a world of physical force, operating within terms of physical limits, and if one person gets more than his share, another must get less. He sees this system as ultimately both exploitative and destructive, and he depicts the evil of the system in the very best of the novels which make up the *Rougon-Macquart* series: *L'Assommoir, Nana, Germinal, La Bête humaine, La Terre,* and *La Débâcle.*

L'Assommoir is one of the first French novels to depict the life of true working-class people—a subject the novel did not seriously entertain before Zola, which perhaps explains why this novel received so much critical attention when it was first published. "I wanted," says Zola in his preface, "to depict the inevitable downfall of a working-class family in the polluted atmosphere of our urban areas" (*L'Assommoir,* 21). The context for this novel is the same as for *La Curée* and *L'Argent;* in *L'Assommoir,* money also sets the limits to the lives of the characters, although it affects the working class more brutally. Zola praises Coupeau's and Gervaise's initial energy and delight in their work; he symbolically has Gervaise keep her bankbook in the back of a grandfather clock—and money and time wisely spent become equated in this novel. But such energy seemingly cannot be sustained, especially in the face of continued accidents and disappointments; first Coupeau and then Gervaise herself become more passive, surrendering to drink and then finally to self-abandonment. Zola quantifies their experience: he does not morally condemn Gervaise—he only shows life weighing more heavily upon her day by day until the weight trips the balance and the scale falls. The accumulated effect of living destroys these characters, whose existence is limited to food, sex, and drink. The scene in which the wedding party goes to a museum establishes a brilliant contrast between their lives and a bourgeois setting: they are totally out of place, in awe of the polished expanse of floor and puzzled by the paintings on the wall that have no connection to their life.

Gervaise Macquart's fourth child—Anna, known as Nana—is perhaps the most famous character in the *Rougon-Macquart* series. Born in 1852 when Gervaise was married to Coupeau, Nana is the product of the Parisian streets. She has a child by an unknown father when she is sixteen; at eighteen, she is the mistress of a wealthy Russian merchant who spends the winters in Paris. All of this is prelude to Nana's eventual success in the Théâtre des Variétés, where she comes to the attention of men in high government and high society, all of whom destroy themselves financially and physically in their obsession for her. Nana later conquers the East as she conquered Paris. When she returns to Paris in 1870, her sickly son, Louiset, is dying of smallpox, a disease she contracts from him. Coming on the eve of the Franco-Prussian War, Nana's death—her body covered with suppurating sores—symbolizes the corruption of the Second Empire. Her own degenerate nature and the degenerate nature of the body politic are one. And the death of her sickly son marks the end of one of the Macquart lines, now totally played out in mental and physical degeneration. The death of the imbecile and/or sickly child will become a literary insignia in the naturalistic story of personal and cultural decline—a representative event written into nature itself and manifest on every page of Zola's *Rougon-Macquart* novels.[3]

Zola concentrates in *Nana* on depicting a public world—the world of the theater, the restaurant, and the hotel—in which Nana can come from nowhere and become the center of attention once she displays her body and sensual charms. Zola also focuses on the upper realm of the bourgeoisie and the aristocracy: we quickly move from city streets to luxurious salons, and Nana's rooms at the peak of her success are as luxurious as any. In this context, Zola exposes the shallowness of upper-class life, the emptiness of such people, whose money and power comes from the work of others, whose lives lack substance and direction, and who dissipate energies on sensuous pleasures that lead to a fateful decadence. Count Muffat is the character who best embodies this process, and his gradual decline from respected aristocrat to masochistic plaything of Nana's enlists as much sympathy from the reader as disgust.

Disgust is the end product of this world, the reader's final response—disgust at Muffat and the empty world of the aristocracy; disgust at Fontan the actor, whose violence seems as necessary a consequence of this world as Muffat's decadence and whose anger leads to sadistic beatings of Nana; disgust at Satin, a gutter rat with whom Nana has a lesbian affair; and, finally, disgust at Nana herself, who is carried away by her own excesses. Almost all of the action that involves Nana takes place in a

---

3. The theme of decline, embodied in the impending death of the last degenerative offspring, is also a major theme of literary modernism, as in Mann's Buddenbrooks and Faulkner's Compson families. Such degeneration and decline are inseparable from the fate of characters like Fitzgerald's Anthony Patch and Dick Diver, but in later novels the naturalistic explanation of such decline is omitted.

world of great luxury—of gold-plated and silver-adorned salons and boudoirs, the money for which comes from the dying world of the aristocracy. This landed, propertied class is represented by Muffat, whose financial and moral defeats become one. Nana and her followers infect each other in a world where death is the only end product. At the end of the novel, her purulent body is inseparable from the corruption of the aristocracy; its death is the harbinger of the call of the mob—"Á Berlin! Á Berlin! Á Berlin!"—which signals the beginning of the Franco-Prussian War and the end of the Second Empire. Zola saw the health of a society inextricably connected with the way its members work and the way it controls the wealth and power that come from work. Once the aristocracy was displaced from the true economic process of a commercial/ industrial world, the seed of death was planted within it. Nana simply exploits the destructive process that is already at work, and since she is part of the process, her own destruction is also guaranteed. In *Nana,* Zola shows an understanding not only of a courtesan in a corrupted world but also of the very reasons for such corruption.

Zola depicts the opposite world in *Germinal:* here he takes us into the northern coalfields where the miners are on strike. Such strikes had occurred at La Ricamarie, Rive-de-Gier, Aubin, and Anzin; Zola actually visited the coalfields of Anzin and used his observations there as the basis for his novel. *Germinal* is a richly detailed, highly charged novel that graphically depicts the woeful life of coal mining. A mining family like the Maheus finds itself caught between two kinds of economic power. On the one hand, we have the owners, investors, and managers, embodied by Grégoire and Hennebeau. Both are well-meaning, decent men but unsympathetic to the worker's plight because any change in the system would be to their disadvantage. On the other hand, we have those who represent the workers. Étienne Lantier, the central character, is the self-educated, idealistic socialist who reads Marx and who believes that the value of a product is created by the work that it brings into being. Rasseneur is the trade unionist who believes a settlement must be worked out within the system by the principals involved. And Souvarine is the revolutionary anarchist who believes the system must first be destroyed and then rebuilt outside the restrictions of capitalism. Zola repudiates the paternalism of a Grégoire, but he also repudiates the radical solution of a Souvarine, for the workers end up as victims of both extremes: Grégoire feeds off their helplessness while Souvarine destroys those who oppose him and their means to work. It is not clear whether Zola finally assents to the positions of Rasseneur or Étienne. He appears to reject both of them as leaders, since the mob of workers turns on each man, on two separate occasions. The workers themselves seem to embody a force—like a force of nature—that will overpower the idle and the destructive and, in some vague Darwinian way, will create a higher purpose able to redeem the system from within.

Zola makes clear that the worlds of *Nana* and *Germinal* are really one—and that the workers who produce the wealth that allow the luxury of Nana possess the means of transforming the system. Almost everything in Zola's world comes back to the nobility of work, but he never addresses the problem of who will lead the new workers and who will control the master who controls the masses. Zola takes us in *Germinal* to the doorstep of totalitarianism without realizing it. He was aware that he was dealing with matters of power—*La Bête humaine* reveals his obsession with that subject—but he never knew who was to be trusted with the power that would eventually come from the fall of a decadent ruling class.

In the *Rougon-Macquart* novels, Zola shows how the effects of a commercial/industrial process transformed the city, the provinces, and the relationship between man and his work. In *La Terre,* he shows how this process reached a peasant world and transformed the land. The main character, Jean Macquart, is the brother of Gervaise of *L'Assommoir* and an uncle of Nana, Étienne, and Claude. His travels have taken him to La Beauce, a small market town in the grain-growing plains, the center of which is Chartres. In *La Terre,* Zola reveals that the feudal system has passed forever; the land has been bought up by the new bourgeoisie like Hourdequin or absorbed by greedy peasants like Fouan and his brutal son, Buteau. Zola depicts a degenerate world, where the possibility of a pastoral past is pure literary invention. Greed and suffering seem to be the by-products of provincial life, and they always have been. But now the small farmer is being bought out by the larger property owners who "use machinery" and, in some instances, participate in "large capital turnover" (*La Terre,* 156). Zola depicts the land as a counterforce with its life-giving rhythms. But he also shows that the land will never be "handed back"—that the farmer, large or small, is part of a process controlled by moneyed interests from the city. As Hourdequin explains, the land is "being crushed out of existence by taxes, foreign competition, the continual increase in labor costs, the flight of capital into industry and the Stock Exchange" (157). The city has reached out and absorbed the land, and the peasants participated in this destructive process. Zola ends the novel with a reference to the inseparability of life and death:

"Here were the Dead, there was the Seed; and bread would be springing from the Good Earth" (500). The bread will be taken to the markets of Paris to feed the city, and the land is now part of a larger commercial/industrial process.

The move from the land to the city is not without violence, and such violence is a part of Jacques Lantier's nature, alienated from himself and the land, as he moves in a seemingly conditioned way from lust to murder. In *La Bête humaine,* Zola superimposes upon this pathology Jacques's obsession with the locomotive of which he is the engineer: "he had loved this engine for all the four years he had been driving it. . . . He loved this one because it had the rare qualities that go to make a worthy woman" (159). Lust, murder, and the machine become connected in a strange and unexplained way; and the train conditions, if not embodies, the sexual violence that Jacques turns back on women. The mechanical power of the train is larger than the world it occupies, as Zola describes it crashing through huge snowbanks and crossing the land in a blur of speed. The tremendous power of the train has political implications. As Jacques Ellul has pointed out in *The Technological Society,* there is a direct connection between a technological and a totalitarian society: efficiency—power that sustains order and control—is their common denominator. But such power, like the rampant power of the crowd, is equally dangerous when uncontrolled. And in *La Bête humaine,* Zola once again closes a novel on the note of blind, undirected power working in an uncontrolled way as the train—"its engine without engineer or fireman, its cattle-cars filled with troops howling patriotic airs"—hurtles through the night "going to war." The train symbolizes the new commercial, industrial, technological society without true leader or direction: "Without a master, through the blackness, a blind, deaf beast, unleashed with death, it sped on, and on, loaded with cannon-fodder, with soldiers stupid with exhaustion, drunk, singing" (384).

La Débâcle picks up where *La Bête humaine* ends—with soldiers going off to fight in what will prove to be the disastrous Franco-Prussian War. Zola realized that violence was necessary if France was to break from Napoleon III, and he anticipated the Franco-Prussian War before it happened. The corruption of the empire, radiating from Paris outward, had been the theme of the major novels, and Zola showed how such corruption had infected every limb of the society—from the aristocracy separated for generations from the land, to the high bourgeoisie in their banks and offices of exchange, to the peasants and mine workers where greed and strife have interrupted the sacred office of work. The 17,000

French soldiers lost in the Sedan become a sacrifice to bureaucratic and military incompetence—and even more to a society that has produced wealth and luxury by exploiting the land and the people. Paris, the geographic center of the *Rougon-Macquart* novels, can no longer energize its extremities. Social discontent is a highly combustible element, waiting to explode, and the final scene in *La Débâcle* is that of Paris burning, "burning like some huge sacrificial fire." The novel closes with the hope of a new Paris that will draw its strength from the land—from the good, simple people like Jean with their love of the earth and their capacity for work. Even Maurice, Jean's friend who has fought against the Republic, sees some hope, and with his dying words tells Jean: "Go and take up your pick and trowel, turn over the soil and rebuild the house!" Zola has the final words: "The ravaged field was lying fallow, the burnt house was down to the ground, and Jean, the most humble and grief-stricken of men, went away, walking into the future to set about the great, hard job of building a new France" (*La Débâcle,* 508, 504, 509).

The naturalistic vision promised "renewal" through "eternal nature, eternal humanity," and toil. In the *Rougon-Macquart* novels, Zola showed how deeply political was the nature of this vision, and what could happen when an old feudal and a new commercial society were cut from the land while the city compromised the vitality of redemptive work.

V

Despite the compellingness of the naturalistic vision, such a view of life limited the sense of human complexity by reducing characters to behavioristic and deterministic realms. The naturalistic hero is usually inarticulate, devoid of deep subjectivity and moral reflection, subject to poverty and suffering, the product of his biological makeup and immediate environment, and the victim of an inevitable sequence of events usually triggered by mechanistic forms of chance.

As the Enlightenment came into being with the commercial city, so literary naturalism came into being with the industrial city. And a mediator between naturalism and the industrial process was Karl Marx (1818–83). As industrial output rose, Marx (like Ricardo) predicted that profits would fall. Capitalists would exploit workers to make up the difference, and workers in turn—always separated from goods by surplus value—would not be able to buy the products of their own labor.

The crisis of overproduction would eventually cause the working class to rise in revolt, overthrow the capitalists, and use the means of production themselves to create the socialist state.

Marx was not challenging the mechanisms of capitalism, only its ends. He gave priority to the element of work over that of investment capitalism, and he believed that work was the matrix that transformed nature into the built environment—turned raw goods into finished products and untamed land into cities. Marx believed the worker was getting less and less of the benefits his labor brought into being, and he saw the class struggle as the antagonism that characterized every society. Disagreeing with Herbert Spencer's emphasis upon the survival of the fittest, he felt the need for the working class to generate wealth by controlling the means of production, and he believed that history was moving toward this end.

Marx was both prescient and historically blind. He misjudged, for example, the power of the middle class, especially its ability to absorb labor. He also misjudged the solidarity of the laboring class and the pull of nationalism. He thought international labor would rise and unite against capitalism, but when war came in 1914 and 1939 laborers in Britain went to war against laborers in Germany. Moreover, he failed to see what would take place beyond imperialism—a world economy that would be capitalistic in nature, excluding Communism (e.g., the Soviet Union and the Warsaw Pact nations) from the great wealth of the world market. And he did not recognize the compelling nature of the "good" (that is, the material) life—new homes, modern appliances, luxury cars, mobility and travel, the fantasy values—often fatuously called "the American dream."

But despite what he did not see, Marx was amazingly prescient in other ways. Lenin's theory of imperialism followed from Marx's concept of accumulation—that is, as industrial capitalism increased it would need to find an outlet in a world economy. When production and distribution became centralized in great trusts, when banking and industrial capital became merged, and when capitalistic powers divided the world into phases of influence, a further struggle would ensue (Lenin anticipated World Wars I and II in these terms) between such states as they strove to redivide the world. In the commercial stage of capitalism, credit institutions are relatively undeveloped. Much of the world is precapitalist and the role of money is limited. As a result, capital at this stage moves in the form of trade, which eventually develops a world market for capitalist production. Manufactured goods are traded to precapitalist societies for raw material and food products. Marx argued that such a practice rigidified relationships between capitalist and precapitalist societies, and Lenin added the belief that it blocked the development of capitalism in colonial areas, creating a rivalry between developed countries as well as the dependency of the undeveloped on the developed countries. In the industrial stage, surplus value and centralization of capital together with the development of credit institutions led to monopoly capitalism (sometimes called "finance" or "late" capitalism) and intensified competition between capitalist countries. Marx and Lenin believed that the combination of monopoly capital and intensified competition brought about imperialism.

Literary naturalism gave life to many of these ideas. Zola, as we have seen, also extolled the process of work, constantly showing, as in *Germinal,* how the workers were cut off from the wealth they created. He also depicted the lower classes as held in submission by an economic system that was a distortion of the workings of nature. The Enlightenment depicted the city as a powerful grid superimposed upon the natural, and the romantics questioned what that grid repressed: the naturalists, who shared the romantics' doubt, depicted the city as an energy system and an alienating mechanism that inculcated a degenerative process by creating a diseased center outside of nature.

As a narrative method, naturalism eventually gave way to another movement, literary modernism. Modernism challenged the basic assumptions of naturalism, moving away from scientism toward a mythic/symbolic base, substituting cyclical for linear time, allowing a Bergsonian kind of subjective reality to replace scientific empiricism, and creating an elitist distinction between high and low culture. It is true that naturalism relied heavily upon symbolism, but it was a symbolism that reinforced a natural reality, in contradistinction to the literary symbolism of, say, Joyce in *Ulysses,* which became a prism through which reality was seen. We view Leopold Bloom through the symbolic lens of the Homeric Ulysses, and the contrast between the two men marks the Viconian differences in the cyclical sweep from a heroic to a demotic era. The naturalistic city is centripetal: life is controlled from a center of urban force; the modernist city is centrifugal: the center moves us outward to symbolic correspondences in space and time. The naturalistic narrator observes forces at work from a center; the modernist narrator finds the center becoming more complex and opaque, his or her own vision more subjective. The difference in literary perspective is a difference in urban reality.

CHAPTER 5

The Inward Turn

I

Two kinds of urban reality emerged from literary modernism: the city as constituted by the artist, whose inner feelings and impressions embody an urban vision, and the city as constituted by the crowd, which had a personality and urban meaning of its own. There were three general ways of looking at the crowd: Gustave Le Bon showed how a crowd mentality transformed an individual's state of mind and became the vehicle of a charismatic leader; Sigmund Freud showed how the crowd developed a consciousness and unconsciousness of its own, taking on an atavistic quality; and Elias Canetti argued that the crowd created a field of force that pulled a leader into its realm, the crowd creating the leader rather than vice versa.[1] As the crowd became more extensive, the artist's vision of the city became more opaque, more mysterious and uncanny. The crowd became a metonym for the city in modernist discourse, and a great deal of urban study is given over to the study of the crowd: the subject of the *Grosstadt* dominates the thought of Georg Simmel, Max Weber, and Walter Benjamin. Modernism intensified the awareness that the individual and the crowd were separate entities with separate modes of being. The crowd was not a composite

---

1. See Le Bon's *The Crowd* (1896), with the useful commentary of Robert Nye, *The Origins of Crowd Psychology* (1975); Freud, *Group Psychology and the Analysis of the Ego* (1922); and Canetti, *Crowds and Power* (1962).

of individuals but constituted a separate being with its own motivations. The crowd easily became the mob, and the mob was indistinguishable from the masses. What gets lost in mass society is the individual: alienation is inevitable; the individual feels alone even in the crowd. And a mass society, when controlled, is a totalitarian society.

The frenetic rhythms of the crowd take on the nervous quality of the city. As Simmel has suggested, the intensification of nervous stimulation induced by rapid crowding led to "onrushing impressions." The individual is absorbed into such energy. One way of responding to this onslaught of impressions is to become insensitive to it, to become Robert Musil's "man without qualities," as indifferent to value as is the metropolis itself. In Musil's work, a world of color becomes gray. In "The Metropolis and Mental Life" (1903), Simmel describes this condition as "the blunting of discrimination"; he believes it stems from "internalizing money" to the point that "all things float with equal specific gravity in the constantly moving stream of money" (quoted in Tafuri, 87–88).

Another way of responding to the nervous stimuli of the city induced by rapid crowding is that of Baudelaire (1821–67). Well aware of the interconnections between urban uniformity and the need for diversity, he single-mindedly looked for such diversity in the crowd, especially, as Walter Benjamin notes in *Charles Baudelaire,* in the arcades and other commercial centers of Paris where one could find the flaneur. In the first edition of *Les Fleurs du mal* (1857), Baudelaire's poetry is mostly introspective. After a court order demanded the removal of six poems on grounds of indecency, Baudelaire wrote a series of poems he added to a second edition (1861), in which he begins to make use of the city as his main subject. The observer in these poems identifies with an urban subject, usually someone who steps out of the crowd, and then through a process of association and memory connects this impression with his own experience. In "The Seven Old Men" ("Les Sept vieillards"), the observer seemingly sees an agent from hell step from the crowd and internalizes this sense of the uncanny; in "The Swan" ("Le Cygne"), a swan, escaped from his cage, steps into the Paris streets recently redesigned by Haussmann—a symbol, "ridiculous and sublime," of the new Paris and of a dozen other thoughts that by association flood the poet's mind. The observer, in other words, finds in the crowd or the Paris streets an object that triggers his imagination or memory and thus is internalized (see figure 5). We move inward from the street to the crowd to an impression drawn from the crowd to the associations that

Figure 5. Gustave Caillebotte, "Paris Street: Rainy Day" (1877). When Hauss-mann, using the "Artists' Plan" of 1793, transformed Paris in the Second Empire, he accommodated the artist-flaneur, allowing a turn from the pastoral to urban reality and legitimating the city as an object of modern art. Courtesy of the Art Institute of Chicago, Charles H. and Mary F. S. Worcester Collection.

impression evokes in the mind. Baudelaire believes in the reality of evil, in experience as sordid and nature as inherently fallen and yet re-deemable through art. Man is drawn toward both God and Satan—and they both can be found in the crowd. The poet thus goes to the crowd to find versions of himself.

Baudelaire in the crowd embodies the artist in the city, the move from an objective to a subjective view of the city—the move, that is, from nat-uralism to modernism. Baudelaire explicitly saw the city from a subjec-tivity within the crowd. *The Spleen of Paris* (*Le Spleen de Paris,* 1864) is a sequence of prose poems about the city that he composed after *Les Fleurs du mal*. In a section titled "Crowds," he confirms that artistic subjectiv-ity is grounded in the crowd, that the poet's imagination is fueled by cityscapes:

Multitude, solitude: equal and convertible terms for the active and fecund poet. He who does not know how to people in solitude will not know either how to be alone in a bustling crowd.

The poet enjoys the incomparable privilege of being able to be himself and others. Like those wandering souls which search for a body, he can enter every person whenever he wants. For him alone, everything is empty. . . .

The solitary and pensive walker draws from this universal communion a singular sense of intoxication. (*Paris Spleen*, 20)

Like the urban detective, the flaneur is the observer, the man who takes in the city at a distance. But unlike the detective, he goes to the arcades to be stimulated by the crowds. The crowd contains the potentiality for experience: meeting a lover or a friend or experiencing a spectacle. But the flaneur is discontented because the city offers more experience than he can assimilate. He always feels that he is missing out even in the process of experiencing: his state of mind is restless dissatisfaction, aimless desire, qualities we find in many of Dreiser's and Fitzgerald's characters. When this sense of potentiality becomes frightening, it threatens stability and leads to the kind of neurasthenia we find in Eliot's writing; when the threat becomes personal, it leads to the paranoia that informs Pynchon's novels. And paranoia takes us to the doorstep of the uncanny. As Baudelaire demonstrated and Walter Benjamin noted, the uncanny—the mysterious and eerie—is born out of heterogeneous crowds, which is really to say that it is born out of the city: out of the stranger who steps from the crowd, out of the familiar becoming strange, out of the return of the repressed, out of the primitive that returns as, say, superstition, out of the postcolonial migrant who returns as alien.[2] As Freud saw in "The Uncanny" (1919), the uncanny is "something which ought to have remained hidden but has come to light" (quoted in Vidler, 14). When the city gives up its secrets, we enter the realm of the uncanny. From Euripides' Dionysus to Dickens's Orlick to Joyce's Walpurgisnacht at Bella Cohen's to Pynchon's Tristero, the literary imagination has revealed the urban uncanny. As the modern city became more impenetrable, the hidden as something hostile and "unhomely" (*Unheimlichkeit*) informed the literary text.

II

In France, the reaction to naturalism was called decadence; in England, aestheticism. Both movements were eventually seen

2. An important discussion of the uncanny is Anthony Vidler's *The Architectural Uncanny: Essays in the Modern Unhomely* (1992).

as forms of symbolism. All of these terms are twentieth-century labels for nineteenth-century literary movements; eventually they lost their distinctions and were combined into the idea of modernism. As a decadent, Baudelaire was the first modern European poet. All the themes of *Les Fleurs du Mal*—Satanism, dandyism, exoticism, eroticism, everything the bourgeois regarded as decadent—were taken over by the symbolists. And yet Baudelaire's dandyism is both a mockery and a by-product of middle-class values. As Wylie Sypher has pointed out, the dandy is "a substitute for the aristocrat who had lost caste. The dandy is a middle-class aristocrat, a figure who could make his entrance only in the cities that were becoming the milieu for the bourgeoisie" (Sypher, 36). The dandy is a product of a consumer society, which he then feels superior to because of his privileged self-fashioning. The dandy distances himself from the bourgeois values that brought him and his culture into being. The desire for distance led Baudelaire to explore new poetic possibilities for treating the huge modern metropolis. Most important in this list was nostalgia for a spiritual homeland or city that existed beyond the visible world, which explains his obsession with Poe. Such nostalgia accompanied a sense of decay and decline. When this sense of decline was internalized, the resulting impression was so strong that it often dominated the way the city was perceived.

In England, Walter Pater reworked many of these themes. In his conclusion to *Studies in the History of the Renaissance* (1873), he speaks of modernism as a self-fashioning, in pursuit of sensations and impressions rather than abstractions: "To burn always with this hard, gemlike flame, to maintain this ecstasy, is success in life" (511). The hero of his *Marius the Epicurean* (1885) cultivates the pleasures of the mind and spirit. Nineteenth-century British inquiries lie beneath Marius's Roman exterior, and second-century A.D. Rome conceals the late Victorian British Empire. Pater sees a similar kind of superimposition, a layering of memory, in Leonardo's *Mona Lisa*. Oscar Wilde (1854–1900) continued the connection between French decadence and English aestheticism by modeling *Dorian Gray* (1891) upon Joris Karl Huysmans's (1848–1907) *À Rebours* (1884). Wilde wrote about the city in "The Decay of Lying" (1889): "Where if not from the Impressionists, do we get those wonderful brown fogs that come creeping down our streets, blurring the gas-lamps and changing the houses into monstrous shadows?" (33). Wilde's remarks apply particularly well to Joyce's method of recording Stephen Dedalus's impressions of the city: as Stephen walks through Dublin every place becomes an aesthetic object or text; his impressions are controlled by his sense of art and beauty. Such symbolic thinking takes us to Arthur Symons's *The Symbolist Movement in Literature* (1899), which discussed the French poets' influence upon English poetry. This book had an immense influence on T. S. Eliot, who read it in 1908 when he was at Harvard and through it discovered Verlaine and Corbière.

Before modernism replaced romanticism, it had to go through the decadent/aesthetic and symbolist experiences: the first created a reality so sour that it turned the aesthetic vision inward to escape reality; the second moved to a private, autistic state of mind, shutting out the urban, commercial, and industrial world that had become hostile. Under such pressure the city as a physical place gave way to the city as a state of mind. This process had been long in the making. In England, William Hazlitt had shown that Wordsworth's poetry was founded on an opposition between the natural and the artificial, between a spirit of humanity and a spirit of fashion.

Baudelaire's poetry also works within the realms of innocence and self-fashioning. Throughout there is a sense of the fall—a fall that antedates history and consciousness and is comparable to original sin. Such a fall can be understood through art, since it is the artist who "recreates rather than discovers nature" (Jouve, 39). The move from sentiment to sensibility takes Baudelaire close to the Flaubert of *L'Education Sentimentale* (1869), where we move from natural to self-fashioned feelings. This realm of artifice helps explain *Les Fleurs du Mal,* where "nothing connects with nothing," to paraphrase T. S. Eliot, who expressed in *The Waste Land* the same sense of fragmentation and isolation. The city no longer encouraged imaginative coherence. Both Baudelaire and Eliot believed such disconnection was a by-product of a system of profit and loss; both rejected material progress because it led to a cycle of desire, doomed to endless escalation. The city was nature inverted, transformed by capitalism. Thus both poets saw modern man caught in an essentially self-destructive urban process: the commercial city became the modern equivalent of Dante's Inferno. Salvation depended upon breaking the circle of materialism. Baudelaire believed one could do this by transforming the self as if it were art; Eliot saw Christ, not the dandy, as the means of escaping material desire.

Decadence assumed that civilization was exhausted and running down. Thus the theory of entropy played into the decadent movement. Entropy involves the transition from the systematic to the random, leading to a disordered future. The decadents—and those who followed them—were wary of the future and looked back to a prior time before the process of decline set in. Modernism owed much to the decadent legacy: Henry Adams, for example, looked back to the ideal of the twelfth century; Ezra Pound to the fifteenth; T. S. Eliot to the seventeenth; F. Scott Fitzgerald, William Faulkner, and John Dos Passos to the ideal of a Jeffersonian republic. Aestheticism was an essential part of "the inward turn," the movement of modernism away from physical reality toward inward process and subjectivity. The city became the place where the sensitive artist experienced acute isolation from ordinary people, as Andrew Lees points out, even as he mingled with the crowd (Lees, 81–82). When he was alone in the crowd, he found that reality gave way to his impressions of the city. And Eliot and Pound began to feel less comfortable in the crowd—amid the walking dead—than did Baudelaire. Out of this disdain for common experience came the modernist's sense of elitism—the willingness to separate oneself from the crowd even to the extent of approving reactionary forms of power.[3]

III

The two major themes of modernism—the artist and the city—begin to emerge. Perhaps the major modernist theme is that of the artist, or the equivalent of the artist, in the city. By *equivalent* I am suggesting an observer who brings a distinct consciousness to the city (as we have with Joyce's Dedalus and Fitzgerald's Carraway) or a consciousness in pursuit of the effect of urban activity on another location or place (as with Conrad's Marlow in Africa). As the modern city became more complex, reading it became more difficult. Part of the problem stemmed from the modernist belief that the self was anchored only in consciousness; an object was created by the act of perceiving it. This was the basis for Wyndham Lewis's attack on modernist time. The self became a bundle of sensory impressions precariously grouped together, its reality constantly threatened with dissolution (Ryan, 5).

Impressionism was the main means of moving from naturalism to modernism—from an impersonal, objective realm to the personal and subjective. The distinction between descriptive detail (the detail controlling the mind) and impressionistic detail (the mind controlling the

---

3. For a discussion of the modernists' move toward reactionary politics, see John Harrison's *The Reactionaries* (1967) and William Chace, *The Political Identities of Ezra Pound and T. S. Eliot* (1973).

detail) is useful to a point. But that point is reached as soon as we consider impressionistic paintings in which a change of sunlight changes the impression—that is, in which the setting itself seems inseparable from the impressionistic response. Joseph Conrad's Marlow sees his world getting morally darker as he speaks (an impression), but he is telling his story at dusk and his world is getting physically darker (a descriptive detail). Henry Fleming's infamous "wafer in the sky" is a metaphor that links descriptive detail and a mental impression. As Denis Donoghue has pointed out in a discussion of Pater, "'Impression' is Pater's word for that event which is neither objective nor subjective but compounded of both considerations. An impression is an impression of something, but it is well on the way to becoming independent of its source" (*Walter Pater,* 49–50). At what point such "independence" takes place is perhaps an arbitrary judgment, but an impressionistic narrator reveals his own sensibility and thus turns his narrative into something uniquely his own. Conrad could never have written *Heart of Darkness* or *Lord Jim* without Marlow's impressionistic stamp. And it was Conrad who influenced Stephen Crane, and Crane Hemingway.

It is no accident that literary subjectivity and impressionism in art coincided. Along with impressionism, cubism broke up the nineteenth-century ideal of photographic realism. Cubism, with its overlay of images, is the artistic equivalent of the superimposed layers of reality in Joyce's *Ulysses,* Eliot's *The Waste Land,* and Pound's *Cantos.* In collapsing space and time, the use of montage produced a new sense of reality. Under the influence of impressionism, naturalistic reality began to take on a subjective quality, as when in Crane's fiction a personal response—a character's impression—is overlaid on a more objective account of events. Such views brought an end to what Zola called the "experimental" novel, did away with naturalism and the "objective" scientist as narrator, and moved toward a new fiction, a narrative that could not separate Paterian impressions from narrative consciousness. In his early fiction, Hemingway mastered this technique, reconciling objective reality with subjective vision, just as Conrad prescribed in his preface to *The Nigger of the "Narcissus"* (1897) and as Ford Madox Ford demonstrated in *The Good Soldier* (1915).

Both the modernist self and impressionism were urban phenomena: impressionism discovered the landscape quality of the city and depicted the world through the subjective eyes of the city dweller, reacting to the external impressions with the overstrained nerves of modern technical man or woman (Hauser, 168). As the impressionistic view became more intense, the ability to see the city objectively became paradoxically more difficult, and an intensity of personal feeling often was accompanied by a more opaque sense of one's surroundings. Thus the views of Conrad's Marlow and Fitzgerald's Nick Carraway give way to darkness or to the opaqueness that Nick himself describes.

The modernists' inward turn challenged the main assumptions of both the Enlightenment and of Darwinism. The modernists, insisting upon mythic and symbolic reality, could not reconcile theories of cyclical history with a belief in linear evolution and mechanical progress, could not accept a mechanistic reality that gave priority to the realm of science at the expense of art and mind, and could not accept the notion of humanity based upon a purely rational theory of cognition and motives. The challenge came from many directions and over a long period of time. Flaubert's *Bouvard et Pécuchet* (1881), for example, satirized bourgeois self-sufficiency, ridiculed the encyclopedic mentality, and suggested that man had minimized rather than enlarged the human self by defining it within such restricted limits. Sir James Frazer (1854–1941) helped catalogue the old myths so that James Joyce and T. S. Eliot could see their relevance to modern times. Heinrich Schliemann (1822–90) discovered what he believed to be Homer's Troy and thus fueled an interest in the old mythology as well as a belief in the relevance of the archaeological layering of time. The interest in archaeology found an important complement in the literary use of landscapes, particularly urban landscapes. In *Salammbô* (1862), Flaubert superimposed Carthage upon the specter of Paris in the Second Empire, an anticipation of cubist technique that influenced James Joyce, who loosely superimposed the heroic world of Ulysses upon modern-day Dublin.

This use of simultaneity (what the modernist called spatial form and the postmodernist the synchronic) negated—to the dismay of Wyndham Lewis—the linear world of naturalism. Henri Bergson, in particular, challenged the priority of a mechanistic, Darwinian evolution that robbed the universe of a creative unfolding and man of the corresponding creative power of a deep subjectivity within which the mythic, the primitive, and the intuitive could reign supreme. Bergson helped deepen the divide between an Enlightenment and modernist mentality. Through intelligence, man created the instruments and tools by which he adapted to and then eventually controlled his environment. Intelligence involved an "outward"-looking process; it looked onto the material world, interested in instrumentality, action, and the organization that permitted social order and progress. When intelligence turned inward, it did what it could to resolve "the organized into the unorganized," but it could not "think true continuity, real mobility, reciprocal penetration—in a word, that creative evolution which is life" (Bergson, 162). To understand the inner realm of being, we must turn to intuition, which Bergson defined as "instinct that has become disinterested, self-conscious, capable of reflecting upon its object and of enlarging it indefinitely" (176). Such activity brought into being an aesthetic faculty, which accessed the inner reality of things as pure being rather than as a category or principle of mechanical organization. Bergson saw this inner reality as the "being" of time, referred to it as *durée,* and connected it with "real" life.

Intelligence turned outward accounted for Enlightenment belief in instrumentality and progress. Intelligence turned inward—that is, intuition—accounted for the modernist belief in an inner, artistic reality inseparable from the realm of form. The penetration of inner reality owed as much to the principles of art as to cognition because the movement of intelligence beyond instinct, and then intuition beyond intelligence, led to a heightened plane of reality shared with art and pierced the outer veil. Intuitive intelligence was thus the highest form of cognitive power as well as the force that drove evolutionary life ahead of it. The weight of this force carried the totality of the past to the moment—and to memory—and the creation of both the universe and the self in Bergson is inseparable from the functioning of intuition and memory. Thus, for Bergson, mind both directed and accessed life. With this idea he challenged the notions of mechanism and teleology, undercut both Enlightenment and Darwinian assumptions, gave weight to the modernist belief that art is the highest activity, and helped establish the modernist assumptions that the universe is inseparable from mind and that the self is created out of memory.

Bergson's distinctions are important to any "idea" of the city. Intelligence turned outward was directed at the instrumentality of the city, its institutions, and the way it functions as a commercial or industrial system. Intelligence turned inward moved toward intuitive truths pertaining to a realm of being, an elemental reality, that precedes the city. Thus the deeper the inner reality intuited by narrators like Conrad's Marlow or Fitzgerald's Nick Carraway, the more opaque becomes the outer reality. Joyce would call this perspectivism the parallax view: when we focus on the foreground, the background becomes vague; when we focus on the background, the foreground blurs. The more these narrators intuit the inner meaning of form, the more blind they become to the mechanical (that is, the urban) world around them. Eliot had said all this in his use of Tiresias, an observer who is often re-presented in modern urban literature.

IV

A text Bergson could have used to document these conclusions is Poe's "The Man of the Crowd" (1840). The narrator of the story is sitting in a London hotel, looking at his immediate surroundings as well as the city street he sees through a bow window. He is convalescing from a recent illness, which has left him with intensified sensory powers, making him an impressionistic narrator. As he looks around him, the people who make up the crowd take on a complex nature, which he tries to organize in terms of their professions, their class, and other characteristics of meaning. Suddenly his eye catches an elderly man who emerges out of the crowd, and on impulse the narrator follows him for a full night and day through the city: into a bazaar, down to the Embankment, past a theater, into a slum, then into a pub, until he returns full circle to the hotel from which they started. The whole process has involved a hermeneutic circle, which the narrator concludes is unreadable: "This old man . . . refuses to be alone. He is the man of the crowd. It will be in vain to follow; for I shall learn no more of him, nor of his deeds. The worst heart of the world is a grosser book than the 'Hortulus Animae,' and perhaps it is but one of the great mercies of God that 'es lässt sich nicht lesen' [it can't be read]" (*Selected Poetry and Prose,* 162). The man of the crowd *is* the crowd and, metonymically, the city as well. While the narrator's sense of acute impression leaves him with an indelible picture of the man of the crowd, the circular journey which encompasses—that is, encloses—the city finally breaks down short of meaning, and we are left with a sense of the mysterious and the uncanny. As the narrator tells us, "I shall learn no more" (162). As Denis Donoghue has perceptively seen, Poe's "story is a parable of imagination and reality, of what Wallace Stevens called the violence within in its dealings with the violence without." That imagination breaks down when it "finds the reality it confronts impenetrable" (*Being Modern Together,* 9, 12). The narrator is thus left with intense impressions of the man of the crowd (that is, impressions of the city), but what such sensory data may mean beyond the realm of impression—what they tell him about the meaning of the city itself—he cannot say. Poe's story, which deeply influenced Baudelaire, ends on the same note as *Heart of Darkness* and *The Great Gatsby,* two novels that also make use of impressionistic narration—impressions that never quite do justice to and that limit our final understanding of urban complexity.

CHAPTER 6

Urban Fantasies

I

Many of the ideas of the city came to us in the form of Enlightenment speculation. As we have seen, the Enlightenment highlighted two ideological shifts. It stressed reason and rationality, science and technology; and it shifted the emphasis from birth rights to the natural rights of the individual. The Enlightenment became the ideological cornerstone of the new nation of America and the basis for what would become the liberal tradition—the right to pursue, relatively unencumbered, a sense of self. A fantasy that anticipates much of this ideology is Francis Bacon's *The New Atlantis* (1627), a tale that radically revises Thomas More's *Utopia* by creating a utopia run totally by scientists who have mastered processes of refrigeration, the production of artificial metals, the study of soils, the crossbreeding of plants and animals, and much more. Each member of the community has a scientific function: traveling, collecting experiments, compiling experimental results, finding practical applications for new inventions, formulating laws, and so on.

Such faith in the scientific process created on both sides of the Atlantic its own opposition, much of which was codified under the name of romanticism. In America, Hawthorne stressed the need for scientific limits in works like "Rappaccini's Daughter" (1846) and "The Celestial Railroad" (1843). In England, Mary Shelley challenged the scientist's desire to create new life (short-circuiting the process of childbirth and rendering women superfluous) in *Frankenstein* (1818), a tale in which the monster rebels against his creator, Victor Frankenstein, and kills the scientist's closest friend, his bride, and eventually Frankenstein himself. Despite the enormity of the monster's crimes, Walton, the tale's narrator, realizes that Frankenstein's is the greater crime because he created the monster separate from any other living species, separate from mate and companionship—without love or friend or soul. Mary Shelley, in other words, tried to curb runaway science by insisting upon human limits—defining the human as that beyond which science should not go. But the Enlightenment emphasis upon rationality was too strong to be so easily displaced. Arthur Conan Doyle created the very epitome of the rational detective in Sherlock Holmes, and Holmes uses that rationality to help safeguard another Enlightenment legacy: the imperial city.

II

Detectives bring the city back to human scale. Dickens's Inspector Bucket, Conrad's Inspector Heat, Doyle's Sherlock Holmes—all give the city a human dimension. Doyle was an admirer of the detectives created by Edgar Allan Poe (Auguste Dupin), Émile Gaboriau (Monsieur Lecoq), and Wilkie Collins (*The Moonstone,* 1868; *The Woman in White,* 1860). Doyle modeled his detective on one of his medical school professors at Edinburgh University, a Doctor Joseph Bell, whose empirical abilities and reasoning powers were legend. Doyle wrote: "Reading some detective stories, I was struck by the fact that in nearly every case their result was achieved by chance. I thought I would try my hand at writing a story where the hero would treat crime as Doctor Bell treated disease, and where science had taken the place of chance. The result was Sherlock Holmes" (quoted in Eyles, 10–11). The Sherlock Holmes stories are thus a testimony to the power of the new science (what the Victorians called scientific rationalism) and technology.

Much of nineteenth-century science was involved in reconstructing past events from modern clues. Through induction, scientists reconstructed prehistory. Darwin drew conclusions about adaptation by observing pigeons, Curvier about the anatomy of prehistoric animals by examining a few surviving bones. In a famous lecture "On a Piece of Chalk" (1886), Thomas Huxley began with his lecturer's chalk and worked back to a geological map of prehistoric times. Huxley's method, as Ian Ousby has pointed out, is re-presented in Holmes's article "The Book of Life," quoted in *A Study in Scarlet:* "From a drop of water . . . a logician could infer the possibility of an Atlantic or a Niagara without having seen or heard of one or the other. So all life is a great chain, the nature of which is known whenever we are shown a single link of it" (Ousby, 154). In *The Sign of Four,* Holmes deduces from Watson's watch, inherited from his brother, a sad story of alcoholism and wasted talent. With his tendency to review a problem as an abstraction, Holmes often overlooks the personal pain behind his observations. He is able to connect clues, but he is often blind to what stands behind or beneath such evidence. The city is the embodiment of order in these stories because Holmes is often blind to a disorder—a chaos—deeper than the surface he unfolds for us. But despite his inability to see how many archaeological layers a city might have, Holmes finds no piece of evidence too trivial in the great scheme of connected meaning. His powers of observation lead to a new sense of excitement about the physical world that it begins to demystify. For example, Holmes frees people from superstitious beliefs in vampires and demonic possession in "The Sussex Vampire" (1895) and "The Devil's Foot" (1910).

Sherlock Holmes appears in sixty narratives: fifty-six short stories and four novels. Nearly all of these were published in *The Strand Magazine* before being collected into separate volumes between 1891 and 1927. Sherlock Holmes was born on January 6, the Feast of the Epiphany. When his father, an officer in the East India Company, returned to England, the family settled in Mycroft in Yorkshire. There Holmes prepared for Oxford, tutored by James Moriarty. After Oxford, Holmes traveled in America and came to think of London as the center of the world and America as an extension of England. On his return, he settled in London and became a private detective. Holmes is a gentleman, polished in manners, reclusive and eccentric, intensely individualistic. He is a misogynist, at least to the extent that he distrusts the emotional nature of women. He once told Watson, "Women are never to be entirely trusted—not the best of them" (*Sign of Four,* 83). Later in the same novel, he warned Watson of the perils of marriage: "Love is an emotional thing, and whatever is emotional is opposed to that true cold reason which I place above all things. I should never marry myself, lest I bias my judgment" (138). Holmes is sexless, scorns the family, uses cocaine, and is manic-depressive. Like many of Dickens's deformed characters, he is cold, rational, unfeeling, and without family. While his inductive rigor aligns him with the scientific community, his spells of dreamy languor and melancholy brooding, his extemporizations on the violin, and his drug-induced fantasies align him with the genius of the decadents' theory. And despite his remarkable range of learning—he is informed on such topics as miracle plays, medieval pottery, the Stradivarius violin, Buddhism in Ceylon, and modern warships—he is ignorant of Carlyle and of the Copernican theory of the solar system. Since so many adventure novels involve a hero and an associate, Doyle invented John A. Watson—character and narrator—as Holmes's sidekick. Watson is a medical doctor, recently discharged from the army. A friend whom he meets at the Criterion Bar at Piccadilly Circus introduces him to Holmes, with whom he agrees to share lodgings. Holmes's foil is James Moriarty, who heads an international crime ring and comes to embody the international evil that threatens the city and by extension the nation and the system.

Holmes exists to protect London, to root out evil in the center of the imperial world, whether it arises from the machinations of a crime ring or from an isolated crime. The system must be made secure; Sherlock Holmes both embodies the system and helps keep it intact. He is always willing to come to the defense of upper-class values, as he does for Sir Henry Baskerville, heir to the Baskerville estate. In restoring Sir Henry to his estate, Holmes is protecting the right to property, an institution basic to the meaning of England as a nation. Doyle's politics are right-wing. In *The Valley of Fear* (1915), set in an American mining town notorious for its exploitation of labor, Doyle clearly sympathizes with the management on whose side Holmes intervenes.

A Study in Scarlet (1887) has acquired a special meaning because it is the novel in which Doyle introduces both Holmes and Watson. Discharged from the army as a medical officer after being wounded in the shoulder (in later novels the wound is to the leg) and later overcome by enteric fever during the second Afghan war, Watson has returned to London. In the opening pages he refers to London as a "wilderness" and a "great cesspool into which all the loungers and idlers of the Empire are irresistibly drained" (*Scarlet*, 10). Holmes and Watson meet in a chemistry laboratory where Holmes has "found a re-agent which is precipitated by haemoglobin," thus allowing him to identify blood stains. The two men take rooms together at 221B Baker Street, where Watson learns that Holmes is a manic-depressive, plays the violin erratically, and has other eccentricities as well, including the long walks he likes to take "into the lowest portions of the city" (17).

The city is only one of Holmes's many interests. He has written an essay in which he claims "all life is a great chain, the nature of which is known whenever we are shown a single link of it" (22). Moreover, he declares that "there is nothing new under the sun. It has all been done before" (22). Holmes comes at truth from the other end of God's telescope. While God knows truth from all time, Holmes must reconstruct it inductively. One knows all beforehand; the other knows all after the fact: Doyle suggests that the two have much in common. Holmes substitutes induction for romantic intuition when he redefines genius as "an infinite capacity for taking pains" (36). His rational powers seem even greater because he is always ahead of Watson, and his powers contrast with those of two bumbling Scotland Yard detectives, Lestrade and Gregson.

A Study in Scarlet involves London and America, as *The Sign of Four* involves London and India. Doyle, who believed in the future of England as a great empire, saw America as playing a part in that plan. He believed that the separation of America and England in the American Revolution was a mistake that would be corrected because the destinies of America and England were entwined. Behind this, of course, was his belief in Anglo-Saxon supremacy as well as in manifest destiny. In *A Study in Scarlet*, the evil that comes into London is embodied by the two murdered men, Enoch Drebber and Joseph Strangerson; their murderer—Jefferson Hope—is a man who eventually wins our sympathy. We thus have in this novel a story within a story: a murder mystery set in London, and the motives for the murders determined in the desert of the American West. Hope has come to Europe in search of Drebber and Strangerson, Mormons who are responsible for the death of Hope's fiancée and her father; he finally catches up with and kills them in London. At his arrest, he tells Holmes, "You may consider me to be a murderer; but I hold that I am just as much an officer of justice as you are" (128). Doyle seems to agree; dying of a burst aneurysm the night of his arrest, Jefferson Hope is never brought to trial.

Mechanical and contrived as a story, *A Study in Scarlet* nevertheless offers us a view into the meaning of the city in the Sherlock Holmes legend. The two plots establish two different worlds: one belonging to Holmes the rationalist in London, the other to the Mormons in Salt Lake City. The Mormons are presented as derelict and evil because Doyle thought of them as a cult; they justify their existence on the basis of secret truths, handed down to them from the past, that they now use to secure power over their followers. Such mystical power is anathema to both Doyle and Holmes, which explains their sympathy toward Jefferson Hope. Holmes's London, a maze containing over four million people, is at the center of an empire; Brigham Young's temple city of Salt Lake City is at the edge of a desert, near the end of the frontier pilgrimage. For all London's limitations, Doyle, with a sense of noblesse oblige, believed that the city extended the gift of civilization to the lesser countries of the world, while the Mormons arrested the spirit of democracy (the hope of a new Jeffersonianism) by bestowing power on those who claim cult knowledge. Doyle connected the movement westward in America with the spirit of imperial expansion. Thus, in solving the murders of Drebber and Strangerson, Holmes both demystifies cult fanaticism and removes an impediment to true democracy. In London, Jefferson Hope becomes a double of Sherlock Holmes. He tracks down Drebber, and he breaks through the maze of the city to seek revenge. In Hope and Holmes the empire and the frontier meet and become symbiotic; between them they make it possible for civilization to advance. The two men are from opposite ends of the world, but Hope still represents urban destiny, albeit its outer reaches. Each has done what he can to preserve London's historical function as the center of this world.

In *The Sign of Four* (1890), trouble comes into London from India. Jonathan Small, an imperial soldier, becomes involved in an ill-advised adventure when he is persuaded to kill an emissary of a wealthy rajah and steal a box of exquisite jewels worth half a million dollars. Like Kurtz in Conrad's *Heart of Darkness,* Small does not become a criminal until he reaches the edge of empire, in this case India. Although his group hides the jewels before they are arrested, Small and his accomplices are convicted of the murder and imprisoned for life. After two officers promise help in their escape, Small and his three conspirators disclose to Major Sholto and Captain Morstan where the jewels are hidden. Major Sholto goes to verify their existence, breaks his agreement with the band of four and with Captain Morstan, and takes the jewels back to England; there he lives in splendor until Morstan and Small, aided by Tonga, an Andaman Island native, come in pursuit.

Once again, *The Sign of Four* involves an imperial adventure told against the world of London. Knowing the city by heart, Holmes can follow the streets and squares when he and Watson are taken to the outskirts for a secret meeting with Sholto's son Thaddeus. Watson cannot follow the maze of streets traveled, but he provides his impressions of late Victorian London lighted by gas lamps as the fog rolls in on an autumn evening. This passage is important because it is the basic literary way of seeing the city from Baudelaire to Eliot. We see a mind recording its impressions of the city, with fog, muddy streets reflected in muddy clouds, the pale and yellow light from shop windows, the sad and glad faces of the crowd absorbed by surrounding gloom. The cumulative effect is felt by both the narrator and the reader: a city beset by apprehension and nervousness, haunted by a sense of the eerie and ghostlike—the uncanny:

It was a September evening and not yet seven o'clock, but the day had been a dreary one, and a dense drizzly fog lay low upon the great city. Mud-coloured clouds drooped sadly over the muddy streets. Down the Strand the lamps were but misty splotches of diffused light which threw a feeble circular glimmer upon the slimy pavement. The yellow glare from the shop-windows streamed out into the steamy, vaporous air and threw a murky, shifting radiance across the crowded thoroughfare. There was to my mind something eerie and ghostlike in the endless procession of faces which flitted across the narrow bars of light and so back into the gloom once more. I am not subject to impressions, but the dull, heavy evening, with the strange business upon which we were engaged, combined to make me nervous and depressed. (*Sign of Four,* 25)

The play between mind and descriptive detail ends in a series of impressions (despite Watson's disclaimer) that represent the urban mind. This technique would be refined by Joseph Conrad and taken up by Ford Madox Ford and other modernists like Stephen Crane and Ernest Hemingway who transformed the omniscient narrator of naturalism. Such a technique not only provides the literary equivalent of impressionistic painting but also gives us an urban narrator whose response to the city moves us from an objective to a subjective realm, as well as from a shared to a private reality. The meaning of the city comes from within such a special realm of perception. T. S. Eliot later indicated that when he came to depict the city, he found Doyle's method reinforced the engaged sensibilities he had associated with Baudelaire and Conrad.

The eerie, ghostlike city anticipates the story of Jonathan Small and Tonga, the criminal and the savage who stalk the city in *The Sign of Four.* They embody the chaos brought into the city from the outside—especially Tonga, whose "savage instincts . . . had broken out" (68). Tonga is pursued to the Thames, which (as in Conrad) connects London to the world; there the threat culminates in a boat chase, during which Watson sees Tonga for the first time. As he describes the scene, a bundle on the deck "straightened itself into a little black man—the smallest I have ever seen—with a great misshapen head and a shock of tangled, disheveled hair." Watson refers to him as a "savage, distorted creature" with a face that "was enough to give a man a sleepless night." It is "marked with all bestiality and cruelty[;] . . . his thick lips . . . writhed back from his teeth, which grinned and chattered at us with half animal fury" (101, 102). Tonga is an evolutionary throwback—not just to animality, but to the realm of savagery that, according to Freud, is linked to a sense of the uncanny, which we suppress when we enter society. Guardians of the city think it can be eradicated. Consequently, Holmes and Watson draw their revolvers, shoot Tonga when he raises his dart gun, and watch his body fall into the Thames. "I caught," Watson tells us, "one glimpse of his venomous, menacing eyes amid the white swirl of the waters" (102). Through the agency of Holmes and, to a lesser extent, Watson, the river that connects London to the world becomes a repository, cleansing the city of the evil it has brought forth, including the prized jewels, which Small scatters over the river water.

Tonga embodies the savagery that Doyle saw lurking on the imperial frontier. Small describes a mutiny that broke out in northern India and led to the death of the plantation owner who had befriended him after a crocodile took his leg when he was swimming in the Ganges. The soldier speaks to both cultural and racial differences when he tells us, "One month India lay as still and peaceful, to all appearance, as Surrey or Kent; the next there were two hundred thousand black devils let loose, and the country was a perfect hell" (115). At Agra, Small joins the Third Bengal Fusiliers, which then retreats to a fort across the river to help stop the rebellion. Agra itself is indefensible because the city had never moved beyond the most primitive realm. "The city of Agra is a great place, swarming with fanatics and fierce worshipers of all sorts," Small confides (116). When on duty at the fort, Small would look "down on the broad, winding river and on the twinkling lights of the great city. The beating of drums, the rattle of tomtoms, and the yells and howls of the rebels, drunk with opium and with bang, were enough to remind us all night of our dangerous neighbors across the stream" (118). In contrasting order and disorder, Doyle clearly sets the meaning of the civilized city against primitive savagery. The latter had to be eradicated so the former could progress, and Holmes is the agent of this process. Doyle shares the late Victorian urban distrust of the Dionysian element, and Sherlock Holmes keeps his own London distanced from such primitive expressions.

The death of Tonga and the arrest of Small restore a sense of urban balance and equanimity. The police can claim credit for solving the case, Watson can court Miss Morstan, and Holmes can praise the power of reason, even as he opens his cocaine bottle. The cocaine obviously adds to the narrative equation an ironic dimension of which even Holmes seems unaware: more Dionysian than Apollonian, it overpowers the rational. Moreover, it suggests that the irrational is a realm that we cannot fully escape as it works its will within Sherlock Holmes and the somber city that Doyle has given him to protect.

III

The popularity of the Sherlock Holmes stories in late Victorian times was surpassed only by the popularity of Rider Haggard's novels. These very different works play dialectically off each other, testimony to the fact that a reading public can put adventure above ideology and readily accept conflicting cultural positions. In the character of Sherlock Holmes, Arthur Conan Doyle depicts the supreme rationalist and looks to a progressive future. In the characters of Ludwig Holly and Allan Quatermain, Rider Haggard depicts the scholar and white hunter whose interests are archaeological and anthropological and who look to a glorious past that contains universal truths. Doyle demystifies the past and challenges cult meaning; Haggard suggests that there are secrets buried in the primitive past that can unlock historical meaning. Such secrets are usually connected with a lost primitive society or cult that has made use of its power and handed it down in hieroglyphic—encoded— ways. (Pynchon's *The Crying of Lot 49* makes use of this same device to enshroud the historical past in mystery.)

Haggard's best-known novel, *She* (1887), has a narrative frame: it is supposedly an edited manuscript sent to a publisher. The plot involves Ludwig Horace Holly, who becomes the guardian of Leo Vincey, who in turn traces his heritage back two thousand years to a Greek named Kallicrates, murdered for love by Ayesha, the She of the novel. They journey back to the land of She, located in the mythical city of Kor, where Ayesha has been alive for two thousand years and Leo is revealed as the reincarnation of Kallicrates. She leads Leo and Holly to the Pillar of Fire that is responsible for her immortality, but when she steps into the fire, time is reversed, and she is consumed by the flames.

Ayesha rules the Amahanggers, a primitive tribe now in control of the once imperial city of Kor, which is carved out of solid rock. She has been living in her hidden city without news of the outside world (Holly brings her up to date with a quick history of Judea, Greece, and Rome). A fertility figure, Ayesha is associated with fields and crops. Haggard was tap-

ping the late Victorian interest in archaeology and anthropology that culminated with Frazer's monumental *The Golden Bough* (1890–1915). He
moves from his own urban and industrial age back thousands of years to
a primitive, agrarian society that constructed a magnificent city out of the
rocked earth. Holding the secret to eternal life, Ayesha can go beyond
human limits. But the city that she controls is a rebuilt ruin, a reminder to
late Victorians of how vulnerable are even the greatest powers. The novel
conjectures that the original inhabitants of Kor were destroyed by a pesti-
lence from which they were unable to recover. Morton Cohen speculates
that Haggard may have had in mind the remarkable ruins of Zimbabwe,
"an inscrutable stone metropolis that has puzzled archaeologists since its
discovery in the late nineteenth century" (108).

Haggard uses his story to suggest the power of primitive cults to control their world and to build monuments to their own ingenuity. The
suggestion is that great truths exist from the beginning of time and that
when the past is unlocked, the meaning of such mysteries unfolds.[1] That
Ayesha is finally consumed by the same fire that gave her eternal life is a
leap into narrative fantasy, but such a leap could be read as exemplary by
his audience: perhaps at the edge of the British Empire was an exotic
realm like Kor that had ancient truths to unfold for a modern audience.
Haggard, in other words, brought two plots into conjunction: he supplies us with a journey into the heart of central Africa that unlocks a
realm of mystery and intrigue, and he brings to that realm a narrator
who, as a professional scholar, can interpret its significance.

Haggard repeats this pattern in *King Solomon's Mines* (1885), when
Allan Quatermain and his friends, in their search for Lord Henry Curtis's lost brother, journey to Kukuanaland. One lost city often precedes
another in Haggard's novels, and on the way they discover the ruined
city of Ophir, which has now lapsed back into darkest barbarianism, the
secrets of its past awaiting rediscovery. Quatermain and his group travel
on to Kukuanaland, another cave city. It is carved out of pure rock with
passages cut to allow Solomon to bring his mined treasures back to
Judea. In the process of restoring the rightful king to the throne of
Kukuanaland, Quatermain and his friends also travel deep into this cave
city—partly a necropolis, partly a treasure house—where they discover
colossi thousand of years old that document the ability of prehistoric

---

1. Freud is said to have been reading *She* while working on his essay on the uncanny;
certainly the return of the repressed—the inevitable revelation of past meaning—is one of
Haggard's most pronounced themes.

man to create permanent beauty. A magnificent road, a tremendous feat of early engineering, once connected this city to the rest of the world. But the road has been buried under desert sand, and the city, like all of Haggard's cities, becomes a symbol of lost magnificence. The past is there as a reminder of human limits: savagery and civilization interpenetrate parts of the same human nature.

In *Allan Quatermain* (1887), Haggard is quite adamant about these themes: "Civilization is only savagery silver-gilt. A vainglory is it, and, like a northern light, comes but to fade and leave the sky more dark. Out of the soil of barbarism it has grown like a tree, and, as I believe, into the soil like a tree, sooner or later, it will once more fall again, as the Egyptian civilization fell, as the Hellenic civilization fell, and as the Roman civilization fell and maybe others of which the world has now lost count, fell also" (420). The reason for this congruence between primitivism and civilization is that truth, like human nature, is eternal. We are nineteen parts savage and one part civilized, Haggard tells us, and "we must look to the nineteen savage portions of our nature, if we would really understand ourselves, and not to the twentieth, which, though so insignificant in reality, is spread all over the other nineteen, making them to appear quite different from what they really are, as the blacking does a boot" (421). Although we see the past only through the prism of the present, the past can be read and decoded, offering us a re-presentation of events. Human nature, he believes, is "Like an iron ring": "you will never, while the world endures and man is man, increase its total circumference. It is the one fixed unchangeable thing—fixed as the stars, more enduring than the mountains, unalterable as the way of the Eternal" (420).

In *Allan Quatermain,* as the eponymous hero and his friends travel across central Africa, they come to Charra, on the Tana River, where they once again find a ruined city; in Old Testament times, it might have been part of a trade route to India and elsewhere. The rise of the slave trade altered the existing trading pattern and led to the decline of the city, for a city is always dependent on its function, on some controlling purpose outside itself. The city—its rise and fall and the tenuousness of its power—supplies an emblem of meaning: "'Gone!, quite gone! the way everything must go. Like the nobles and ladies who lived within their gates, these cities have had their day, and now they are as Babylon and Nineveh, and as London and Paris will one day be. Nothing may endure. . . . In this ruined and forgotten place the moralist may behold a symbol of the universal destiny . . . hurled into the sea of the Eternal'" (432).

Haggard stops the evolutionary clock and sees a spectrum of meaning that extends from human origins to the present. Such meaning is to be found by those who can journey back in time. The journeys of Haggard's characters function like Wellsian time machines, displacing them not only spatially from England to Africa but temporally from the modern industrial world to the primitive world, in this case to a lost feudal agrarianism. The move across continents is also a move from the post-Enlightenment to pre-Enlightenment, from the industrial city to the early agrarian cities, whose being is held together by myths from which modern man has become distanced.

Haggard's narrative devices are used by many of his contemporaries, often for different narrative purposes: Bram Stoker will use them to take us into the edge of empire and again to make contact with the undead (as in *She*); Conrad takes us into the heart of the Congo, where the mysteries of the universe are revealed—not in the fire that illuminates Kor, or the mine city painfully carved out of pure rock in *King Solomon's Mines,* or the engineering that made Milosis a monument to the Sun in *Allan Quatermain*—but in the darkness that consumes Kurtz. The journey is always either from or to a city, and the narrative takes us from the present to a realm of the past, often containing a savagery that throws light on the vulnerability of the city—even a city like London at the high point of imperialism. Just as the citizens of Kor and their queen were subject to the mysteries of death, modern London is subject to the universal principles that come to us as mysteries: the worlds have changed but the underlying tenets remain the same. The modern city will re-present the cities of old because the same forces have worked throughout history. Whereas Arthur Conan Doyle believed in an underlying causality, Rider Haggard believed in the future as the continuation of the past. One is a mechanistic, the other a teleological view. One puts the emphasis on causes realized in time; the other on ends fulfilled. One led to a materialistic, the other to an idealistic city. Literary naturalism (from Balzac and Zola to Norris and Dreiser) took us in one direction, romantic idealism (from Spengler to Toynbee, Emerson to Hart Crane) in the other.

IV

Fantasy literature in the late Victorian period dealt with the meaning of the past, perhaps because the rate of change during this era was so great that readers desired to get a sense of what needed to be kept at a distance. In these fantasies, the past is often held together by mythic beliefs enforced through the power of cults. The modern journeyer confronts these beliefs and tries to demystify them. While Haggard sees some universal truths located in these realms, Doyle subjects such claims to the test of rationality and scientific scrutiny. Bram Stoker, however, distributes his truths between the realms of religion and of science: his investigator is half priest and half scientist.

Count Dracula was a historical figure, a Romanian count who massacred his Turkish enemies by impaling them on spears and leaving them to die. Dracula is a direct descendant of Attila the Hun. He takes pride in having been a bulwark against the Turks, and he claims to have fought for the men who would now destroy him, an assertion the novel never refutes. His castle is located near the border of three Balkan territories (Transylvania, Bukovina, and Moldavia) in northern Romania. This region's history of bloody strife has taken its toll on culture and cut it off from Europe. Dracula turns to Europe—especially England—to remedy this isolation. As Van Helsing tells us, Dracula finds England a most promising realm, where he can create a new social life in a country with strong political institutions. In his strange dialect (which makes Van Helsing as much a foreigner as Dracula), Van Helsing concludes that England is for Dracula the "place of most promise" because its Enlightenment laws and customs will conceal his demonic activity.

Dracula's destructive evil will thus fester and poison England, especially London, from within. His army will conquer its victims unaware. Stoker's *Dracula* (1897) is a story of the undead, those who are neither saved in heaven nor damned in hell but exist somewhere in between. Casting no reflection, they are both material and immaterial: they can creep through small spaces and take the form of bats and wolves. Blood is their food of life, and they exist by drinking the blood of live victims, a phenomenon that connects them in an inverted way with the story of Christ's redeeming blood and with the Christian sacrament of the Eucharist. In line with such an inversion, vampires take their being from the devil. Common belief has it that suicides become vampires; furthermore, everyone who is killed by a vampire becomes a vampire in turn. Such transformations lead to a community antithetical to the living, a community that comes to stand for a principle of disorder within a society of order.

Like the Dionysus legend, the vampire story comes from Asia Minor—that is, from the West/East divide. The West seems threatened by the evil of the East. This theme is further documented by Lucy West-enra's name: the light (life) of the West is put out by Dracula. Almost half the story takes place in London, where Dracula is the irrational element, a modern avatar of Dionysus. Like Dionysus, he embodies the principle of chaos within the city, a system of supposed order. In this sense, he is analogous to the plague or some other catastrophe that comes into the city. For the city to exist, such forces must be suppressed or, as Freudians—sensitive to both the sexual and the uncanny overtones in the Dracula story—would say, repressed.

Dracula works his way to England as a stowaway aboard the Russian ship *Demeter*, which runs aground in a storm before it reaches its destination of Whitby, Yorkshire. Once Dracula lands in England, the endogamous nature of the novel (the characters are linked as members of one family) becomes apparent. Miss Lucy Westenra—engaged to Lord Godalming, beloved by Dr. Seward—is Dracula's first victim. She becomes his servant in death, living off children in Hampstead. He then takes an interest in Lucy's closest friend—Mina Harker, a kind of sister—who eventually escapes Dracula's power. Van Helsing, also an outsider, is surrounded by women, just as is Dracula in his castle. The novel sets up two great father figures in Dracula and Van Helsing (although Dracula actually gets younger rather than older as he feasts on new blood), and they struggle for family dominance: the primitive and the modern world—the power of the cult and the power of science—engage each other in perpetual battle.

As a demonic force, Dracula finds his foils in urban men, including men of science and Jonathan Harker. Harker is a lawyer and expert in London real estate, although initially he works out of his mentor's office in Essex. He is sent to Transylvania to close the deal involving Dracula's purchase of a crumbling estate in Purfleet, east of London, from which Dracula plans to build a vampire empire, and he ends up as Dracula's prisoner. Harker would kill Dracula if he had the chance (his fears revive his suppressed primitive instincts), but he barely escapes as a broken man, sick near to death. He comes to fear a kind of reverse imperialism: the threat that the primitive will colonize the civilized world. Harker's experiences in Dracula's castle breaks down his Enlightenment trust in a rational world. When one leaves the city, one leaves behind the protection it offers. Harker finds relief when he reenters London, but only by repressing his memories of the evil that lies beyond. As he tells Mina, "You know I have had brain fever, and that is to be mad. The secret is here [in a journal], and I do not want to know it" (Stoker, 114). Once he realizes that Dracula is planning to overrun London with his legion of the undead, he joins with Professor Van Helsing and Dr. Seward to keep the city safe from the demonic presence that now threatens it. But he will never again bring to his life the optimism and trust he displayed at the novel's beginning.

Professor Van Helsing, a practicing Catholic, is also a man of European science whose storehouse of information includes the latest discovery in medicine as well as pertinent lore on fighting vampires. While he never doubts the power of science, he is also a man of faith who believes "that we should have an open mind, and not let a little bit of truth check the rush of big truth" (249). He does not deny the mystery of life—and believes, in fact, that there is a "fate amongst us still, sent down from the pagan world of old" (175)—but he also believes that such mysteries can be understood through both the power of revealed religion and the truths of science. Also trusting in what the records of the past can reveal, he relies heavily on the diaries of Jonathan and Mina Harker, believing that "by accurate knowledge of all details he will light upon some clue" (347).

Dr. John Seward, custodian of the lunatic asylum, establishes the connection between Dracula and insanity and thus somewhat demythologizes and secularizes the story. He is skeptical of Van Helsing's belief in the supernatural and assumes that all mystery can be explained through advances in science. While he analyzes Lucy's blood, Dracula drinks it (147). He has a hard time believing that a vampire bat can exist in nineteenth-century London (248), as if science had made the city invulnerable to irrational forces. The connection between insanity and Dracula becomes closer when the character of Renfield, a patient in the asylum who eats flies and spiders, is linked to the story. As Dracula's servant, Renfield becomes more cunning and shrewd, his insanity now masked by an awareness of a higher truth. His attraction to animals and pests seems only one step away from the world of wolves and bats within which Dracula disguises himself. Dracula's savagery takes on pagan intensity; it is restrained only by religious devices like the crucifix and garlic leaves (connected with the divinity of Christ). Stoker seems to be suggesting, as Richard Wasson has pointed out, that technological progress has cut humanity off from dark knowledge, making civilization increasingly unaware of and hence vulnerable to demonic powers (Wasson, 24–25). As the novel moves toward its conclusion and the death of Dracula, Seward becomes more open-minded and more aware of a balance between the power of cult forces and of science, recognizing the limits of the latter. He has seen how vulnerable modern institutions are when viewed through the prism of cult primitivism.

Dracula's mission from the outset is to conquer London, and he recalls other forces that seek to destroy or control the city from within. Although he is self-conscious about his accented English, he has become an expert on the workings of the city. As a foreigner, he realizes that he is the outsider, a kind of Dionysian figure, surrounded by worshipping women and capable of destroying the city. As a man of force, Dracula brings to mind Balzac's Vautrin, the power maniac who has no respect for law and order and who threatens the city by inverting the way it works, counteracting the forces that the city has institutionalized. And like the flaneur, Dracula wants to be both part of and separate from the crowd, to participate in the city and yet to have it within his control. He tells Harker that he longs "to go through the crowded streets of . . . mighty London, to be in the midst of the whirl and rush of humanity, to share its life, its change, its death, and all that makes it what it is" (Stoker, 31). Dracula counts on his army of servants to take over London in the name of the undead.

Writing at the height of the British Empire, Stoker touches a nerve here: once again an urban fantasy suggests the threat of danger from the extremity of the empire, from the mysterious, exotic world of the Other, from a counterculture. In *Dracula,* the belief in modern, scientific lore is more vulnerable to primitive cult powers than it was in Doyle or even Haggard. Van Helsing taps all the knowledge of the past and the present—scientific and religious alike—as the city of London reaches out to residual secrets buried in the mystical past in order to combat and defeat Dracula. The future of civilization seems secure: in England it rests safely in the hands of men like Lord Godalming, whose aristocratic privileges fail to separate him from the common man; and in America in Quincey P. Morris, whose heroic activity helps destroy Dracula and whose pragmatic and emboldened qualities establish America as a new link in the march of civilization. By combining modern religion and science, Van Helsing not only brings the Enlightenment and Christianity into conjunction, but he is also successful in challenging Dracula's supernatural powers: he prevents Dracula from colonizing England, from forming his own community of the undead in London. Stoker's novel once again deals with the archetypal struggle within the city itself between two forces as he deals with two outsiders—one embodying order, the other disorder—engaged in a mortal combat that pits the well-being of London itself against the machinations of a protean Dionysus.

V

Joseph Conrad's major fiction deals with the process of colonization. *Heart of Darkness* (1899), *Lord Jim* (1900), *Nostromo* (1904), the Malay novels—all are concerned with colonization, especially as it involves the relationship between civilized and primitive life. In *Heart of Darkness,* Marlow speaks of "[t]he conquest of the earth, which mostly means the taking it away from those who have a different complexion or slightly flatter noses" (10). *Heart of Darkness* appeared as a story in three installments in *Blackwell's* magazine in 1899 and was published in 1902 in a collection of stories titled *Youth,* all involving Marlow's disillusionment as he experiences the tenuousness of universal truth. Marlow comes to see that savagery was the common denominator of history and that civilization only conceals it. Kurtz is able to organize such savagery and turn it into power.

Heart of Darkness treats the disintegrating effect that solitude and the primitive can have on civilized men. Norman Sherry has demonstrated how closely Marlow's experiences paralleled Conrad's own. The Inner Station, desolate and decaying in the novel, is the physical center of the heart of darkness; there Kurtz in his isolation from civilization and his proximity to the savage jungle becomes physically and culturally degenerate. Although Kurtz had spent a year alone, Conrad found the actual Inner Station—far from consisting of a decayed hut on a hill—a bustling place, although its chief, a man named Klein, was seriously ill and, like Kurtz, died during the return journey. Despite these similarities, Sherry believes that the model for Kurtz was Arthur Eugene Constant Hodister, a charismatic, highly successful commercial agent and explorer, who also died in the jungle. As Sherry puts it, "Hodister's fate was not precisely that of Kurtz, but it might be said of both men that their faith in their ability to command the 'exotic Immensity' of the Congo jungle led to their being destroyed by the same Immensity—by its inhabitants in the case of Hodister and its primitive customs in the case of Kurtz" (111). It is, however, unlikely that Conrad ever encountered the hostilities that Marlow describes. Sherry points out that the natives in this region were under the influence of the Congo Arabs, who would not take orders from a European such as Kurtz (53). Moreover, neither Klein nor Hodister, unlike Kurtz, was alone; no actual agent could have presided over what the novel calls "unspeakable rites" (Sherry, 67).

Marlow gets his Congo position when the previous captain, who had been in the jungle a bit too long, "asserted" himself against the local chief and got a spear in the back for his lapse. The incident establishes at once what the jungle can do to one's perspective and bears witness to the violence it harbors. When he arrives at the Central Station, Marlow witnesses the chaos the jungle can wreak on order. Drainage pipes, all broken, had been tumbled into a ravine: "it was a wanton smash-up" (Conrad, 20). Marlow soon meets the Company's chief accountant, who, in order to protect himself from degeneration, wears clothes washed and starched daily; with the sick and the dying housed beside him, only a clean white shirt separates him from death and disorder, just as only the fragile institutions of the city separate it from a residual savagery.

Finally meeting Kurtz, Marlow discovers that he was partly educated in England and that his mother was half-English, his father half-French. An accomplished musician, Kurtz at one time was sensitive to the best in culture. We are, in fact, told that "all Europe contributed to the making of Kurtz" (50): he is the end product of civilization. Kurtz's presence had unified the natives, whom he organized for his attacks on elephant herds and other tribes. His camp is piled with mountains of ivory, and the skulls on the fence that face his hut are both homage to his misused power and a symbolic reminder that greed and death are often companions. On returning to the Company, Marlow is told by a journalist who knew Kurtz that he had the power to "electrify" large meetings, making him a cult figure who energized the masses for his own political agenda. With insight into the nature of the charismatic leader and the nature of mass psychology, Conrad, like Stoker, takes us in this novel to the heart of empire, beyond which lies totalitarianism.

Marlow's narrative is introduced to us by another narrator. *Heart of Darkness* begins with an unnamed speaker, setting the scene and then introducing Marlow, who tells his story to a group of men who in their professional capacities embody the meaning of the city. The use of dual narrators creates an inverted form of Greek tragedy: Marlow is not telling his story to an engaged audience (a kind of Greek chorus) but to a disinterested, perhaps unsympathetic, group—one that seems only mildly interested in the story and unable to apply its conclusions to themselves. Conrad is really aiming the story outside the frame, at the reader.

The meaning of *Heart of Darkness* cannot be separated from its telling. As a number of critics have pointed out, Conrad's affinity to mechanistic thought brought him at times close to the teachings of Darwin. But

Marlow's impressions allow an inward view of Kurtz. The outside description depends heavily upon a theory of degeneration abstracted from Darwin and his followers, especially Max Nordau. But the inside look takes us deeply and solely to the subjectivity of Marlow, who sees an Enlightenment world grow darker and darker as his faith in progress diminishes. Commentators have connected the quality of Marlow's thoughts with that of Pater's Marius, and Ian Watt has read Conrad's preface to *The Nigger of the "Narcissus"* as a Pateresque statement of aesthetics. But while Pater is concerned with the cumulative force of impressions, Conrad, as Allan Hunter has suggested, is also interested in what he himself called "the permanence of memory" (*Notes on Life and Letters,* quoted in Hunter, 11).

Marlow's experience is a journey back into time as well as a study in degeneration: Conrad takes us on a journey back beyond civilization into the origins of existence. There we find the primitive forces that civilization still employs but tries to conceal. Conrad tells us that there is little difference between civilization and savagery; savagery simply operates beneath the surface of civilization. Once Marlow gets deep into the jungle, he sees in Kurtz the rapaciousness that drives life. Cities work by relying on institutions that simply re-present this primal struggle. Just as the city employs technology and bureaucracy to control its inhabitants, so both Marlow and Kurtz find the means to control the savages: Kurtz by becoming their god, Marlow by releasing the energy of the steam engine. Religion and science, Conrad suggests, are the means by which rulers have maintained their power since the beginning of time, in the city as in the jungle.

The city of Brussels has organized the chaos and horror of life. Marlow refers to it as "a whited sepulchre" (Conrad, 9), a sepulchral city: a city of the dead. The city is a monument to power, but Marlow sees that it cannot be separated from the reality of death and the forces that pull us back to the primitive, back to the earth. Death and degeneration are laws of life, setting limits to the meaning of the city and to life itself. As an Enlightenment entity, the city tries to deny its limits and emblematizes its capacity to rule the world, but Marlow sees beneath this arrogant surface. Kurtz also sees at once the beginning and the end: the basis upon which civilization rests and the tenuousness of the human condition.

As Ian Watt has argued, Conrad's thinking is a product of his era. Science assumed that the earth had originated as an incidental by-product of cooling gases from the sun, and according to the second law of thermodynamics (formulated by Lord Kelvin in 1851) the earth would eventually freeze through the diffusion of heat energy. The understanding of entropy now had cosmic relevance: the universe could run down like a machine, like an overwound clock. In 1897 Conrad himself spoke of the universe as a machine which had "evolved...out of chaos...and behold!—it knits....It knits us in and it knits us out. It has knitted time, space, pain, death, corruption, despair and all the illusions—and nothing matters" (quoted in Watt, *Conrad,* 153). (This knitting machine is evoked in Marlow's description of the knitting women in the director's office in Brussels.)

Such cosmic pessimism led to the belief that civilization was grounded on a residual contradiction. In his *Romanes* lecture in 1893, Thomas Huxley claimed that a cruel divide exists between the ethical sense perpetuated by civilization and the laws of nature. One suggested the perfectibility of man; the other insisted on base human limitations. Freud carried this idea even further, arguing that modern man became more civilized by suppressing the baser instincts. But such instincts could never be fully or completely repressed, and they had eventually to express themselves as part of the uncanny, always at the expense of civilization. Kurtz himself illustrates these ideas. In the city, Kurtz—a poet, a painter—embodied civilization; in the jungle he reverts, in a devolutionary way, to a primal savagery. The thinking here is consistent with the debate over evolution. Herbert Spencer claimed that evolution would lead to progress and improvements, but Max Nordau argued that it could lead to degeneration.

Kurtz's last words were "The horror! The horror!" When Marlow tells the Intended that he "heard [Kurtz's] very last words," she says, "Repeat them." Marlow lies in order to spare her the truth, telling her, "The last word he pronounced was—your name" (Conrad, 78–79). The lie is necessary for life—indeed, for civilization—to go on: the ugly reach of the city into the jungle is concealed by sentiment. If the Intended is to keep her sentimental sense of love, she must not know of Kurtz's African mistress, nor of the greed, the death, the degeneration; if the imperial mission is to continue, men must be sent out in her name. Truth, kept separate from the uncanny, is founded upon civilized lies. With these perceptions, *Heart of Darkness* penetrates more deeply into the secrets of the universe than Rider Haggard's *She;* Conrad, as Allan Hunter believes, "is putting the record right about a large number of what he identifies as popular fallacies" (Hunter, 15). Conrad thus takes us to the dead end of doubt, to the destructive element that must become a way of life for the truly initiated. We end on a boat in the Thames River: the story has come full circle. The Thames, we are told, runs into the Congo, creating a seamless reality that connects the modern city with the primitive jungle, the familiar with the uncanny. Like the Buddha in the frame narrative who has seen through to the secrets of life, Marlow has perceived the mystery of existence.

Conrad may be working with one of the main ideas of Herbert Spencer: that the evolutionary movement is from the homogeneous to the heterogeneous, from the simple to the complex, from the undifferentiated in form and function to the differentiated. The difference between the jungle and the city is thus a matter of degree rather than of kind; as the city becomes more complex so does its means of organization, but such organization is always being tested by the primitive urges that it tries to suppress. Conrad therefore challenges Spencer on his own terms, denying that history progresses, as Kurtz degenerates rather than evolves. A look at other novels by Conrad supports this conclusion: the moral squalor of Verloc's London, the chaos after Jim's death in Patusan, and the tyranny in Razumov's Russia do not suggest progress. Built into nature are physical limits beyond which humans cannot go, and the metropolis, as heterogeneous and complex as it may be, is subject to the same laws as the jungle village.

Conrad, like Stoker, challenges Doyle's Enlightenment trust in reason and Haggard's trust in a mystical past. Stoker depicted the power that cult worship still had in a civilized realm. But Conrad goes one step further and reveals the thin line between civilization and savagery, suggesting how tenuous are the forces of order when facing the degenerative forces of chaos, and how vulnerable both from within and without is the infected city.

CHAPTER 7

Joycity

I

James Joyce is the paradigmatic modern, the novelist whose works have moved through the narrative modes of literary modernism. Such movement takes us from the pretense of the real in fiction (the life portraits in *Dubliners* and in Chekhov's short stories) to a literature of artistic self-consciousness with its sense of the indeterminate, a literature of narrative play and self-referentiality as well as the disruption (often parodically) of discourse in general (as one might argue we find in *Finnegans Wake*). As a literary movement, modernism evolves from romantic realism, naturalism, and neo-realism to aestheticism and mythic symbolism controlled by cyclical theories of time and Bergsonian consciousness and then to versions of postmodernism. Postmodernism emphasizes consciousness as part of a linguistic or other structure, with a methodology that transforms the way we think of both nature and history as it substitutes signs for substance, relation for external reality, and hermeneutics for absolute meaning. Joyce's development as a novelist prospectively recapitulates the way the novel has been conceptualized in the twentieth century.

Joyce's connection to literary naturalism was remote and indirect, but nevertheless real. It was most directly mediated by George Moore (1852–1933), whose early novels were written under the influence of Zola and whose works like *The Lake* (1905), *The Untilled Fields* (1903), and *Vain Fortune* (1891) Joyce knew well. Joyce often disparaged aspects of Moore's work; for instance, in *The Lake,* Father Oliver Gogarty's sexual awakening results from his nude swim across a lake in County Mayo, and Joyce thought such a transformation was a bit much. But like Moore, Joyce believed that Ireland was in the grip of ecclesiastical paralysis, that the moral timidity of the nation undercut the drive for home rule and independence, and that the parochialism of the country kept it locked in a peasant mentality. The Irish were obsessed with sex and death, suppressing one and celebrating the other. Caught in the tensions of such self-destructive play, young men and women of Ireland were destined to express their energies neurotically, to desire escape while blocked by invisible walls that held them.[1] Joyce did not have to look far to find in Moore counterparts to such stories of his own in *Dubliners* (1914) as "Eveline," "A Little Cloud," "Counterparts," and "The Boarding House." And Moore's significance was technical as well as thematic, for he had moved away from the omniscient point of view of Zola's novels toward stories narrated more psychologically—stories that unfold through a central consciousness.

Joyce realized that the unfolding of such consciousness could be the basis for a new kind of novel—a novel with an aesthetic hero for whom sensibility was more important than sentiment, and who sought self-definition in the context of the beautiful rather than in the naturalistic context of a determining commercial/industrial environment. Flaubert's *Sentimental Education* had shown Frederic Moreau playing sentiment out to its final absurdity. Flaubert had also shown in *Salammbô* and *The Temptation of Saint Anthony* (1874) how an aesthetic consciousness could transform the novel. But the greatest catalyst for Joyce was Walter Pater. In *The Renaissance,* Pater had written, "What is important . . . is not that the critic should possess a correct abstract definition of beauty for the intellect, but a certain kind of temperament, the power of being deeply moved by the presence of beautiful objects" (509).

Henry James had given us such a novel—one that turned on a character who could be deeply moved by beautiful objects: in the presence of St. Mark's Square in Venice, Hyacinth Robinson in *The Princess Casamassima* (1886) abandons his anarchistic plans because he comes to believe that it is more important to create, especially to create the beau-

---

1. Later, in a letter to his brother Stanislaus, Joyce wrote: "Sometimes thinking of Ireland it seems to me that I have been unnecessarily harsh. I have reproduced (in *Dubliners* at least) none of the attractions of the city" (quoted in Hart, 122).

tiful, than to destroy. This commitment to aestheticism became one of
the controlling ideas behind literary modernism. Virginia Woolf, Marcel
Proust (whose early imagination was deeply influenced by Pater), and
Thomas Mann would turn this impulse into a literary movement; and
Joyce used it as the basis for rewriting his bildungsroman, *A Portrait of
the Artist as a Young Man* (1916), a novel that turns in its famous beach
scene on Stephen Dedalus's commitment to the beautiful. As Stephen
walks through Dublin—"dear dirty Dublin"—objects take on impressionistic meaning as he begins to see through aesthetic eyes. Stephen
realizes that urban objects have an equivalent for him in aesthetic and literary terms, that cityscapes evoke the spirit of the literary artist: "His
morning walks across the city had begun: and he foreknew that as he
passed the sloblands of Fairview he would think of the cloistral sil-
verveined prose of Newman; that as he walked along the North Strand
Road . . . he would recall the dark humor of Guido Cavalcanti and smile;
that as he went by Baird's stonecutting works in Talbot Place the spirit
of Ibsen would blow through him like a keen wind" (*Portrait*, 204).

As we have seen, if the two great subjects of modern literature are the
artist and the city, then the one great subject has to be the artist in the
city—an aesthetic consciousness in the midst of the mob, a controlling
sensibility within the maze. Joyce, Mann, Proust—all share this theme.
And if one can interpret the Tiresias figure broadly, then Baudelaire's *Les
Fleurs du Mal*, Eliot's *The Waste Land*, Hart Crane's *The Bridge*, and
William Carlos Williams's *Paterson* are the poetic expressions of this
theme.

The subject perhaps owes most to Flaubert. In *Bouvard and Pécuchet*,
Flaubert ridiculed the bourgeois mind, seeing it as encyclopedic empiricism in pursuit of commercial ends. In *Sentimental Education*, he dis-
pensed with the subject of sentimental education, which had controlled
the novel for almost two hundred years. And in *The Temptation of Saint
Anthony*, he wrote one of the first purely aesthetic novels—a novel that
turns on sensibility and not sentiment. As Pound was quick to see,
Flaubert was the father of modernism. Modernism as a literary movement turned away from the commercial world by moving either toward
aestheticism or toward an upper-class kind of experience that excluded
the trials of the middle class and below—such as could be found in Virginia Woolf's Bloomsbury or in the salon world of Henry James and
T. S. Eliot. Modernism sought a world uptown rather than downtown,
removed from the crassness of commercial pursuits, made up of refined
men of leisure and of women "who come and go / Talking of Michelan-

gelo." The "inward turn," exemplified by Prufrock in the salon and Stephen Dedalus in the city, takes us into modern consciousness.

Joyce never went beyond the commercial/industrial city; the subject of the imperial, totalitarian city was left to other moderns, mostly writing in London. Indeed, Joyce's interests were even more specific, centering on the commercial more than the industrial city. There was perhaps a good reason for this. In 1904, Dublin had a population of between 350,000 and 400,000, while London had a population approaching seven million. Dublin, in fact, was closer to a peasant than an industrial world—a fact Joyce caught nicely in *Ulysses* with the old milkwoman at the beginning of the novel, with Mr. Deasy on foot-and-mouth disease, and with the cattle crossing the street that stop the funeral procession on its way to Glasnevin cemetery. If one wants to argue that there is an inseparable connection between literary modes and historical process, the evidence here seems to bear the thesis out. Joyce's writings share the concern of late-nineteenth-century realism with the transition from an agrarian and landed to a commercial and urban world. What Joyce saw in Ireland, Ibsen saw in Norway, Hauptmann in Germany, and D'Annunzio in Italy—and all of them influenced Joyce; and what Joyce saw in Ireland, Zola had seen in France and Chekhov in Russia—both of whom seemed to have had little direct influence on Joyce. (The connection between Joyce's *Dubliners* and Chekhov's short stories argues the complexities of the indirect, shared historical moment.)

Many of these writers were considering in literary terms what Marx and Engels had taken up in economic terms: the land question; the displacement of a peasant class; the entrapment of a commercial class in a new kind of city controlled by money and commodity relationships; the breakdown of the family as the young leave the land; the effect of this transformation on women; the rise of the criminal as an urban type; the rise of urban institutions like the boardinghouse, which in the city substitutes for the nuclear family; the effect on human consciousness of the expanding city; the city as maze, seemingly beyond human scale.

Dickens, Balzac, Gogol, and Dostoyevsky had all created versions of this new city—had shown the influx of the young men and women from the provinces in search of a heightened essential self, as well as the breakdown of the family as the hero went his lonely way in search of success in a new moneyed, commercial world. Events turn on the melodramatic, especially the crime of an overreacher like Balzac's Vautrin or Dostoyevsky's Raskolnikov, and on the detective who cuts through the anonymity and the chaos—for example, Inspector Bucket in Dickens's *Bleak*

House—fathoming the maze, restoring the city to human scale by personalizing it. Hugo tells us that "it is from the fruitful union of the grotesque and the sublime that the modern spirit is born—so complex, so various in its forms, so inexhaustible in its creations, and quite opposed, in so being, to the uniform simplicity of the classical spirit" (quoted in Fanger, 229). As Hugo suggests, the modern city partakes of both the grotesque and the sublime: it distorts nature in the name of a different reality.

II

Joyce saw the narrative possibilities of the sublime and the grotesque unfolding through an aesthetic consciousness. He thus came into his own as a novelist by going beyond nineteenth-century realism and literary naturalism. But there were two narrative elements that he had to purge before he could find his voice—sentimentality and melodrama. Dickens's world turned on sentiment, the belief that social evil could be overcome by the capacity of the human heart to do good; but this notion could not long prevail in an urban environment with its diminished sense of the individual. When literary conventions exhaust their credibility, they give way to parody; so Joyce parodies Dickens's sentiment in the "Oxen of the Sun" chapter in *Ulysses*. Also in the center of Dickens's city is the melodramatic man of mystery—a Jaggers or a Tulkinghorn—with secret information locked in vault-like places. He has keys to drawers or cabinets that contain other keys to secret places, and the plot almost always turns on the disclosure of documents that he keeps hidden—that is, it turns on information that he uses as power. In *Dubliners,* as in Chekov's stories, the melodramatic elements were reduced. The narratives turn on everyday events, turn on the commonplace—indeed, commonness is the key to these stories. Common people, doing common tasks, on a common day: Joyce's fiction had this quality even before *Ulysses*.

Much in Joyce stems from the workings of shared prejudice and gossip. Gossip is to Joyce's world what melodramatic information is to Dickens's. Gossip, the commonplace information that by its nature includes and excludes people from a group, relies on shared meaning. A few shared whispers exclude Leopold Bloom from the group at Paddy

Dignam's funeral. His remarks on the virtues of a quick and painless death meet silent resistance because they do not allow the possibility of last rites being administered, while talk of the evil of suicide discomfort him and Mr. Cunningham, who knows how Bloom's father died. "What a town Dublin is!" Joyce told Frank Budgen. "I wonder if there is another like it. Everybody has time to hail a friend and start a conversation about a third party" (Budgen, 60).

Dickens's London takes its being from an imposition of the melodramatic upon the city's commercial nature. Joyce's Dublin takes its being from an imposition of commonality upon the city's commercial nature. It can be no accident that Bloom is a canvasser of advertisements—a more commercial pursuit could not be found for this last remnant of the epic hero. Bloom is preoccupied all morning by the need to place an ad for Alexander Keyes's tea, wine, and liquor store. At the cemetery, the caretaker's keys remind him of this unattended chore, and after the funeral he takes copy to the newspaper office. All of this business, including his getting Keyes to renew the ad, takes place in the center of the city—an area once reserved for the religious sanctuary but now replaced by the newspaper, the modern city's commercial voice. There were two newspapers in Dublin on June 16, 1904, the morning *Freeman's Journal* and the evening *Telegraph.* Joyce used both of these papers, relying heavily in *Ulysses* upon the *Telegraph.*

While for Hugo the nineteenth century revealed the grotesqueries of the sublime, the twentieth century for Joyce revealed the grotesqueries of commercialism. In his walk through the streets, Bloom sees men wearing sandwich boards advertising HELY'S stationer's store. The contrast between commercial and human ends creates coincidences upon which Joyce builds, often leading to an ironic juxtaposition of the sacred and the profane. Bloom later sees a placard advertising the Micus bazaar to raise funds for Mercer's hospital, the hospital for which Handel's *Messiah* was first performed. Still later, he sees the statue of Tom Moore, erected over a public urinal, and thinks of Moore's famous song, "The Meeting of the Waters." Such contrasts lead to a use of the grotesque very different from that of the Victorian novel.

And if one can juxtapose the events and experiences of urban life with ironic effect, one can also juxtapose literary conventions and methods with the same effect. This can be seen in the stories that Joyce added late to *Dubliners.* Florence Walzl and Bernard Benstock have convincingly shown that Joyce superimposed the symbolism of the Feast of the

Epiphany (January 6) on the story of "The Dead" (Walzl, 449; Benstock, 165).[2] By 1914, Joyce had learned that he could transform the reality of literary naturalism by superimposing the symbolic upon the realistic. Jackson Cope maintains that he learned to do this from Gabriele D'Annunzio, whose books he bought with the money he received from his essay on Ibsen. Cope believes that the novel *Il Fuoco* (1900) and the play *La citta morta* (1900) were most influential with their complex interplay of realism and symbolism, biography and myth, all set in an archaeological realm of layered reality. Cope argues that "Joyce learned from this a way to raise Stephen Hero beyond the limitations of the Bildungsroman" (60).

In *Stephen Hero* (1904), Stephen realizes that certain fixed moments illuminate the meaning of a city—that Dublin, or London, or Paris has an essence that reveals itself in its accidents. An inchoate, trivial conversation overheard revealed the essence of urban love, "and this triviality made him think of collecting many such moments together in a book of epiphanies" (*Stephen Hero,* 211). Such was Joyce's intention when he began *Dubliners.* But in the later *Dubliners* stories, Joyce realized that a symbolic overlay on naturalistic detail distanced the harsh realism, added an ironic dimension, and created comic effect. As comparisons between *A Portrait* and *Stephen Hero* clearly show, Joyce moved away from modern realism toward modern aestheticism—two different modes of narrative reality. But even as he abandoned neo-realism, Joyce clung to the belief that objects in nature unfold their meaning. Such a process of unfolding was inseparable from the idea of the epiphany—and a theory of symbolism.

Joyce went beyond both literary naturalism and symbolism when he began to control symbols in the context of myth. The aestheticized birdlike girl who supplies the epiphany in chapter 4 of *A Portrait* takes on symbolic meaning because *A Portrait* is controlled by the Daedalus-Icarus myth—that is, by the myth of birdlike flight. In moving from aestheticism to mythic symbolism, Joyce moved from the early stages of modernism to what today we think of as high modernism, and the novel that best reflects this movement is, of course, *Ulysses* (1922), where Joyce brings all of these narrative elements into play and whose naturalistic

---

2. Examples of Joyce's use of the symbolic method can be multiplied. A. Walton Litz has shown how "Two Gallants" is a mixture of realism and symbolism, Joyce making use of "stock responses and illusions of romantic fiction" (Litz, "Two Gallants," 63, 65). And Marvin Magalaner and Richard Kain have shown how Joyce superimposed a Dantean grid upon the story of "Grace" (Magalaner, 100–101; Kain, 147).

plane of reference is symbolically held in place by a mythic structure superimposed upon it. *Ulysses* is the literary complement to what was happening in archaeology—the discovery of layered cities, the realization that different cultures were superimposed upon each other in time. Heinrich Schliemann's discoveries in Troy (1871) and Arthur Evans's in Crete (Knossos, 1876) had a tremendous influence on the works of D'Annunzio, which in turn influenced Joyce. In George Moore's *The Lake,* Nora Glynn participates in such an archaeological dig. Schliemann discovered as many as nine cities superimposed on each other in Troy: cities 7A and B are the city of Homer. The archaeological structure of Troy found its equivalent in *The Waste Land, The Cantos,* and especially *Ulysses.*

III

Joyce's interest in the Mediterranean world may have been motivated by another source. As early as 1907, he believed that there was a connection between Mediterranean and Irish culture. In a lecture he gave at the Università Popolare in Trieste in April of 1907, he argued not only for a connection between Iberia and Ireland (long speculated) but also for a direct connection between Ireland and the early Phoenicians and later Egyptians, based on a theory of sea trade and on common elements of language. Speaking of the special nature of the Irish language, he began:

The language is oriental in origin, and has been identified by many philologists with the ancient language of the Phoenicians, the originators of trade and navigation, according to historians. This adventurous people, who had a monopoly of the sea, established in Ireland a civilization that had decayed and almost disappeared before the first Greek historian took his pen in hand. It jealously preserved the secrets of its knowledge, and the first mention of the island of Ireland in foreign literature is found in a Greek poem of the fifth century before Christ, where the historian repeats the Phoenician tradition. The language that the Latin writer of comedy, Plautus, put in the mouth of Phoenicians in his comedy *Poenulus* is almost the same language that the Irish peasants speak today, according to the critic Vallancey. The religion and civilization of this ancient people, later known by the name of Druidism, were Egyptian. The Druid priests had their temples in the open, worshiped the sun and moon in groves of oak trees. In the crude state of knowledge of those times, the Irish priests were considered very learned, and when Plutarch mentions Ireland, he says that it was the dwelling place of holy men. Festus Avienus in the fourth century was the first to give Ireland the title of *Insula Sacra;* and later, after having undergone the invasions of the Spanish and Gaelic tribes, it was converted to Christianity by St. Patrick and his followers, and again earned the title of "Holy Isle." (*Critical Writings,* 156)

This passage suggests why Joyce was eventually attracted to Victor Berard's theory that the Ulysses story was deeply influenced by Phoenician culture, hence making it a Jewish poem. Joyce's belief in the symmetry between ancient Phoenicia, Greece, Crete, Egypt, and Ireland played into his eventual acceptance of the Viconian theory of history.

Joyce's interest in Vico's theory has been generally connected with *Finnegans Wake,* but Richard Ellmann has shown that Joyce was already interested in Vico while he was working on *Ulysses.* This connection is not surprising given Joyce's interest in Flaubert—especially novels like *Bouvard and Pécuchet,* which indicts the supremacy of the rationalistic, Enlightenment mind that trusts in factual accumulation. Even more to the point is *Salammbô,* which reveals Flaubert's own use of Vico: one order of space and time (Catharge at the time of the Punic Wars) reflects another order of space and time (Paris in the Second Empire). Vico believed that there are three cycles of time and then a *ricorso*—the age of the gods, of heroes, and of men; or the primitive, semihistory, and the historic—characterized by rites first of religion, second of marriage, and third of burial. The first turn in the cycle took place before the Trojan War, the second during the Trojan War, and the third at the time Athens and Rome became republics. The ancient reflux or the *ricorso* occurred with the fall of Rome, whereby civilization gave way to a new barbarism, which in turn led to a new age of feudal or medieval heroes, and then to the Enlightenment democracies that Vico observed in his own day. The modern reflux began with the end of the Enlightenment, resulting in the commercial paralysis and moral decadence from which modernism could not extricate itself.

Viconian cycles lead inevitably to the parallax view, to use a term that, like *metempsychosis,* is important in *Ulysses.* According to Zack Bowen, "Parallax, as explained by Sir Robert Ball [whose work "The Story of the Heavens" Bloom thinks of as he looks up at the Ballast Office Clock], is the visual sensation received when one holds up a finger in front of one's eyes and observes a far object. The finger appears to be doubled. Conversely, if one looks at the finger, the far object appears to be doubled. In the astronomical sense of parallax, distant heavenly bodies observed from different points on the planet appear to be in different positions even though their positions remain the same" (469). This notion is significant to Joyce's new way of thinking about narrative. The parallax view creates two areas of activity, a foreground and a background, one of which blurs when the other is focused upon—which is to say that the positioning between the two is subjective, held together by historical consciousness. Joyce, as we have seen, used something like this method in "Grace," "The Dead," and *A Portrait;* but in *Ulysses* the method dominates by calling attention to itself.[3]

IV

Joyce had originally conceived of *Ulysses* as part of *Dubliners.* In a letter to his brother from Rome in September of 1906, he speaks of writing a story about a Dublin Jew named Albert Hunter, who had taken him home on June 22, 1904, after a street fight. So far as we know, Joyce never wrote such a story, but he carried the idea in his head for seven years, when he began *Ulysses.*

The Homeric parallels were important to Joyce because they held Dublin as a city in suspense between the sacred and the profane, the ancient and the modern world. As Michael Seidel observes, "Joyce knew precisely where to go when he wants obstacles to the fulfillment of epic form. He goes to the streets" (102). To flip the heroic coin is to find Bloom, whose story is too insignificant for even the newspapers to tell correctly. We are told that L. Boom was at Paddy Dignam's funeral along with M'Coy and Stephen Dedalus (who were not), together with McIntosh (who was and wasn't). For Joyce, gods in the world have given way to a canvasser of advertisements; the sacred has become profane because so much has to be siphoned through the crowd, of which the citizen in "Cyclops" is the embodiment.

Perhaps the most successful of such juxtapositions of the past and the present occurs in the "Wandering Rocks" chapter. On first look this

3. The argument over the importance of the Ulysses legend to Joyce's novel has gone on since its publication; critics like T. S. Eliot and Richard Ellmann emphasize the mythic parallels while those such as Ezra Pound and Hugh Kenner minimize them. But if Joyce believed a parallax view stemmed from his use of Vico, then there need be no disagreement. The two planes of the novel, the foreground and the background, the realistic and the symbolic, are very much in play (as Eliot and Ellmann claim), but they cannot be held in focus at once (as Pound and Kenner perhaps intuited).

seems to be the most realistic of all the chapters in *Ulysses,* close in its details, as many commentators have pointed out, to *Dubliners.* In a remark to Frank Budgen, Joyce apparently confirmed this impression, as he spoke of writing it with a map of Dublin before him. But, as Richard Ellmann has demonstrated, Joyce overlaid this landscape with the geography of the Mideast: the Liffey becomes the Bosphorus, the strait dividing Asia and Europe through which Jason's Argo has to sail. Now, however, there instead floats a throwaway advertising the new Elijah in the person of J. Alexander Dowie, the evangelist from America. The details are important: he is the new Elijah from the New World whose coming is announced in an advertisement proclaiming the word of God to the masses. The newspaper is now part of the religious equation.

In the "Aeolus" chapter the newspaper headlines speak from "THE HEART OF THE HIBERNIAN METROPOLIS." The newspaper has become the geographical center of the commercial city. In the holy city, which provides the original idea of every city, the center was the sanctuary. Such cities as Ur and Uruk served as sacred burial places where desert tribes could return to worship their dead. Each city had its network of gods and of priests who communicated with them. Through a series of overlays, Joyce takes us through a newspaper advertisement that calls Bloom's attention to a German company planning citrus groves in Israel to thoughts of how the holy cities gave way to secular ends and were corrupted. Cities built to worship the dead have become dead in themselves: "A barren land, bare waste. Volcanic lake, the dead sea: no fish, weedless, sunk deep in the earth. No wind would life those waves, grey metal, poisonous foggy water. Brimstone they called it raining down: the cities of the plain: Sodom, Gomorrah, Edom. All dead names. A dead sea in a dead land, grey and old" (*Ulysses,* 61).

How the sacred cities of the old have been transformed is a matter of interest to Bloom. Later, in the "Lestrygonians" chapter, as Bloom walks the commercial streets of Dublin, his thoughts return to this subject. These sacred cities of old have been corrupted from within; they have allowed their sacred functions to become profaned. Palestine gave way to Sodom and Gomorrah, Heliopolis to Babylon. The commercial city, too, precedes a final collapse. And in *Ulysses,* the sacred, heroic cities of the past and the secular, commercial cities of the present are held in mutual suspension: the novel is formed by such a parallax view. The biblical Elijah went to war against the false god of Baal and the property-obsessed Ahab; the new Elijah hands out ostensibly religious but actually commercial throwaways in the center of Dublin. Befitting the new city's status as a commercial rather than a sacred place, the life-giving river carries the fraudulent message of the new Elijah, Alexander J. Dowie. Bloom superimposes these ideas upon each other, as in the city modern life flows in its pursuit of money:

Cityful passing away, other cityful coming, passing away too: other coming on, passing on. Houses, lines of houses, streets, miles of pavements, piled up bricks, stones. Changing hands. This owner, that. Landlord never dies they say. Other steps into his shoes when he gets his notice to quit. They buy the place up with gold and still they have all the gold. Swindle in it somewhere. Piled up cities, worn away age after age. Pyramids in sand. Built on bread and onions. Slaves. Chinese wall. Babylon. Big stones left. Round towers. Rest rubble, sprawling suburbs, jerrybuilt, Kerwan's mushroom houses, built of breeze. Shelter for the night. (164)

Since Bloom embodies the commercial city, it is not surprising that his vision centers on its commercial function. Built into these passages is a sense of cyclical history. Cities rise and fall like the cultures that inform them. Ezra Pound believed that cultures began to decline when they cut themselves away from the land and became commercial, creating systems of money and usury that separated workers from their work, artisans from their craft. Bloom seems to be suggesting something similar, but Joyce is far vaguer than Pound on how history works. *Ulysses* moves from Mr. Deasy's Christian Hegelianism (history works to reveal the manifestations of God) to Stephen's sense of entrapment (history as a nightmare from which he is trying to wake). When Stephen tells Deasy that God is a shout in the street, he is not far removed from describing the way *Ulysses* functions as a novel. Most of the action is inseparable from the street and from the commercial processes that transform street activity. The man in the brown macintosh reinforces this point. He appears and disappears mysteriously at Paddy Dignam's funeral, and again in the "Circe" chapter, where his Christ-like presence gives way to intimations of nightmare. The man in the macintosh represents the carnivalesque; he is the mysterious stranger, another version of the Dionysus figure, the outsider who challenges his surroundings by suggesting a force larger and more mysterious than the daily order.

Like Dublin itself, the man in the macintosh is part of a larger continuum, part of the history whose cycles create the diminished present, the commercial nightmare from which Stephen is trying to wake. The "Circe" chapter is Joyce's representation of this nightmare world. As many critics have pointed out, it is a Walpurgisnacht, an expulsion of mental and emotional turmoil for both Stephen and Bloom, a catharsis that allows them to go on in the face of urban discontinuity (*Finnegans Wake* served the same ongoing purpose for Joyce). And "Circe" leads to "Ithaca," in which both Stephen and Bloom are compared to stars flowing through the heavens and thus are placed in the larger universe. Throughout the novel, Bloom has been obsessed with the flow of people through cities, Stephen with the flow of history. As they stop in the "Ithaca" section to urinate, both are less than sanguine about where the "flow" is taking them. The great "yes" to the flow comes, of course, from Molly, whose energies have a sexual base and whose joy is inseparable from maternal processes. Her reverie anticipates that of Anna Livia Plurabelle in *Finnegans Wake*, where the woman is transformed into the river flowing to the sea, thus replenishing the cycle of life. Crudely put, Joyce in *Ulysses* creates a cyclical vision of the city, caught in the flow of rise and fall, which can give way either to a nightmarish vision of history or to joy in the energies that perpetuate life. Each point of view finds its embodiment in the novel: Bloom's vision of the city, Stephen's vision of history, and Molly's impulse to sustain the ongoing rhythm of life itself.

V

If the starting point of *Ulysses* is the story of Ulysses or the Wandering Jew,[4] the starting point for *Finnegans Wake* (1939) is the Osiris story, perhaps the most basic myth of the gods. Murdered by his brother Seth, his body dismembered and the parts scattered, Osiris is reassembled and brought back to life by his sister-wife, Isis. At that time she conceives their son, Horus, who lives to revenge his father's murder (a story that is an analogue to that of Tammuz, Adonis, Dionysus, and Christ). Rise and fall, fall and rise—such is the pattern of *Finnegans Wake*, where Finn McCool of Irish legend gives way to Humphrey Chimpden Earwicker. The correspondingly fundamental heroic myth is

4. The Wandering Jew, who rebuked Christ at Calvary, is fated to walk the world and neither die nor find rest until the Second Coming. As Chester Anderson has pointed out, he is sometimes connected with Enoch, Elijah, and Al-Khadir, who in Semitic mythology was a vegetation god (C. Anderson, 11). Beginning with Al-Khadir and moving through Enoch to Leopold Bloom completes a Viconian cycle. Once Joyce became aware of Victor Berard's theory of the Phoenician—that is, the Semitic—influence on the Ulysses legend, he collapsed the Wandering Jew story into the story of Ulysses. So it is appropriate that his modern Ulysses is Jewish, just as it is apt, once he had connected Ireland with the Mediterranean, that his modern Dedalus is an Irishman.

the Tristan and Isolde story: old King Mark is replaced by his nephew Tristan, who steals the love of Mark's wife, Isolde. In *Finnegans Wake* the Tristan and Isolde story finds its equivalent in the struggle between the father and the brothers over the love of Iseult (sometimes called Issy, which suggests the Osiris legend). Both her name and the setting of the novel in Chapelizod (Isolde's chapel) reinforce the Isolde connection.

During the writing of *Finnegans Wake,* Joyce began to think of his characters in relational terms: he devised a series of signs, or sigla, for his major characters, and thought of many of the sigla as interchangeable. The meaning of the main characters of the novel changes, depending upon what phase in the Viconian cycle they inhabit. For example, Earwicker is variously the dismembered god, Oliver Cromwell, a Norwegian ship captain, a man named Buckley in the Russian Revolution, and a Chapelizod pubkeeper. His secret act in Phoenix Park partakes of Adam's original sin re-presented as a sordid act in the modern city. The two brothers—Shem and Shaun, penman and postman, bohemian and bourgeois, one a wasteful gracehopper and the other a prudent ondt, one a member of the Gripes and the other of the Mookse—represent polarized space and time (Joyce vs. Wyndham Lewis, England vs. Ireland) before they eventually are reconciled on the level of universal consciousness. As the sigla change, so do the characters, until it is difficult to know, as one commentator puts it, "who is who when everybody is somebody else" (quoted in Bowen and Carens, 595).

Thus the difference between *Ulysses* and *Finnegans Wake* is immense and has major relevance to the way the city is depicted and emerges in Joyce's fiction. First, in a work organized archetypally, like *Finnegans Wake,* we lose our sense of foreground and are left with only background. Dublin and Ireland and the people who comprise the city begin to disappear or become flatter and thinner to the point of invisibility. It becomes harder to identify with characters, we lose a sense of the everyday and of a specific place, and what is abstractable from the events becomes more important than the events themselves. Such flattening is the direction the novel has taken since *Finnegans Wake,* and we will see the influence that Joyce had, directly or indirectly, on twentieth-century novelists from Samuel Beckett to Thomas Pynchon.

Second, *Finnegans Wake* presents a narrative realm that is relational rather than centered. One can talk about the Osiris legend or the Egyptian *Book of the Dead* as the novel's center, or one can substitute the Oedipus legend, as Margot Norris has done, and show how it serves exactly the same function. *Finnegans Wake* is intertextual, taking its meaning from other narratives as well as itself. The sense of resulting play is almost endless, as the reader soon finds. The letter the hen digs up in the chicken coop parodies the story of the *Book of Kells,* which was buried, dug up, and reinterpreted; it also parodies the Osiris myth and its cognates, and its subjection to Freudian and Marxist interpretations mocks exercises in modern literary criticism. Such practices constantly disrupt the story. Joyce makes draft after draft more linguistically complex, until he creates almost a pure example of the deferral, dispersal, and difference characteristic of postmodernism.

And last, in analyzing the movement of Joyce from *Ulysses* to *Finnegans Wake,* we can see that disruption came not by rebellion or revolution but from within his own system. The lesson here is that every system of organization necessarily contains a principle of disorganization. Within the Viconian organic theory of nature and history is a structural theory that emerges as Joyce begins to think of universal time and in monomythic terms. The journey from "The Dead" through the "Proteus" and "Circe" sections of *Ulysses* to *Finnegans Wake* is thus a matter of transformation, a shift within rather than a dismantling of a paradigm; it is a shift of which Joyce himself may not have been consciously aware. Aware or not, the deed was done: Joyce's novels instantiate the transformations in modern narratives. He is, to use a metaphor apt to his work, the father of us all, the man who saw the way before there was a way to be seen, who both made and unmade the modern novel, and whose narrative departures it took a generation to learn to read.

VI

In *Ulysses,* myth is superimposed upon a modern city; in *Finnegans Wake,* myth is superimposed upon a dream. "It was Joyce's lifelong endeavor," Harry Levin writes, "to escape from the nightmare of history, to conceive the totality of human experience on a simultaneous plane, to synchronize past, present, and future in the timelessness of a millennium" (198). The ending of *Ulysses* thus carried Joyce toward *Finnegans Wake* as the ending of *A Portrait* had carried him toward *Ulysses.* *Ulysses* locates two historic moments and keeps them suspended for ironic purposes. The layered results of these epochs appear in mutant display—that is, *Ulysses* depicts the remnants of an age of heroes and priests in the diminished reality of men like Bloom and Father Conmee;

the last gasp of an aristocracy in the person of Haines and other English occupiers;[5] and the rise of commercial structures that grip the city, control its voice journalistically, walk its street with humans strapped into display signs, and encircle its life with trams. In contrast, *Finnegans Wake* transforms one historical moment into another and obliterates the difference. *Ulysses* symbolically accommodates a material world; *Finnegans Wake* mythically transforms such a world. Put differently, *Ulysses* is the metaphoric vision, *Finnegans Wake* the metamorphic: the metaphoric vision leaves the material world untouched, while the metamorphic vision transforms it. As Harry Levin argues, "street life and Homeric legend are scrupulously differentiated through *Ulysses*. [But] the locus for *Finnegans Wake* is that point in infinity where such parallels meet" (142). When the parallels do not meet, the result is mock-epic; when they do, we have universal history. Bloom is metaphorically (and ironically) Odysseus, while Earwicker is metamorphically all men from all time. Dublin remains Dublin in *Ulysses*—the city at the end of its cyclical sweep of time—while containing all cities from all time in *Finnegans Wake*. *Ulysses* is a naturalistic/realistic vision, the material world symbolically overlaid; *Finnegans Wake* is a mythic / antirepresentational vision, the material world organically transformed.

In March of 1912 in Trieste, Joyce gave two lectures at the Università Popolare on the subject of "verismo ed idealismo." He illustrated these two literary extremes by discussing Daniel Defoe and William Blake. Defoe's Robinson Crusoe was Joyce's practical, mechanical, commercial—that is, modern—man; Blake's Albion was the romantic visionary who goes beyond the physical contradictions to an organic, external

---

5. In his monumental *Inventing Ireland* (1995), Declan Kiberd argues that Joyce saw Ireland through colonial (really postcolonial) eyes, that his Ireland "is just another of those modern places where there is no *there* any more" (337). Joyce thus anticipates Rushdie, Naipaul, and Marquez (339). My own reading of Joyce is radically different from Kiberd's. I see him portraying Ireland as rooted firmly within the history of continental Europe, with connections to a mythic Mediterranean. If his portrait of Ireland seems centerless, it is because he depicts Ireland through different literary modes, creating a series of different realities (or realisms). As he takes us from the edges of literary naturalism to the verge of postmodernism, Joyce's historical consciousness, including the history of Ireland, is far more rooted than Kiberd is willing to acknowledge; I believe that Joyce sees British colonialism as more an accident than an essence of that history—more the product of Viconian cycles than a sign of colonial destiny. To be sure, Ireland would never recapture its own lost culture, but for Joyce that was not totally without benefit, for Ireland had been moved more toward the center of Europe. Kiberd's argument, though intelligent and informed, plays to present critical fashions; a more traditional reading of Joyce is bound eventually to challenge its appeal.

sense of unity. *Ulysses* is Joyce's great fusion of the realistic and symbolic vision, and *Finnegans Wake* is his great romantic vision—a work that takes mechanical reality beyond itself and moves modernism into a new literary dimension. Like the romantics, Joyce created a universal self out of memory; substituted the organic for the mechanical, the mythic for the symbolic; and insisted on the inseparability of man and nature. In *Ulysses* the citizens flow through the city, but in *Finnegans Wake* Earwicker and Anna Livia Plurabelle become the city. The Hill of Howth becomes a giant foot, Dublin a giant belly, the Wellington monument a giant phallus, and Anna becomes the River Liffey—all time flowing through these physical and human channels. Earwicker transformed is Adam, Tristan, Cromwell, and Parnell. When Joyce was writing *Ulysses*, he was using Giordano Bruno's theory of an ultimate unity and its terrestrial division into contrasts and opposites. By the time he came to *Finnegans Wake*, he had consented to Blake's belief that "eternity is in love with the productions of time."

In *Finnegans Wake*, Joyce went beyond the mechanistic view of his early stories and the symbolism of *Ulysses*—methods that held in contrast the tensions of the commercial city. Instead, he not only postulated a Viconian swing back to the mythic city of the past but created in his metamorphic power a redeeming vision. In so doing, he unearthed a city of the sacred dead—just as the great archaeologist Schliemann had done when he resurrected the dead city of Troy, a city inseparable from the story of Ulysses. Both T. S. Eliot and Ezra Pound would contrast the walking dead, going about their tasks in the secular, unreal city, with the redeeming power of a mythic realm or with the vision of Ecbatana, the heavenly city—as Bloom speculates on the profit of transporting cattle by train at the same time as he communicates with the dead in Glasnevin. But in *Ulysses*, Dublin never gives way to Bloomusalem as it seems to in *Finnegans Wake*, as life flows from a death watch, from a fatal fall in the city as well as from the fallen city.

VII

As the mind moves inward, the physical world, including the city, becomes a subjective reality. Joyce's Dublin takes on the meaning projected on it by Stephen Dedalus and Leopold Bloom or assumes the extended quality of dream and language that characterizes *Finnegans*

Wake. Reworked by Samuel Beckett, Joycean reality gives way to phantasmagoria and the spectral, shrivels to the compass of an isolated room or barren ruin as we see when the city becomes prolapsed in late modernist work such as that of Samuel Beckett. As a student at Trinity College, Dublin, Beckett became extremely interested in Descartes, keeping a large loose-leaf notebook full of philosophical commentary on him and his critics. Beckett's interest eventually extended to Descartes's contemporaries and to the ideas of the Enlightenment.

As we have seen, one response to the Enlightenment was the kind of self that Wordsworth created out of memory; later, deeply intensified through the philosophy of Bergson, it led to modernists like Proust, the subject of Beckett's first book. The end product of modernism, that is, led to an aesthetics of self, as defined in one context by Oscar Wilde and in another by Joyce. Wilde's aestheticism created the dandy, the self as the equivalent of an art object; Joyce through Stephen Dedalus—whether taken literally or ironically—established a realm in which beauty unfolds as an epiphany and reality is transformed by the imagination. Early on, Joyce took the Enlightenment agenda as his object of attack, seeing in such works as Flaubert's *Bouvard et Pécuchet* a critique of the mentality that glorified science and the encyclopedic mind. Leopold Bloom is a more humane version of Bouvard and Pécuchet—a Charlie Chaplin figure, who is unintentionally amusing when he sees through scientific eyes. Bloom looks around Dublin and, in Enlightenment tradition, finds solutions to major problems, from bottling the gas generated by the corpses in the cemetery to creating a rail line from the stockyard to the docks. Bloom is a sympathetic character whom we come to admire immensely, but at moments in Joyce's novel we laugh more at him than with him, particularly when he suggests that the scientific mind can order and control its surroundings.

Beckett's fiction begins with epistemological doubt. Like Descartes, Beckett wants to split mind from body, and then mind from its surroundings. But unlike Descartes, Beckett believes the mind is too infused with surrounding reality ever to be separate from it. Further, Beckett questions where our mental process is leading us. While Descartes conceived of creation as a hierarchy of creatures moving toward a final cause and the ultimate form of God, Beckett saw how tenuous the connection is between mind and body and between mind and anything like final form.

Life in Beckett's works proceeds like a game of chess. His characters become trapped between their desire to die and their fear of death. A life force—a remnant of Schopenhauer's cosmic will—drives them on, despite their will to die. Beckett's characters are thus in a perpetual halfway house. In earlier naturalistic novels, under the influence of Darwin, it was assumed that humanity existed halfway between a lost animality and an evolutionary process that was moving toward a more perfect future, but in Beckett the past and the future cannot be qualitatively differentiated: there is only the emptied present between blank walls of time. His characters are thus caught in a process of discontinuous time—separated from a past that offers no traditional way of meaning and a future that has already been discounted. Both an Enlightenment and a romantic sense of self are negated: Beckett's characters find no order in their minds by which to impose meaning on the world, no means to create a personal identity through memory and past experience, and no source of beauty stemming from their own being, the natural world, or the creative process of the imagination.

Many modernists have tried to find a way out of this kind of radical nihilism. Nietzsche believed that consciousness freed from rationality could better come to terms with reality; Beckett's Parisian contemporary Jean-Paul Sartre tried to fill this temporal and personal vacuum with the distressed, existential self, whose will can fill the void; Michel Foucault went one step further than Nietzsche and saw consciousness as a form of discourse, inseparable from culture, and held in place by power, especially by social institutions. Beckett found all of these ways of coping with the self too heroic, too much under the control of forms of consciousness, human will, or institutionalized power. More than any of his contemporaries, his onslaught on post-Enlightenment man was total. He limited rationality and the imagination; he questioned the human will; he robbed time of both linearity and cyclicality; he took from nature any process by which it could complete itself; and he recognized (long before Derrida) the tenuousness of language, which he saw perpetually canceled by competing claims on the mind. Joyce's exile was geographic; Beckett's was metaphysical. He emptied the modern self of any residual meaning—and refused any means of reinstating what he had completely subverted. Under such an onslaught, there is no self, no community, no history, and no city, as we turn inward to a consciousness that negates the outward world of urban reality.

CHAPTER 8

Urban Entropy

I

We have moved in the twentieth century from apocalypse to entropy. The first two laws of thermodynamics explain the nature of entropy: first, the amount of energy in the universe is fixed, and energy can never be increased or diminished, only transformed; second, every time energy is transformed from one state to another, there is a loss in the amount of energy available to perform future work. Entropy is that loss of energy in a closed system. In an open system, negative entropy supplies an added source of energy; plants, for example, absorb energy from the sun. A city is a closed system: nothing provides it energy outside itself.

Writing against the realms of science and technology, Jeremy Rifkin argues in *Entropy: A New World View* (1989) that at every stage of production, whatever energy is extracted from the environment "ends up in one form or another as waste" (129). The result is growing disorder: "The massive flow-through of energy in modern industrial society is creating massive disorder in the world we live in. The faster we streamline our technologies, the faster we speed up the transforming process, the faster available energy is dissipated, the more the disorder mounts" (80). Rifkin points out that it took millions of years to exhaust the environment that supported a hunter-gatherer society, thousands to exhaust the agriculture environment, and only hundreds to deplete the industrial environment (67). Whatever is taken in as raw material (available energy) ends up as unusable waste (unavailable energy) (58). Three hundred trout are needed to sustain a human for a year; the trout consume 90,000 frogs; the frogs consume 27 million grasshoppers; the grasshoppers live off 1,000 tons of grass. Thus, Rifkin concludes, "in order for one human being to maintain a high level of 'orderliness,' the energy contained in 27 million grasshoppers or a thousand tons of grass must be used.... [E]very living thing maintains its own order only at the expense of creating greater disorder ... in the overall environment" (54).

In *The Waste Land* (1922), Eliot's "waste" encompasses more than what Rifkin is talking about. Eliot is working with vegetative myths in which the land has been depleted because of drought and other natural disasters, lore that in turn involves sacrificial myths. But Eliot superimposes these primitive myths onto modern-day London where they overlay—and take on the meaning of—the depletion of an urban and industrial society, as seen in its emotionally exhausted citizenry. Moreover, Eliot suggests that the process of waste has speeded up since the Renaissance, a view that Rifkin also argues. Thus, while Eliot and Rifkin start with different assumptions, their conclusions are remarkably similar.

II

Eliot's use of the wasteland landscape in Rifkin's industrial sense was anticipated by other urban writers. Dickens believed that as the city went beyond a human scale, it became a destructive entity, organizing its citizens around impersonal institutions and the desire for money. The railroad changed the scale in *Dombey and Son;* Pip betrayed his human instincts in the city; Bleak House became property in a Chancery game; justice gave way to the Circumlocution Office; the prison replaced the home in *Little Dorrit*, where houses slide into dust; and death competed with life in *Our Mutual Friend*. Dickens's city inverted the ur-city: the fortress became the prison; the sacred burial ground, the necropolis; and the meeting place, the railroad station. Jaggers and Tulkinghorn, the agents of the city, pursued money and had access to enormous power through secrets and other information at their command. As values became increasingly materialistic, there was less room for love and friendship; time was measured by fashions, defining the citizens externally according to what they could buy. And because fashions always change, there was no inner stability, no sense of residual identity; a nervous emptiness became a way of life. Empty citizens, desperately seeking something to give life meaning, inhabited a grotesque landscape, which was an inversion of nature: Dickens's wasteland ends where Eliot's begins.

Dostoyevsky also anticipated the wasteland. In *Crime and Punishment* (1865), he demonstrated how the meeting place—where the citizens were supposed to come together in human and communal terms—had been lost as the marketplace dominated. Dostoyevsky disliked St. Petersburg: he thought of it as an artificial city, without roots, that had descended from the sky rather than taken its origins from the earth (as did Novogorod and Kiev). In an act of violence, Peter had taken the land from Sweden and constructed a city, like Amsterdam or Venice, on the inhospitable marshes of the Gulf of Finland. Peter's cathedral—with the cross on top of its steeple—stands like a ship with its mast symbolically pointed toward the West, which offered landlocked Russia access to Europe and to European secular thought, especially the utilitarian ideas of Mill and Bentham. St. Petersburg became a monument to Peter's dominance over the land as well as the center of the government bureaucracy needed to keep an empire. *Crime and Punishment* is Dostoyevsky's most direct treatment of the city, and one can follow the action step by step through the streets of St. Petersburg. Many of the key events take place in public: Sonia's solicitations, Marmeladov's death, Svidrigaylov's suicide, Raskolnikov's kissing the earth and his confession in Haymarket Square. Dostoyevsky makes use of the contradictions built into St. Petersburg. Much of the action takes place within crowds, yet this is a novel of terrible isolation and inner solitude. The city, a monument to the Enlightenment West, possesses great architectural beauty; yet the streets are rife with drunkards, debauchers, prostitutes, madmen, and murderers: there is a terrible contradiction between what the city symbolizes and the human reality it has generated.

Raskolnikov killed for ideological reasons: to prove that he stood outside the community of man, that he was extraordinary—and for psychological reasons: to prove that he could do it. In contrast to radical Western ideas that had moved into Russian intellectual thought, Dostoyevsky postulated the idea of Russia (the East), based upon the earth, love, and the communion of the people—the ur-idea of the marketplace. Thus Raskolnikov had to go through two stages of development: he had first to overcome his radical individualism and then consent to the idea of humanity. As he publicly acknowledges this change, the idea of

Christ's cross and the idea of the crossroads meet. Lazarus and the New Jerusalem come together when Raskolnikov kisses the earth in Haymarket Square and when he is with Sonia outside the prison, in the last scene in the novel. Dostoyevsky thus allowed the city to be redeemed through the absorption of self into the people—into a community—and through the idea of Christ and of a common humanity. The communal self is the basis for the New Jerusalem. Dickens took us into a nineteenth-century version of the wasteland, but Dostoyevsky helped show a way out. Eliot was reading both *Our Mutual Friend* and a French translation of *Crime and Punishment* while he was working on *The Waste Land,* and each influenced him immensely.

The sense of decline that Eliot found in Dickens and Dostoyevsky was sustained by other nineteenth-century commentators—especially Cesare Lombroso and Max Nordau. Though Eliot is not usually linked with a social observer like Nordau, there is a clear connection that reveals an affinity of mind. In *Degeneration* (1892), dedicated to Lombroso, Nordau tells us that modernism is the dead end of decadence. Decadence, he argued, stemmed from the rise of the overwrought city, the source of nervous fatigue and mental exhaustion. This urban state of mind was extrapolated into such decadent literary forms as mysticism, egomania, and literary realism and naturalism. Wagner, Tolstoy, Rossetti, and Verlaine were guilty of mysticism, which was characterized by vague and incoherent thought, erotic excitability, and religious enthusiasm. Huysmans, Baudelaire, and Nietzsche were guilty of egomania, revealed by an obsession with self, taking drugs or using other stimuli, and obsessive and defective thought. And Zola embodied naturalism, marked by pessimism and licentious ideas. According to Nordau, these three forms of degeneration shared common ground and could be attributed to "a brain incapable of normal working, thence feebleness of will, inattention, predominance of emotion.... From a clinical point of view ... these pathological pictures are nevertheless only different manifestations of ... exhaustion[,] ... an exhausted central nervous system" (536).

The modern literary brain had become infected, and what it expressed was pathologically defective. Nordau was especially sensitive to works like Huysmans's *À Rebours,* which revealed modern man working "against the grain," "against nature"; he insisted that Nietzsche wrote his major works when he was clinically insane; and he attacked Zola even as he agreed with him that the city was encouraging the survival of the unfittest—an emotionally exhausted overclass and a bestial underclass. Nordau was distressed by the loss of individual autonomy, and he believed that the personal breakdown revealed a national breakdown. The vision of destiny possessed by a cohesive people with an organic sense of the land had been lost. (He would later become deeply involved in the Zionist movement, looking for a Jewish homeland that would render this sense of land and community.)

Oswald Spengler, who would share and extend many of these concerns into a new commentary, also perceived a short-circuiting within the modern city. Seeing the roots of human life in the soil, Spengler believed that the city bankrupted the country and was diminished in return. Cut off from a source of nourishment beyond itself, the city became a closed system, caught in an entropic process that depleted its energy; it fed on itself, producing degenerate ideas and human suffering. As a result, man's instinct was replaced by reason, intelligence, and consciousness; his sense of nature and myth, by scientific theory; and his sense of the natural marketplace (barter and exchange), by abstract theories of money. Spengler concluded by discussing "the sterility of civilized man" and the end of Europe, which would be replaced by an emerging nation—perhaps from the Mideast, perhaps Russia.

Spengler gave birth to his own version of the wasteland, as a sense of a vital community gave way to mechanical, dead institutions. Eliot's portrait of London in *The Waste Land* and Ezra Pound's portrait of the empire city in the *Cantos* have much in common with Spengler's city. Pound also discussed the need for a homogeneous community to ward off cultural entropy. The *Cantos* depict what happens when a culture loses contact with the land, man with his work, and the city with a community of shared values. Such a moment of loss comes with usury, when money makes money, when an abstract theory of money becomes the basis of economics, and when national banks and other urban institutions dominate the city. Jefferson had fought the rise of the national bank in America, and because of that struggle he became one of Pound's heroes. But when it was clear that the Hamiltonian vision had won, Pound shifted his allegiance to Mussolini and to his new belief in the cooperative state. *The Pisan Cantos* (1948) would be his testimony to the memory of such historical loss.

A source that Eliot and Pound shared with Spengler was other works that emphasized cultural decline, like Henry Adams's *Education* (1907) and Hermann Hesse's *Blick ins Chaos* (1920). Eliot refers to *Blick ins Chaos* in *The Waste Land*. Like Spengler, Hesse believed that the old world was playing itself out and would be replaced by a new world, and that an uncivilized state of being lay dormant in culture. When it awakened, our animal instincts would be aroused, and then the Karamazovs would emerge. He argues that the Karamazovs were a primeval, occult, Asiatic ideal that had begun to devour the spirit of Europe, and he labels that ideal "the decline of Europe. This decline is a turning back to Asia, a return to the mother, to the sources, . . . and of course will lead like every earthly death to a new birth. It is only we who experience these phenomena as 'decline.' . . . It was the Karamazovs that he [the Kaiser] feared, it was the infection of Europe by the East, it was the reeling home of the weary mind of Europe to its Asiatic mother that he so greatly and so very rightly feared" (Hesse, 71, 75). Hesse believed that the decline of Europe came about when it began to absorb an Asian influence: "Already half of Europe, at least half of eastern Europe, is on the road to chaos; intoxicated with a divine madness it makes its way along the edge of the abyss and sings, sings drunken hymns the way Dmitri Karamazov sang. The citizens laugh indignantly at these songs, the holy man and seer listens to them with tears" (85). Both Spengler and Hesse believed in the decline of the West: Spengler feared the influences of the new industrial urbanism; Hesse warned of a discordant element— a new Dionysianism—that was creeping into European culture from the East. Eliot's *The Waste Land* brings life to these assumptions.

III

The Waste Land, centered in modern London, functions on three levels of reality: the individual, the historical, and the mythic-religious. The city, the culmination of Western history, embodies a state of individual consciousness and reflects a complex plane of existence. London is one of several cities caught in the process of rise and fall:

Falling towers
Jerusalem Athens Alexandria
Vienna London
Unreal

(ll. 374–77)

Each city represents the high point of a culture or an empire that falls to barbarians in a moment of violence. Eliot has just referred to

hooded hordes swarming
Over endless plains, stumbling in cracked earth

Ringed by the flat horizon only
What is the city over the mountains
Cracks and reforms and bursts in the violet air[.]
(ll. 369 – 73)

These lines are Eliot's gloss on *Blick ins Chaos:* "half of Europe . . . on the way to chaos," singing as it goes like drunken Dmitri Karamazov. Western man has used up or exhausted history; again and again, the city has shown a falling away from an ideal, an exhaustion from within as its inhabitants succumb to the secular ends of profit and loss, each person locked within a prison of self.

In order to understand what the "prison of self" means to Eliot, we must turn for a moment to seventeenth-century epistemology. For Descartes, reality entailed keeping two worlds—the objective and the subjective—separate; his was a divided consciousness, a compartmentalization that modernism undid. Already in the eighteenth century, Hume had challenged the long-standing myth of the unitary personality by reducing individual identity to a bundle of discrete sensations. In the conclusion to *The Renaissance,* Pater accepted Hume's epistemology, with Hume's "sensations" giving way to "impressions": "The objects of the physical world dissolve into a group of impressions—colour, odour, texture—in the mind of the observer." These impressions, "unstable, flickering, inconsistent, . . . burn and are extinguished with our consciousness of them" (Pater, 235). Such an epistemology was the basis of both impressionistic art and literary modernism and gave rise to the feud over fictional reality between H. G. Wells and Henry James. For Virginia Woolf, it was a way out of the omniscient consciousness of naturalism. Impressions thus become a way of seeing the city. The city became a personal, often isolated experience, with each inhabitant caught in his or her own subjectivity. What they see— whether Conrad's Marlow, Fitzgerald's Nick Carraway, or Eliot's urbanites—is an extension of themselves. And when they see more than they can accept, they disclaim reality, like Marlow lying to Kurtz's Intended; or they turn away, eyes clouded and opaque, like Nick at the end of *The Great Gatsby;* or they turn inward, locked into the self.

An understanding of Eliot's use of landscape, particularly his use of the city, thus begins with a theory of mind as well as place. Eliot's use of setting is grounded in his reading of F. H. Bradley, the philosopher who was the subject of his doctoral dissertation at Harvard, and the relationship between their ideas is complex. Bradley distinguishes between two planes of reality—the ideal and the real, the human and the divine, the immediate and the transcendental. Eliot quotes a key passage in which Bradley questions major Enlightenment assumptions:

How can the human-divine ideal ever be my will? The answer is, Your will it never can be as the will of your private self, so that your private self should become wholly good. To that self you must die, and by faith be made one with that ideal. You must resolve to give up your will, as the mere will of this or that man, and you must put your whole self, your entire will, into the will of the divine. That must be your one self, as it is your true self; that you must hold to both with thought and will, and all other you must renounce. (Eliot, *Selected Prose*, 202)

The Enlightenment put emphasis on linear time and progress, did away with hierarchy in the name of equality, and put the greatest emphasis on each individual's ability to create him- or herself. This sense of individual potentiality worked against the idea of the community, and in an industrial culture it led to an atomistic population—the locked prison of self. Bradley wanted to break that lock by giving up the "private self," renouncing the individual will in the name of a higher reality. Eliot invokes this Bradleyan ideal in almost all of his poetry and shows how one moves toward or away from it. It results in his double image of the city—both the City of God and the city of man, both a holy and secular place, both New Jerusalem and Dis.

IV

In his essay on Dante, Eliot writes that he learned from Baudelaire how to use the city in his poetry to evoke a sense of an urban hell in the modern world. Baudelaire revealed "the more sordid aspects of the modern metropolis,... the possibility of fusion between the sordidly realistic and the phantasmagoric, the possibility of the juxtaposition of the matter-of-fact and the fantastic" (Eliot, *To Criticize the Critic*, 126). While nineteenth-century novelists had used the city realistically, no previous poet had drawn on the approach of Dickens, Balzac, and Dostoyevsky in this way. Baudelaire's view confirmed Eliot's early impressions of the city: "In my childhood... my urban imagination was that of St. Louis, upon which Paris and London have been superimposed" (Eliot, "The Influence of Landscape," 420).

Eliot was not afraid to confront urban degeneration. He read with interest James Thomson's *City of Dreadful Night* (1874) and the minor

French novelist Charles-Louis Phillipe's *Bubu of Montparnasse* (1901). Bubu, an apprentice cabinetmaker in Paris, becomes a procurer. His is the story of little people caught and helpless in a web of poverty that brutalizes what might otherwise be love. Much of the detail is similar to Eliot's description of the urban poor—to "lodgers who drink the slimy water of cheap hotels" (35; cf. Prufrock) or who "masticated great mouthfuls of food that swelled his jaws" (53; cf. Apeneck Sweeney). But even as Eliot graphically depicts the modern, secular city in his poems, that city takes its meaning from Saint Augustine's *City of God*. And it was Baudelaire, once again, who corroborated the connection between urban damnation and urban salvation. Eliot maintained that Baudelaire saw the limits of the Enlightenment agenda, saw that progress could not change man's nature or condition; indeed, the spirit of progress would only increase greed and vulgarity, thus strengthening the worst in humanity. Eliot saw the need to overcome "the ennui of modern life. It is this, I believe, that Baudelaire is trying to express: and it is this which separates him from the modern Protestantism of Byron and Shelley. It is ...sin in the permanent Christian sense that occupies the mind of Baudelaire" (Eliot, introduction, 19, 20).

The connection between the secular and religious city may be more obvious to Eliot than to the general reader, but such a connection had been deeply cut in Eliot's own mind. In the chorus II from *The Rock,* he wrote:

> "Our citizenship is in heaven"; yes, but that is the model and type for
>   your citizenship upon earth.

When we lose sight of the relationship between the two realms

> Then [we] could set about imperial expansion
> Accompanied by industrial development.
> Exporting iron, coal and cotton goods
> And intellectual enlightenment
> And everything, including capital
> And several versions of the Word of GOD:
> The British race assured of a mission
> Performed it, but left much at home unsure.
> (chorus II from *The Rock,* in *Collected Poems,* 100–101)

Thus Eliot summarizes the spirit of mind that led to the modern city— the mind bent upon the control of nature in the name of wealth, which violated the idea of community:

When the Stranger says: "What is the meaning of this city?
Do you huddle close together because you love each other?"
What will you answer? "We all dwell together
To make money from each other"?

(chorus III from *The Rock*, in *Collected Poems*, 103)

The Waste Land expresses the depth of such materialism, the sense of
a secular hell when the crowd of the living dead flowed over London
Bridge and into King William Street (the Wall Street of London),
church bells tolling secular pursuits. As Eliot's narrator travels up and
down the Thames, he passes the Church of St. Magnus Martyr, the
magnificent Wren construction that was in danger of demolition as the
poem was being written (see figure 6). He travels through Billingsgate,
London's district of fishmongers, a place that reinforces the connection
between the mythical Fisher King and the idea of Christ, the fisher of
men whose apostles were themselves fishermen. When he crosses London Bridge, he passes the monument to the 1666 fire. As we know from
the poem's facsimile edition, Eliot connected the monument with Dryden's *Annus Mirabilis* (1667), the poem written after the Great Fire to
celebrate the meaning of London, which both poets saw as a religious
city (cf. Kenner, "The Urban Apocalypse"). Eliot located his cultural
ideal in Dryden's seventeenth-century world, from which he believed
there had been a falling away.

Eliot's view connected him, at least indirectly, with the philosophical
position of decadence—the view running from Huysmans through
Baudelaire to Wilde that turned toward what was degenerate or
depraved in culture. "The Love Song of J. Alfred Prufrock" (1915) draws
heavily upon that tradition. Prufrock is the American equivalent of the
decadent: he suffers from abulia, an inability to act decisively; he puts art
ahead of life, living in the world of the salon where women come and go
talking of Michelangelo; and he is sexually inhibited, unable to pose
questions of love. While the pure decadent identified with the spirit of
degeneracy, Eliot looked for redemption from it; for him, the depraved
secular city was overlaid with remnants of the religious past. But both
the decadents and Eliot saw the modern world in decline from a more
perfect moment, whether in, say, medieval Europe or Dryden's London
before rationalism had brought about the split between religion and science. Eliot connected this break—the "dissociation of sensibility," as he
called it—with the loss of the mythic imagination, which empiricism had
helped to supplant. He decried the rise of empiricism with its emphasis

Figure 6. Magnus Martyr. This church by Christopher Wren—a spiritual icon with its "inexplicable splendour of Ionian white and gold"—was in danger of being destroyed at the time Eliot was writing *The Waste Land*. Courtesy of the Frances Loeb Library, Graduate School of Design, Harvard University.

on the random and the disconnected, and he used his sense of such discontinuities to describe the modern, secular city that had given birth to rampant, solipsistic individualism.

Eliot presents in *The Waste Land* not only London but the collective history of the city, beginning in Athens. This progression accounts for the cast of characters in the poem: Tiresias (Athens), Christ (Jerusalem), Cleopatra (Alexandria), Marie Larisch (Vienna), and Queen Elizabeth (London). His work, in other words, partakes of the archaeology of history, the superimposition of one layer of time upon another—a technique that presupposed a cyclical process of time and that accommodated his use of myth, Bergson's idea of durée, a sense of simultaneity, and a belief in history as repeated process. All of this Eliot located in the poem through the idea of the city.

V

As the city became increasingly removed from the life of the land, its social institutions became more powerful and it no longer was part of the rhythms of nature. The romantics tried to restore the relationship between man and nature by treating nature as part of a larger force, by creating a *Volksgeist,* and by putting the individual mind at the center of a symbolic universe. They turned to myth, to a theory of the organic, and to an idealized sense of experience to be discovered as history. Up to the Renaissance, reason was considered as part of nature; but empiricism separated reason from the workings of nature and assigned it to the mind, as did Descartes. This split accounts for the difference between mythic and scientific process. The mythic process intensifies the identification between humans and nature, but the scientific process clearly distinguishes between the two: nature works in terms of its own laws, and humans observe and describe those laws. Once nature was viewed as a system of laws, the magic was gone: the workings of matter were repeatable and hence mechanistically predictable.

Eliot decried the loss of the mythical imagination, and he put a new emphasis on literary mythology to prevent modern man from being reduced to interpreting disconnected signs. Eliot suggests that as the city lost touch with the land, with the rhythms and the psychic nourishment of nature, a spiritual meaning was lost. The result was an urban wasteland and historical entropy, whose metaphorical equivalent is the desert, as the city was cut off from the redeeming water, the mythic impulses of life. Such a context makes explicit the assumptions that Eliot brought to *The Waste Land*—assumptions that can be documented from Eliot's literary criticism. The poem moves from the medieval world of Chaucer to the modern world of the neurasthenic woman and others locked into the isolated self ("We think of the key, each in his prison"; l. 414); from "the dead land" (l. 2) to the city of the walking dead; from communal hope to the city of frayed nerves, of urban anxiety and panic ("'My nerves are bad to-night. Yes, bad'"; l. 111). Eliot depicts emptiness in cluttered space and loneliness in the crowd. Women sit spiritually exhausted in the pub; the young man carbuncular enters an untidy flat to make indifferent love.

We have changed how we measure humanity, from relying on the rhythms of the land to using urban mechanisms. Behind such mechanics lies the destructive desire to conquer nature in the name of money, a desire revealed in the facsimile edition of *The Waste Land*. Its fourth book—a kind of Melvillean or Conradian journey to plunder the North Pole—leads to the destruction of the ship and the death of the crew. This deadly journey expands the theme of the "profit and loss" (l. 314) that is left more implied than developed in the final version of the poem.

So far we have been examining the literary influences as they worked upon Eliot's imaginative views of the city. Equally important to Eliot's urban views was his interest in the new sciences—especially archaeology and anthropology. Eliot documented his debt to Frazer's *The Golden Bough* in his "Notes" to *The Waste Land*. In 1890, Sir James George Frazer (1854 – 1941) published the first two volumes of *The Golden Bough*, which he then compiled into twelve volumes between 1895 and 1915, followed by an "Aftermath" in 1936. *The Golden Bough* was a study of the sacred grove in Nemi, outside of Rome. The grove was the domain of Diana, protected by a priest who, using the golden bough, would fight all intruders. If victorious, the intruder became the next protective priest. Frazer's study revealed two important aspects of anthropology. First, he depicted the connection between the primitive mind and magic, and he documented the primitive belief that when the king ages or declines, or when the land is laid waste, the king must die and be replaced by a more virile leader. Thus the theme of sacrifice enters primitive belief very early and anticipates the salvific function of Christ. Second, as Frazer's knowledge of the primitive world increased, he was able to work most of his information into his discussion of the sacred grove. The Nemi location, in other words, grounded what he had to say about other cultures literally all over the world. One was the microcosm of the macrocosm: the Nemi group was the particular that revealed the universal. Like Joyce after him, Frazer superimposed one realm of history on another. Eliot was aware of both Frazer's achievement and his technique.

There were three ways anthropologists related to the past. Some looked to a pastoral past and saw the present as a fall from an idealized time. Others believed in progress—the movement forward in linear time to more advanced forms of life and technology. And others saw a stable relationship between the savage past and the civilized present—insisting that there was a thin line between the two and that civilization was merely a way of concealing the primitive nature of reality. Eliot primarily opted for the first and third of these views. As he read Frazer and other anthropologists, he became interested in primitivism as the origin of religion. He saw the connection between the Osiris legend and its cognates and the Christ story. He could follow Frazer up to a point: the Frazer who looked back to primitive origins much interested him; the Frazer who saw religion giving way to more advanced forms of science did not. Eliot's use of anthropology was thus a matter of justifying his own religious and philosophical beliefs.

Eliot's use of Frazer and Weston thus had a double purpose. It was not only a way of getting back to the past; it was also a way of asserting the moral value of myth and ritual highlighted by the Cambridge Ritualist school of anthropology, who took Frazer as their mentor. This group included Jane Ellen Harrison (1850–1928), Gilbert Murray (1866–1957), and Francis Cornford (1874–1943). Frazer contended that human thinking about the cosmos evolved through three stages: magical, religious, and scientific. His research (mostly based on questionnaires to missionaries) supported his belief that there was a primitive connection between the renewal of infertile land and the sacrifice of the king.

Throughout, Eliot uses such myth to show what modern man has lost in trying to control the land. Eliot's major sources depict man in his most elemental contact with the land. The priest is the king because he can predict and control the rise of the river, which brings life-giving water with it. Jessie Weston examines the connection between the meaning of the land and the stories of Tammuz, Adonis, and Christ:

We know that the cult of the god Tammuz, who, if not the direct original of the Phoenician-Greek Adonis, is at least representative of a common parent deity, may be traced back to 3,000 B.C. . . . The woes of the land and the folk are set forth in poignant detail, and Tammuz is passionately invoked to have pity upon his worshipers, and to end their suffering by a speedy return. . . .

[H]is influence is operative, not only in the vernal processes of Nature, as a Spring god [note the opening of *The Waste Land*] but in all its reproductive energies. (37–38)

These mythical elements, which Weston treats in great detail, are incorporated into *The Waste Land*. The Fisher King is a product of this cult of life, as is the Grail legend with its questing knight, especially the Percival version (which Eliot uses) of Robert de Borron: "during the wandering of that holy man and his companions in the wilderness, certain of the company fell into sin. By the command of God, Brons, Joseph's brother-in-law, caught a Fish, which, with the Grail, provided a mystic meal of which the unworthy cannot partake; thus the sinners were separated from the righteous. Henceforward Brons was known as 'the Rich Fisher.' It is noteworthy, however, that in the Percival romance, ascribed to Borron, the title is, as a rule, Roi Pêcheur, not Riche Pêcheur" (Weston, 116–17).

Eliot's poem is a catalogue of Weston's details. The tarot pack is the means by which the priest predicted the rise and fall of the water. The Chapel Perilous is the destination of the questing knight. The Percival knight arrives at the chapel, which is perilous because a Blackhand knight has slain three thousand knights and buried them in the adjoining cemetery. He arrives during a storm, out of which a voice speaks (cf. "What the Thunder Said"), and proceeds to a belfry filled with bats. If the knight can overcome the Blackhand, he can—in the tradition of the Fisher King story—restore the harmony between man and the land and bring new life. In Eliot's poem, the Percival knight quests across an urban landscape before he arrives at the Chapel Perilous. Eliot superimposes the vegetative myth upon a description of the modern city because he realized the unbreakable connection between the two. The megalopolis not only had destroyed the symbiotic relationship between man and the land, but in controlling the land it had trapped humanity within a monument of self. That Eliot ends his poem on a note of doubt shows his awareness that he could not go beyond history and free modern man from the perils of urbanism.

VI

The city both contained and organized vital energy. When morally complete, the container brought material and spiritual energy into centripetal harmony; when morally depleted, it dissolved into centrifugal chaos. Always beneath the order was a disorder waiting to erupt. Eliot's world, especially his view of the city, is a constant attempt to keep a primitive energy in check. This is why Eliot was so taken with Conrad's *Heart of Darkness* and its sense of savage energy barely contained by a civilized veneer. Humanity was in a halfway house between order and disorder, the spiritual and the material, the City of God and the city of man, the savage Sweeney and the decadent Prufrock. He believed that there were realms where these levels of being met: man and God met in Christ; man and the animal in Sweeney; desire and inhibition in Prufrock; the city of order and disorder, the primitive and the civilized, in Elizabethan London. He could then address the religious and mythic aspects of the city—Augustine and Dante's city of God, Frazer and the city of fertility and waste—before moving to the modern city, which had abandoned the original meaning of the city.

The solution for Eliot was a religious one: return to our religious roots and restore Christian culture. The superimposition of religious assumptions upon a secular culture leads to the confusion common in his last period of writing, which was preoccupied with this theme. For example, he writes in "Burnt Norton" of the continuity of human time that does not allow anything beyond itself:

> Time present and time past
> Are both perhaps present in time future,
> And time future contained in time past.
> If all time is eternally present
> All time is unredeemable.

The city cannot redeem itself:

> Eructation of unhealthy souls
> Into the faded air, the torpid
> Driven on the wind that sweeps the gloomy hills of London,
> Hampstead and Clerkenwell, Campden and Putney,
> Highgate, Primrose and Ludgate. Not here
> Not here the darkness, in this twittering world.
>
> ("Burnt Norton")

To understand these lines, we must understand that the temporal and the infinite are bridged by Christ, who becomes the source of redemption—personal and collective. As Eliot says in "The Dry Salvages," "the past has another pattern, and ceases to be a mere sequence" once we "apprehend / The point of intersection of the timeless / With time." It all comes back to the

———Incarnation.
Here the impossible union.
Of spheres of existence is actual,
Here the past and future
Are conquered, and reconciled[.]
          ("The Dry Salvages")

The question involving temporal and eternal time asked in "Burnt Norton" is answered in "The Dry Salvages." Moreover, the living and the dead constitute an earthly-unearthly community of souls that unites the city of man and the City of God, completes the circle, connects the end with the beginning.

VII

Many of the questions that Eliot raised in his prose and poetry were also explored in his verse drama. *The Family Reunion* (1939) takes place on a declining estate, Wishwood, held together by Lady Monchensey, who refuses to have anything changed until her eldest son, Harry, returns to take over and preserve the house. Harry, who has been gone for eight years, returns to England on the ship over whose side his wife has fallen (or was pushed by Harry) and drowned. Once back at Wishwood, Harry realizes that he cannot find his lost innocence there—his childhood has gone like the prized hollow tree by the river, cut down to build a summer house. Harry barely remembers his father, who left the estate when Harry was a child, apparently with Aunt Agatha, with whom his father lived until he died five years later. Each generation seems to repeat the history of the previous generation: Harry's father also wished his wife dead. And like Agatha, in love with Harry's father, Mary, in love with Harry, has come to live at Wishwood. Driven by guilt and pursued by its embodiment, the Eumenides, Harry decides to leave Wishwood, at which time his mother dies; he realizes that the family, the house, and an idealized past will not be perpetuated.

The Family Reunion is Eliot's testimony to a world of radical, modern change. Lacking any meaningful function, the estate cannot be held together. Instead we are left with the empty, desolate lives of its modern inhabitants, most of whom are not even capable of the guilt that haunts Harry. Eliot treats the past as both haunted and betrayed, as Wishwood is betrayed by culture as well as by individuals. Agatha suggests that suffering must be communal and not private, but there is no basis for community anymore. The possible bridge goes unrealized, and Eliot ends his play short of offering the religious hope that he allows in his later poetry.

The Cocktail Party (1949) takes Eliot back to another familiar theme: loneliness, the isolation that separates individuals. Just before guests arrive for their cocktail party, Edward Chamberlayne discovers that his wife, Lavinia, has left him. One guest is unidentified, a mysterious stranger who seems to possess strange powers. He turns out to be Henry Harcourt-Reilly, a psychiatrist, who helps Edward and Lavinia reconcile. Edward is the man who cannot love and Lavinia the woman who cannot be loved: their disabilities make them a perfect match.

While the Edward-Lavinia story provides a comic plot, a more serious element is introduced in the person of Celia Coplestone, in love with Edward, whom she does not understand. She in turn is loved by Peter Quilpe, whom she also does not really know, and who has projected on her an image to meet his own needs (*Cocktail Party*, 382). Set in London, the play introduces us to Eliot's urbanites: they consider each other good friends, but they know only each other's exterior and never make genuine contact. The "other" is often a projection of their own imaginations or needs—"a dream," as Celia comes to call it. She tells Edward:

> I see another person,
> I see you as a person whom I never saw before.
> The man I saw before, he was only a projection
> I see that now—of something that I wanted—
> No, not wanted—something I aspired to—
> Something that I desperately wanted to exist.
>
> (327)

Such a projection was necessary, we learn, because she was so alone, a victim "Of solitude in the phantasmal world / Of imagination, shuffling memories and desires" (365).

Celia joins a community of nuns, a decision that takes her to her death in Africa. For Eliot, the missionary provides a way of redeeming the sterile desert, by bridging the savage and the civilized and by connecting primitive myth and the Christian church. Celia's death is meant to carry symbolically much of this meaning. Her journey to Africa is at the expense of her dream of success in Hollywood, a place that combines two cultural extremes—the commercial metropolis and the savage village—so that "the savage and the Christian are joined in reproach of the oversophisticated city" (375). A good deal of this meaning is supplied by Sir Henry Harcourt-Reilly, whose title and last name suggest a connection between the city and the savage (Harcourt the establishment, Reilly the uncouth Irishman). As Eliot once told an interviewer, Harcourt-Reilly is "a god *in* the machine" (quoted in Crawford, 235).

The comic elements in the play reduce the melodramatic effect of Celia's death—a death which allows Eliot to suggest once again that the way out of self is through community, the community of both the living and the dead. In *The Cocktail Party,* Eliot makes an important distinction between city and community: the city brings a herd of people together in the pursuit of material goods and well-being; a community brings a small number of people together whose shared values support actions that can carry them beyond their own sense of well-being. The play also returns to Eliot's theme of the connection between the primitive and the religious, his belief that myth is infused with a sexual energy that religion spiritualizes. Dr. Harcourt Reilly is in touch with this energy and so was Celia before her death; they were separated from the city dwellers who have been sealed off from these redeeming powers. As Robert Crawford has put it, "[Eliot] saw this society as increasingly menaced by industrialization which, particularly in the cities, where power was now centralized, was cutting off the population from its roots" (201).

Recent criticism like Crawford's has become sensitive to Eliot's attention to anthropology and to the connections between the savage and the city. Crawford has documented Eliot's interest in such books on religion and primitivism as Emile Durkheim's *The Elementary Forms of Religious Life* (1915), F. B. Jevon's *Introduction to the History of Religion* (1927), and E. B. Tylor's *Primitive Culture* (1889), as well as the writings of Levy-Bruhl, Frazer, Spencer, and F. J. Gillen (Crawford, 18, 25, 72, 91). The connection between modern and primitive man informed literary texts as different as *Tarzan of the Apes* (1914) and *Heart of Darkness.* So too these issues shaped Eliot's concern with literary figures such as Sherlock Holmes: Holmes is both the rational and the urban man, but he must confront, as we have seen, the irrational and the preternatural. Eliot shared Conrad's belief that there was an intersection of "horror" between the civilized and the savage, the primitive and the city—a confrontation represented in the Fisher King and the landscape of the desert in *The Waste Land,* in the persons of Celia and Dr. Harcourt-Reilly in *The Cocktail Party,* and in his Apeneck Sweeney.

Eliot refers to Sweeney in five works: "Mr. Eliot's Sunday Morning Service" (1918), "Sweeney Among the Nightingales" (1918), "Sweeney

Erect" (1919), *Sweeney Agonistes* (1932), and Sweeney at Mrs. Porter's in
The Waste Land (1922). In the first poem, Sweeney is in his bath. In the
second, he is in a house of prostitution with two women and a strange
man, who becomes suspicious of the women, leaves the room, but reap-
pears "Outside the window, leaning in," while the nightingales (prostitutes?) sing in the bloody wood where "Agamemnon cried aloud," stain-
ing his "dishonoured shroud" with their excrement. In "Sweeney
Erect," the connection between Sweeney and ancient Greece is made
even more explicit; Eliot suggests the heroic world depended upon the
very violence that Sweeney embodies and that the modern world sup-
presses, giving us Prufrock in its stead. The New England mind—from
Emerson to Henry James, Eliot is suggesting—never came to terms with
Sweeney, the representative of the Irish immigrants who invaded
Boston in the nineteenth century:

> (The lengthened shadow of a man
> Is history, said Emerson
> Who had not seen the silhouette
> Of Sweeney straddled in the sun.)
> ("Sweeney Erect")

Despite his primitive nature, Sweeney is constantly connected with
the city: he embodies the latent violence of urban man, the sexuality that
modern life has so completely repressed. Sweeney recounts the story of
a city man "who did a girl in" and then kept her body, preserved in
Lysol, in a bathtub. The city blurs the differences between life and death.
When, in *Sweeney Agonistes,* Sweeney proposes to carry Doris off to a
cannibal isle, *The Cocktail Party* is recalled; he will be the cannibal and
she, suffering the fate of Celia, will be his "missionary stew," as they both
revert to the primitive.

As Eliot's use of Sweeney suggests, at some point the distinction
between the primitive and the civilized begins to fade, for reasons that
seem contradictory. On the one hand, the closer we return to the primitive, the closer we come to the animality of humans, as embodied by
(Apeneck) Sweeney. On the other hand, the closer we return to the
primitive, the closer we come to a kind of sexual energy, which—when
spiritualized—Eliot believed was redemptive. The positions reflect the
difference between Enlightenment and romantic assumptions: the
Enlightenment distrusted the primitive, while the romantics saw in
primitivism a suppressed vitality. However, Eliot had no trouble recon-

ciling these not totally consistent views: his idealized Christian culture always had its darker, more primitive side. His ideas were supported by the writings of Christopher Dawson, especially his books *The Making of Europe* (1932), *Beyond Politics* (1939), and *Religion and Culture* (1950); the last book made clear that Dawson, like Eliot, believed in the connection between primitive religion and Christianity. Most important for both men was the city, a container that cut its inhabitants off from the deeper realms of primitive meaning and being.

Eliot thus created a complex version of the modern city, locating it between an earthly (sometimes infernal) and a heavenly realm, between the reality of a declining Europe and the ideal of a Christian culture, and between lost sexual prowess and redeeming vitality. Made up of a faceless crowd that never quite becomes a community, his city was cut off from a primitive, spiritual energy that combined sexuality and myth into a saving power. Throughout his career Eliot tried to bring these elements together—tried, that is, to arrest urban entropy and to ground in moral values the unreal city.[1]

VIII

Close to Eliot's view of the city is W. H. Auden's. The two poets' careers have remarkable symmetries. Eliot was born in America and moved to England; Auden was born in England and moved to America. For each, the secular voice that characterized his earlier poetry gave way to a religious one. And both poets spent much of their later career in search of an idealized Christian community—what Auden called the just city.

In his early poetry, Auden was indebted to Marx, Freud, and the psychologist Homer Lane. When he left Europe in 1938 and settled in America, the physical move was matched by an ideological change; his religious beliefs increasingly showed the influence of Kierkegaard and Reinhold Niebuhr. This transition also marked his movement from Communist sympathizer to renewed Christian. A Christian image of the

---

1. Jeffrey M. Perl, *Skepticism and Modern Enmity* (1989), and Kenneth Asher, *T.S. Eliot and Ideology* (1995) treat the continuity of Eliot's ideas: one puts the emphasis on a pragmatic skepticism, the other on Eliot's response to Charles Maurras. Neither sees a continuity between Eliot's early interest in myth and his later attempt to define a Christian culture.

city began to emerge, as Auden sketches two possibilities. Human will, if exercised, could turn the urban community into the just city, the good place, the City of God; or passivity could let the city degrade and decay.

Auden's poetry offers many images of the modern city. In "Paysage Moralisé" the city is the opposite of the island, symbolizing social life as opposed to isolation and escape. In poem XXII of *Poems* (1934), Auden depicts the city as an industrial ruin: smokeless chimneys, damaged bridges, deserted power stations. In poem XXXI of *Look Stranger!* (1936), the city, built by the "conscience stricken, the weapon making," is a place where "Wild rumors woo and terrify the crowd" in a world menaced by hatred and fear. The modern urban society is like a desert— expanded desolation, a place without limits. In *City Without Walls* (1969), Auden insists that the "walls of tradition, mythos and cultures . . . have crumbled . . . [leaving] modern man's life directionless and meaningless. Urban humanity has turned into compulsive hermits in caves of steel and glass" (35). But even though Auden's actual city is disordered, dirty, and immoral, he always depicts a redeeming ideal. "Spain" (1937) entertains the possibility of the just city, a social ideal he will later identify with the religious ideal of the City of God. In "In Memorial for the City" (1949), Auden tells us that the City of God is attainable only through "full acceptance of faith." His earthly city is the secular and material city of the Greeks; his City of God is a Christian city with an eternal component that allows the moment to become an "eternal fact." The heavenly city of faith may redeem the earthly city.

Auden moved from secular humanism to religious belief, insisting the spiritual was often released by the profane. Auden believed that the carnival was relevant to the fallen city. The carnival was a cathartic release of repressed discontent; it encouraged a protest element. The carnival involved a comic acceptance of human earthiness—a form of laughing *with* and *at* ourselves. It offered a recourse to a higher realm of life, a realm of faith, from which suffering emerges as an occasion for grace. In *The Sea and the Mirror* (1944), Auden uses Shakespeare's *The Tempest* as an object lesson for the modern condition. Prospero needs both Caliban and Ariel, the earthy and the airy, just as the industrial city needs its smokestacks and an idealized antithesis. As failed artist, Prospero runs the risk of turning from aesthetics to politics and becoming a despot, the Hitler figure of modernism. In the center of Auden's world is the opposition between art and politics; while the failure of one encouraged a reliance on the other, religion provided an alternative. This confluence of history, as we shall see, was not without peril.

CHAPTER 9

Beyond Liberalism

I

    T. S. Eliot saw modernism as the last efforts of an old world rather than the first struggles of a new. Disillusioned with the Enlightenment city, he believed that the modern city could be redeemed by a radical change of mind as the old materialism was tempered with a new spirituality. The individual, no longer autonomous, needed to find a new source of energy and needed to ground anxiety in a shared community. Writers like Eliot and Auden looked to religious ideals to replace the Enlightenment view of radical egoism, the liberal belief that the individual—rational, pragmatic, and inventive—was free to remake the self in a world that guaranteed unlimited progress.

    Like Eliot, Fyodor Dostoyevsky (1821–81) could not accept an Enlightenment agenda. In 1862 he traveled through Europe, becoming increasingly disillusioned with Western capitals like Paris and London, which he saw as materialistic and decadent. Throughout his later life, he remained opposed to liberalism and capitalism, which he believed together created the autonomous self grounded in money. Dostoyevsky anticipated many of Eliot's concerns: he distrusted rationalism, condemned the belief in progress, and was similarly impatient with science. He said that man without God would build a tragic civilization, and for him God was embodied in an idealized agrarian order, founded upon the Russian peasant. As Michael Harrington has aptly put it, "When Dostoyevsky speaks of man without God, he really means man torn from the land, and his condemnation of atheism is an indictment of cities. . . . The Megalopolis which came after him is inhabited by a rootless, confused people. The ancient God, the traditional wisdom, the old institutions have either shattered or vanished" (157). Dostoyevsky saw two aberrant character types emerging from the new urbanism: the Underground Man and the Grand Inquisitor. The Underground Man takes us toward alienation and isolation, the Grand Inquisitor toward totalitarianism: the two are inseparable, simply different sides of the same coin.

Dostoyevsky's *Notes from the Underground* (1864) may be his response to Nikolay Chernyshevsky's *What Is to Be Done* (1863), a utopian novel that propounds radical individualism—what Chernyshevsky called "rational egoism"—as the solution to social problems. Dostoyevsky believed that Chernyshevsky's Enlightenment ideals had already infected St. Petersburg, which he called "the most abstract and intentional city in the whole world" (183). By "intentional" he meant artificial rather than organic—an "anticity," built in violation of the laws of natural growth.[1] Not only is St. Petersburg the product of rationalized urban planning, situated unnaturally in a swamp, but it is illuminated by the northern lights, which produce an eerie glow and destroy the natural break between darkness and light. Dostoyevsky's Underground Man is a product of this world: he is disassociated from life, rejects any sense of community in which to ground himself, and suffers from hyperconsciousness and disconnected thinking. In *Notes from the Underground,* Dostoyevsky attacks the belief in a society organized on a rationalistic basis, divorced from the Russian people, especially the values of the Russian peasants. He bewails Enlightenment trust in reason and progress, insisting that imperfect human nature undercuts any hope for utopia; moreover, political change without prior change in the individual makes community impossible. The Underground Man represents the ultimate outcome of isolation: he embodies a chaos of conflicting emotion that cuts him off from his own feelings; when he drives away Liza, destroying his best hope of redemption, he demonstrates how removed he is from human emotion, from an ability to love or return love.

In *Crime and Punishment,* Dostoyevsky drew directly on other nineteenth-century novels, especially Balzac's *Père Goriot.* His portrayal of Raskolnikov's desire to become Napoleon, the extraordinary man of

---

1. "Intentional" is sometimes translated as "premeditated." Both words suggest a state of disembodied mind, separate from physical process.

genius, relies in large part on Vautrin, the individual who defies moral limits. His most radical change in the formula of the earlier novel involves Porfiry Petrovich, the police magistrate. Unlike Dickens's Inspector Bucket, who solved the case by intimate knowledge of the city, Petrovich succeeds by psychological cunning, by knowing how Raskolnikov's mind works. He knows that Raskolnikov's guilt will eventually betray him—that a confession at the crossroads is inevitable. Raskolnikov kisses the ground there to get back to the earth, back to the people, the peasants. For Dostoyevsky, redemption is in the people and not the city. Raskolnikov sinned against humanity by glorifying radical individualism, his belief that he was extraordinary and could kill with impunity, and it is to the human community that Raskolnikov must return to expiate the murder. In that effort, he is assisted by Porfiry Petrovich, who embodies the secular authority of the city, and Sonia, who embodies the religious spirit of the people. Petrovich brings him before the law; Sonia, before the human community—concretized in Christ, where final redemption awaits. In *Crime and Punishment*, Dostoyevsky reconciled the Grand Inquisitor and the Underground Man, authority and isolation, the secular and the religious. Only a mystical community can redeem the fallen city. But when the mystical community is extended to the idea of the nation-state—with its own political agenda and sense of national destiny—such a solution, as we shall see, becomes fraught with political problems.

As Eliot and Dostoyevsky reveal, once Enlightenment ideals are called into question, there is a desperate urge to find a substitute ideology. Not everyone could follow Dostoyevsky, Eliot, and Auden toward a religious solution. Some turned to a new aestheticism, but the power of a redeeming art could engender its own skepticism, as Andrey Bely discovered. Bely (1880–1934), initially part of the Russian symbolist movement, tried to reduce the world to a system of correspondences that work on two planes of existence—the actual and the fantastic. St. Petersburg, as we have seen, is an Enlightenment city: planned in 1703, it rose over swampland and dominated wild nature with its cathedral and fort, its city blocks and impressive canals. Yet there is something inimical at work in the city, as Pushkin had already seen in the early part of the nineteenth century. In *The Bronze Horseman* (1833), whose title of course refers to the westward-looking Peter the Great, Pushkin saw St. Petersburg embodying a combination of "West" and "East" that gave the city an uncanny feeling, a sense of homelessness that challenged national identity.

In *St. Petersburg* (1913), Bely conveys this sense of two worlds pulling at each other. He questions Peter's Enlightenment enthusiasm and rejects the authority of science that robs life of its mystery. The novel suggests the need to break away from abstractions and return to the creative force of nature; it particularly suggests the need to rely more on intuition than on reason. The novel takes place between September 30 and October 9, 1905, but events from the past creep into this time span, creating a kind of time warp. On one level, St. Petersburg is a healthy city, the capital of the world's largest land empire. But, on another level, the city is spectre-like. Russia has just been defeated by Japan, and it is suffering a series of urban uprisings and strikes. Old values are being superseded by new realities. The city is rootless and artificial, on the verge of social chaos.

The bureaucrat Ableukhov and his son Nikolay Apollonovich correspond respectively to Dostoyevsky's Grand Inquisitor and to the Underground Man. A terrorist group has given Nikolay a bomb to blow up his father; the bomb, in a sardine tin with a crude timing device, ticks away in Nikolay's room after he "inadvertently" sets it, and it will go off in twenty-four hours. The clock, the mechanism that orders Western civilization, is connected to an explosive device: destruction is built into time, and Bely's novel has its apocalyptic moments. (This literal bomb goes off harmlessly; the real bomb is within Nikolay.)

Bely rewrites James's *The Princess Casamassima*, a novel in which aestheticism wins over politics: Hyacinth Robinson refuses to participate in the anarchist's plot because he finds the order of beauty more important than the disorder of political revolution. In contrast, Nikolay finds it unrealistic to turn to an aesthetic solution and thus has nothing to put in place of violence. The road to aestheticism was not without its perils; indeed, it was often a fatal journey (as with Mann's Aschenbach, Fitzgerald's Gatsby, Pater's Marius, Wilde's Dorian Gray, Huysmans's Des Esseintes). But aestheticism was a way of grounding an otherwise culturally emptied self. Bely takes us to the end of liberalism—the modern fear of fragmentation, the fear of losing one's individuality. Nikolay becomes lost in a maze of his own psychic chaos, as his mind seems to take on qualities of the city itself.

The city mystifies rather than allows a larger sense of self. Even the commercial process is no longer grounded in the "unreal city." Money begins to make money. Similarly, in Gogol's *Dead Souls* (1842), there is no connection between value and the commercial process. Chichikov goes into the countryside to buy up dead souls (that is, the titles on dead peasants), which he then mortgages at the bank, turning the city of the dead into a commodity. The commercial system promotes schemes that exploit the system rather than encourage useful production. In "The Overcoat" (1842) and "The Nose" (1836), Gogol carries this process to extremes, anticipating Kafka. This sense of the aberrant, when extended to the mysterious and the sinister, transforms the commonplace and adds an uncanny dimension to nineteenth-century realism. Along with Kafka, Ionesco and Genet make the most of this transformed reality in their writings. A more traditional critique of urban capitalism comes from Thomas Mann.

II

With the breakdown of a homogeneous urban community, we are left with the problem of giving identity to a mass populace in a secular society, a question Thomas Mann (1875–1955) often addressed. Mann believed, for example, that music was most vital when it was a part of religion. In the Renaissance, however, music was severed from its religious purposes and became a cultural force of its own. This secularism reached a high point with Beethoven and Wagner, who drew music into nineteenth-century religious liberalism and turned it into the human. Mann saw individualism and liberalism as the basis for modernism, part of a cult that led to the degeneration of culture. His characters seem initially satisfied with their middle-class status, but this satisfaction turns out to be blind complacency. When they try to penetrate beneath their social routine, their social customs, to regain a lost vitality, the attempt usually takes them to or near death. Mann wanted a moderation of both pure rationality and pure mysticism. His *Buddenbrooks* (1900) depicts the decline of a bourgeois family, the collapse of its material "calling," and the emergence of a powerless artistic temperament. The artist is a part of the degenerative, decadent process, aesthetic transfigurations accompanying biological decline, a subject Mann treated in *Death in Venice* (1913). *Tonio Kröger* (1903) attempted to reconcile artistic and bourgeois values, but the artist—cut off from ordinary people and life—becomes an urban outcast. Mann believed that the weakening of one's inner idea of self ate away personality from within. His artist, like decadents generally, becomes weary and yearns for death.

Aschenbach is an older Tonio; because he transforms reality into an impossible ideal, he loses contact with life. *Death in Venice* is a story of repressed homosexuality, but it is also an allegory of the decay of an old world that has lost direction in the face of modernism. Venice, like von Aschenbach, is dying from within: both try to keep their illness a secret from the world. Mann pointed to the absence of vital myth as a fatal quality of modern existence, emphasizing the need to realize our irrational nature within a rational society. He saw that beneath the assumed order of the modern city was a destructive disorder at work. *Death in Venice* is perhaps Mann's first use of the mythic method—giving shape to contemporary history by manipulating its parallels with antiquity. Many readings of this story emphasize Mann's use of the Dionysus myth. Some critics even go so far as to see a connection in names: Aschen (ashes) Bach (Bacchus), and Tadzio (Sabazios, another name for Dionysus). The stranger that Aschenbach sees in the cemetery is a Dionysian figure (he even disappears ghostlike into one of the Greek statues), and the cholera that infects Venice is a plague often connected with the appearance of Dionysus. Even the pomegranate juice that Aschenbach drinks with dinner has relevance, since pomegranates supposedly first grew from the blood of Dionysus. Aschenbach's dream is more directly connected with the Dionysus story; both include wild music and dancing, shrill cries of the votaries of the god, uniform dress of the maddened women, and the eating of raw flesh and drinking of warm blood of the sacrificial animal. Moreover, it is the irresolvable discord between reason and emotion—the heart of the Dionysus myth—that lures Aschenbach to cholera-ridden Venice. When Aschenbach fails to come to terms with his decadent world, when he overidealizes Tadzio, he becomes subject to a process of decline. Like the city, which insists on a false order, he fails to come to terms with the chaos within himself. As Conrad knew, art, like civilization, hides a destructive process. The fate of the artist, like that of all great cities, inescapably moves toward death: Eliot's "falling tower" theme dominated the modern imagination. The darker, Dionysian forces of life overwhelm Aschenbach.

Reflections of a Nonpolitical Man (1918) attacks liberal belief in progress. In particular, Mann recognizes the greatness of Germany but is also aware of its evil potentiality. These themes return in slightly different form in his later works. In *The Magic Mountain* (1924), the rational, Enlightenment, liberal position is given to Settembrini. He is opposed by Naphta, an Eastern European Jew abandoned in a pogrom and adopted by the Jesuits; a crypto-Communist and proto-Nazi, capable of mixing Catholicism and terrorism, Naphta seems to be Mann's adaptation of the Grand Inquisitor. One believes in while the other distrusts the nation-state. The dispute between Settembrini and Naphta—between belief in an old-line radical individualism and belief in an emerging totalitarianism—ends unresolved and leaves us with an amorphous idea of mass man.

In *Dr. Faustus* (1948), Mann brings this stalemated struggle to a dead end of conflict, and the liberal agenda gives way to cultural madness. Adrian Leverkühn's story is told against the rise and fall of Nazism: he makes a pact with the Devil, willfully contracts syphilis, and finally goes insane. In his depiction of Leverkühn, Mann drew heavily on his knowledge of Nietzsche, who justified existence as an "aesthetic phenomenon," equating self with the freedom of art. Such freedom is an extension of the liberal ideology, and Leverkühn illustrates the destructiveness of carrying it to an extreme in radical individualism. As modern life became more rationalized, mechanized, and industrialized, art was driven underground—back to the primitive, mythical, and irrational. In his earlier work, Mann was sympathetic toward mythic explanations, relying heavily upon the myth of Dionysus and embracing Nietzsche's idea of eternal return—that history would continue to re-present itself. But Leverkühn's use of atonalism or the twelve-tone musical system moves him further away from any kind of grounding of the self in traditional art; he takes primitivism to a radical extreme, and his belief that culture must be grounded on pagan cult aligns him with the mystical nationalism that Mann connected to the Nazis. His story is told by Serenus Zeitblom ("time bloom," suggesting inevitability); himself a product of the Enlightenment, Leverkühn's romantic excesses puzzle him. Both complicit and helpless in the face of Leverkühn's runaway energy, Zeitblom provides a rather sorry end to Enlightenment ideology.

By its very nature, the Faustus myth is a celebration of destructive individualism. To the traditional story of Faustus (first given literary form in 1587 by Johannes Spies in Germany and made famous by Christopher Marlowe and Goethe), Mann adds issues of disease, art, and cultural disintegration. As Leverkühn discovers the impossibility of compromise between the forces of individual genius and the forces of totalitarianism, he embodies both the artist and the nation that wills its own destruction. In showing us the impossibility of Augustine's *City of God,* the impossibility of community, he represents the opposite of Mann's political hopes in *Reflections of a Nonpolitical Man.* As Michael Harrington points out, "In *Faustus,* the world is so mad that madness is the only sensible reaction to it. The old definition of decadence as the triumph of society over community, of *Gesellschaft* over *Gemeinschaft,* returns in tragic form to define the situation" (64). The city destroys itself from within when its inhabitants share such a state of mind. There is no longer a possibility of harmony in Leverkühn's world of music. As Harrington rhetorically asks, "In a completely secular world, devoid of transcendence and filled with war and upheaval, what ground is there for harmony? Conventional beauty is a lie, the artist is faced with unrelieved chaos" (65). In *Faustus,* Mann takes us to the inevitable end of Enlightenment and romantic individualism, to the city as the destructive end product of the liberal agenda.

Enlightenment man pursued power; romantic man, freedom. The romantic breaks bourgeois restraints in the name of a privileged self, and Nietzsche mediates the transition from Enlightenment man, who is part of a system, to romantic man, who celebrates his own genius. In *Faustus,* Mann was working within a rich tradition of the romantic self. Leverkühn looks back to Balzac's Vautrin, Byron's Manfred, and Dostoyevsky's Stavrogin, as well as Nietzsche's superman. All of these men of radical freedom are self-destructive. Stavrogin commits suicide; his disciple, Kirilov, kills himself to free humanity from God. Alone on the peak of the Jungfrau, isolated from humanity, Manfred says, "I was my own destroyer." Having read both Dostoyevsky and Byron, Nietzsche came away with the notion of heroic rebellion. Ungrounded, such romantic freedom had no place in the new bourgeois society, especially in the city, where order and conformity were nearly synonymous. Wylie Sypher understood this fundamental point, asserting that "the romantic belief in liberty proved incompatible with the liberal belief in programs for the progress of society" (26). Ortega y Gasset also grasped this truth when he charted the romantic-liberal's decline toward mass man, the romantic hero giving way to the bourgeois technician. And it is this phenomenon that Robert Musil captures in *The Man Without Qualities* (*Der Mann ohne Eigenschaften,* 1930–43): Ulrich is the new functionary, defined from without by circumstances; the center of gravity no longer lies in himself but in the relations between things. We have moved, as Sypher argues, from romantic individualism to liberal collectivism: "The liberal program for society finally negated the significance of the person. Freedom became an organization, and a middle-class organization at that" (26). The move from mass to master was only another step; when extended, romantic freedom, after it was absorbed by the nation-state, fed into totalitarianism, a process mediated by Carlyle's Teufelsdröckh and the belief that the romantic hero was the source of political stability.

In moving from Robert Musil and the end of romantic individualism to mass man and Bertolt Brecht (1898–1956), we follow links in the same chain. Brecht was unsympathetic to Mann's *Reflections of a Nonpolitical Man,* which sought an inspired nationalism—an organic sense of community—rather than the Enlightenment hope of Settembrini or the centralized power of Naphta. Rejecting both liberalism and totalitarianism, Mann hoped, at least initially, for some middle-class stability, but he ended up with an inchoate sense of mass man. Brecht, seeing no hope in a middle-class resurgence, embraced the idea of mass man and moved toward Communism. And yet Mann and Brecht shared common ground: both distrusted the new megalopolis. In *The Jungle of the Cities (Im Dickicht der Städte,* 1924), Brecht describes the degeneration of the Garga family, which moved from a European village to the jungle of Chicago in a misplaced hope of a better life. And in *Rise and Fall of the Town of Mahagonny (Aufstieg und Fall der Stadt Mahagonny,* 1929), he argues that the city is man's destiny: the same laws apply to both. The supreme law is money: governing all activity, controlling human relationship, dividing the citizenry into exploiters and exploited. In *Mahagonny,* Brecht even attacks the myth of the Wild West, seeing its fraudulent individualism as attracting the naive to a world already corrupted by money. Brecht's antiurbanism is complete but not original; his attack on urban materialism was anticipated by H. G. Wells. Wells also moved us from romantic freedom and the liberal agenda, through the idea of mass man, toward the totalitarian superstate.

III

As the city becomes more chaotic, less friendly and more hostile, the inhabitants become more alienated, more lonely and isolated, the landscape more grotesque, and the urban process itself more absurd. H. G. Wells (1866–1946) carried this idea even further in *Tono-Bungay* (1909); the patent medicine that makes Uncle Ponderevo wealthy is only slightly injurious to the health of those who use it, and schemes, like the search for quap, move commerce into a state of imperialism (characterized by the invasion of the wilderness, the killing of the natives, and the exploitation of natural resources). Conrad and Eliot begin right here: Conrad with the imperial adventure eating at the heart of the city, Eliot with Tiresias's voice of warning from the city of the dead.

The anxiety over where science and technology were taking humanity created an opposite response—the belief that technology would help us adapt to our environment, help direct human evolution, and become the basis for progress. The new city would be a product of such evolution, according to Wells. In *The Time Machine* (1895), his narrator describes in fascinating detail the earth cooling and humans devolving as the traveler journeys into the future. Among his discoveries are two forms of life that have diverged from each other: the Eloi, who have become so aestheti-cized that they are near extinction; and the Morlocks, who have become so brutalized that they have sunk beneath the animals. In *The Island of Dr. Moreau* (1896), Wells recasts this plot, showing Dr. Moreau actively engaged in vivisection, by which he has transformed the island animals surgically, giving them the rudiments of humanity (that is, the ability to think and to use language). But when some of the animals revert to their basic nature, they revolt against Moreau and kill him and his assistant. This story, like many of Wells's tales, is narrated from the point of view of a participant-observer; before he escapes the island, he witnesses the animals slipping further and further back toward a natural violence, until the last vestiges of their humanity are gone.

Despite the fate of Dr. Moreau, Wells came to believe that evolution-ary progress could be made under the enlightened leadership of a scien-tist leader, a Platonic philosopher-king. But Wells's movement toward this position was slow and deliberate, unable at first to get beyond the notion that such a leader would simply be an unethical tyrant. His first fantasy expression of this idea is *When the Sleeper Wakes* (1899), the story of a man who awakens 203 years in the future to find himself in a city that is part of a totalitarian state. Graham, the sleeper, discovers to his amaze-ment that his earthly investments have accrued over that period of time until he owns half the world—but the real power is in the hands of Ostrog, who believes in the Overman whose function is to subdue the weak and to keep the inferior and the bestial in check. Graham, who car-ries into the future his Enlightenment beliefs, cannot accept such a polit-ical view and challenges Ostrog's power, although the story is unclear on whether or not he is successful.

When the Sleeper Wakes is a fantasy version of Edward Bellamy's *Look-ing Backward, 2000–1887* (1888), the dream vision of another sleeper who is taken to an idealized, industrialized society where all human wants are satisfied by machine technology and the state is ruled by an engineer dic-tator. Mark Twain in *A Connecticut Yankee in King Arthur's Court* (1889) and William Morris in *News from Nowhere* (1891) responded to Bellamy's vision of the future. The apocalyptic ending of Twain's fantasy reveals his fears of what happens when technology ignores ethical limits.

Wells shared some of this apprehension. As early as *A Modern Utopia* (1905), he criticized both democracy and the nation-state. He attacked democracy because it rested too heavily on individualism and encouraged the economic exploitation of nature; he attacked the nation-state because it required a top-heavy bureaucracy and enslavement by "the State official" (*Modern Utopia*, 79). He believed the way out of this impasse was a World State that encouraged a common good: "As against the individual the State represents the species; in the case of the Utopian World State it absolutely represents the species" (80). Wells's idea of utopia was inseparable from his belief in Darwinian evolution. But Wells qualified Darwin's ideas, because he did not believe that nature was working for human benefit; instead humanity had to inform nature with the directing intelligence that might come from the built environment. In that context, he saw the state as a form of higher development than the individual, and he saw the World State as a form of higher development than the nation-state. He believed that the nation-state had come to the end of its natural development and pointed to imperialism as proof: since each nation-state advanced at the expense of others, such a process, he correctly predicted, would have to end in world war. Within the ideal World State Wells placed four classes of people: the Poietic (intellectuals), the Kinetic (administrators), the Dull, and the Base. Such groupings recalled his earlier distinction between the Eloi and the Morlocks, except here the extremes between the highest and the lowest are not racial (that is, based upon biology and heredity) but instead involved educational distinctions to which "people drift of their own accord" (236). The new intellectual class—the Samurai, as Wells called them—would supply the directing intelligence needed in the evolutionary process. Wells had no faith in democratic ideals; for him, hope lay with the race, not the individual. He came to believe in what he called the "Mind of the Race," which involved the merging of individual minds into racial memory and a collective mind. Thus, like Samuel Butler and later Aldous Huxley, he adopted a vitalist position—a belief that matter was informed with mind. By this point in his thinking, he had sacrificed liberty to order, democracy to authority.

Wells promulgated these ideas for almost forty years. But eventually the weight of twentieth-century events wore him down, and he radically revised his sense of the fantastic; cosmic optimism gave way to cosmic pessimism in *Mind at the End of Its Tether* (1944). In this book, written two years before his death, Wells not only repudiated the efficacy of a racial mind, he predicted the end of the universe as we know it: "Our universe is not merely bankrupt; there remains no dividend at all; it has not simply liquidated; it is going clean out of existence, leaving not a wrack behind. The attempt to trace a pattern of any sort is absolutely futile" (*Tether*, 17). Wells believed that we had come to the end of a cosmic process: "The Radium Clock gives us a maximum period of far less than ten and probably far less then five thousand million terrestrial years for the career of life. During this period there has been a constant succession of forms, dominating the scene. Each has dominated, and each in its turn has been thrust aside and superseded by some form better adapted to the changing circumstances of life" (24). Now we have reached the end of man, as we know that species: "homo sapiens . . . is in his present form played out. . . . Ordinary man is at the end of his tether. Only a small, highly adaptable minority of the species can possibly survive" (18, 30).

The reason for such pessimism is not hard to see. Wells was disillusioned by the events in Hitler's Germany and Stalin's Soviet Union. In his distrust of the nation-state, Wells may indeed have anticipated the rise of Hitler and Stalin, but he never came to terms with the way totalitarian power could be abused; furthermore, his idea of an advancing racial mind had no basis in historical fact. Wells's thinking imploded, undercutting two powerful constructs within which he had been working: the Enlightenment construct, which he had repudiated, and the Darwinian construct, which he had radically revised. Once faith in these traditions was gone, he had nothing left.

The debate that went on within Wells himself went on in modernism generally. As we have seen, at one point Edward Bellamy had opposed Mark Twain and William Morris. The Czech writer Karel Čapek endorsed many of Wells's ideas, but he maintained that Wells never saw the dangers of fascism; Yevgeny Ivanovich Zamyatin raised more questions from within the Soviet Union, where he had already seen enough to make him doubt the totalitarian state. Later Aldous Huxley and George Orwell added to the chorus of criticism. By 1948, Wells's ideas—sometimes unfairly distorted—had been totally discredited.

IV

Once the city took its being from commercial rather than land-based activity, attempts to address its shortcomings became more radical, focusing on the need to centralize power. As an urban artistic consciousness turned inward, outer political reality became more authoritarian. The Enlightenment city had given birth to liberal individualism, but that sense of the self was radically modified as the modernists either turned away from or gave consent to various forms of totalitarian control.

One of the earliest visions of the totalitarian state was Zamyatin's *We* (1924), a dystopian novel set in the twenty-sixth century, in a state made "perfect" by science and technology. The Single State, as it is called, is ruled by a dictator, the Well-Doer or the Benefactor, and a bureaucracy, the Bureau of Guardians. The citizens live in glass houses so that they can be watched by the political police. The State works on the assumption that in the Garden of Eden humans were happy until they sought freedom; by removing freedom, the Single State restores happiness. But freedom is not so easily repressed and returns in the desire for love (outlawed by the state) and in other "primitive" urges that are a residual part of human nature. Once Zamyatin negates the city, he finds his subject in what is precivilized.

We, almost certainly inspired by H. G. Wells and Jack London, was written at the time of Lenin's death; the object of Zamyatin's satire thus appears to be the industrial state generally rather than Stalin's regime or the Soviet Union. The Well-Doer is modeled, at least in part, on Frederick Winslow Taylor, the father of scientific industrialism. In his *Principles of Scientific Management* (1911), Taylor formulates the strict division of labor that subsumes the individual to the machine. However, while the effects of technology may be his main theme, Zamyatin nevertheless anticipates the evil of Stalinism: he depicts the fate of would-be individualists in a highly organized conformist society, a theme treated earlier by Dostoyevsky in "The Legend of the Grand Inquisitor" and later by Huxley and Orwell. There is, in fact, a direct line of descent from the Grand Inquisitor to the Well-Doer to Mustapha Mond in Huxley's *Brave New World* (1932) and O'Brien in Orwell's *Nineteen Eighty-Four* (1949). In all of these works, the individual is sacrificed to higher authority: in order to guarantee conformity, the state must eliminate the autonomous self.

The entire city is surrounded by a glass wall that divides the rational from the irrational, the urban from the wilderness; its collapse would lead to the reunion of humanity and nature, the reconciliation of reason and intuition, the renewal of the autonomous self. As in most depictions of the sterile city, the realm of nature here is heightened: Zamyatin's nature is wild energy, infused with the passion of instinct from which the individual has been cut off. Inside the wall the inhabitants suffer from urban entropy; outside the wall is the threat of perpetual revolution. Order versus disorder, entropy versus revolution are the dichotomies of urban existence. Zamyatin's futuristic city is both bleak and hopeful: bleak because the inevitable loss of the autonomous self leads to forms of totalitarian control; hopeful because a residual primitive force in the individual fights such control and, as with the fall of the Roman Empire, revolution is always an option. Both entropy and revolution are built into the superstate; order always rests upon disorder.

While Zamyatin's city depends on bureaucratic control, there is always the tug to get outside the city, back to a residual self: the Ancient House embodies this escape. Revolution works at the margins of the city, where individuals, like Dostoyevsky's Underground Man, put their hope in the release of the repressed. In the meantime, the forces of order and control rule the day. The rise of the superstate leads to the collapse of individualism, and thus the collectivist impulse signaled the loss of the subject long before postmodern thinkers took notice and made the issue prominent. The city brings us the masses, industrial order, and collectivist politics. In Zamyatin, the journey to self-authenticity involves reversing direction, going back through the city into the realm of the primitive.

V

When Zamyatin's idea of going back to an era before the city was put to practice, the results were disastrous, for that was precisely Adolf Hitler's objective for the Third Reich. Through National Socialism, Hitler (1889–1945) established totalitarian rule in Germany from 1933 to 1945. He saw himself carrying on the tradition of the First Reich, the medieval Holy Roman Empire, and the Second Reich, Bismarck's Prussian rule after the defeat of France in 1871. His appeal to power took two forms: he called for the reunification of German-speaking nations separated by the Treaty of Versailles, and he attracted the masses by invoking national destiny. Hitler's rise was aided by the defeat of Germany in World War I, which exacted large reparations and left the German people politically frustrated, and by the global depression of the thirties, which increased their economic plight. He transformed the

German Workers' Party, which was sympathetic to his political aims, into the National Socialist German Workers' Party—the Nazis. Hitler consolidated his power by creating a network of hated enemies; the "Other" was primarily the Marxist and the Jew—for him synonymous terms. Since these enemies were mostly urban dwellers, Hitler came to hate the cities. In *Mein Kampf* (1924), he wrote: "To me the giant city seemed the embodiment of racial desecration.... The longer I lived in this city [Vienna, later Munich] the more my hatred grew for the foreign mixture of peoples which had begun to corrode the old site of German culture" (quoted in Shirer, 49).

Dionysus mesmerized a city; Hitler mesmerized a nation by working from within the nation-state, connecting it to a sublime destiny of his own creation. Hitler brought into play almost all that was in opposition to the city: he emphasized the rural over the urban, the *Volk* over the crowd, cultural homogeneity over diversity. Appropriating and twisting the intellectual and cultural ideas of the past, he distorted Nietzsche's idea of the superman to suit his own purposes, instituted a mystical notion of the German state based on his special use of Wagnerian and other myths, created a social hierarchy based on a misinformed notion of race, and turned the political frustrations of the past into a call for military conquest. Then, once the city was in his control, he—like rulers before him—transformed it into a monument to his power and control. Whether we pass with Napoleon III into the imperial city or move back through the *Volk* with Hitler into the totalitarian city, we remain in the realm of the city as defined by the masses.

VI

Zamyatin wrote *We* before the rise of the superstate; George Orwell (1903–50) wrote *Nineteen Eighty-Four* after the defeat of the Third Reich. While Orwell knew Zamyatin's *We* and even wrote an appreciative essay about it, he looked both back to an earlier generation of writers (Stevenson, Kipling, Butler, Gissing, and Galsworthy) and forward to the possibility of future superstates. Orwell had a sense of historical continuity that Zamyatin lacked—the advantage of being able to see the interplay that had historically occurred involving the nation-state, imperialism, and totalitarianism. (And today we must read his futuristic novel in terms of the past.)

Orwell's superstate begins as an Enlightenment construct, born of the need to control nature; the state then extends this control over the general population. The superstate is part of the evolutionary development of capitalism, and its end product is power. This explains the need for mind control, manipulation of the past, and the collapse of language, for the aim of the superstate is to destroy individualism. Orwell believed that modern history went wrong with the failure of socialism to offer a difference. Instead of working for individual equality, the state created another kind of inequality based on position, on its own hierarchy: Big Brother took the place of wealth; the superpoliceman replaced the business tycoon. As control became an end in itself, hope for an urban community gave way to the reality of masses under the control of a master.

In *Nineteen Eighty-Four,* a mysterious Inner Party led by Big Brother controls the superstate of Oceania. Orwell contrasts the superstate with the nation-state by humanizing, even sentimentalizing, the past, as represented by the junk shop—with its double bed and grandfather clock. Winston's frame of reference is the past, and he is the only character in the text who can be read novelistically. The rest, including Julia, are political ciphers, without past, without mind. His nostalgia marks a desire to return to a time before things went so wrong, a desire to replay history in the hope of a better outcome. But Winston's is a lost cause: when he abandons his love for Julia (in a scene that looks back to Zamyatin's *We*), he loses his last link to humanity. Orwell's original inclination to title his novel *The Last Man in Europe* suggests that Winston embodies the last vestiges of humanism, the last trace of individualism. Just as the irrational Naphta makes substantial inroads in the enlightened argument of Settembrini, so O'Brien seems to get the better of Winston. Both Naphta and O'Brien see the powerlessness of the individual as prelude to the end of humanism, and the loss of the subject in postmodern discourse only confirms their argument.

O'Brien challenges Winston's distinctions between individual and mass, past and present, community and party. He knows that Winston believes "that the Party did not seek power for its own ends, but only for the good of the majority . . . because men in the mass were frail, cowardly creatures who could not endure liberty or face the truth," and he finds this stupid; turning up the pain meter, he tells Winston: "The party seeks power entirely for its own sake. We are not interested in the good of others; we are interested solely in power" (Orwell, 216–17). One does not establish a dictatorship to safeguard a revolution; one makes a revolution to establish a dictatorship. Power is its own justification. Orwell brilliantly saw that totalitarian power required a static society, a society inimical to change. Orwell's Oceania shares world power with two other superstates—Eastasia and Eurasia; the three constantly realign themselves politically and are continually at war. Orwell realized that a totalitarian state must engage in perpetual war: it must waste the products of advanced technology before they can raise the citizens' standard of living and thus destroy social hierarchy, the basis of power.

To read *Nineteen Eighty-Four* as a novel puts Winston at the center of what is happening; to read it as dystopia puts the state at the center. Orwell's emphasis is on the state, on what went wrong in the transition from Enlightenment city to nation-state to empire to totalitarian regime. He claimed that the novel was a general warning about the dangers of totalitarianism rather than an attack on a specific totalitarian state, an expression of his concern with the failure of Enlightenment democracy. Orwell blamed this failure on the breakdown of liberalism with its faith in individuality, and then the additional breakdown of modern socialism and communism: first individual greed splintered the state, then totalitarian power dehumanized it. In each case, a political system failed to produce a community.

The modern state has misused power. What Orwell saw so clearly was how power structures all else: it subsumes consciousness, language, sex, history, and even nature, reducing landscape to the vistas that the state allows to be seen. Power in the form of Newspeak destroys difference: war is peace, freedom is slavery, ignorance is strength. Logocentrism gives way to power, and language, an extension of the state, means what Big Brother tells us it means. What went wrong at the level of the state infects everything—the city, the masses, language, consciousness, art. Orwell, like Wells, takes us to the logical end of the Enlightenment legacy. The city begins by organizing power and ends by being consumed by the power it organized.

VII

Modernism was primarily an aesthetic movement. Matthew Arnold was among those who saw literature replacing religion. But some modernists (e.g., Bely) saw aestheticism itself as an exhausted cultural alternative. As a result, some (Eliot and Auden) turned back to religion; others (Wells and Brecht) moved toward a world state or forms of totalitarianism. Thus, as Mann, Zamyatin, Orwell, and others revealed, the liberal agenda, especially the fate of the individual, gave way before nationalism or totalitarianism. The superman and the super-state: two sides, as it turns out, of the same coin. The forces that liberated the individual (the rise of urbanism) eventually led to the nation-state, and both impulses played out destructively. The *Übermensch* carried destruction within him, just as extreme nationalism (encouraged along with the *Übermensch* by Wagner, Nietzsche, and Heidegger) led to *Götterdämmerung* or national death. In *The Politics of Cultural Despair* (1961), Fritz Stern has chronicled the destructive outcomes of the liberal political agenda. The attack on liberal capitalism came from the right via the mystical nationalism that rose in Germany, and from the left via a social utopianism that was grounded in Marx—the dispute that went on *between* Mann and Brecht and *within* Wells and Orwell. The attack on liberalism and bourgeois capitalism was a continuation of romanticism, and it was in all of its phases antiurban. It was picked up by Nordau, who influenced Spengler, and later by Hitler and (despite the seeming contradiction) by neo-Marxists who saw cities as part of an insidious web of international capitalism. Thus the city was either attacked as the source of degeneration and decadence, or it was turned into the labyrinth—the maze—of late capitalism, the characteristic shape, as we shall see, of the postmodern city.

A number of modernists tried to ground an urban self in established institutions, such as the Communist Party or the church. These ideologies became the basis of idealized cities projected into space, into the future; they were more a matter of hope than of realistic expectation. Such projection was a continuation of what I have called the "inward turn," the modernists' movement toward a subjective reality, the tendency to create an idealized place in the mind. Postmodernism attacked this kind of transcendent reality—what has been called metafiction and master narratives—insisting on an ungrounded reality. But ironically, the modernist mind never quite died; it surfaces in ghostlike ways when, despite the loss of transcendent meaning, characters acknowledge an outside authority—as do Thomas Pynchon's Oedipa Maas and Paul Auster's Quinn, as we shall see. Moreover, as the city became more mysterious, it also became more menacing; the sense of mystery heralded a frightening unknown, the unpredictable. Orwell's Big Brother was less in evidence, but the uncanny state of mind that he produced remained and reappeared in the new fiction; a postmodern anxiety usurped other authority.

The liberal ideal broke down: the self needed to be grounded in something larger than its own self-reflexivity and autonomy; the city needed a theoretical justification, an informed ideology. But institutions—the church and the state—subsumed rather than liberated the individual. Once art, religion, and politics were thrown into question, the problem was this: what would take the place of the liberal agenda? Postwar existentialism—returning to the realm of radical individualism by reworking the idea of the romantic hero phenomenologically separated from nothingness by only the mind—offered a short-lived response.[2] The problem was ultimately a question involving mass society. When Europe provided no definitive answer, the question was asked again in America.

2. For a discussion of the connection between the romantic hero and existentialism, see my *A Dangerous Crossing,* 1–12; for a discussion of the self-destructive quality of the existential hero, see my "Demonic Quest."

PART 4

American Re-presentations

CHAPTER 10

The City and the Wilderness

I

The city in America was different, more a re-presentation than a duplication of the European city. In Europe, the city had to define itself against its medieval origins and the transformations from feudalism; in America, against the wilderness and the frontier experience. The term *frontier* also had quite different meanings, signifying the line at which two powers met in the Old World and open space and opportunity in the New. In America, encountering the frontier meant encountering the wilderness, which correspondingly took on a new thematic importance. On the East Coast, American cities looked to Europe for their model, especially to London; cities in the Ohio and Mississippi Valleys in turn modeled themselves on East Coast cities. The trackers and hunters came first, followed by the farmers, followed by the clerks and professional people who transformed the farming village. To move beyond this frontier was to move into the wilderness—and into all that wilderness conveyed, to settlers mindful of the biblical idea of founding a city in the wilderness. The story of Jerusalem offered a biblical parallel to the Puritans who came to the new wilderness, and to the frontier people who moved across a continent. The city on a hill was their dominating trope.

Walter Prescott Webb in *The Great Frontier* (1952) analyzed the relations of modern Europe to the rest of the world, describing a political system connecting the metropolis to a frontier. Webb saw the two as interrelated: while the metropolis was a cultural center, serving as a depository for Western civilization, the frontier acted upon it, wearing away its institutions—entails, titles, primogeniture. The power of the frontier lay in its attractions: "The frontier experience from 1500 to, say, 1900 was without doubt among the most memorable adventures mankind has had in modern times. On the rim of the Metropolis, always its yonder edge, the beacon fire of its Great Frontier was luring men outward, stirring them to mighty deeds, achievements and sacrifices" (Webb, 280). As Martin Green has put it, "after 1850 the American imagination turned decisively toward the West and the continent" (144).

The move in America from colonies to a republic was also a move from Christian to Enlightenment ideology: the Constitution and the Bill of Rights are Enlightenment documents. Benjamin Franklin and Thomas Jefferson were instrumental in "inventing" America. In fact, the Jeffersonian vision dominated American intellectual debate for two hundred years even as it was eroded by the rise of Hamiltonian federalism and the industrial state. Jefferson's ideas were informed by several factors: he loved the farmer's life, was a product of the Enlightenment, and gave priority to matters of national interest. Jefferson argued for a simple, frugal agrarian republic. He feared that the powers set in motion by the Revolution could be misapplied, turning democracy into a new authoritarianism brought about by capitalistic competition, urban development, and the birth and growth of an urban proletariat. "Those who labor in the earth are the chosen people of God," he insisted in *Notes on Virginia* (164–65). Fearing the results of the industrial revolution, especially as he had witnessed it in Europe (he had spent five years as ambassador to France), he discouraged manufacturing in Virginia, arguing that workshops should remain in Europe. His dislike of the city stemmed more from what it had become in Europe than what it was in America of the 1780s. He especially feared the mob, which, he maintained in *Notes,* had corrupted both the people and government: "The mobs of great cities add just so much to the support of pure government, as sores do to the strength of the human body" (165).

Although he began as a Federalist, Jefferson became one of the founders of the Republican Party once he perceived a too-strong central government as a threat. His beliefs leagued him with James Madison and James Monroe, his fellow Virginians, and brought him into conflict with Alexander Hamilton of New York. While Hamilton supported the royalty of England, Jefferson sympathized with the French pursuit of a republic and wanted to break with the economic dependency upon England that Hamilton thought essential for the new nation. His view of the domestic economy was also different. As a southerner, Jefferson feared the industrial, capitalistic North with its infrastructure of banks and factories. As president, he arranged the Louisiana Purchase, which not only gave America possession of French New Orleans but opened up the Mississippi Valley from the Mississippi River to the Rocky Mountains and leagued the South and the West politically.

Jefferson did his best to keep religion and the state separate, and his abiding belief in an American destiny helped secularize the idea of a New Jerusalem. His holy city was a product of rational thought. Like many Enlightenment thinkers, Jefferson had been influenced by ancient, especially Roman, thought. He saw heroic classicism as a European myth to be made American. Jefferson was instrumental in getting the services of Pierre Charles L'Enfant to help design the federal city, and he played a role in the planning of Washington, including the designing of the White House and the Capitol.[1] Later in life, Jefferson saw the need for an industrial America, but he insisted that such industry must be subordinated to and accommodated by an agrarian economy. After the War of 1812, however, he saw the country moving toward an industrialization that would not be reversed. The Civil War—which came thirty-four years after his death—culminated this movement.

Jefferson's fear of the European city was shared by a number of major American writers. In *The Bravo* (1831), James Fenimore Cooper (1789–1851) depicted Venice as a center of intrigue and corruption;[2] Herman Melville (1819–91) would describe a heartless London in *Redburn* (1849); and Nathaniel Hawthorne (1804–64) saw modern Rome be-

1. L'Enfant modeled the American capital after Versailles with its grid pattern and streets broken by diagonal boulevards that radiated from a center. Jefferson presided over the competition for the design of the capitol building, choosing the plan of William Thornton with its rectangular classical proportions and its Roman dome. Jefferson's own plan for the design of the executive mansion was modeled on a Palladian villa, with dome and porticos, much like Monticello—a plan that James Hoban modified. The capital that Jefferson helped build on the banks of the Potomac contained more classical buildings than any city in the world outside of Rome (Risjord, 78).

2. *The Bravo,* dealing with a Venetian assassin, was the first novel in a trilogy by Cooper set in Europe. While his sympathy was with the European gentry, Cooper felt that the center of historical gravity had shifted to America. Despite his identification with an American aristocracy, he also believed in the promise of American democracy (see *An American Democrat,* 1821), a belief that he more or less abandoned in his later years. His Leatherstocking Tales depicted the evolution of the American frontier, from upstate New York to the prairie.

yond redemption in *The Marble Faun* (1860). If the American city were to thrive, there had to be a break with the European past, the creation of a new urban reality. But that vision was conflicted from the outset. All of these authors had serious reservations about the nature of city living. A city was a city, whether in Europe or America, and American cities were already beginning to show similarities to their European counterparts. In *The Blithedale Romance* (1852), Hawthorne depicted the implausibility of fulfilling utopian expectations. Coverdale is an American flaneur, who describes his routine in the city: "I felt a hesitation about plunging into this muddy tide of human activity and pastime. It suited me better, for the present, to linger on the brink, or hover in the air above it" (161). A disembodied spirit within the city, his need for isolation made Blithedale too sociable for him. Like Baudelaire, Coverdale comes to the city to be alone in the crowd—that is, to be alone among people who are no longer individuals, who have become things, urban objects, stripped of human identity.

Hawthorne, like so many of his contemporaries, saw the city as a means of restraining the wilderness. *The Scarlet Letter* (1850) is set against both the emerging city, with its putative order, and the wilderness, with its sense of the unrestrained. When Hester goes outside the village, she is tempted in a kind of frenzy into having sex, which results in her being ostracized from the community. She spends her subsequent years living between the village and the wilderness. The wilderness in Hawthorne's fiction carries much of the meaning of the Dionysus story. What is unpredictable and untamed comes into the village from the wilderness; it is the realm of the Indians, who provide a dialectical opposition, embodying a chaos that Puritan order tries to suppress. Like Jefferson, Hawthorne put great emphasis upon a sense of a redeeming community; but also like Jefferson, he saw the limits such a community must have, especially in the face of the natural condition it was man's task to confront. Built into the order of the city was the disorder of nature; neither completely contained the other. Already Hawthorne, as his "Celestial Railroad" and other stories suggest, saw limits to the Jeffersonian vision: the community was flawed by the condition of human nature, which in itself compromised the very idea of the New Jerusalem.

Jefferson's was a failed vision of what America might have become— a vision that dominated the literary imagination of the moderns. Henry Adams wrote a nine-volume history of the Jefferson administration. Ezra Pound saw Jefferson as the last hope of America. F. Scott Fitzgerald set his idealized America in the realm before the city—that is, in the world of Jefferson. John Dos Passos wrote three books idealizing Jefferson. Faulkner centered his fallen, fictional world in a Mississippi town called Jefferson. And, as a number of critics have suggested, Frank Lloyd Wright's organic sense of architecture owed much to Jefferson.[3]

II

Edgar Allan Poe's (1809–49) fiction takes us to a city beyond the New Jerusalem and the Jeffersonian utopia. More extreme than other romantics, Poe believed that the city contains a destructive force that causes a process of dissolution. His city, whether it be a buried city of the distant past or nineteenth-century London or Paris, is inseparable from the inevitability of death. In "The Mystery of Marie Roget" (1842), Poe transferred the murder of Mary Rogers from Staten Island to Paris because Paris was more mysterious and sinister, more capable of evil. "Mellonta Tauta" (1848) is a fantasy projection of New York in 2848, transformed by natural disaster, religion, and democracy (the mob).

In 1848, Poe wrote "Eureka," which he called a "prose poem," a long philosophical, quasi-scientific explanation of the universe. This work, written eighteen months before his death, has been used by a number of critics as a key to the meaning of his earlier works. Reading backward from one work to explain another raises certain critical problems, but in the case of "Eureka" such a practice also brings rewards. In this work, Poe asserts that God is His own creation, the product of His own will. The universe has been constituted from a "primordial particle" willed by God. The particle has expanded to the outer limits of the universe, from where it has the tendency to return inward to its source. As the universe expands it experiences multeity; as it collapses into itself it experiences unity. Matter thus desires its own entropic destruction: everything is wearing down to a final unity. Such a philosophy relies on the belief in a double motion of the universe, which can be detected in the general workings of human experience. The prime motion of creation, expulsion and impulsion, reveals the conflict between Eros and Thanatos, between the life wish and the desire for self-destruction. Daniel Hoff-

3. See J. M. Fitch's *Architecture and the Esthetics of Plenty* (1961); see also Vincent Scully's *American Architecture and Urbanism* (1969) and *The Rise of American Architecture* (1970).

man has called it a double truth: "expansion and contraction.... Life and Death. All is Double" (295).

Everything in Poe, in other words, is moving toward death, which again brings into being the original unity. Such a philosophy explains Poe's obsession with the death of beautiful young women, who are being called to a special realm. And it explains the vision of the city that we find in such poems as "The City in the Sea" (1831). The city, like Atlantis, exists as a symbol of unity beneath the sea, and there the dead have returned:

> Lo! Death has reared himself a throne
> In a strange city lying alone
> Far down within the dim West[.]

This city resembles nothing on earth. It is a "wilderness of glass," illuminated from light that comes upward from the bottom of the sea, and it is ruled over by Death, who looks down on the city from his "proud tower." The poem ends with a suggestion of the magnetic attraction that the city has for the living: it is a kind of counterforce to heaven, more powerful than Hell. Once again we see the city as inseparable from the realm of death; negative entropy brings the city back to an initial inertia.

Poe demonstrates the working of negative entropy in his short story "Mellonta Tauta," written in 1848 but set one thousand years ahead in 2848. The story involves a balloon trip to a New York now in ruins. The initial disruption seems to have come about in the year 2050 through an earthquake, resulting in urban degeneration intensified by internal weaknesses. Such limitations stemmed from giving too much power to the churches—"a kind of pagoda instituted for the worship of two idols that went by the names of Wealth and Fashion" (*Complete Works,* VI, 291)—and to the mob, which Poe equated with misguided democracy in America. Almost every reference to a city in Poe is accompanied by a reference to a body of water: "Mellonta Tauta" ends with the balloon collapsing and falling into the sea, that great vortex that consumes all time, as does the whirlpool in *The Narrative of Arthur Gordon Pym* (1838) and the maelstrom in "A Descent into the Maelstrom" (1841).

In Poe, the city is always outside of time, a relic of the past toward which all future life paradoxically flows. Edward H. Davidson believes the new interest in archaeology influenced Poe's lost city of death. Such a city undid time as a "linear continuum, a parceling of history into ages and periods," and led instead to time "as a vast amorphous idea in which the objects from the past assumed a timeless reality." Death and its city become like a work of art: a unity unto itself, immune from time (Davidson, 117–18). Because Poe's city was outside of time, critics had trouble pigeonholing him. Vernon Parrington could not bring Poe within the confines of the liberal tenets he brought to American literature, and F. O. Matthiessen could not reconcile Poe's vague use of landscape with the visionary America of Hawthorne, Melville, and Whitman. William Carlos Williams sought to incorporate Poe into the American grain, but his unconvincing attempts failed to account for the peculiar position of Poe's landscapes, on the brink of if not outside the realm of time. Poe constantly calls us back to a nothingness. The city is thus that strange home, beyond the wilderness, to which we are ultimately called. Built into such a vision was Poe's distrust of the gospel of progress, a distrust that played into his doctrine of ruin and decay. Like other romantics who view the city, Poe insists on limits to the physical world and leaves us with a sense of the uncanny, the disintegrated city being that mysterious home to which our limits guarantee that we, like all life, will return.

III

Unlike Poe, Herman Melville grounded the city in the here and now. Melville's city is located between the wilderness, from which it sprang, and the dissolution toward which it seems to be working—that is, it must be read in terms of the differences between nature and civilization. In his early works, Melville showed great distrust of civilization, especially as it worked its will on primitive people, upsetting the cultural balance of natives living in simple peace. In *Typee* (1846) and *Omoo* (1847), he was especially critical of the missionaries, who brought a religious message that challenged the indigenous beliefs of the tribes. Good and evil were clearly distinguished in these novels.

In *Typee*, the narrator, Tom, after many months at sea, arrives in the summer of 1842 at Nukuheva, one of the forbidding Polynesian islands in the Marquesas group of the South Pacific. His patience exhausted by bad treatment aboard the *Dolly*, the narrator—along with a friend, Toby—decides to jump ship, even though the natives, the Typee, are known to be cannibals. When they enter the jungle and fall into the hands of the Typee, they become witnesses to a society that is complex and self-sustaining. Although there were no roads in the valley, only "a labyrinth of footpaths, twisting and turning among the thickets without end" (*Typee,* 222), the natives communicate with each other from one end of the island to another by posting men in coconut trees who pass on verbal messages. Tom also discovers a kind of Stonehenge structure built many generations before that explains the "creation" of the universe. Tom concludes that "human beings were living in the valleys of the Marquesas three thousand years ago [parallel to those] inhabiting the land of Egypt" and that in intelligence and cultural sophistication they were equal to the Egyptians and Greeks (179). Like the Egyptians, the Typees have constructed impressive burial grounds. The priests claim knowledge of mystical secrets that allow them special powers. True, the Typees practiced cannibalism on the bodies of slain enemies; but though he disapproves, Tom comes to believe that such a practice did not destroy their moral sense (228).

The island, a cornucopia of grains and other foods, produces a healthy people. Tom comes to see advantages of the primitive over the civilized life; the self-sufficiency of the island contrasts with the poverty and dependency of life in the city. The natives live in harmony with the land, sharing it in common, and each individual is strengthened by a sense of community. While there is personal property, there is no such thing as real estate; and as sufficient goods are available for all, poverty is nonexistent. As a result, "there were no foreclosures of mortgages, . . . no beggars; no debtors prisons . . . to sum up in one word—no Money! That 'root of all evil' was not to be found in the valley" (141–42). But despite the attractions, Tom and Toby return to the port city of Nukuheva and eventually back to civilization. The Typees supply Melville's modern audience a point of contrast to the limitations inherent in the urban, civilized life; but modern humanity is a product of the city, and no escape to the primitive past can last long.

In *Redburn,* Melville looked through the other end of the telescope to view the evil of the city itself. If there are truths built into nature, the truths built into the city must be different, for the city is a human construction and subject to human change. If the hand of God has left its message in nature, then the hand leaving a message in the city is human. Redburn becomes aware of urban instability when he realizes the great difference between the city of the past and the present. When he first arrives in Liverpool, he is carrying the guidebook his father had used fifty years previously. Redburn soon discovers that there is no correlation between the Liverpool his father experienced and the Liverpool he is witnessing. This change creates a tremendous sense of displacement, a feeling of double loss—both of his father when Redburn was a child and of the father's world now that he is an adult.

In Melville, the father's legacy is always tenuous, a theme he will treat again in *Pierre*. The closest Redburn can get to his father is to walk, as his father did, through the stone arch at the end of Church Street. But this route takes him to a statue that reminds him "that the African slave-trade once constituted the principal commerce of Liverpool; and that the prosperity of the town was once supposed to have been indissolubly linked to its prosecution" (*Redburn,* 149). His father's world was not only physically different, it was also morally different. The prized guide-book, he realizes, "was next to useless. Yes, the thing that had guided the father could not guide the son.... Here now,... thought I, learn a lesson, and never forget it. This world, my boy, is a moving world.... Every age makes its own guide-books, and the old ones are used for waste paper" (150–51).

Redburn becomes aware not only that cultures are built on shifting sands and changing values, but that evil indelibly inheres in their structures. Redburn is overwhelmed by the poverty and the squalor of Liverpool. He sees a mother and her three children, seemingly dead, in a hole just off a busy city street. A slight motion tells him that the mother and two of the children are barely alive, but "dumb and next to dead with want" (174). Ragpickers in the neighborhood are indifferent to the mother's plight: "'She desarves it,' said an old hag, who was just placing on her crooked shoulders her bag of pickings, and who was turning to totter off, 'that Betsy Jennings desarves it—was she ever married? tell me that.'" A policeman is equally indifferent: "'It's none of my business, Jack,' said he, 'I don't belong to that street.'" When he asks the watchman at the warehouse for help, he is told that property comes before human life: "'You're crazy, boy,' said he, 'do you suppose, that Parkins and Wood want their warehouse turned into a hospital?'" The otherwise generous landlady of his own boardinghouse tells him "that she gave away enough to beggars in her own street... without looking after the whole neighborhood" (175). Redburn manages to get some bread from the cook; when the children respond convulsively, he realizes that he is doing more harm than good by prolonging their ordeal. Indifference to human suffering has become an urban way of life. The large number of people in misery has hardened the heart of the city to individual pain and cheapened the idea of life. On the third morning, Redburn discovers that the mother and children are dead; later in the day their bodies have been removed, and in their place "a heap of quick-lime was glistening" (178).

Melville's novels speak to each other: the passage detailing deadly urban want in *Redburn* contrasts tellingly with the passage describing the abundance of food in *Typee*. The natives have only to go to nature to satisfy their wants; the city dwellers must rely on a distribution system inseparable from money. And money is the foundation of civilized law. As he walks through the dock area of the city, Redburn witnesses more human derelicts, including a young man who was chewed up by industrial machinery, "his limbs mangled and bloody" (180). Pawnbrokers are as plentiful as sharks in the sea and equally compassionate. Urban hardship has no redress; modern law protects property and not life, at least not the life of the indigent.

In his course through the center of Liverpool, Redburn becomes aware of another urban truth: all cities are alike. Cities, whose form is determined by their function, have the same structure and begin to look like each other, especially in their wealthier part: "Liverpool, away from the docks, was very much such a place as New York. There were the same sort of streets pretty much; the same rows of houses with stone steps; the same kind of side-walks and curbs; and the same elbowing, heartless-looking crowd as ever" (195). The Leeds Canal reminds him of the Erie Canal, St. John's Market of Fulton Market, and Lord Street of Broadway. All cities also intensify the evil that accompanied the Fall from Eden, and the appeal to law and other bureaucratic institutions is as fruitless as the appeal to the "heartless" crowd. Indeed, the crowd and the law, two forms of urban reality that abstract and distance citizens from humanity, are what Melville, like Dickens, comes to mean by the city. Redburn has become aware that death lurks literally beneath the sidewalks of the city, making a mockery of urban life and the institutions that sustain such order. Melville's Pierre will learn the same lesson.

Pierre (1852) is a perfect example of what has been called romantic realism. Melville constructed a symbolic reality that he then superimposed on various realistic settings, especially the city of New York at midcentury. In *Pierre*, Melville takes his antipathy to the city to another level. The story itself is a strange one. Pierre Glendinning is living a bucolic life with his mother on a farm in the Berkshires when he discovers that his father has had an affair with a beautiful French emigrant and abandoned both her and their child. Trying to redeem the sins of his father, Pierre breaks his engagement with Lucy Tartan and marries Isabel, his half-sister; he takes her and Delly Ulver—a young woman she knows who has recently borne an illegitimate child (now dead) and who thus also seems related to the story of his father—to New York, where he hopes to make a living as a writer. These events lead to his mother's disinheriting him and to his cousin, Glendinning Stanly, rudely breaking with him.

In New York, Pierre and his ménage (he is eventually joined by Lucy) live in the Apostle Church, which has been converted into a rooming house for artists. Thus Melville does not simply sustain Balzac's idea of the boardinghouse as a substitute for the lost family: the house is a transformed temple, emphasizing the distance between the religious and the secular, housing the new observer of the city, the artist. It is here that Pierre comes in contact with Plotinus Plinlimmon, whose pamphlet, "Chronometricals and Horologicals," he had found in the coach that took him to the city. The pamphlet explains that a Greenwich clock does not tell the time in China and that Christian (chronometrical) conduct is not consistent with our modern (horological) culture. The pamphlet, in other words, teaches what Pierre has already learned: moral truth is both relative and ambiguous, and good cannot be separated from evil. Pierre comes to learn that heaven on earth is impossible.

After *Pierre,* good and evil would no longer be separate realities for Melville. As Marius Bewley has pointed out, in *Moby-Dick* (1851) Melville made an effort "to introduce order into his moral universe, and to establish a polarity between good and evil." But in *Pierre* and *The Confidence Man* such distinctions were replaced by a sense of ambiguity. As a result, "moral action . . . became an impossibility. With no metaphysical poles of good and evil, and no dialectical pattern on the pragmatic levels of life to guide them, Melville's heroes became incapable of development or progression. They became the passive victims of their situation in life, trapped in the endless unfolding of moral ambiguities whose total significance was to drain all possible meaning from life" (Bewley, 94–95).

The city that Pierre enters embodies this ambiguity and intensifies the worst in the human condition. The first light that Pierre sees when he enters New York is that of a prison and the first person is a harlot; the chanting mob gives the city the appearance of Babel and its amorality makes it a Babylon. When Pierre kills Glendinning Stanly, his metaphorical brother, he becomes Cain, the founder of all cities; he dies in the Tombs, the jail that is the bowels of the city, and causes the deaths of Isabel and Lucy. Pierre's journey, like Redburn's, has been from innocence to experience, from pastoral well-being to urban death.

Much of the meaning in *Pierre* comes, as in many urban novels, through reference to art, although Pierre is more the philosopher than the artist in the city. He becomes obsessed with a portrait of his father (made on the sly by his cousin) because he believes it may hold the secret of the father he never really knew. In a New York museum, Pierre and Isabel come across a painting that seems to be identical to that portrait, which Pierre destroyed before leaving home. And on the wall directly opposite this portrait is a portrait of the Cenci. Beatrice Cenci (1577–99), an Italian noblewoman, was executed after she procured the death of her vicious father, and the physical juxtaposition of the pictures emphasizes the parallels between the stories. Like Beatrice, he seeks justice in the face of the father; like Beatrice, he murders in the name of that justice; and like Beatrice, he dies for his deed. The Cenci story gives romantic validity and universality to Pierre's. When myths are superimposed upon the discordant city, the ambiguity of character and the ambiguity of place become one. Try as it might, the city cannot escape the reality that connects human existence to moral ambiguity and death.

In "Bartleby the Scrivener" (1853), Melville explicitly treats the state of mind that takes us to death once the logic of the city is questioned. The narrator is a Wall Street lawyer dealing in bonds, mortgages, and deeds—the city's essential business, by which property is claimed or transferred. Such work calls the modern city into being: a capitalist society could not function without such agency. Because he has been given additional work, the narrator hires Bartleby to join his other scriveners, Old Turkey and Nippers, and a young office boy named Ginger Nut. All goes well until one day the narrator asks Bartleby to proofread a document, and Bartleby replies: "I would prefer not to." If the city is to function as a commercial system, a hierarchy of cooperation is necessary from the lowliest clerk to the most powerful entrepreneur. In refusing to participate in the system, Bartleby challenges its very being.

Bartleby is an analogue to the mysterious stranger. We know little about his background, but chaos does trail him, for "the scrivener was the victim of innate and incurable disorder" ("Bartleby," in *Selected Tales*, III–12). Such disorder separates Bartleby from the workaday world and, we are told, "he seemed alone, absolutely alone in the universe" (116). Bartleby's story is one of walls. Not only is the setting Wall Street, but the office is surrounded by the walls of other buildings: the narrator's window looks out at a "lofty brick wall, black by age"; at the other end of the office, Bartleby looks "out, at his pale window behind the screen, upon the dead brick wall" (93, 111). In a world of limits, where death is the final reward and good is tainted with evil, there is no basis to claim that one course of action is superior to another. Bartleby's "I would prefer not to" makes as much sense as Nippers's drunken mornings and Old Turkey's irritable afternoons.

Bartleby divorces himself from the crowd and, by extension, the city—refusing to assent to their ultimate purpose. Such behavior challenges the city. The narrator can no longer sustain his sense of social superiority in the face of it. He tells us that Bartleby's behavior cost him a sense of identity, "unmanned me as it were" (109). He begins to feel the "disorder" that Bartleby is generating and fails to go to church that Sunday because "the things I had seen disqualified me for the time from church-going" (112). Bartleby's state of mind becomes contagious, as everyone in the office unconsciously begins using the word "prefer." Terrified at where these events could lead, the narrator moves from Wall Street to offices closer to City Hall. When the new tenant finds Bartleby still lodged in the old office, he tells the narrator, "you are responsible for the man you left there" (124). The narrator makes desperate pleas to Bartleby, promises other kinds of jobs, and even offers to bring Bartleby home with him, but once again all his offers are rejected. Upset, the narrator takes flight into the city: "for a few days I drove about the upper part of the town and through the suburbs[,] . . . crossed over to Jersey City and Hoboken, and paid fugitive visit to Manhattanville and Astoria" (127). The trip itself seems needed to confirm to the narrator the palpability of the city in the face of Bartleby's challenge to it. On returning to his office, he learns that the landlord has called the police: Bartleby has been arrested as a vagrant and is now in the Tombs, the inverted fort on which the city relies to distance itself from internal threats. The narrator finds Bartleby in the prison yard, standing on a small plot of grass under a blue sky and facing "toward a high wall" (128). The city has reduced nature to a minimum. Nevertheless, the narrator, still a fountain of hope in the face of Bartleby's despair, leaves money for special food. Perverse to the end, Bartleby stops eating and eventually dies.

We are told at the end that Bartleby may have been "a subordinate clerk in the Dead Letter Office at Washington, from which he had been suddenly removed by a change in the administration" (131). From the death of communications to the death of the capitalistic system is a small step in Melville's story, as it will be in Pynchon's *The Crying of Lot 49*. Entropy works at the heart of this urban order, exhausting it from within; Bartleby has intuited the truth of this process, and so has the narrator whose compassion at the end is as much for himself as it is for Bartleby.

In "The Paradise of Bachelors and the Tartarus of Maids" (1855), Melville creates another narrative involving urban order inseparable from disorder, urban wealth as the end product of industrial poverty, as he counterpoints two stories. The story of the bachelors takes place at the Templars' modern cloisters. The Templars, knights who had fought in the holy lands, are re-presented in the story as lawyers whose temple is a club where they are served a sumptuous dinner. The same man narrates the second story, involving a New England papermill whose monstrous machines are tended by blank-looking, pale girls. He finds that one scene recalls the other, connecting the world of the wealthy lawyers to that of the impoverished maidens and linking the documents that sustain the system to the industrial inferno that produces the paper on which they are written. As the "Bartleby" narrator finds himself morally connected to Bartleby, so the bachelors are morally connected to the maids. In a commercial/industrial system, urban heights sit uncomfortably close to urban depths.

Another story involving dichotomies is "The Two Temples," which Melville was unable to publish in his lifetime because of its attack on Grace Church in New York. The narrator is arrested after he sneaks back into a new, richly fashioned Gothic church from which he had been turned away; there he hears the black-robed priest praise his wealthy congregation as "the salt of the earth" ("Two Temples," 1246). His treatment at the church contrasts starkly with his reception by a London theater crowd, who treat the narrator generously. Indeed, the theater in the Strand reminds him of the church in New York: the topmost gallery resembles the church tower; the orchestra recalls the church organ; the audience far below consists of jeweled ladies and handsomely dressed men; Macready, the actor, resembles the black-robed priest. Two temples: the secular temple in a strange land offers him charity, the religious temple at home offers hostility. Melville's fiction thrives on such dichotomies.

His deliberate counterpointing indicts the social system that was the end product of the Enlightenment revolution, and many of Melville's stories, including "Bartleby the Scrivener," can be read as condemning both the city and its Enlightenment legacy. Bartleby, for example, comes to realize that the differences between nature and culture have been collapsed into each other and that in an Enlightenment culture we have put a premium on the rational will, believing it can control the physical realm and produce wealth—as it does on Wall Street. But the lowly scrivener has seen through this cultural construct to nature—not romantic nature, but a more ambiguous nature that opens onto the metaphysical void presented in stories like "The Paradise of Bachelors and the Tartarus of Maids." Thus his "prefer not to" is a willed passivity in the face of a problematic social agenda, and it raises an ethical question: what is the nature of duty when a dubious cultural demand shuts us off from chaos and an ambiguous universe? In this reading, Bartleby becomes a far more active agent than critics have often found him, as his behavior is seen as a willed, existential questioning of our Enlightenment agenda—an agenda that gave the authority to pillage the frontier (the same authority that Conrad's Marlow saw as inseparable from imperialism). "Bartleby the Scrivener" is Melville's testimony that the world is now city and the frontier closed.

It is thus fitting that one of Melville's last stories, *The Confidence Man* (1857), looks back on the human cost of closing the frontier. The events in the novel, set aboard the *Fidèle* at St. Louis, begin on April Fool's Day. A number of characters board or leave the ship as it makes its way twelve hundred miles down the Mississippi River, on the edge of the open West. The novel often pauses to offer stories within stories. One such narration involves Colonel John Moredock's harangue, "Containing the Metaphysics of Indian Hating, According to the Views of One Evidently Not so Prepossessed as Rousseau in Favor of Savages." Perhaps more mythical than real, Moredock, as the story goes, is the son of a pioneer woman who lost three husbands to attacks from Indians. As she made her way with her nine children toward a settlement in Illinois on the western bank of the Mississippi, her party was attacked and—with the exception of her son John—killed by Indians. John's task becomes that of avenger. He pursues the "twenty renegades from various tribes, outlaws even among Indians" (*Confidence Man,* 133), eventually killing them all. But instead of satisfying his desire for revenge, this experience only whets his appetite for the death of more Indians. Moredock has become, like Captain Ahab, obsessed with destroying all embodiments of the wilderness, first in the name of revenge and then in the name of civilization. Moredock's desire to wipe out the Indians reenacts Ahab's desire to impose his will upon the white whale. As in his other novels, Melville here takes on the moral problem of exploitation, of the human desire to control and subordinate what is wild in nature in the name of its own authority. As in *Typee,* the wilderness itself seems a threat to those who either have come from or are going to the city. Some critics believe that Melville's *The Confidence Man* was his sequel to Hawthorne's "The Celestial Railroad." Just as Hawthorne warned about the dangers connected with a belief that we could arrive at perfect urban happiness, either temporal or eternal, so Melville, like Poe, depicts the city of man as inseparable from the city of death. The city comes into being at the expense of the conquered wilderness, intensifying the ambiguity that urban inhabitants play out, making it a new kind of fate.

CHAPTER 11

The Urban Frontier

I

As a reading of Melville anticipates, one of the major disputes regarding the growth of cities in America is the question of how independent the city was from the American frontier. Frederick Jackson Turner believed the frontier created its own reality, which formed the character of America as a nation. "The true point of view in the history of this nation is not the Atlantic Coast," Turner argued in his famous essay of 1893, "it is the Great West" (1–2). For over a generation, the Turner thesis set the terms for conceptualizing the relationship between the city and the frontier. In *The Rise of the City* (1933), Arthur M. Schlesinger, Sr., offered a competing paradigm, arguing that "the cities marched westward with the outposts of settlement" (210), and that the frontier experience was never independent of urban America. Schlesinger contended that the differences between city and country led to the first national parties under the Constitution: Hamilton's Federalist scheme favored urban financial institutions while Jefferson's Republican scheme favored farmers. Developments like the Erie Canal, completed in 1825, proved that the city-country relationship was symbiotic. The canal opened eastern markets to farm products of the Great Lakes region, fostered immigration to the Old Northwest, and urbanized the Midwest. In return, once the canal had connected New York City with its hinterland, New York became the principal East Coast city, far outdistancing Boston, Philadelphia, and Baltimore in population and financial growth. New York had only 60,000 inhabitants in 1800; by 1860, it had 800,000. Once the railroad extended the canal, the city grew even more. Schlesinger's thesis was further developed by Richard Wade, first in a dissertation and then in an influential book, *The Urban Frontier* (1959). Wade was concerned with the cities of the trans-Appalachian West from 1790 to 1830. In cities like Pittsburgh, Cincinnati, Lexington, Louisville, and St. Louis, the city dweller soon followed the farmer, and the network of large cities on major waterways — from the Ohio River to the Mississippi — facilitated trade and transportation from the East Coast to the Mississippi Valley. Wade points out that "by quickening transportation and cutting distances, steam navigation telescoped fifty years' urban development into a single generation" (70). These cities took their structure and meaning from eastern cities like Philadelphia, thus carrying the influence of the East across the country.

After the Civil War, another group of cities, which were located on the Great Lakes, became the industrial centers of the country: Buffalo (iron and steel), Pittsburgh (steel), Cleveland (oil), Detroit (automobiles), Chicago (steel and oil), and Milwaukee (beer). In 1866, the extension of the telegraph and the laying of the Atlantic cable made the East Coast the link between the Midwest and Europe. In the meantime, the steam engine had revolutionized industry: no longer did factories have to be located on rivers to have a source of power. And as factories moved into cities, so did a rural population. By 1920, there had been a dramatic population shift: the census return showed that for the first time in the country's history, more than half of the population lived in urban areas. Masses of people reared in rural areas had to adapt to the new, hectic pace of city life. Dr. George M. Beard, anticipating the problem in his *American Nervousness* (1881), coined the word *neurasthenia* to describe the mental instability attributable to the pace and pressures — the stress, the competitiveness, the intensity, the lack of community, the hostility, the anonymity, the mental stimuli, the distractions, the noise — of city life.

With urban change came the rise of political machines (for example, the Tammany organization in New York, which, under the influence of "bosses" like W. M. Tweed and Richard Crocker, dominated city politics from 1854 to 1932). As immigrants came to America from Europe, both the native and immigrant population became discontented. The New York riots of 1863 came about primarily because Irish workers resented being sent to fight in the Civil War when the well-to-do could buy a substitute for $300. As the crime rate rose, many attributed the change to the rise of immigrant poverty. The growth of organized crime was a part of this phenomenon. In a 1953 essay, Daniel Bell demonstrated that organized crime was a means of social mobility for immigrant groups. In the last half of the nineteenth century, the Irish and East European Jews controlled New York crime; after 1920 the control passed to Italian Americans and the Mafia. Despite the social stigma, crime—as Fitzgerald's Gatsby knew—was another way of climbing the American ladder of success.

Once the emphasis shifted from rural to urban America, the city became the primary political and cultural arena. The major social problems of today—from inner-city decline to immigration and minority problems, crime and gang wars, zoning, public housing, transportation, unemployment, and welfare—are city problems: the city is our destiny and has been since the end of the Civil War, as a number of major writers clearly saw. The works of William Faulkner, Mark Twain, and Willa Cather reveal in literary terms the meaning of the shift from an agrarian to an urban America.

II

William Faulkner, perhaps more than any other American writer, took the wilderness as his subject, but the wilderness does not offer a morally untainted starting point. As long as there were human occupants, the land was corruptible. The fate of Ikkemotubbe—as it emerges in the stories, especially those collected in *Go Down, Moses* (1942)—reveals such corruption. As the last of the Chickasaw chiefs of the area that become Faulkner's Yoknapatawpha County (the historical Lafayette County), he tricked his way into power. When he loses a courtship battle, he leaves the plantation and lives for seven years in New Orleans, where he claims to be the Man, chief of his People, and acquires the name "Doom" (from the French *du homme*). Thoroughly citified, he returns to the plantation and tricks the legitimate Man into stepping down and allowing him to become chief. In *Go Down, Moses*, Ikkemotubbe is the father of Sam Fathers, born of a quadroon woman. But in "A Justice" (1931), Sam is the illegitimate son of a Chickasaw named Crawfish-ford and a black woman, who was married to a black man. In this version, Ikkemotubbe names the child Sam Had-Two-Fathers. Relying on his knowledge of New Orleans real estate practices, Ikkemotubbe sells parts of the wilderness to the various settlers and planters. The fam-

ilies who eventually make aristocratic claims—the Compsons, Sar-
torises, De Spains, Sutpens, and McCaslins—all come by their land
through such transactions. Once the land is turned into property, something to be bought and sold, the serpent is in the garden. And the selling
does not stop with the land: Ikkemotubbe sells his son Sam Fathers to
Lucius Quintus Carothers McCaslin. Sam remains a man of the wilderness and initiates Cass Edmonds and Ike McCaslin into the sacred rituals of the woods.

Sam is born in 1808 and dies in 1883, a span of time during which
urbanized industry comes to control the region and destroy the wilderness—a story that Faulkner dramatically relates, primarily in "The Bear."
The death of the bear, followed shortly by the death of Sam Fathers, represents the passing of the old order as the South is transformed by new
industry after the Civil War. Boon and the dog Lion destroy the bear, just
as the timber company destroys the forest. The death of the bear and the
death of the wilderness are one event, yoked together by Faulkner's language. With the man and the dog straddling the bear, Boon's knife prob-
ing for the bear's heart, the bear "crashed down. It didn't collapse, crum-
ple. It fell all of a piece, *as a tree falls,* so that all three of them, man, dog,
and bear seemed to bounce once" (in *Go Down, Moses,* 241; italics mine).

The death of the wilderness is told against the rise of Memphis, both
in "The Bear" and in Faulkner's other fiction. Memphis's human representative is Popeye, whom we meet in *Sanctuary* (1931) and who embodies the modern mechanized world. A man afraid of nature, he is
described in mechanical terms (his face is like stamped tin, his eyes like
balls of rubber). He is evil incarnate, degenerate (the son of a syphilitic),
and unnatural (impotent, he rapes Temple Drake with a corncob). Temple falls into his hands when she is abandoned by Gowan Stevens, who
betrays whatever elements of chivalry are left in the South. Popeye takes
her to a Memphis brothel, where he provides her with a lover so that he
can watch them have sex. The sanctuary, once the spiritual heart of the
city, has become the brothel. The connection between ritual sacrifice and
sex (that is, between religion and sex) was present from the beginning:
as Flaubert demonstrated in *Salammbô,* the temple housed priestesses of
the moon, who had sexual functions. But, as with Richardson's Clarissa,
Temple's imprisonment reveals a degeneracy both Richardson and Fielding connected with the city. Moreover, whatever the old, aristocratic
world might have been in reality, its ideals have now all been inverted:
Temple is a caricature of Southern femininity, fraudulently playing the
role of Southern Womanhood victimized (Faulkner returned to this

theme twenty years later in *Requiem for a Nun,* 1951); Gowan Stevens, a drunken, cowardly playboy, is a caricature of Southern chivalry; the sanctuary, now evil, houses a desecrated vessel; and the town of Jefferson, a caricature of its name, courts respectability over truth, more interested in the appearance of virtue than in virtue itself. The center of this world is now the Memphis underworld of Popeye—antinatural, mechanical, exploitative, beyond justice if not law (Lee Goodwin dies for a murder Popeye committed, while Popeye is executed for a murder he did not commit). In Faulkner's Jefferson, much of the evil comes from Memphis, down the railroad tracks (tracks that his great-grandfather helped build).

In Faulkner's later fiction, this outside evil is embodied in the Snopes family, especially Flem Snopes; they come from somewhere outside the South and filter into Jefferson through Frenchman's Bend. Like Popeye, Flem is sexually impotent and without moral scruple, totally motivated by greed. He works his way up from a clerkship in Varner's store to become president of the Merchant and Farmers Bank in Jefferson. His activities mirror the new commercial and industrial base: he opens a greasy spoon, oversees the power plant, and takes over Manfred de Spain's bank and house (the mansion). Each time he moves ahead, he brings in another Snopes to fill his former position, until the aristocrats are displaced and the town is overrun with Snopeses.

Such events exemplify an American form of the gothic. The rise of the city and the passing of an agrarian world led to the gothic novel not only in England but also in America. The change occurred in the North before the Civil War, in the deep South after. Hawthorne's *The House of the Seven Gables* (1851) and Poe's "The Fall of the House of Usher" (1839) thus anticipate the fiction of Faulkner. As the South became urbanized after the Civil War, energy was drawn from the estate, which then rapidly declined. In *Absalom, Absalom!* (1936), Faulkner treats this subject directly. The world of the father—in this case, Thomas Sutpen—is perverted: brother kills brother, brother and sister fall incestuously in love, and the family degenerates until the last of Sutpen's heirs is demented. When Henry Sutpen secretly returns to the mansion and roams its empty rooms like a ghost, the gothic element is intensified. The fire that burns the mansion to the ground destroys what was already dead.

Faulkner's world can be located between the realms of gothic fiction and the Southern equivalent of Eliot's wasteland. A decline has been in process from some moment in the past. Exactly when it started is a matter of speculation: When the land became property? When human beings became property (slaves)? When the postbellum South became commercial and industrial? When honor gave way to greed and courage to respectability, the old virtues becoming caricatures of themselves? Or perhaps, since these matters are inseparable from a fundamental rapacity, they all may be stages of a single phenomenon. In any case, Faulkner's wilderness is inexorably degenerating. The bear as object of the hunt has given way to the squirrel; the last of the Compson family is the idiot Benjy; the last of Sutpen's heirs is the deformed James Bond; the old aristocracy, whatever their faults, have been replaced by the Snopeses in what is clearly a change for the worse; hope is emptied from the name Jefferson, now overshadowed by Memphis; and a tired passivity negates even the suggestion of a redeeming energy.

III

Mark Twain, who died in 1910, thirteen years after Faulkner was born, carried on the sense of an older world lost to a newer one. His was an age of transition from an agrarian to an urban America, an age in which the frontier was fast closing. Twain never came to terms with this era, despite his attempts in works like *The Gilded Age* (1873); he felt that urban life was becoming more and more impersonal, that cities were repressing the inner life of individuals, who then concealed their true state of mind. In 1882, he wrote in his "Notebooks": "Human nature cannot be studied in cities except at a disadvantage—a village is the place. There you can know your man inside and out—in a city you but know the crust; and his crust is usually a lie."

Twain saw humans as born with a Rousseau-like innocence that was debased by institutions: what we think of as "moral sense," a conscience, was acquired through a training that was morally corrupting and destructive. He briefly hoped that the industrial age might raise men morally by creating a utopia, a world of plenty. But he soon realized that instead of decreasing greed, the new technocracy, with its newer forms of power, extended greed, increased the possibility of technological misuse, and made the human species more destructive than ever before. Man, always capable of great evil, now had the physical means to cause even greater harm, as Hank does at the end of *A Connecticut Yankee*. Twain believed that it was increasingly difficult to remain innocent in the face of the new industrial, urban world—themes that emerge in works like "The Mysterious Stranger" (published posthumously in 1916) and "What Is Man" (1906). The devil in "The Mysterious Stranger" tells the boy that behind the illusion is a set of causes, a set circumstances already in play in the devil's mind, and that the boy is acting out the devil's dream.

Innocents Abroad (1869) and *Roughing It* (1872) deal with the two poles of nineteenth-century American life: Europe, from which the immigrants came, and the West toward which their descendants were moving. Twain saw the failings of both. He had a natural distrust of monarchy and hereditary aristocracy and was suspicious of imperialism wherever he found it. England's actions in the Boer War, Russia's attempt to annex Japanese land, and American dealings with Cuba and the Philippines equally aroused his wrath. Western missionaries from all countries were targets because they usually preceded the gunboats. For Twain, imperialism was merely the logical outward extension of capitalism; looking inward, he believed that urban America was becoming too controlling and that democracy would fail in the face of the mob and of central government.

In the unpublished "Notes for a Social History of the United States from 1850 to 1900," Twain maintained that America became money-mad after 1850. He believed that the California gold rush brought on the desire for sudden wealth, an attitude that was intensified by the Civil War, which was financed by Wall Street bankers and railroad promoters. They were unscrupulous men who wanted above all to "Get rich; dishonestly if we can; honestly if we must." *The Gilded Age,* written with Charles Dudley Warner, depicts a corrupt America, a country that had betrayed its sense of promise. Demonstrating that the frontier cannot be separated from an urban influence, the book supplies an impressive account of the connection between the frontier and Washington, D.C. By 1873 Congress had given away almost two hundred million acres of public land to the railroad corporations. Oakes Ames, brother of the president of the Union Pacific and a Massachusetts congressman, offered stock at inside prices to other congressmen. Turning his attention to New York, Twain cites the Tweed ring, which robbed the city of almost two hundred million dollars by renting armories that did not exist, billing for repairs never made, and demanding inflated payments for building both done and not done.

The Gilded Age also reveals the connection between the frontier and the capital necessary to exploit it. Colonel Sellers, who wants to build the "city of Napoleon upon a prairie mud flat," says: "All we need is the

capital to develop it. Slap down the rails and bring the land into market"
(133). Behind that capital, of course, is Wall Street and the Washington
politicians—that is, behind the capital is the city. George Washington
Hawkins takes over the dream of his father Si, the belief that speculation
in Tennessee land will bring in an eventual fortune. But when the older
Hawkins buys the land in the hope of reselling it for a profit, it becomes
a curse. Referring to John Locke's belief that work turns land into property, his son tells us that if the land had been worked the story would
have been different. Central to the novel is the land, its use and its misuse, which frustrates and ruins the speculators: Si and Washington
Hawkins, Colonel Sellers, and Harry Brierly. Land speculation also leads
indirectly to Laura Hawkins's ruin when she becomes involved in one of
Washington's schemes to get rich, in this case by selling the land for a
Negro college. Philip Sterling also speculates with the land, though
significantly he finds coal when he is working the land himself, after his
men have left. In appending a happy ending, Twain gives back with one
hand what he had taken away with the other. The American get-rich
dream, denied in the story of Laura and Washington Hawkins, is senti-
mentally reaffirmed in the Philip Sterling–Ruth Bolton plot.

In *Life on the Mississippi* (1883), Twain contrasted the new and old
river. He had returned to the Mississippi, after a twenty-year absence, to
get firsthand impressions for what was to be the setting of *Huckleberry
Finn* (1885). What he saw filled him with nostalgia, particularly for life on
the river during the age of the riverboats, which had now been almost
totally replaced by the railroad.[1] Twain, like Huck, tried desperately to
hold on to his innocence in a world fast giving way to conformity and
dull routine. In his "Notebooks" (February 20, 1891), Twain fantasized
about what might happen if Huck and Tom came back, now sixty years
old, "from nobody knows where—and crazy. [Huck] thinks he is a boy
again, and scans always every face for Tom and Becky. Tom comes...

---

1. Twain's *Life on the Mississippi* reworks a Rip Van Winkle–like American habit—that
tendency to locate ideals in a world that cannot accommodate them. We have dozens of
such books—works like James's *The American Scene* (1907), Dreiser's *Hoosier Holiday*
(1916), Pound's "Patria Mia" (1911), Eliot's *After Strange Gods* (1934), Fitzgerald's "My Lost
City" (1932), and Henry Miller's *Remember to Remember* (1947)—in which a writer returns
to an American scene, usually after an absence of twenty years, to find that world sadly
transformed and the values he considered so deeply American transformed with it. To be
sure, such an experience is in great part subjective, since one person's diminished world
becomes the basis for another's ideal. Yet in each case the author conveys a vivid sense that
we have used up a moment of possibility that will never come again—a sense that we have
betrayed the promises of the past.

from wandering the world. . . . Together they talk [of] old times; both are desolate, life has been a failure, all that was lovable, all that was beautiful is under the mould. They die together."

Twain saw that human destructiveness had long been reworking the wilderness. Appropriately, he connected this state of mind with Daniel Defoe. In *A Connecticut Yankee in King Arthur's Court,* Twain's Yankee compares himself to Defoe's Crusoe: "I saw that I was just another Robinson Crusoe cast away on an uninhabited island, with no society but some more or less tame animals, and if I wanted to make life bearable I must do as he did—invent, contrive, create, reorganize things—set brain and hand to work, and keep them busy. Well, that was in my line" (33). Ironically, like Locke, the Connecticut Yankee believes that the wilderness *is* waste, that the wilderness is redeemed by work; but, like the McCaslins in Faulkner's "The Bear," he proves the opposite—the wasteland is what is left when the wilderness is gone.

IV

Willa Cather gives us another account of the lost frontier, depicting the pioneer immigrants who were attracted by the "free land" available after the Civil War. The Union Pacific Railroad had been completed by 1869, and the Burlington Route entered southern Nebraska; between 1870 and 1880, thousands of settlers arrived on the Nebraska prairie. *My Ántonia* (1918) describes their lives, both lonely and communal. They were alone on the land and yet more easily assimilated into a community than immigrants who remained in the city. Many were destroyed by the experience, such as Mr. Shimerda, whose homesickness for Bohemia led to his suicide. Many survived by simply enduring—especially Ántonia, who not only perseveres but sustains her husband (in a way her mother could not sustain her father) until a second generation is firmly in place.

In her novel Willa Cather delineates four landscapes. The first is the prairie and its farm, where Jim Burden lives at the beginning of the novel, where his grandfather displays a moral authority, and where Jim witnesses the hardships of the Shimerda family, who literally live in the ground. Second is the town, once removed from the land, where life becomes slightly more abstract, ritualized, and conventional—ruled more by the money of people like Mr. Harling and Wick Cutter than by moral authority. Third is a Midwestern city like Lincoln, once further removed from the land, the seat of a large university and a live theater— a place where intellectual and aesthetic interests can be accommodated. And fourth is Cambridge, Massachusetts, and New York City, at yet another remove, the opposite of the land—the locations respectively of Harvard University, where Jim will get his law degree, and of the home office of the corporation for which he will work.

For Cather, the frontier is the true melting pot of America. People have to work together to survive: whatever prejudices they bring from the Old World get resolved in the process of establishing a new community. As we move away from the frontier into the town, we find such prejudices more deeply entrenched. The families from Virginia feel superior to the foreign families and the servant girls, who nevertheless eventually triumph socially because—like Lena Lingard and Tiny Soderball—they work harder and refuse to give up. While some succeed on the land, others do not; and the story that Jim Burden tells is sad, as is his own. For as he moves further and further away from the land, he feels diminished. The road had taken him in a circle, and although he has moved far beyond the life of Ántonia and the land, he has been conditioned by the past that he shares with her, and he will always be different from other city dwellers and the better for it. The novel ends with Jim telling us: "I had a sense of coming home to myself, and of having found out what a little circle man's experience is. For Ántonia and for me, this had been the road of Destiny; had taken us to those early accidents of fortune which predetermined for us all that we can ever be. Now I understood that the same road was to bring us together again. Whatever we had missed, we possessed together the precious, the incommunicable past" (*My Ántonia*, 272). As Cather was writing *My Ántonia*, she realized that whether her characters survived or were destroyed, the frontier experience was gone. By the story's end, Ántonia was a native daughter. What was left of the pioneer experience was controlled by money and by the Wick Cutters, who have been the source of evil from the beginning. Cutter, who has lost contact with the land and the people, lives only for money. In his obsession to keep his money from going to the wife he has perpetually tormented, he murders her and commits suicide; what is left of his estate is eaten up by lawyers. Ántonia leaves a living legacy in her eleven children; Wick Cutter leaves nothing.

In *A Lost Lady* (1922), Cather treats once again the difference between the frontier and the city, the past and the present, in a work that deeply influenced the way F. Scott Fitzgerald conceptualized the differences between the lost frontier and the new city. In Cather's novel, the meaning of the frontier is carried by Captain Forrester, who came to the plains after the Civil War and helped the railroad cut through that country. The spirit of the frontier is carried on by his young wife, Marian, who comes from California, marries the captain after he has had a serious accident, and becomes to Niel Herbert, the Jim Burden figure in the novel, a symbol of all that is good. Although Niel does not narrate the story, he establishes a moral presence that carries its meaning. His scorn is focused on Frank Ellinger, who embodies the use of force, and on Ivy Peters, whose moneygrubbing makes him the counterpart of Wick Cutter. When Niel learns that Mrs. Forrester has had an affair with Ellinger, and when he later discovers that she has turned over her business dealings to Peters, he is totally disillusioned. He sees passing a way of life that he equates with the West, a way of life that ends with the death of the captain and the corruption of Mrs. Forrester. We are told at the end of the novel that Niel "had seen the end of an era, the sunset of the pioneer. He had come upon it when already its glory was nearly spent. . . . This was the very end of the road-making West. . . . It was already gone, that age; nothing could ever bring it back" (*Lost Lady*, 168–69). Niel cannot forgive Mrs. Forrester for betraying the spirit of this vision. He condemns her for not dying "with the pioneer period to which she belonged," for preferring "life on any terms" (169). Like Gatsby, Niel wants Mrs. Forrester to sustain an ideal even after it has been exhausted.

Cather once again offers a choice between an idealized past and a diminished present in *The Professor's House* (1925); here the contrast between frontier and city is drawn by setting the primitive Cliff City (modeled on Mesa Verde) against Washington, D.C. The lost city goes back thousands of years; located in the Southwest (on the border between Colorado and New Mexico) and dug out of rock cliffs, it was built over a long period of time. It may have held as many as 70,000 inhabitants, who reached advanced stages of civilized life and learning (especially astronomy). But as the citizens of Cliff City gained more material goods, they became more refined and less militant, less able to defend themselves. Seemingly outside the larger network of tribes, the city was probably destroyed by a less civilized, more savage tribe, which was jealous of its advanced state. The lost city was found by Tom Outland, whose inability to get Washington to declare it a national monument speaks to the contrast between these two worlds. Tom's own story reflects the spirit of the West at the same time as he is the new man (the scientist/engineer who invents a new engine). The two forces, the old and the new, battle within him, and the novel suggests that we can either control the land or live in peace with it.

The professor's eight-volume study of the Spanish conquest of America is the thematic opposite of the story of Cliff City—a story of military victory, not defeat. But the professor himself is set against Tom. As the professor sees his own family becoming more and more materialistic, he becomes more passive, more tired, more resigned to his death. When his family leaves for a Paris vacation, he stays behind, moving into the attic study in the old house. The wind that blows out the stove pilot light facilitates his own unconscious wish to die. He is saved by Augusta, the devoted family servant, who is the Ántonia figure in this novel: she embodies the simple will to live, the will of the cliff dwellers, the spirit of the pioneers, the spirit of the present. The novel delineates two states of mind: an Enlightenment mentality, a desire for control and for pursuing material goods; and a frontier mentality, a desire to live in simple harmony, at one with the land. Both Tom and the professor struggle to sustain this spirit of life, embraced so simply by Augusta and by the early inhabitants of Cliff City. One goal (harmony with the land) enriches life; the other (material pursuits) leads to death. At the end of the novel, the professor realizes that two phases of his life (youth and middle age) are over, but he now has the courage to face the last phase. Unlike the bureaucrats in Washington, unlike his own family, unlike even Tom Outland, he has finally come to terms with the contradictions between the present and the past.

Cather repeatedly treated the theme of the lost past, especially the lost frontier. While perhaps the frontier movement was initially also an urban movement, as Richard Wade argues, at some point—according to Faulkner, Twain, and Cather—the city began to dominate and to destroy whatever symbiosis there may have been. The close of the frontier ended a way of life, locking America into an urban destiny, into urban powers.

CHAPTER 12

Urban Powers

I

What often goes unnoticed in the discussion of French and American literary naturalism is that writers like Frank Norris and Theodore Dreiser shared a historical moment with Balzac and Zola. All of these novelists set their novels in a world that was becoming more and more industrial. Key to the international character of literary naturalism is that the aftermath of the Civil War in America paralleled the changes taking place in France between 1848 and 1870, as both economies moved from a landed to a commercial/industrial world. In America this period witnessed the rapid growth of cities, the rise of corporate businesses, the influx of immigrant labor, and the spread of wretched working conditions. Like Zola's writings, American postbellum novels move from the boardrooms of power and wealth to the salons where the wealth is displayed; to the legislative forums that the wealth controls; to the mills, factories, and mines that produce the wealth at great human sacrifice and suffering. An analysis of cultural influence, however, can take the discussion only so far. A search for direct literary influence is even more limiting: literary works are too complex to "derive" from any one source. But Zola did more than write several dozen novels: he also developed a narrative methodology, a way of seeing reality, that left its mark on both sides of the Atlantic. French and American literary naturalism share the same narrative mode, displaying their differences within a shared spectrum of meaning.[1]

Like Zola, Frank Norris and Theodore Dreiser wrote novels that (in different ways) take their being from a naturalistic biology. Characters like McTeague and Vandover are products of an animality that leads to decline and degeneration, especially when their more debased instincts are stimulated by alcohol and dissipated living. McTeague tries to fight off the beast within him: his resolve vanishes for a moment when he has Trina helpless in his dentist chair, under the narcotic spell of gas. But it is not until his office is shut down and he is thrown onto the street that he comes under the destructive influence of alcohol, which accelerates the degenerative process. Poverty has the same degenerative affect on Trina and McTeague in *McTeague* (1899) that it has on Gervaise and Coupeau in *L'Assommoir*, and it brings to the surface the same homicidal tendencies that we see in Jacques Lantier in *La Bête Humaine*. What we see in Norris is the biology of greed, a desire for money and gold so extreme that it can create an illusionary reality and a pathology of murder. A degenerative process is latent in both the individual and the environment. But once degeneration begins, the social and individual components reinforce each other, speeding moral and physical decline.

Norris was not content to depict the pathology of naturalism. By March of 1899, in a letter to William Dean Howells, Norris described his idea for an "epic trilogy" dealing with wheat—its production (*The Octopus*, 1901), distribution (*The Pit*, 1902), and consumption (the never-completed *The Wolf*). Like Zola, Norris wanted to write a series of nov-

---

1. There have been many attempts to link French and American literary naturalism. See Ahnebrink, *The Beginning of Naturalism in American Fiction;* see also Biencourt. Ahnebrink also includes a study of Zola's influence on Frank Norris in *Essays and Studies on American Language and Literature.* Another critic who sees a direct connection between French and other kinds of naturalism is George J. Becker; see *Realism in Modern Literature.* Such a reading brought about a diverse reaction from a number of American critics who stressed the indigenous nature of American literary naturalism, such as Charles Child Walcutt, Donald Pizer (*Realism and Naturalism in Nineteenth-Century America*), and William Dillingham. Walcutt believed that American naturalism was influenced by transcendentalism; Pizer saw it more as a by-product of American realism. Both Pizer and Walcutt stressed the formal aspects of naturalism, as did Dillingham. More recently, there has been a movement back to the idea of literary naturalism as an international movement. See Chevrel and Baguley. In a 1984 essay ("American Literary Naturalism"), I tried to reconnect American and French literary naturalism by showing how they shared the same narrative mode.

els describing the economic forces that were changing society's base from agrarian to urban. He also wanted to work out his idea of the West—his belief that the direction of modern civilization, with some starts and stops, had been moving along a western frontier, jumping the Atlantic after the Crusades, progressing across the American continent, and then jumping across the Pacific after the American West was settled. Dewey's exploits at Manila and the landing of United States Marines in China during the Boxer Rebellion in 1900 were significant events in the documentation of this thesis (Norris, "The Frontier Gone at Last," 71, 74, 77), which Norris restates in *The Octopus* (227–28). Reversing the process, his trilogy would begin at the present cutting edge of the frontier (California), move eastward to the commodity markets where wheat was bought and sold speculatively (Chicago), and end where the movement westward originally began (Europe). What Norris wanted to show was how modern capitalism had created a world city: how economic events thousands of miles removed from each other had life-threatening consequences for markets all over the world. Thus in *The Octopus,* he describes the telegraph lines that connect the ranchers

by wire with San Francisco, and through that city with Minneapolis, Duluth, Chicago, New York, and at last the most important of all, with Liverpool. . . . The ranch became merely the part of an enormous whole, a unit in the vast agglomeration of wheat land the whole world round, feeling the effects of causes thousands of miles distant—a drought on the prairies of Dakota, a rain on the plains of India, a frost on the Russian steppes, a hot wind on the llanos of the Argentine. (44)

Norris's unfinished trilogy telling the story of wheat was his attempt to show how the newly fashioned world city was based on the principles of biology. While his sympathies in *The Octopus* were clearly against the railroad and with the ranchers, he showed how the ranchers were also corrupted by money, how they were exploiting the land for immediate gain, and how they were also leaving a legacy of greed, of bribery, and of deceit. There were no innocents in this economic process—only the working of the wheat, embodying the great force of nature itself. What used to be a symbiotic relationship between city and countryside has broken down; the city feeds off the land, depleting resources without restoring them. Like Zola, Norris depicted the movement away from the land to the city—the wheat itself, now handled as an abstraction, being funneled through the city to markets all over the world. In his next novel, *The Pit,* Norris further develops this theme, convincingly showing Chicago as a center into and out of which energy flows: Chicago was a "force" that "turned the wheels of a harvester and seeder a thousand miles distant in Iowa and Kansas," the "heart of America," a force of empire that determined "how much the peasant [in Europe] shall pay for his loaf of bread" (*The Pit*, 62, 120). But as central as Chicago and wheat speculation are to Norris's story, the wheat is a force even greater than both. This is a world of physical bounds: when Jadwin tries to raise the price of wheat beyond its limit, the market breaks and he is a ruined man. Every person and every social institution has its limit, and even abstract matters like wheat speculation are governed by laws that ultimately come back to nature—back to the land, back to wheat, and ultimately back to the forces out of which life germinates, another theme Norris shared with Zola. Because the third volume remained unfinished, Norris never took his story to Europe where the consumption of wheat would be the final step in the cycle of life. But thematically a third volume was unnecessary: Norris had already shown how the growing and selling of wheat touches the lives of everyone, and he had clearly documented both the biological basis of economics and the process of degeneration that can occur when civilization loses touch with the rhythms of the land.

II

Like Norris, Theodore Dreiser felt that the workings of the city could not be divorced from natural processes. He came by this idea in the summer of 1894, an intellectual turning point in his life. At that time, as a reporter on the Pittsburgh *Dispatch*, he spent his free time in the public library reading Herbert Spencer (1820–1903) and Honoré de Balzac, an experience, he has told us, that "quite blew me, intellectually, to bits" (*Book About Myself*, 457). It is hard to imagine Dreiser, with only a semester of college and no formal training in philosophy, reading Spencer in any sophisticated way. But Dreiser made great use of Spencer—first in his philosophical essays in "The Prophet," and later in *Sister Carrie* (1900). Spencer's philosophy is a combination of nineteenth-century mechanistic and romantic beliefs. Like Thomas Hobbes, Spencer believed that we live in a world composed of matter in motion, the natural process of which is repeatable and hence describable in scientific, mechanical terms. Like the romantics, he also believed that nature symbolically reflected its inner meaning, so to read the universe was to read the unfolding of nature and to understand such correspondences as those between the human and the animal worlds.

The key to Spencer's philosophy was his belief in force: not a life force as in Bergson, where the impetus comes from within, but a force that manifested itself from without. We are surrounded by physical forces that limit our mental ability and our capacity to act without restraint. As we become more powerful agents of force ourselves, we can widen those limits and move beyond previous physical restraints—up to a point, which Spencer awkwardly called the point of "equilibration" and Dreiser the "equation inevitable." Once this unbreachable limit is reached, there is momentary stasis followed by a reversal in the flow of matter and a process of dissolution. But while each individual follows a cyclical pattern (birth and growth leading toward development and maturity, followed eventually by physical and mental decline leading toward death), the race is fated to move onward and upward.

The idea of cycles within the march of time was central to Spencer's belief in evolution: humanity could advance even while the individual was circumscribed within physical limits. All matter was thus passing from homogeneity to heterogeneity—that is, from the more simple toward the more complex; once the point of equilibration is reached, dissolution and new forms of homogeneity follow, as the cycle repeats itself. Such evolution also occurs in society, which is an organic unit subject to undirected physical or man-made forces (Spencer, 226). Spencer saw humanity as moving away from slave and military societies characterized by uniformity (homogeneity) toward industrial societies characterized by varied skills (heterogeneity) and specialization. Yet even in industrial societies we cannot escape our essential relationship to nature. We are all affected by such primary events as harvests and droughts: a bad wheat crop affects every member of a society, from farmers to dwellers in gigantic cities. As in nature, the fittest will survive (a Spencerian idea often attributed to Darwin). Spencer was not a man of sentiment: that creatures insufficiently adaptable are eliminated is simply the law of nature.

Spencer's *First Principles* serves as a key to understanding Dreiser's first novel, *Sister Carrie*. It is an exercise in the principle of matter in motion—Carrie illustrating the move toward completion; Drouet, a form of stasis or equilibrium; and Hurstwood, a process of dissolution. The main force at work in the novel is that of the city, seen first in a less complex form (Chicago), and then in a more complex, heterogeneous form (New York). Dreiser's city is most vivid at night, when its lights, like the light of the sun, suggest a kind of inner energy. The city is commonly described as a magnet, possessing a compelling attraction that draws people to it with pulsating energy. Urban crowds are matter in motion, sweeping onward, like the sea, through space and time. Nor is the city unaffected by natural forces; the pull of the sun and the moon, which creates the tides of the sea, marks the rhythm of the flux of the crowd, as well as Carrie and later Hurstwood rocking in their rocking chairs.

All of the novel's characters are caught in an urban materialism: the self is defined externally. Take away Drouet's clothes and, as Dreiser writes, "he was nothing" (*Sister Carrie,* 72–73); so too with Hurstwood's managerial position, and Carrie's connection with the theater. Carrie is able to enlarge her circumference of being, as Hurstwood's gets smaller and smaller, leaving him little room to operate and finally no choices. As a heliotrope turns toward the sun, so all of Dreiser's characters turn to the lights of the city; within the city they are moved to material desires that they cannot resist. As the sun heats the land and creates the convectional winds that condense vapor to clouds—the clouds changing to rain, the rain to wetted land, the land to harvested crops, and the crops to sustained life—so the city is an energy source, creating the institutions (the sweatshops in which Carrie first works) that bring forth material goods (the clothes and the trinkets she desires) and the social play (life in the theater, the hotels, the restaurants) that she finds compelling. And just as the planets cannot go beyond the limits set by their solar system, Dreiser's characters cannot go beyond the limits set by money: Carrie's rise and Hurstwood's fall are both measured by their changing incomes. The meaning of one scene in the novel becomes the motives for the next: a cause–effect–cause progression. Thus, like Spencer's, Dreiser's world is one of physical limits—a world in which the self constantly tests such limits, a universe held in a process of expansion and contraction, which establishes the physical realm beyond which the individual, the crowd, the city, and even the world cannot go.

III

Dreiser's narrative view of the city corresponds to the theories of a group of urban historians who were also interested in how physical laws applied to social phenomenon. Robert E. Park maintained that the city was externally organized in terms of laws of its own. His colleague Ernest W. Burgess illustrated this point when he insisted that the city grows in concentric rings—spreading out from the central business area to an area of poor housing and low rents, a slum; to the working-class area, which will become the next slum; to a residential area of high-class apartments; and finally to a commuter zone, a suburban area, or satellite sites within thirty to sixty minutes of the central business area.[2]

Both Dreiser and Park and his school drew from nineteenth-century positivistic thought as they approached the city, and everything in *Sister Carrie* can be accounted for in such terms. Chicago is a series of concentric circles with the business area in the center, surrounded by factories, where Carrie works; surrounded by cheap homes for the workers, where she lives with the Hansons; surrounded by more expensive apartments, where she lives with Drouet. Beyond these are the richest homes, at which Carrie marvels, and finally the suburbs, where Hurstwood lives with his ungrateful family. In the tradition of Balzac, Dreiser saw the city as a magnet luring young men and women from the provinces because only there could they realize the fullest sense of self. He begins the novel with this point: "To the child, the genius with imagination...the approach to a great city for the first time is a wonderful thing. Particularly if it be evening....Ah, the promise of the night" (*Sister Carrie,* 7). Within the confines of the city, Carrie's role is purely mechanistic; she is matter controlled by principles of physical laws. We live within material confines and the imbalances created by such limits: on the physical level, heat exists only where there is also cold; on the social level, wealth exists only where there is also poverty. The force with which the pendulum moves in one direction determines the force of the return swing: what goes up in Dreiser's world produces what comes down.

These assumptions set the terms of the strict causal sequence that takes Carrie to the New York Waldorf and Hurstwood to Potter's Field: reverse any one scene in *Sister Carrie* and the action stops. If Carrie had met Hurstwood and not Drouet on the train from Columbia City to Chicago, there would have been no story. Nor would there have been a story if she had not met Drouet after she lost her factory job and was on the verge of being sent home by the Hansons; nor if she had not been

---

2. Followers of Park and Burgess (Nels Anderson, Walter Reckless, F. M. Thrasher, H. W. Zarbaugh, Louis Wirth) have written books on each of these areas, describing the physical laws at work in different zones.

disillusioned with Drouet at the moment she met Hurstwood; nor if Hurstwood had not been feeling threatened by his wife when he met Carrie. Each scene supplies the cause for the next effect, taking the characters in spiraling circles (one of the key images of the novel) beyond themselves as they move from Chicago to New York, a larger city where the laws work with even greater force, taking Carrie higher than she could go in Chicago and Hurstwood to the lowest urban depths. Since the city takes its being from the production and consumption of goods, the people who make up the city are subject to the laws of production and consumption, both in the factories (production) in Chicago and the lavish shops (consumption) in New York. Dreiser set the New York scenes in 1894, a depression year that reveals the harsh reality of capitalism at work. All of Dreiser's characters participate in a larger process. He believed that for every Carrie living in luxury and elegance, there was a Hurstwood sleeping in a flophouse or worse. He told the story of people whose lives cannot be separated from an urban context, the laws of which he believed in as faithfully as did the most deterministic urban historian.

IV

All of the major characters in *Sister Carrie* come to the city, usually on a train. The city, which has become more and more like a machine, is even accessed by one: this blurs where the machine begins and ends in the industrial city. Dreiser begins *Sister Carrie* with Carrie Meeber coming into Chicago from Columbia City (Green Bay, Wisconsin, in the holograph) on the train where she meets Drouet. In the middle of the novel, Carrie is on another train—this time with Hurstwood, who is taking her to Montreal and later to New York. At the end of the novel, Mrs. Hurstwood and her family also come into New York on a train. In the tradition of the Balzac novel, the city reaches out its iron rails and entices the pilgrim to a realm of desire that only it can offer and probably never fulfill.

Robert Ames tells Carrie to read Balzac (in one of the last scenes she is reading *Père Goriot*), especially *The Great Man from the Provinces* sequence. His choice is highly appropriate, for Dreiser's novel falls into the same subgenre, a narrative formula also used by many nineteenth-century novelists, such as Dickens in *Great Expectations*. The young-man-from-the-provinces novel involves a predictable sequence of events. First, the provinces or the estate is played out, and the city is where the young must go in order to realize a romantic sense of self, an essential being. Urban flight in turn causes a break with the family, whose residual values the hero takes to the city, where he or she learns that they must be abandoned. Love and friendship prove insubstantial in a place where almost everything turns on money and where personal relationships are inseparable from commodity relationships. The city is so much larger than the individual that the human scale is lost—as are its values—and the hero spends much of the novel trying to reinvest energy in a system that is both a compelling lure and trap. Such novels often address the need to find an alternative set of human values, but attempts to redeem the city usually are unsuccessful; the main character typically is left confronting the city, after becoming experienced, wary, and disillusioned.

Dreiser employs this narrative pattern in the naturalistic mode rather than the mode of comic realism of Balzac or Dickens. As a result, there are radical differences between novels like *Sister Carrie* and *Lost Illusions*. First, Dreiser pays little attention to the reason Carrie leaves her family to go to the city: it is assumed that the city is where someone with her disposition and temperament would go. There is hardly a reference to Carrie's mother in any draft of the novel, and her father appears only as a thought as her train passes the flour plant in which he works as a laborer. Carrie will live with her sister and her sister's husband in Chicago, so the novel does not begin with a total break from the family. But the Hansons are such dour people—both gloomy and unyielding— that Carrie soon understands that she cannot have the kind of life she has dreamed about with them.

Carrie soon discovers that almost every relationship she incurs is connected with money. She quickly realizes that the Hansons have invited her to live with them because they expect to use the bulk of her pay for their household expenses and to increase payments on the land they have bought. Her first experience of the city is her job in a shoe factory, where she works a machine on an assembly line from 8 to 6, with a half hour for lunch, for $4.50 a week—a nine-and-a-half-hour workday for a little over seventy cents a day. (There is about a forty-to-one difference between the value of the dollar in 1890 and today; so Carrie would be working for less than $30 a day in current terms.) Given the weight that money has in this world, Drouet's offer of twenty dollars is an immense amount (the equivalent of about $800 today), a sum worth over a month's salary. To analyze relationships between characters in these terms catches both the spirit and the method of Dreiser's technique: almost everything is quantified, and usually in monetary terms. It is not accidental, for example, that when Carrie leaves Hurstwood, she will also leave him twenty dollars, the same sum that Drouet gave to her. Everything, including love and friendship, has a price in this novel.

V

The city formed Carrie, acting as a catalyst to bring out elements dormant in her personality. She came to the city in pursuit of a self that was waiting to be born. In *The Social History of Art* (1951), Arnold Hauser describes "the inner strife of the romantic soul [that] is reflected nowhere so directly and expressively as in the figure of the 'second self'" (181). The second self involves the self as unknown, as an uncannily remote stranger, as romantic possibility. Dreiser's characters move compulsively toward this sense of romantic possibility at the same time as they are restrained by their own physical limits. With hidden acting talent, and hence mobility, Carrie has a larger, unknown self, not shared by Drouet and Hurstwood. This hidden self has capabilities that she was unaware of in Columbia City and that she discovers only when she goes on the stage as an amateur actress in Chicago. All kinds of mysteries lie buried in the city, including the mystery of the inner self. Carrie is energized by the city and its mechanical extensions, intuits the power of the train, feels its flow embodied in the crowds that she watches from Hanson's doorstep as well as in public spaces (avenues, parks, restaurants, hotels), and is aware that it is creating in her a larger sense of self. Ames encourages her to take this sense of self as far as her abilities allow. But her abilities have limits—just as the novel graphically shows Hurstwood's limits—and at some point Carrie's expanding desire will give way to frustration, a point the novel treats in the coda.

The connections among Carrie, the stage, and the city have not always been fully understood. In an otherwise extremely rich reading of the novel, Philip Fisher argues that Carrie's acting involves a limitless potentiality of self, as vast as the city itself: "Dreiser is the first novelist to base his entire sense of the self on the dramatic possibilities inherent in a dynamic society.... To some extent acting in *Sister Carrie* always serves to preserve a freedom of the self from its appearance, and it is to that degree that it records a higher version of the possible or prospective self in defiance of the momentary 'role' or 'part' that it is compelled to play and be recognized in" (167). Fisher moves us toward a postmodern reading of a naturalistic novel. Like a new historicist, he textualizes history, seeing all aspects of culture—legal, artistic, behavioral—as forms of representation to be read like fiction.[3] Carrie on the stage and Carrie on the street become manifestations of one and the same experience. And there are elements in the novel that support Fisher's reading. Dreiser stresses the connection between the stage and the city. When Drouet takes her into a restaurant to buy a sumptuous meal, they sit by a window and watch the crowd flow by as if the city were a stage. Hurstwood repeats this scene at the end of the novel when he also looks out the large window of a New York hotel at the panorama of the city. And when Carrie walks down Broadway, she feels that she is part of a larger theater: "Such feelings as were generated in Carrie by this walk put her in an exceedingly receptive mood for the pathos which followed in the play" (*Sister Carrie*, 227).

But the play forces Carrie to look within herself, the restaurant window outside herself. To be sure, the two experiences can reinforce each other—the city does intensify personal feelings—but they are not identical, as Hurstwood realizes when he is pulled off the streetcar by the angry mob of strikers. He is drawn into an energy outside of himself, a force like that of a roiling sea, while Carrie must draw upon emotions within herself, which is not quite the same process as inventing a second self. Carrie effectively portrays Laura because she empathizes with Laura's plight. If she is to grow as an actress, she must—as Ames tells her—re-create experience in her imagination, live vicariously. The city has its own physical laws, but Carrie is not subject to them in the same way when she is onstage. Carrie is energized, Hurstwood exhausted by the city; Carrie is an actress, but Hurstwood's role in the city is no less dramatic in the literary sense than Carrie's. To go beyond herself, Carrie must distance herself from the physical city and make its drama a state of mind. It is when the city is internalized that its force is most powerfully felt. The city and the stage come together: the play gives meaning to the

---

3. Other recent books that attempt to read Dreiser without invoking literary naturalism are Walter Benn Michaels, *The Gold Standard and the Logic of Naturalism* (1987); June Howard, *Form and History in American Literary Naturalism* (1985); and Lee Clark Mitchell, *Determined Fictions* (1989). Postmodern readings often create a tropological, idealized, synchronic, formal language system to read mechanistic, causally structured, diachronic, empirically grounded texts. This creates an incongruity between literary text and critical method, collapsing one narrative mode with great confusion into another.

city, Carrie gives meaning to the play, and *Sister Carrie* gives meaning to all three—the city, the play, and Carrie.

That there is more to know about the city, that there are higher planes of artistic reality than the Broadway stage—this is the lesson toward which Ames points Carrie. Ames, like Inspector Bucket or Inspector Heat in Dickens or Conrad, functions to humanize the city. In an early draft of the novel, Ames calls Carrie's attention to conspicuous consumption at Sherry's and points out how many people lead inauthentic lives by displaying themselves as a commodity. (Later the novel will show Mrs. Hurstwood "displaying" Jessica.) If the city instills desire, then Carrie will be subject to that desire so long as she is part of that environment. As the coda of the novel reveals, such desire will never be satisfied; the logic of the city is to excite and stimulate, to postulate a realm of simultaneous and contradictory compelling possibilities.

But Ames believes such materialism can be softened with discernment, with taste. Dreiser's city is most often characterized by its lights, which brighten the night: Ames, the electrical engineer, has invented a new kind of electric light, a new mode of illumination. Hence Ames adds to the city lights at the same time as he metaphorically illuminates the world for Carrie, giving her the means to see. In stark contrast, when Hurstwood commits suicide, he does so at night, in a room without a window, giving himself to the "kindness" of the night; the energy drained from him was not replenished. The night here embodies the other side of the city's energy, the motion that has taken Hurstwood full cycle back toward dissolution and decay. The resulting failure is the consequence of negative entropy: like a cold, dead satellite, Hurstwood can no longer be warmed by the urban sun.

Carrie and Hurstwood are unaware of the processes they enact. Dreiser uses characters who are inseparable from the evolutionary process, subject to the forces of their environment, and unconscious of the gestalt that holds this process together. They live in an evolutionary halfway house—no longer the products of pure animal instinct, they also lack fully developed reason. In some ways, they embody the worst in the evolutionary process. *Sister Carrie* depends on a philosophical observer—a kind of Herbert Spencer telling a Balzacian story about life in urban America at the end of the nineteenth century. In the tradition of Balzac and Zola, Dreiser subjects his characters to the physical impulses of the city: their existence is circumscribed by its reality, urban and personal motives as one.

CHAPTER 13

Urban Destiny

I

In *The Great Gatsby* (1925), F. Scott Fitzgerald was working with many important subtexts, perhaps most importantly the fate of
Enlightenment optimism and Enlightenment man. As we have seen, the
breakdown of the feudal world caused birthrights to give way to natural
rights, which is another way of saying that a new kind of person was free
to be invented. Almost simultaneously with this radical change, the
American continent invited the adventurous to a new world, where was
spawned a new nation based on a heightened sense of self and an open
frontier. When the frontier was closed, a dimension of self—as well as of
place—was lost. The frontier's movement, of course, was east to west,
but it was accompanied by a major cultural change caused by movement
in the other direction, as wealth moved from the land (the West) to the
city (the East). With its primary function to process wealth, such a city
gave rise to social institutions, class hierarchies, and role stratification
that only loosely existed on the frontier.

A young man like Gatsby came to the city to realize his heightened
sense of self; the city of Tom Buchanan and Meyer Wolfsheim, not the
frontier world of Dan Cody and James J. Hill, was the new arena in the
battle for success. Gatsby never understood this important cultural
change—but Fitzgerald did. Gatsby's sense of romantic purpose might
have prevailed on the frontier, but it lacked urban sophistication: the
lure of the city was for him also a complex trap. Fitzgerald saw in the

passing of Gatsby the end of romantic readiness, a sense of unlimited potential. Just as the sense of wonder of the first sailors who saw the American shore was lost when the continent was settled, so the hope of attaining an object commensurate with romantic promise had been lost with the closing of the frontier and the end of the Jeffersonian vision, and with the corresponding rise of the new city and triumph of the Hamiltonian view. *The Great Gatsby* is thus much more than a novel about the last of the romantics; it is also a novel about America—the state of mind, concept of self, and realm of possibility that made America possible.

The allusions and narrative meaning built into *The Great Gatsby* recapitulate the history of the American frontier, which was rendered mythic in the popular genre of the western long after it was a lived experience. That history was told in a still different and highly influential form by Frederick Jackson Turner, who argued in 1893—based on his analysis of the 1890 census reports—that the frontier was already closed. Trained at Johns Hopkins University, teaching at the University of Wisconsin (his native state), he challenged the prevailing notion of history, which located historical meaning in political and economic institutions and saw the development of America as an extension of European ideas, brought to and then institutionalized in the East, whence they spread through the country. Turner defined the frontier as that realm that "lies at the hither edge of free land. In the census report it is treated as the margin of that settlement which has a density of two or more to the square mile" (Turner, 2): it provided an escape hatch and a way of assimilating, settling, and defining America—an argument that is contested today. The colonist became part of a new species when he entered the frontier. "The wilderness master[ed] the colonist," Turner claimed. As the settler's European trappings were stripped from him, so also were "the garments of civilization." He found himself in hunting shirt, moccasins, and log cabin, planting Indian corn and plowing with a sharp stick. He was transformed by the frontier before he transformed it. The outcome was "not the old Europe.... The fact is, that here is a new product that is American" (2). In short, America became the end product of the frontier: "It was the nationalizing tendency of the West that transformed the democracy of Jefferson into the national republicanism of Monroe and the democracy of Andrew Jackson" (14).

For Turner, the frontier embodied that sense of wonder which is inseparable from America. With it came a new sense of hope, an engendering of desire; expectation was more important than actual fulfillment.

The romantic emotion Nick Carraway calls up at the end of Fitzgerald's novel is different only in rhetorical intensity from the passion Turner expresses at the end of his famous essay:

Since the days when the fleet of Columbus sailed into the waters of the New World, America has been another name for opportunity, and the people of the United States have taken their tone from the incessant expansion that has not only been open but has been forced upon them.... [N]ever again will such gifts of free land offer themselves. For a moment, at the frontier, the bonds of custom are broken and unrestraint is triumphant.... And now, four centuries from the discovery of America, at the end of a hundred years of life under the Constitution, the frontier has gone, and with its going has closed the first period of American History. (18)

Like Nick, Turner locates an idealized America in the dead Jeffersonian past. With the end of the frontier, the city became the new nexus of power. The ending of *The Great Gatsby* registers each of these ideas. Nick tells us that Gatsby's dream is dead, that it "was already behind him ... in that vast obscurity beyond the city"—that is, "before" the rise of the city and "beyond" it in the frontier. There "the dark fields of the republic"—that is, the lost hope of Jefferson—"rolled on under the night" (*Gatsby*, 182). In different ways, both Turner and Fitzgerald were suggesting that with the end of the frontier—and with the rise of the new city—the dynamics of progressive history were shifting along sectional lines, particularly those of East and West. And it is precisely to this point that Nick returns in the last pages of the novel, when he deliberately and effectively contrasts what the East and the West now mean to him. Like Turner, he finds the provincialism of the West reassuring, while the anonymity of the East is deeply disturbing.[1]

Like T. S. Eliot, Fitzgerald looked back to an idealized moment, now lost in time. For Eliot, that was seventeenth-century London; for Fitzgerald, the America of the new republic. But such a return is more illusory in Fitzgerald than in Eliot. Fitzgerald is less intent on recapturing an original innocence than on seeing when and why the promise of America was betrayed. That moment came during the Civil War when Jefferson's vision gave way to that of Hamilton, a major theme in Fitz-

---

1. The Turner thesis would have been reinforced for Fitzgerald by Van Wyck Brooks's *The Ordeal of Mark Twain*, published in 1922, just before he began writing *Gatsby*. Brooks argued that the robust sense of reality that Twain had brought from the West was gentrified under the influence of Twain's wife and people like William Dean Howells. A spirit of rugged individualism had moved to the West, had conquered the land, and then had been transformed by genteel money in the East.

gerald's fiction; the agrarian hope is absorbed by industry and by the financial institutions that industry brought into being. Such institutions give birth to the Tom Buchanans and their world of privileged money. (In *The Beautiful and Damned,* this theme is carried by Anthony Patch; in "The Diamond as Big as the Ritz," by the Washington family; and in *Tender Is the Night,* by the Warren family.)

The city plays an immensely important role in *The Great Gatsby* because it marks the last link in a historical process from feudalism to modernism. Enlightenment natural rights replaced feudal birthrights, only to be subsumed by the privileges and advantages of wealth. We move from Crusoe, to Benjamin Franklin–Thomas Jefferson, to Daniel Boone–James J. Hill–Buffalo Bill Cody, to John D. Rockefeller–Jay Gould. We move variously from a world of peasantry to the bourgeoisie, from explorers to pioneers, from feudal faith to Enlightenment optimism, from landed aristocracy to robber baron, from frontier village to modern megalopolis—from one power structure to another. And presiding over the last is Tom Buchanan. The novel says all of this both directly and indirectly, with references to Franklin, Boone, Cody, and Rockefeller, as well as to the pastoral origins of the city. (The original owner of Tom's mansion is named Demaine or "tomorrow," suggesting that the future is Tom's; the former owner of Gatsby's mansion could not get the townspeople to thatch their roofs and behave like peasants.)

The center of gravity was now in the East, especially New York. Gatsby comes East to stake out his fortune in the dens of the underworld. Nick's motives are quite different, as he walks the streets of New York trying to unlock the mystery of the city: he comes to understand that such a world feeds on the labor and energy of others, like the Wilsons, that the city both attracts and destroys, and that the lonely clerks in the empty evening streets are all young romantics with tenuous dreams. The image, like many in *The Great Gatsby,* is derived from *The Waste Land,* and Fitzgerald's novel ends with the narrative equivalent of Eliot's Unreal City. Like Eliot's Tiresias, Nick finds his physical vision blurring as his inner vision becomes more acute. Fitzgerald's romantic world unfolds with blindness toward violence and the grotesque.

Fitzgerald's city looks simultaneously back to the frontier of Frederick Jackson Turner and to the wasteland of T. S. Eliot. Eliot depicted postwar Europe experiencing radical change: cities like London, Paris, Brussels, Berlin, and Vienna had been weakened from within as imperial boundaries were extended, until one empire after another disintegrated—the fall of the Hapsburgs anticipating the end of imperial Great

Britain. In London the rich had nerves on end; middle-class housewives were trapped in sterile and purposeless lives; and lower-class clerks sought gratification, no matter how mechanical or unfulfilling. Like Henry Adams, Eliot believed that societies needed mythic meaning to give them both center and direction; material pursuits and an obsession with profit were destructive. In the post-Enlightenment world of science and technology, an earlier spiritual and primitive vitality was exhausted.[2] Gatsby cannot function outside these imperatives, nor can he sustain the religious conception of self (that he is a son of God, even if that God is his own imagination) that Fitzgerald originally brought to the novel. The creation of an "aesthetic" self relies on urban accommodation.

A sense of romantic exhaustion was inseparable from the postwar sense of world weariness that appears in both the story that Nick Carraway tells in *Gatsby* and the story Tiresias tells in *The Waste Land*. As we have seen, Eliot drew on a host of books that addressed cultural decline: Nordau's *Degeneration,* Adams's *Education,* Herman Hesse's *Blick ins Chaos,* and Oswald Spengler's *The Decline of the West*. Nordau, Adams, and Hesse all reinforced Spengler's pronouncements, and his most famous work provided Fitzgerald and Eliot with common ground. The religious and romantic intensity that they felt slipping away, Spengler saw embodied in Faustian man.

II

The argument in *The Decline of the West* (1918–22) comes to us coated in a heavy German romanticism that owes much to Goethe's theory of *Urphänomen*—the belief in cultural morphology (that forms adhere to rules of development)—and to Nietzsche's idea of "eternal recurrence." Like many romantics, Spengler was trying to escape

---

2. In *The Medievalist Impulse in American Literature,* Kim Ileen Moreland discusses Fitzgerald in the context of Mark Twain and Henry Adams (also Hemingway). Her argument is that these authors turn to the Middle Ages (perhaps Hemingway less so) out of an intellectual nostalgia for a different reality. This is true to a point, but central to this issue is first their disillusionment with the Enlightenment, especially the new commercialism and the vast materialism that made inroads upon the aristocratic mind. It was the loss of the "old courtesies" that drove Adams and Fitzgerald back beyond the Enlightenment to a nostalgia for the Middle Ages and a lost aristocracy—to a realm that no longer had palpability, serving best as a mirage, as Fitzgerald suggests at the end of *Gatsby:* "So we beat on, boats against the current, borne back ceaselessly into the past" (182).

the influence of the Enlightenment, especially the Enlightenment insistence on mechanism and causality. In their place, he substituted biological connections: he found the history of a culture analogous to the growth, maturity, and decay of a plant. For Spengler, maturation gave way to decline when a Culture gave way to a Civilization. Each culture takes its being from the land, from the countryside, from the village and town. Like a plant, it draws sustenance from its roots—from the soil that nourishes it. As it grows it transforms and is transformed: nature yields to artifice; the town gives way to the city. Spengler saw the rise of an urban center as marking the turning point for every culture:

World-city and province—the two basic ideas of every civilization—bring up a wholly new form-problem of History, the very problem we are living through today. . . . In place of a world, there is a *city, a point,* in which the whole life of broad regions is collecting while the rest dries up. In place of a type—true people, born of and grown on the soil, there is a sort of nomad, cohering unstably in fluid masses, the parasitical city, traditionless, utterly matter-of-fact, regionless. (Spengler, I, 32)

Elsewhere Spengler intensified his idea: "Beat and tension, blood and intellect, Destiny and Causality are to one another as the country-side in bloom is to the city of stone, as something existing per se to something existing dependently" (II, 102). Much in Spengler appealed directly to Fitzgerald's personal sense of mental and physical instability, of dissipation and weariness. Such a state of mind was reinforced by the sense that a culture had played out an essential element of history on the battlefields of World War I and that the German economy was on the verge of economic depression.

The Decline of the West begins and ends with an organic theory of society. Each culture follows a biological pattern of growth and decline, vitality (stemming from the land) and decadence (spreading from the city). As one moves away from the natural rhythms of the land, instinct is replaced by reason, nature and myth by scientific theory, and a natural marketplace (barter and exchange) by abstract theories of money. As Spengler put it: "Intelligence is the replacement of unconscious living by exercise in thought, masterly, but bloodless and jejune. . . . Hence . . . the substitution of scientific theory, the causal myth, for the religious. Hence, too, money-in-the-abstract as the pure causality of economic life, in contrast to rustic barter, which is pulsation and not a system of tensions." He ends this discussion by noting "the sterility of civilized man" (II, 103).

Spengler discussed three cultures that had experienced growth and decay: the classical or Apollonian; the Mediterranean or Magian; and the medieval or Faustian. Each culture was independent of the other; their histories were similar because of a common process at work, not a causal connection. Apollonian man was generally self-satisfied; conceived of himself as living in a local, finite space, in a tangible present; lived on the human scale, as represented by the life-size nude statue and the small-columned temple; limited political life to the city-state; and burned rather than buried his dead to remove the body from eternity. Magian or Arabian man was torn between forces of good and evil; viewed the world mysteriously, as a cave in which light fought against darkness; and expressed himself with interior-oriented architecture and a religion that was magical and dualistic.

Faustian man longed for the unattainable and had no sense of his limits. His imagination, like his Gothic cathedrals, soared to encompass the idea of infinity; his paintings made use of distant perspectives, his music the expansive form of the fugue; his adventurers were long-distance sailors and explorers; and his modern heirs tried to conquer space or create vast empires. When Faustian man lingered into the modern age, he was transformed by the Enlightenment, which brought with it empiricism and the need for quantitative measurement: the sense of the infinite gave way to cold reason, science, and technology. Man, no longer at one with the land, moved to the new money-centered city. The rise of a new breed of money brokers turned the old world destructively upside down: Faustian man became Enlightenment man; the priest-king became the new Caesar, the man of money and power; a primitive sense of race was lost in the decay of civilization.

All of these Spenglerian ideas infuse *The Great Gatsby,* giving special meaning to Fitzgerald's declaration to Maxwell Perkins, "I read [Spengler] the summer I was writing *The Great Gatsby,* and I don't think I ever recovered from him" (*Letters,* 289).[3] Fitzgerald further documented his interest in Spengler's view of culture in an interview he gave the New York *World* (see the issue of April 23, 1927). While he does not belabor

3. Robert Sklar has questioned Fitzgerald's claim to knowledge of Spengler. The *Decline* was published in 1918 (vol. 1) and 1922 (vol. 2), Fitzgerald did not read German, and there were no English translations until after *Gatsby* was written. But there were over nine commentaries on Spengler's work prior to the publication of *Gatsby,* including an 8,000-word essay by W. K. Steward in *Century* magazine—a periodical that Fitzgerald often read—which appeared in the summer of 1924, exactly when Fitzgerald said he was reading Spengler.

the point, *Gatsby* clearly shows how an artificial, urban world has replaced a natural landscape. The valley of ashes, for example, is a "fantastic farm" that brought forth ashes, which "grow like wheat into ridges and hills"; nature has given way to "grotesque gardens; where ashes take the forms of houses and chimneys" (*Gatsby*, 15). The process of nature has been inverted—distorted—as Spengler maintained happened when the city transformed the countryside. Beneath the city street lay a lost world implied by Fitzgerald's description of Fifth Avenue as "so warm and soft, almost pastoral, on the summer Sunday afternoon that I wouldn't have been surprised to see a great flock of white sheep turn the corner" (18).

That the city takes its being from money is one of the main themes of the novel. Money ultimately differentiates Tom Buchanan and Gatsby as characters, and explains why Nick Carraway describes New York as "the city rising up across the river in white heaps and sugar lumps all built with a wish out of non-olfactory money" (45).[4] Gatsby never understands the meaning of Nick's words; never realizes that there are different kinds of money—East Egg or established money, for example, as opposed to West Egg or new riches; never comes to see how his connection with the crooked bucket shops contrasts with Tom Buchanan's brokerage houses; and never understands why Meyer Wolfsheim's world of Broadway pool halls cannot lead to the Long Island world of polo ponies and private clubs. The novel moves to the moment when these truths unfold—to the scene in the Plaza Hotel that hot afternoon when Tom plays his trump card by revealing to Daisy the source of Gatsby's money.

What Gatsby created was never consistent within its own terms—nor was it compatible within the meaning of the America being transformed by the new city. Modeling himself on Dan Cody, who combines the history of the wilderness and frontier—Daniel Boone first enters the wilderness, and Buffalo Bill Cody turns the frontier experience into a commercial Wild West show—Gatsby brought a frontier spirit to an unaccommodating city. In a premarket economy, money follows power; in a market economy, power follows money—and in the world market economy of New York, the established money of Tom Buchanan, with his Yale and high-society connections, separated Tom from Gatsby, with his Meyer Wolfsheim "gonnegtions," just as the bay separated West Egg

---

4. In Roman times, laundry soap was made from refining sewage. When Tiberius was asked how he felt about profiting from such an enterprise, he responded, "Money doesn't smell."

from East Egg. Understanding this, Nick saw in what ways Gatsby's imagination failed him when he entered an urban world that he never comprehended. Gatsby's supposed Oxford background remains at odds with his pink suits and silver ties, just as the stories he tells of his past are full of contradictions. Nick smiles inwardly when Gatsby tells him that he comes from a wealthy Midwest family in San Francisco, and that he had lived "like a rajah in all the capitals of Europe—Paris, Venice, Rome—collecting jewels, chiefly rubies, [and] hunting big game" (43). Even in his imagination, Gatsby cannot reconcile the new city with his sense of romance, and that ungrounded imagination is the source of his larger failure. What Gatsby creates of himself belongs to a lost order, to the frontier of the past, a realm less circumscribed than the modern city. Like Faustian man, he has a fate connected with what Spengler called Destiny—that historical process that subjects citizenry and culture to national forces.

The rise of the machine and the demise of Faustian man were accompanied by a reversal in the human relationship with nature, from the time of the printed book to the steam engine. The machine separated humans from nature, transformed the landscape, helped create the modern city, and enlarged the scale on which people lived as life became less human. Dickens documented the psychic transformation that came with this enlarged scale, as did Fitzgerald when he shows Nick, like the flaneur, lonely in the city, dwarfed by gigantic buildings that overwhelm even as they evoke a sense of mysterious power. Although Nick, in the young-man-from-the-provinces tradition, is attracted by the power of the city, he also shares the "haunting loneliness" of poor young clerks at dusk (38).

By 1920, the Western world was more urban than rural. Spengler referred to the city as "*a point*" where energy collects, absorbing all around it, and this point is inseparable from money (I, 25–26). Spengler's theory glosses Fitzgerald's text. Tom is a broker; Nick has come to New York to study the business by working in a brokerage firm. Before Daisy appears at their fateful reunion, Gatsby reads from a book on economics, an appropriate way to spend time waiting for a woman whose voice is full of money. Gatsby and Tom Buchanan thus play out key Spenglerian ideas: Gatsby recapitulates the story of Faustian man, while Tom embodies the rise of the new, moneyed Caesar who has come to power after Enlightenment science has transformed the mind.

Once we see its Spenglerian nature, the novel takes on added meaning. As Spengler put it, "Race, Time, and Destiny belong together. But the moment scientific thought approaches them, the word 'Time' acquires the significance of a dimension, the word 'Destiny' that of causal connection, while Race . . . becomes an incomprehensible chaos of unconnected and heterogeneous characters that . . . interpenetrate without end and without law" (II, 131). This passage explains what might otherwise appear accidental and gratuitous in Tom's character: his need for "scientific" explanations. Not only is he unable to relate directly to the world of nature, he is also unable to relate directly to others outside his class and race. In fact, Tom feels so threatened by blacks that he has bought into a "scientific" theory of race according to which, as he says, "Civilization is going to pieces" (*Gatsby,* 9). The sense of racial disharmony, so evident in Tom, illustrates Spengler's view of what happens to a race when it is removed from its own soil and transplanted into another culture. "A race does not migrate," he tells us: "Men migrate, and their successive generations are born in ever-changing landscapes" (Spengler, II, 119). Eventually the land can transform the uprooted into a new culture, but such integration has not happened in post-Enlightenment America, where race has become "an incomprehensible chaos" (II, 131). The promise of the New World has given way to disharmony, both cultural and racial, which Fitzgerald links with the phenomenon of a Gatsby in the new city. Crossing the Queensboro Bridge in Gatsby's splendid car, Nick observes a funeral procession (here Fitzgerald juxtaposes the "wild promise" of the city with death) made up of immigrants from southeastern Europe "with tragic eyes and short upper lips," followed soon after by a limousine "driven by a white chauffeur, in which sat three modish negroes" (*Gatsby,* 45). The popularity of such books as Madison Grant's *The Passing of the Great Race* (1916) and Lothrop Stoddard's *The Rising Tide of Color* (1920)—racial attacks prompted by the large influx of immigrants[5]—led to restrictions set forth in the immigration acts of 1917, 1921, and 1924. "America must be kept American," insisted Calvin Coolidge when he signed the 1924 act that limited immigration to 150,000 people a year (Mowry and Brownell, 30).

As the new, moneyed Caesar, Tom not only replaces the Faustian Gatsby but is subject to the threat of the "rising tide of color" because, as Spengler would have it, contemporary Caesars, like the Roman Caesars, would eventually be overcome by the new barbarians. Spengler connected these conquerors with what today we would call the third world: emerging peoples who can employ modern technology, which they will eventually use against the Western world. At one point, Tom is

---

5. Between 1880 and 1920, over twenty million immigrants came to America.

described as if "he saw himself standing alone on the last barrier of civilization" (*Gatsby*, 130). Tom's racism is thus consistent with his dominant but vulnerable position in the Spenglerian scheme of history.

Civilizations break under the weight of urban chaos. Both Fitzgerald and Spengler believed that the movement from an agrarian to an industrial and urbanized realm could not be reversed and that modern man was in the last stage of a sealed fate, participating in a cruel destiny. Gatsby brings his great expectations to a city where his sense of the possible is a mirage. Fitzgerald located an impossible ideal in an exhausted past and, like Spengler, saw modern man as victim of a nostalgia for an old, untainted world that the modern city had rendered impossible.

These feelings come together once more in *Tender Is the Night* (1934), a novel in which Fitzgerald makes conscious use of its European setting: Switzerland ("the true center of the Western World," 115), the Riviera, Paris, and Rome. Fitzgerald depicts the breakup of the European aristocracy following World War I; the aristocracy is replaced by the Warren (war end?) family, whose money gives them control over others and makes them grand consumers. Trains crisscross the country carrying goods to satisfy Nicole's wants (*Tender*, 113). All of these elements have Spenglerian reference. In the ancient world, Greek culture gave way to Roman civilization; in that cycle, Pericles marked a historical beginning point, Alexander a turning point, and the rise of Julius Caesar and his followers a terminal point. Similarly, in modern history, Charlemagne marked a beginning point and Napoleon was a turning point in Western culture; his passing anticipates the coming of the new Caesars. In each case, the turning point is the passing of control from a landed aristocracy to an urban money center. In this context, the details of Fitzgerald's novel take on added significance. It is no accident that Dick's final decline takes place in Rome, against a backdrop of decadence (consider, for example, Baby Warren's experience with the ambassador who comes down the stairs with pink cold cream on his face, Dick's treatment at the hands of the police, and his argument with the taxi driver—appropriately enough, over money).

When Dick leaves Rome, he is a defeated man, and now Tommy Barban again enters the novel. When the new "barbarian" takes Nicole from Dick, a kind of literary archaeology is at work. There are numerous parallels to Spengler's description of the end of the Apollonian and Magian cycles: the new barbarian comes with the end of every civilization— Roman or Arabian, for example—and conquers the Mediterranean, where Fitzgerald's scene takes place. When Nicole abandons herself to

Tommy, she becomes passive in the face of a now-dominant male energy that turns the past order into anarchy.

Dick's decline, coming as it does in Rome, involves a superimposition of one period of time upon another—the modern upon the ancient. With the end of World War I, new Caesars began to rise in the money markets of London, Paris, Berlin, and New York. The battle of the Somme is "a love battle" for Dick because here the aristocracies of Europe went to war with themselves; the novel documents the helplessness of their postwar condition in the sanitarium in Switzerland as well as on the shores of the Mediterranean, where they most clearly reveal their mental decline and deracinated condition. The power of Europe is passing to a new-moneyed class represented by the Warrens, who have come out of the industrialized West, and to a new breed of exploiters, who have come out of the emerging countries of the East (Eliot comes to the same view of history in *The Waste Land*). That Tommy Barban has become a stockbroker is highly pertinent, as is Mary North's marriage to an Asian, newly rich with manganese money. The description of the Shah of Persia's car (*Tender,* 138) also reinforces this theme. As the West (Europe and later America) loses its vitality, a new threat to its barricades comes from the East: the fall of Rome anticipates the fall of London, Paris, and New York. Fitzgerald is working closely with Eliot's theme of falling towers: the Paris scenes in *Tender Is the Night* reveal the decadence of that city; the Anglophile Baby Warren testifies to the growing sterility of modern London (233–34); and Abe North's death in New York marks the beginning of an age of new brutality.

The fate of both Abe North and Dick Diver indicates that Fitzgerald did not limit his sense of decline to the capitals of Europe. In an earlier version of the novel, Abe North was named Abe Grant, stressing his connection to the fate of the industrialized, capitalistic North after the Civil War. The Civil War was a conflict between two radically different cultures, pitting a landed aristocracy against industrialized capitalism. In *A Connecticut Yankee in King Arthur's Court,* Mark Twain contrasts modern technology and medieval feudalism: in Europe, the contrast between the nineteenth and sixth centuries was a matter of time; in America, the contrast between North and South was a matter of cultural space. Spengler understandably had more to say about Europe than America in his discussion of decline; Fitzgerald filled in the gaps. In historical function, Grant paralleled Napoleon, and in 1865 just as in 1815 rising finance capitalism and new technology transformed the landscape; thus, by 1865, Paris and New York were systemically interchangeable.

III

In "My Lost City" (1932), Fitzgerald discussed how he projected success and failure onto New York and created two cities: the New York of his prep school and college days, when the city seemed limitless, and the more sobering postwar New York, when he worked in an advertising firm and seemed confined to "My drab room in the Bronx, my square foot of the subway" (*Crack-up,* 25). New York held its terrors as well as thrills, and he came to realize "that behind much of the entertainment that the city poured forth into the nation there were only a lot of rather lost and lonely people" (28). After his success with *This Side of Paradise* (1920), Fitzgerald returned to the city as a conquering hero; but he found that it had confines, discovering that it "was not the endless successions of canyons . . . but *it had limits*—from the tallest structures he saw for the first time that it faded out into the country on all sides, into an expanse of green and blue that alone was limitless" (*Crack-up,* 32). Where New York stopped, America began, and one could never escape the larger destiny that contained the city itself. The Puritan legacy—comprising both secular business and a religious state of mind—would always remain. Beyond the romantic city was a regularized, provincial, soberly religious workaday world of family responsibilities—with "vulnerabilities," as he put it in "What I Think and Feel at 25" (213–22).

Very early, Fitzgerald created two antiromantic hells: one was a sexual realm, vaguely corresponding to Broadway; the other was the mundane realm of the middle class. In contrast to both was Fifth Avenue, supplying a sense of place commensurate with self. *This Side of Paradise* supplies an exception to this rule as the story ends with a sense of all that impedes the self-creating imagination, including luxurious New York. Fitzgerald's second novel, *The Beautiful and Damned* (1922), picks up where *This Side of Paradise* leaves off. Told against a backdrop of New York, the story follows Anthony and Gloria Patch as they move from a comfortable brownstone apartment in the center of Manhattan to more dreary flats and finally to the Bronx, Fitzgerald's supreme example of middle-class hell. This novel is his most conscious attempt to show how difficult it was to create the romantic self in the face of a Puritan legacy, for Puritanism carried the seeds of its own destruction. Adam Patch, Anthony's grandfather, is a product of the post–Civil War period, that time when the old aristocratic values of Jefferson surrendered to the materialistic values of Hamilton. The country was then remade in an image that would no longer support what Amory Blaine and Anthony Patch found necessary to the result of a runaway imagination.

Fitzgerald rehearsed this theme in many of his short stories. In "The Diamond as Big as the Ritz" (1922), for example, the activities of Fitz-Norman Culpepper Washington parallel the events of American history from 1870 to his death in 1900. He protects his interest, even to the extent of murdering, enslaving, and imprisoning his servants and others during these "years of progress and expansion" (16). In order to get to the diamond mountain one must pass through the town of Fish, where sit twelve somber men who are disciples without a Christ, religious by-products of the Washington (that is, the American) legacy, now without nourishment. The apocalyptic ending of the story further reveals the destructive nature of the legacy that Adam Patch left Anthony, and the land ravaged by exploiters and turned to waste anticipates the valley of ashes.

Fitzgerald's view of the city cannot be separated from his view of America, which engages the larger topics of history and culture. The city is the vortex in which the play of personal and cultural motives takes place. In *Gatsby,* it gives us the established world of Tom Buchanan, the underworld of Meyer Wolfsheim, and the ethnic diversity of new immigrants from southeastern Europe and blacks from the South. The city is both a realm of great vitality and a realm of death, containing at the same time the promise of new life and the exhaustion of the old. The embodiment of the city's exhausted life is clearly the valley of ashes in Queens, with its world-weary, disillusioned custodian George Wilson (modeled in one sense on Woodrow Wilson, whose own disillusioned ideals were played out to sickness and death) and his wife Myrtle, whose vitality is literally extinguished here when she is run over by a car driven by Daisy Buchanan. Built into the city, in other words, is the hope of romantic possibility as well as the reality of physical defeat and death. This image of the city is not new: we have found it in Dickens's *Great Expectations,* Balzac's *Père Goriot,* Zola's *L'Assommoir,* and Dreiser's *Sister Carrie.* The end product of Gatsby's urban hopes is a death in which both romantic and mechanical energy are inextricable.

Modernism was greatly influenced by the romantic idea of history, which was in part a reaction to the Enlightenment emphasis on the empirical and its built-in belief in progress. The idea of science was challenged by the idea of myth; the assumption of mechanistic matter gave way to the idea that matter was infused with mind, which encouraged a belief in a vitalistic nature as well as a sense of historical destiny and cyclical time. The processes of history and nature were one: birth, maturity, and death parallel sunrise, noon, and sunset, and the cycle of events had a correlative in seasonal change. Nature was continuously unfolding, there to be read symbolically, and heroes were called into being by the necessity of the historical moment. Such a view of history can be found with shades of difference in Vico, Hegel, Spengler, and Toynbee—but in Spengler it became the modernist basis for history.

Embedded in *The Decline of the West* is a theory of history both romantic and entropic. Nick Carraway's own growing awareness of the ethnic diversity of New York leads directly into Spengler's idea that race is deeply embedded in a theory of culture. With the rise of ethnic diversity, what is organic and homogenous to a culture breaks down. As these factors drive the move from Culture to Civilization, a process of decline begins. The modern city thus has a shell that promises great vitality (the "wild promise of all the mystery and beauty in the world"), while an inner reality works destructively and pushes us toward death ("a dead man passed us in a hearse"). Hope and promise, decline and death, occur together in the modern megalopolis. Thus Gatsby can bring his sense of promise to the city in which he will die, just as the splendid buildings that Nick sees as the New York skyline coexist with the valley of ashes. Faustian expansiveness gives way to a new set of limits, romantic history to the entropic.

The early Eliot grappled with the same problems that faced Fitzgerald. Obsessed with the question of solipsism that he found in the philosophy of F. H. Bradley, Eliot offered three ways out of this subjectivity. First, there was escape through poetry, especially poetry that embodied what Eliot called the objective correlative. Second, there was escape through myth, especially the Christ myth, which supplied a narrative meaning larger than the self. And third, there was escape through cultural homogeneity—a shared sense of cultural belonging and cultural meaning that Eliot celebrated in his essay *After Strange Gods,* delivered first as a lecture at the University of Virginia in 1933. Fitzgerald, who was then living outside of Baltimore, met Eliot at the Turnbull estate and perhaps even discussed what Eliot told his Southern audience: that they had a basis for cultural unity that New York with its racial diversity lacked.

For Eliot, the escape from self and the way to an ennobling culture lay in a community of like selves. That solution, as we know all too well, is fraught with problems: Eliot's thinking borders on anti-Semitism and racism. But the problem, as he addressed it, was the same one that infused Spengler's distinction between Culture and Civilization. When there was no going back to a romantic past, the modernist saw a solution in forms of totalizing power. Perhaps Eliot hoped to find in Charles Maurras and the Action Française a unifying source of cultural purpose, a grounding of the communal self, and a means of undoing the atomistic influence of urban diversity, which he believed was responsible for the degeneration of culture. The agrarian critics, while they never moved to the political extremes of Eliot, Pound, or Wyndham Lewis, were motivated by the same desire. In *The Great Gatsby*'s concern over shared culture, Fitzgerald had put his finger on an issue that would lead to a lively discourse on the problems of ethnicity on both sides of the Atlantic.

Fitzgerald returned to this subject after his unhappy experience with the Roman police, which confirmed his opinion about the degenerate nature of the Mediterranean. In a letter to Edmund Wilson, he complained about such dark blood "creep[ing] northward to defile the Nordic race." If northern Europe were to avoid similar degeneration, it would have to "raise the bars of immigration and permit only Scandinavians, Teutons, Anglo-Saxons and Celts to enter" (*Letters,* 326). One must be careful not to overread this letter, especially out of its context: Fitzgerald was clearly angry at the beating he suffered at the hands of the Roman police, and his rhetoric is unfortunately inflated. Furthermore, he was writing long before the consequences of such racial thinking had been demonstrated in Nazi Germany. Nevertheless, it is surprising that Fitzgerald resorts to the same argument that he used to discredit Tom Buchanan in *Gatsby*. Tom functioned within the insularity and comfort of his own class, and he felt threatened by urban diversity. Three racial groups supposedly made up the Western world: the Mediterranean, the Alpine, and the Nordic; these were the traditional anthropological ethnic divisions before World War II. According to the built-in hierarchy that Fitzgerald seems to take for granted, any community that absorbs a large percentage of Mediterranean or Alpine people is in danger of cultural degeneration. Such an argument cannot be defended, but its attractions were perhaps more understandable before World War II, when racial arguments were a part of cultural discourse, and when a sense of community was inseparable from a longing for cultural homogeneity and from the modernist belief that a racial element was part of entropic history, responsible for the decline of the city in Western culture.

Fitzgerald's last treatment of entropic history comes in *The Last Tycoon* (1941), which once more features the man of romantic aspiration in a materialistic culture that defeats him. The story of Monroe Stahr, the last of the Faustians, is counterpointed against that of a former Hollywood czar who commits suicide at the "shrine" of Andrew Jackson's Hermitage—a shrine because it was Jackson who fought the rise of the national bank in the name of yeoman culture. The novel makes clear how far America has moved away from the landed, cohesive culture of its origins, and it portrays the destructive conclusion that such a course may signal. The main conflict of the novel involves Stahr's fight with Brimmer, the Communist labor organizer, one of a number of characters who mark the trend toward totalitarianism. The problem with this unfinished novel—a problem Fitzgerald might have corrected in revision—is that the vital Stahr is so quickly drained of his energy by men like Brimmer that it is hard to believe he ever had the powers Fitzgerald claimed for him. The entropic process is so swift that it calls into question the "high point" from which the decline starts. Embedded in the culture is a degenerative process that eats up the romantic individualist from within—it defeats him from the start. The vitality that a Gatsby displays in holding together his sense of self is so greatly diminished in *The Last Tycoon* that the necessary balance between the romantic impulse and degeneration is lost. Fitzgerald's America was a far more barren place when he was writing *The Last Tycoon* in 1940 than it was when he was writing *The Great Gatsby* in 1925. In fifteen years, the processes of entropy had speeded up—and Fitzgerald saw nothing that could stop the downward plunge.

The problems of culture and history that Fitzgerald and his contemporaries faced would be dealt with in different terms after World War II. Romantic history relied heavily on the idea that every culture had a destiny, a unique identity, a coherence that gave it special meaning. Such a belief was a carryover from the old historicism—that method of history as practiced by Leopold von Ranke and Jacob Burckhardt, which insisted that every nation (such as Germany) and every period of time (such as the Renaissance) had an essential meaning—an identity or *Geist*—that could be intuited and that, at the national level, played itself out as destiny. In *The Open Society* (1945), Karl Popper attacked this thinking; he especially criticized it for supporting the totalitarian concern for a national agenda, the belief in a racial community, and the desire to create a cultural "Other" as a political lightning rod.

Instead of starting off with a theory of culture on which it could then build a history, postmodern theorists of history (e.g., the Frankfurt School) look at the elements that make up both high and low culture and think of them as a series of intersecting, informational loops producing cultural meaning that can be both interpreted and evaluated.

Like Michel Foucault, they believe that individual consciousness is collapsed into the culture itself. There are thus no prophets because historical meaning is created rather than embedded in time. History is no longer simply "there," waiting to be discovered. As a result, there should be neither romantic destiny nor entropic history—only a series of disconnected events. But literary texts are not always philosophically consistent, and entropy remains for postmodernists a major way of describing history. Nevertheless, we have come a long way from the F. Scott Fitzgerald who saw a romantic idea of destiny and a mechanistic idea of entropy unfolding together to produce the story of America. Perceiving the "idea" of America as both visionary and flawed, Fitzgerald believed that in the cities the Enlightenment legacy had been corrupted from within, leading inescapably to disillusionment and waste.

CHAPTER 14

The Urban Vortex

I

F. Scott Fitzgerald looked back to Eliot and Conrad. But there was another tradition in America at work. As America moved into nationhood, it needed a new ideology by which to live, and Ralph Waldo Emerson (1803–82) and Walt Whitman (1819–92) supplied it. They refocused attention from the individual to the nation itself—especially the "humanity" that made up the nation; and they disputed the legitimacy of the old theocracy, challenging Puritanism at its heart, questioning the divinity of Christ, and moving toward a secular religion.

Emerson distinguished between nature and artifact. Nature, he said, "refers to essences unchanged" ("Nature," in *Selected Prose and Poetry,* 4); art, on the other hand, involves the superimposition of man's will on nature. Nature gives us the forest, man the city. Since the city is a human artifact, man is responsible for it. But there is another order of reality: man discovers an order in nature as well as himself, which is an order of the mind. For Emerson, there is no conflict between the practical and theoretical, the humanistic and scientific, religion and science, value and fact, inner and outer, man and nature, character and event: "Man is one, mind is one, nature is one, the world is one" (M. Konvitz, 7).

Emerson's world lacks a sense of transcendent tragedy. In the long run there is no evil: history works toward the fulfillment of good. But such residual harmony coexists with the realm of the everyday, the world of human dealings. Here the imperfections in daily life must be addressed: swamps, for example, must be drained to stop infections. On this level we fashion ourselves in an existential way, creating our sense of history by selecting those events and values that carry significance. As John Dewey pointed out, Emerson was connected with the Transcendentalists, but he believed that we find "truth in the highway, in the untaught endeavor, the unexpected idea, and this removes him from their remoteness. His ideas are not fixed upon any Reality that is beyond or behind or in any way apart" (M. Konvitz, 28). The past has relevance only if it has bearing on the present. From a pragmatic view, seen against the grain, the new urbanism demanded constant attention.

Emerson's interest in urban America grew out of his tours as a lyceum lecturer, which took him to all the major cities in the country. Besides the 250 lectures he delivered in Boston between 1840 and 1860, he delivered 40 lectures in New York and 25 in Philadelphia. In the decade preceding the Civil War, he journeyed west of the Appalachians, speaking in Cleveland, Cincinnati, Columbus, Pittsburgh, St. Louis, and Chicago; in 1871, he lectured in California. Emerson also traveled in Europe and contrasted the two worlds. If America was to become a new and higher culture, he insisted, it must cast off the precedents of Europe and come to terms with its own soil. He saw London mirroring the history of earlier cities, including Rome, all of which seemed destined to repeat a cycle of rise and fall. But Emerson thought the cycle could be broken by preserving what was best in the cities of the past: "Americans need not deny Rome; they needed only select which parts of its foundations they too would build upon, need only decide which elements of its dramas they would adapt to their own roles. The very act of selection was an act of both homage to and liberation from the past" (Cowan, 168 – 69).

While Europe provided the city of Cain, America offered the hope of a New Jerusalem. The theme of the New Jerusalem runs through Emerson's writings: the American people, like the Israelites, had been tested in the wilderness. Emerson linked Jesus metaphorically to the journey from the city of man to the City of God (Cowan, 60, 74, 79). According to Augustine, Cain belonged to the city of man, Abel to the City of God. Cain built a city, but Abel, a sojourner, did not. These events illuminate a major urban archetype: the journeyer from the City of God is by grace a citizen above and a stranger below. The mysterious stranger, whom we have encountered often in this study, carries the weight of two worlds. Like Whitman after him, Emerson secularized the City of God, locating a new and idealized city in the West.

Emerson's world was preindustrial, so he never had to come to terms with the city transformed by the new technology, as did Whitman, Hart Crane, and William Carlos Williams. But Emerson did see the symbiotic connection between the city and its hinterland, the natural and the industrial, the organic and the mechanistic. Like Whitman and Crane, he "wanted to find ways by which the poet might integrate the growing industrial city into an artistic work that professed to embody organic principles" (Cowan, 182–3). That hope, he argued, lay in the new cities of the West, of which Boston was a harbinger. Whitman explored the industrial morass far more deeply, and his city is fraught with problems less easy to reconcile to a heavenly ideal. But it was Emerson who set the foundation for the subsequent romantic view of the American city.

II

Whitman is to American literature what Joyce is to European literature: he changed its direction in midstream. Joyce takes us from Aristotle and Aquinas to Vico and Bergson; Whitman, from Emerson to Whitehead and Dewey. Whitman's philosophy, like Emerson's, turns on a theory of the One and the Many. He believed in One Mind, insisting that the power and privileges that lie in any lie in all, and identified with the crowd, which became a metonym for the city and the growing nation. But in his work the crowd is often individualized. Out of it steps Poe, Lincoln, the poet himself. As he tells us in "Specimen Days" (1875, 1882), he saw Lincoln almost every day when Whitman lived in Washington, "as I happen to live where he passes to or from his lodgings out of town" (*Complete Poetry,* 732–33). And Broadway, his favorite street with its mixed crowd, offered a parade of American history for him, over the course of time generating Andrew Jackson, Daniel Webster, Henry Clay, William Seward, Martin Van Buren, William Cullen Bryant, the Prince of Wales, and Charles Dickens. He also remembered seeing James Fenimore Cooper and Edgar Allan Poe ("it must have been in 1845 or '6") (701).

Although Whitman saw the crowd containing all of humanity, he also noticed the great men who separated themselves from it to enter history as distinct personalities. The particular realized itself in the universal, the Many in the One, Whitman the poet in the crowd. In "A Backward Glance o'er Travel'd Roads" (1888), he claimed that he abandoned con-

ventional themes in *Leaves of Grass* and treated the "broadest average" or
the crowd "in the now ripening Nineteenth Century, and especially in
each of their countless examples and practical occupations in the United
States today" (*Complete Poetry,* 618). He developed this point further:
"Think of the United States today—the facts of these thirty-eight or
forty empires solder'd in one—sixty or seventy millions of equals, with
their lives, their passions, their future—these incalculable, modern,
American, seething multitudes around us, of which we are inseparable
parts!" (661).

Destiny was a collective phenomenon; the species moved on while
the individual passed away; but the great man kept his independence. As
he learned from Emerson: "the great man is he who in the midst of the
crowd keeps with perfect sweetness the independence of solitude"
("Self-Reliance," in *Selected Poetry and Prose,* 170). Each age called forth its
own heroes, and the city was finally shaped by human will. The promise
of America depended on its ability to reconcile the individual and the
crowd: "Only from [the masses], and from its proper relation and
potency, comes [individualism]. . . . The two are contradictory, but our
task is to reconcile them" (Whitman, "Democratic Vistas," in *Leaves of
Grass,* 470). The poet becomes self-sufficient and then extrapolates from
that sense of sufficiency, embodied in the crowd, to the nation itself;
such importance could be placed on the crowd only because America
was rapidly becoming an urban nation. Between 1810 and 1860, the population of the United States grew six times faster than the world average,
reaching 30 million by the Civil War. The proportion of Americans living in cities grew from 6 percent to 20 percent of the total. New York
City's population rose from 124,000 in 1820 to 515,000 in 1850, surpass-
ing a million in 1860. Brooklyn soared from 5,200 in 1820 to well over
200,000 by the Civil War (a number that doubled in the next fifteen
years) as it became the third largest city in America. By 1880, 22 percent
of Americans lived in cities with populations over 80,000. The collo-
quial element of Whitman's poetry was influenced by his contact with
workers who constituted the "b'hoy" element of the Bowery that dominated street life. As David Reynolds has pointed out, "his whole persona
in *Leaves of Grass*—wicked rather than conventionally virtuous, free,
smart, prone to slang and vigorous outbursts—reflects the b'hoy culture" (105; see also 107, 495). Whitman's poetry thus takes its power
from Emersonian ideas transformed into a kind of street speech.

The city becomes a place of mystery and intrigue, hiding secrets of life
itself. To walk through it is thus to immerse oneself deeply in life, as

Whitman suggests in describing his nocturnal wanderings through Washington in "Specimen Days":

Tonight, after leaving the hospital at 10 o'clock... I wander'd a long time around Washington. The night was sweet, very clear, sufficiently cool, a voluptuous half-moon, slightly golden, the space near it of a transparent blue-gray tinge. I walk'd up Pennsylvania avenue, and then to Seventh street, and a long while around the Patent-office. Somehow it look'd rebuke-fully strong, majestic, there in the delicate moonlight. The sky, the planets, the constellations all so bright, so calm, so expressively silent, so soothing, after those hospital scenes. I wander'd to and fro till the moist moon set, long after midnight. (*Complete Poetry,* 738)

And the city can bring repose as well as poetic excitement: "Tonight I have been wandering awhile in the capitol, which is all lit up. The illu-minated rotunda looks fine. I like to stand aside and look a long, long while, up at the dome; it comforts me somehow" (757).

To immerse oneself in the city was to immerse oneself in the crowd, the very embodiment of humanity. And what truths the crowd taught, poetry in turn reflected. *Leaves of Grass* went through nine editions from 1855 to 1890 as Whitman sought to keep up with a changing America. Just as he discovered American heroes in the crowd, Whitman discov-ered himself and his country in his poetry. He re-created America in his imagination by substituting romantic for Enlightenment assumptions, seeing the destiny of America as involving the One and the Many rather than in the rational pursuit of progress. While their influence was only indirect, Darwin and Hegel, in different ways, encouraged him to think in evolutionary terms and helped him preserve hope for a new Amer-ica—at least up to a point.

That point came after the Civil War, when Whitman began to doubt the easy optimism that he had initially invested in democracy. Carlyle's essay "Shooting Niagara; and After" (1867) had a tremendous influence on him. Carlyle argued against a government wedded to the popular vote and was even more critical of what he referred to as the growing "swarms" of people. Nor was his view of the masses free of racism, as he questioned why 300,000 white men had to die in order to give the vote to three mil-lion blacks. Whitman's first reaction was outrage, and "Democratic Vistas" was his attempt at an answer. But the more deeply Whitman engaged Carlyle's argument, the more his doubts grew. As David Reynolds points out, Whitman's view darkened as he moved through drafts, from an early version, "Democracy," to "Democratic Vistas" four years later: "In the later work, Whitman turned his 'moral microscope' on current America and saw 'a sort of dry and flat Sahara,' with 'cities, crowded with petty grotesques, malformations, phantoms, playing meaningless antics.' If the United States continued in its current direction, he wrote, it might well end up 'the most tremendous failure of time'" (478).

His belief in democracy had limits. And while he was opposed to slavery in the free states and celebrated the dignity of blacks who fought heroically in the Civil War, Whitman had reservations about the future of blacks in America, a view that can be found both early and late in his writing. In a *Daily Times* editorial (1858), he carried his Free Soil argument to a racial extreme: "Who believes that Whites and Blacks can ever amalgamate in America? Or who wishes it to happen? Nature has set an impassable seal against it. Besides is not America for the Whites? And is it not better so? As long as the Blacks remain here, how can they become anything like an independent and heroic race? There is no chance for it" (quoted in Reynolds, 372–73). The city was destroying Whitman's idea of community. His attitude toward immigrant Catholics, especially the Irish, was exceptionally hostile. The urban crowd, the very city itself, was becoming ugly. Whitman saw firsthand the great rise of New York, but he believed the future of America was in the West, where perhaps the new capital of America could be relocated ("Democratic Vistas," in *Leaves of Grass,* 480).

Whitman felt equally conflicted over the rise of technology in America, especially after the Civil War. The Atlantic cable and the growth of the railroad encouraged the unification of humanity: technology was collapsing space, bringing together divergent people and cultures. By 1880, over 760,000 miles of telegraph wire and 128,000 miles of railway track had been laid. But such advances also brought rampant materialism, and he had a sense that America was selling its soul for money. The country's total wealth swelled from $8.43 billion in 1850 to $48.95 billion in 1880, and its factory output rose from $1.06 billion to $5.56 billion in the same period—facts that testify to the industrialization and urbanization of America. The federal government and big business were getting stronger as the people were getting weaker. The National Banking Act (1863) and the charter of the Union Pacific and Central Pacific Railroads were commercial windfalls, and the Fourteenth Amendment—aimed ostensibly at protecting the rights of individuals, especially the freed slaves—ironically sped the rise of corporate America. In "Democratic Vistas," he lamented what America was becoming: "The spectacle is appalling. . . . The depravity of the business classes of our country is not less than it has been supposed, but infinitely greater. The official services of America, national, state, and municipal, in all their branches, except

Figure 7. Brooklyn Bridge. The symbol of Hart Crane's hope for an urban unity: built to employ the pull of gravity internally, the bridge literally holds itself up by its own weight. Courtesy of the Frances Loeb Library, Graduate School of Design, Harvard University.

the judiciary, are saturated in corruption, bribery, falsehood, maladministration and the judiciary is tainted. The great cities reek with respectable as much as non-respectable robbery and scoundrelism" (in *Leaves of Grass,* 467). Whitman's vision thus underwent serious modification. A sense of excitement over the new city and a sense of hope in the new nation gave way to skepticism and doubt. His hope never disappeared, but the doubt revealed that the problems of America—the rise of a new commercialism, the growth of the industrial city, the growing influence of money and big business—dimmed whatever urban brightness was left, until even the promise of the West was empty.

III

Hart Crane (1899–1932) inherited Whitman's vision: the hope and the doubt, the order and the chaos. Crane tried to update Whitman. The precursor to *The Bridge* (1930) is "Crossing Brooklyn Ferry" (1856), as the Brooklyn Bridge takes the place of the ferry. The bridge (see figure 7) is a symbol of interconnectedness between the finite and the infinite, the past and the present, East and West, the agrarian and industrial society, and Crane's task is to heal "the iron-dealt cleavage." This attempt had analogues in the work of Lewis Mumford and Van

Wyck Brooks, writers who were connected with *The Seven Arts* magazine. But it was perhaps Waldo Frank who, after Whitman, was the
greatest influence on Crane. As John Unterecker has maintained, it was
Frank who "suggested a way in which industrial America, in which
Crane felt himself inextricably enmeshed, might be somehow transformed into a better world. Only by the artist's involvement with it . . .
might the artist—inheritor and transmitter of the culture of the past—
triumph over the barbarism of an industrial society" (153 – 54).

In his early poetry, Crane was intent on reconciling two myths already
linked by Goethe—those of Faustus and of Helen, reflecting the Teu-
tonic urge to transform the landscape and the Greek urge to reify the
beautiful. Crane's poem "For the Marriage of Faustus and Helen" (1925)
derives in great part from Joyce's *Ulysses.* As Joyce superimposed the
heroic world of Homer on the modern city of Dublin, so Crane superimposed the heroic world of Faustus and Helen on modern-day New
York. His Helen rides in a streetcar; the Dionysian revels of her court
take place on a roof garden with a jazz band; the fall of Troy is re-
presented by World War I. "The importance of this scaffolding may easily be exaggerated," Crane tells us, "but it gave me a series of correspondences between two widely separated worlds on which to sound some
major themes of human speculation—love, beauty, death, renascence"
(quoted in Unterecker, 258 – 59).

Another version of the Faustus-Helen story was Henry Adams's
famous treatment of the opposing forces he called the Virgin and the
Dynamo. Crane believed that Adams had anticipated the major problem
of the modernist world, and he made use of this metaphor in *The Bridge:*
Columbus prays to the Virgin at the beginning of the poem and the airplane falls from the sky near the end. Crane wanted to heal the opposition between nature and an industrial, urban society and to suggest the
way that mythic and technological, scientific modes could be reconciled.
His effort was noble, but his vision could not grasp the reality and the
poem ultimately was overcome by doubt. Crane's attempt revealed the
failure of the romantic vision in an urban era. He believed in an organic
unity, a true monism: all was one, everything related. He tried to create
a poetic vision that would reveal such unity, but his plan was too ambitious. As he worked on the poem, he began reading Spengler, which
curbed his Whitmanesque optimism; *The Bridge* became a fusion of the
optimistic and the pessimistic. The poem moves from the city, to the
early frontier, to the West, and back to the city. The city and the frontier,
the city and the land, interpenetrate; one reinforces the other. The

underlying hope is for a New Atlantis—a new connection between what has been torn asunder and what awaits. Crane tried to steer a course between T. S. Eliot's sense of cultural exhaustion and William Carlos Williams's belief in new beginnings. He wanted to break with the "poetry of negation," so that Eliot's wasteland world could be transformed by the power of the imagination.

The early critics condemned *The Bridge* as disorganized, but in the years since its publication later analysts have unearthed principles of unity. I have already suggested the "Virgin and Dynamo" theme, but a more fundamental concern running through the work is the need to reconcile nature and the machine, the dominating city and the lost frontier. The poem opens by opposing nature and the machine: gulls circle the bridge while elevators rise and fall; the sun leaks from the sky as an acetylene torch sparks the day. Disharmony between the natural and the mechanical leads to psychological instability: the bedlamite jumps from the bridge. Crane then moves from a subway in New York to the transcontinental train on the tracks behind his father's cannery. The poem next moves to the Mississippi, symbol of time's flow to the harmony of the sea as well as symbol of American origins—"the pure savage world," "the primal, physical body of America" (Unterecker, 504–5). Such a return was necessary if urban America was to find roots. The Indian woman with her papoose turns into the frontier woman, the mother of Larry, who goes to sea in the new clipper ships that are the transports of a new America.

The next section of the poem, "Cape Hatteras," is Crane's hymn to Walt Whitman—his attempt to update Whitman's story of America. America, especially urban America, has become even more materialistic than "Democratic Vistas" prophesied. The "Exchange" now controls the "labyrinth"; the "gigantic powerhouse" and "dynamos" dominate Kitty Hawk and the Wright brothers (Crane, 35–36): their flight anticipates the crashed plane that is a harbinger of mechanistic doom ("down gravitation's vortex into crashed…dispersion…into mashed and shapeless debris," 38–39). Crane's plea is to the spirit of Whitman ("O Walt—there and beyond!") that some kind of controlling unity ("O, upward from the dead") will emerge out of such chaos, out of this "debris" to bridge the "iron dealt cleavage" (39):

> And it was thou who on the boldest heel
> Stood up and flung the span on even wing
> Of that great Bridge, Our Myth, whereof I sing!
>
> (41)

Whitman's "vision ... reclaimed," the poet takes to the "Open Road." We then move across the country to California ("This was the Promised Land, and still is," 50), back to New York once more, into the subway tunnel, into the presence of Poe, whose Dionysian presence challenges the more sanguine vision of Whitman. The circle is complete: we have left a city of divided consciousness and emerged into the open air of Atlantis. Crane wrote this part of the poem first, and it is the journey to American roots that now brings us back: the mythical lost land, which had once connected America with the European and African continents, is symbol of the invisible unity on which Crane bases his hope for a new America.

The Bridge was Crane's attempt to reconcile New York to the rest of America, the city to nature, the mechanistic to the organic, visible chaos to an invisible principle of unity. He was grappling with the legacy of Emerson and Whitman: so much of America's promise relied upon the invisible—the supposition of some transcendent power that would resolve the problems of an industrial society. Such reliance on transcendence, like earlier appeals to the lost wilderness, appeared more dubious as America became more urban, until Crane came to question the legitimacy of his vision. In a 1931 letter to his friend Bill Wright, Crane revealed the brooding doubts that haunted his writing of *The Bridge:* "Present day America seems a long way off from the destiny I fancied when I wrote the poem. In some ways Spengler must have been right" (quoted in Unterecker, 644).

In 1931, Crane won a Guggenheim Fellowship and he spent the next year in Mexico, whose primitive culture he hoped to depict. He planned to write a drama on the conflict between Montezuma and Cortez as well as a heroic poem on the theme of the Conquest, maintaining that the Mexican poets were too busy imitating American or European models to come to terms with their own culture. His poem would be a Mexican equivalent to *The Bridge.* Once again he would treat an American civilization overrun by a modern European one. In *The Bridge,* the Indians give way to the frontier; in his Conquest poem, Mexican Indians would be transformed by Spanish Catholicism. Crane was obsessed by such fusion between the primitive and the modern, the Christian and the pagan, and once again he saw the myth turn on the image of the Virgin: "The Virgin of Guadalupe miraculously unites the teaching of the early Catholic missionaries with many survivals of the old Indian myths and pagan cults. She is a typical Mexican product, a strange blend of Christian and pagan strains. . . . She is really the Goddess of the Mexican masses" (1931 letter to Bess Crane, quoted in Unterecker, 708). Like rivers to the sea, religions flow into each other, simultaneously transforming and re-presenting one another. The key to Mexico City, like the key to New York City, is a mythic vision, without which there is no redeeming poetry; he "still . . . harbor[ed] the illusion that there is soil, a mythology, a people and spirit here [in Mexico] that are capable of unique and magnificent utterance" (708). Despite the faltering hope that now seemed to be an illusion, Crane believed that the city was redeemable in visionary terms, that the will was servant to the mind, and that a sense of lost unity could be restored once a culture became aware of the connection between nature and the machine, between myth and the secrets of the city. For all we know that hope was still with him when he took his fatal plunge into the sea.

IV

The view of the city that Hart Crane opposed was embodied by the work of Le Corbusier, who argued that the city needed to dominate nature, to impose its will on its surroundings: "The city! It is a grip upon nature. . . . It is a human operation directed against nature . . . both for protection and for work. It is a creation. . . . The spirit which animates nature is a spirit of order." Thus not only does the city superimpose order on nature but that order, Le Corbusier insisted, is the law of nature. "Man works in a straight line because he has a goal and knows where he is going. . . . A modern city lives by a straight line. . . . The curve is ruinous, difficult and dangerous; it is a paralyzing thing" (*The City of Tomorrow*, xii, 1, 11, 25). Cities grow according to a pattern—a slow accumulation followed by a gradual rise, which acquired a "gravitational pull . . . [a] centrifugal force" of immense power, "bringing the rush and the mob" (93). Seeing the whole of history as evolutionary, he argued that the city evolved until it dominated modern life. The great city in turn determined a nation's fate: "war, peace, and toil. Great cities are the spiritual workshops in which the work of the world is done" (87). When a city came to a dead stop, its country would do the same (96–97).

Le Corbusier's point about the remarkable growth of modern cities can be quickly documented with a population chart of the principal city in four major countries—France, England, Germany, and the United States—from 1800 to 1910 (see table 1). Within a period of 110 years,

Table 1 *The Growth of Urban Centers (population in thousands)*

	1800	1880	1910
Paris	647	2,200	3
London	800	3,800	7,200
Berlin	182	1,840	3,400
New York	60	2,800	4,500

SOURCE: Adapted from Andrew Lees, *Cities Perceived.*

Paris grew almost five times larger; London nine times; Berlin eighteen times; and New York an incredible seventy-five times. Such population increase filled urban space, leading to divergent theories of what the city should be. Le Corbusier wanted a vertical city—buildings that towered into the air and left open space at the bottom for parks and other human activity (see figure 8). Skyscrapers, he maintained, could accommodate 40,000 people and take up only 5 percent of the land (*City of Tomorrow,* 297). New York, he claimed, was a failure because its skyscrapers were not built in parks; it was a vertical city, a product of "the new times. It is a catastrophe with which a too hasty destiny has overwhelmed courageous and confident people" (*When Cathedrals Were White,* 36).

Le Corbusier saw New York as a mystical object that concealed a harsh reality. When his ship arrived in New York, he saw "a fantastic, almost mystic city rising up in the mist. But the ship moves forward and the apparition is transformed into an image of incredible brutality and savagery" (*When Cathedrals Were White,* 34). This sense of the compelling beauty and savagery of New York would be shared by many of its observers, including John Dos Passos.

V

Even though he wrote extensively about the city, John Dos Passos was antiurban, with political and social beliefs rooted in the Jeffersonian vision. Despite America's radical urban transformations, he retained the Jeffersonian fear that individualism would be overwhelmed by forms of power, whether of the military, of wealth, or of centralized government. Dos Passos wrote several books about Jefferson and his era: *The Ground We Stand On* (1941), *The Head and Heart of Thomas Jefferson*

Figure 8. Le Corbusier's Voisin plan illustrates his belief that "the city . . . is a grip upon nature." He desired to control urban space with a series of skyscrapers, destroying the human scale even as he opened up land beneath. Courtesy of the Frances Loeb Library, Graduate School of Design, Harvard University.

(1954), and *The Shackles of Power* (1966). These histories, rather turgid and dry, do not reveal Dos Passos at his best. He accepts the Jeffersonian vision as what America should be and assumes his readers will uncritically assent. Because he fails to suggest why the Hamiltonian opposition came into being or convey a sense of history as a process driven by industrial and nationalistic forces, the drama of the conflict between Jefferson and Hamilton is left out. Dos Passos provides a melodramatic version of history: good guys versus bad guys, with the bad guys responsible for creating the world with which his modern characters can no longer cope.

Early in his career he had defended liberal causes and moved close to the Communist Party, but his motive—like Dreiser's—was to support a system that could counter the power base of Western capitalism. To evaluate communism firsthand, he journeyed to Russia; the trip was not reassuring but neither was it discouraging enough to suggest the need of changing political direction.[1] His moment of disillusionment came later,

1. Like so many of his contemporaries who also made pilgrimages to Russia—e.g., H. G. Wells, Theodore Dreiser, Edmund Wilson—Dos Passos approached the Communist experiment with a sense of hope.

during the Spanish Civil War, when his friend José Robles Pazos was executed by the communists. In *Adventures of a Young Man* (1938), Glenn Spotswood, fighting the loyalists in Spain, is arrested by a party (GPU) agent, accused of Trotskyism, and executed. As Granville Hicks has pointed out, "In Spain Dos Passos had concluded that communism was not merely something he could not support; it was as much the enemy as fascism or any other brand of reaction" (118). The Nazi-Soviet Pact of 1939 could not have come as a surprise to him. Dos Passos's political shift was thus motivated more by a desire to preserve the integrity of the individual against external forces than by ideology. When he felt the individual was threatened from the right, he moved left; when the threat came from the left, he moved right. He eventually realized that the individual was no longer in control of his or her fate—that the liberal agenda had been transformed by new forms of power. Since most of these forces were at work in the city, Dos Passos sent his characters into the urban vortex in order to show how individual consciousness was threatened by a collective consciousness, the individual in a futile search of freedom within the mob.

As Ben Stoltzfus has pointed out, a number of French writers (Baudelaire, Verhaeren, Léon-Paul Fargue, Paul Claudel) had taken as their subject the "collective existence in which individuals are absorbed into the greater entity . . . of the big modern city," but he believes that Jules Romains's *Le Bourg régénéré* (1906) is the first synoptic novel— that is, for the first time "a town becomes the protagonist of a novel" (Stoltzfus, 204, 205). While Dos Passos denied the direct influence of Romains, such writing was inevitable given the rise of the city as an entity unto itself. According to Stoltzfus, "This new orientation to the city as a source of poetic inspiration, sprouting from the very sidewalks of Paris, was to be known as unanimism," a term Romains coined to express the activity and the behavior of groups, "the evolving consciousness of the collective life of groups and the city" (205). Dos Passos in turn revealed that urban consciousness in a way that gave the city a new meaning.

In Dos Passos's early works, individual consciousness was primarily a matter of aesthetics. In *One Man's Initiation* (1920) and *Three Soldiers* (1921), the artist's vision is central. According to Malcolm Cowley, this vision involved the artist's faith in "his own sensibility" and his belief that society is hostile to such sensibility, that the poet is misunderstood by the philistine world, and that the poet triumphs over this material world "by mystically including it within himself" and by creating art as a counterstatement (23). But such an emphasis on aesthetics forced Dos Passos to reject rather than engage his culture. In writing *Manhattan Transfer* (1925), he began to move in another literary direction; having found the means to portray the material realm, he created a social, primarily urban consciousness and showed how it could lead to destructive, indeed degenerate, ends.

Manhattan Transfer expresses radical disaffection with the city. Like Nick Carraway, Jimmy Herf, alienated and lonely, leaves the city defeated by it. Dos Passos's novel conveys a Freudian truth. In *Civilization and Its Discontents* (1930), Freud describes aggressiveness as an inborn feature of human nature. He saw Western culture as essentially the business of men, who were distracted from their work by women and sex. Civilized life inhibited hostility, driving it inward; the city, aligned with the superego, restrained the vitality of the psyche. Life in the metropolis, as both Dos Passos and Freud saw it, thus became more neurotic. They came to believe that freedom and civilization were inherently incompatible. T. S. Eliot had already depicted the neurotic character of modern city man; in the trilogy *U.S.A.*, Dos Passos similarly portrayed inhibited urbanites.

In all three novels, the individual tries to realize himself or herself in an urban environment and almost always fails, leaving us with repeated examples of disintegration. Charley Anderson, for example, becomes more dissolute as *The Big Money* (1936) progresses, increasingly alcoholic and neurotic, until he becomes self-destructive; he dies after he drives drunkenly through a railroad crossing and stalls in front of an oncoming train. There is an irony in his death: Anderson, who made a fortune by inventing a starter for airplanes, cannot start his stalled car before the train hits it. He who lives by the machine dies by it in Dos Passos's novel: the machine and big money determine personal and cultural fate.

In order to control time in *U.S.A.*, Dos Passos used three narrative devices—the "Newsreel," a series of biographies, and the "Camera Eye"—which locked him and his characters into a temporal continuum that defined them. The Newsreel primarily comprised a series of newspaper headlines that established the historical context; the biographies were of people who either contributed to that context or were defined by it; and the Camera Eye involved personal memories, seemingly of Dos Passos himself. Even in the narrative, characters exist first in general time and then are plunged into a more specific historical moment. A typical passage from *U.S.A.* reveals this method:

July was hot that summer, in the office they worked in a continual whirl of electric fans, the men's collars wilted and the girls kept themselves over plastered with powder; only Mr. Dreyfus still looked cool and crisply tailored as if he'd just stepped out to a bandbox. The last day of the month Janey was sitting a minute at her desk when Jerry Burnham came in. (157)

We are first in the month of July during a heat wave, and then suddenly we are in a specific day, the last in July, and involved with Jerry Burnham and Janey. The shift from the general to the particular sets the terms of the relationship between the workings of America—especially the institutions found in the city—and the effect that this world has on Dos Passos's characters, who are thus always predefined by the world in which they function. More than any other modern writer, Dos Passos anticipates the postmodern tendency to collapse consciousness into the culture itself: what we discover in novels like *Manhattan Transfer* and *U.S.A.* is a direct manifestation of urban consciousness, the mind at one with the workings of the modern city.

There may be another connection between individual and collective consciousness. Blanche Gelfant has argued that most of Dos Passos's characters reject the world of the father, which is most often defined by material success: "Success is what the fathers preach, and the world of material ends is what the fathers have created. It follows then that success is what the sons in aversion to the father must reject" ("John Dos Passos," 182–83). In other words, in rejecting the father, Dos Passos's characters reject the world of the father. But a number do seek success: J. Ward Moorehouse becomes the head of a leading advertising firm; Dick Savage becomes an executive in Moorehouse's firm; Eleanor Stoddard becomes a successful interior decorator and marries into Russian nobility; Charley Anderson becomes a wealthy airplane manufacturer; and Margo Dowling becomes a movie star. Such decisions separate them from Wenny, Vag, Jimmy Herf, Glenn Spotswood, and others, who remain social outsiders. But the choice itself is ultimately unimportant: in either case, the final resolution is empty; the process of degeneration and decline is inevitable.

Dos Passos takes us inch by inch into his world: first the crowd with its collective consciousness, then the city with its material pursuits, and finally the choice to embrace or reject the struggle for material success. Such success is the "elixir" (as Dos Passos calls it in *Midcentury*) at the urban heart, the destructive element that cannot be altered whose embrace leads to death. One enters the city at the risk of losing the self in a material realm, of being irretrievably drawn into the self-consuming vortex that awaits the urban pilgrim of Western literature. The titles themselves of his trilogy point to this conclusion: *The 42nd Parallel* (1930), *1919* (1932), and *The Big Money* respectively suggest characters locked into space, into time, and finally into the pursuit of money, a pursuit that takes them to the urban arena and into the game of failure or success. Gelfant believes that Dos Passos finally resolved this destructive process in *Chosen Country* (1951), which she terms "prospective, looking towards a still malleable future in which the founding democratic ideals can yet come true.... The work of creating a civilization out of the wilderness still remains to be done" ("John Dos Passos," 192). But that conclusion contradicts her previous argument, since the world that Jay Pignatelli would accept is the same world that the major novels clearly rejected. Jay's vision is retrospective, not prospective; there was a moment in the past when the "founding democratic ideals" could have been realized, but time has passed him by; the city has overwhelmed the wilderness, and the idealized option no longer exists.

In *Midcentury* (1961), Dos Passos, despite a change in his politics, extends his views of the relationship between the city and nature. The section titled "A Creature that Builds" includes a prose poem regarding the city and its institutions. The desire to build is a natural one, but it involves a process both delimiting (an "abnegation of lives") and degenerating (we build upon a "discarded" past). What we build takes on an institutional reality even at the insect level. "Institutions, so the sociologists tell us, shape man's course," seemingly superseding or at least altering nature. Such a process can be destructive:

> Lecturing on "Social Insects" the late Professor Wheeler of
> Harvard used to point out with some malice to his students
> > that the ants,
> > too,
> > in spite of the predestined perfection
> of their intuitions,
> > suffered what he called "perversions of
> appetite."
> > Their underground galleries and storied
> domes
> > are infested by an array of lethal creatures, thieves and
> predators, scavenger crickets, greedy roaches and rove beetles,
> and one particularly plumed little bug
> > which secretes in its hair an elixir so
> delectable to antkind
> > that the ants lose all sense of self- or

species-preservation
          and seek death in its embrace.

(*Midcentury,* 117 – 18)

Dos Passos anticipates what today is called sociobiology: the assumption that social organization is determined by biological—and genetic—laws written into nature and that what is characteristic of one species may apply to another, including humans. Here within the very "city" that the ants build is an attraction so compelling that it cannot be resisted, even though it leads to the destruction of the city and its inhabitants. The logic of the poem clearly suggests that the human equivalent of this "elixir" is material success. Moreover, the text of *Midcentury,* which describes the rise of powerful labor unions simultaneous with the shift of power to Franklin Roosevelt and the beginning of the New Deal, allows the reader to fill in whatever gaps the poem may leave. The agenda of capitalism created an urban reality in which the forces of the left and the right clash. Dos Passos spent his whole career depicting an urban America that was moving toward decline, caught in a degenerative process that worked secretly and compellingly within that whirlpool of elegant activity which in the name of progress led to death.

Dos Passos was influenced by a number of sources, particularly Joyce and Whitman. But Marshall McLuhan argues for the importance of Flaubert, who first gave us the discontinuous landscape—the relationship between subjectivity and landscape—with the claim that a landscape becomes discontinuous when it is held in place by the impressionistic mind. In *Manhattan Transfer,* Dos Passos's city provides "a phantasmagoric back-drop for [his characters'] frustrations and defeats. The city is felt as alien, meaningless." In contrast, Joyce sees human motives built into the city, where they become "an extension of human functions, as having a human shape and eliciting the full range of human response which man cannot achieve in any other situation" (McLuhan, 154). Put differently, in *U.S.A.,* as we move from city to nation, the relationship between mind and setting becomes mechanical. Joyce's *Ulysses,* which unfolds in a relatively small city, is held together by gossip and communal memory: almost every character has a past involving a shared urban reality. Dos Passos's characters, without a past, are generally anonymous and unknown to each other, products of a mechanistic city that creates a common fate. In Joyce, the city becomes a state of mind; in Dos Passos, the city becomes a mechanical force. Separate and fragmented, Dos Passos's characters lack individual will and are brought together by the force of the urban vortex, not the force of human volition.

VI

William Carlos Williams lived all his life in Rutherford, New Jersey, about thirty miles west of New York City. Unlike Ezra Pound, Williams did not go to Europe in search of himself (though he visited): he insisted that the American poet should turn to America for the subject matter of poetry. He approved of the way Pound tried to improve the language, because he felt that language revealed the essence of culture, but he viewed Pound's attempt to find a cultural ideal in the European past as a betrayal. Williams found his own roots in Emerson and Whitman.

Williams, not a symbolist, believed the poet must create a vision and then—by a concentration on the specific, the concrete—must show how the real, factual world can be lifted to this level by the imagination. He distanced himself from romantic and Victorian poetry, especially the overly rich poetry of Keats and Tennyson, which had influenced his early work. Moreover, he repudiated many romantic assumptions: nature for him is not divinely infused with meaning. The mind held time together, and objects in nature are discrete and separate: the poet gives them meaning, a meaning found not in the object or the mind but in the fusion of the two. Meaning is not built into nature or time. History is discontinuous, a series of new beginnings: the past does not build upon itself. Thus Williams sharply disagrees with Eliot's notion of tradition.

Williams, who wanted American myths to replace European myths, felt that Eliot and Pound had contaminated modern poetry by aligning it with a European tradition of the past. Like Eliot, he sought an impersonal poetry, but not one grounded in high culture. In his introduction to *Kora in Hell* (1920) he called Pound a traitor to American poetry, and in his *Autobiography* (1951) he attacked *The Waste Land* as "the great catastrophe of our letters." He severely criticized its author: "Critically Eliot returned us to the classroom just at the moment when I felt that we were on the point of escape to matters much closer to the essence of a new art form—rooted in the locality which gave it fruit" (*Autobiography*, 146). Joel Conarroe has argued that *Paterson* is "a kind of anti-*Cantos*, an anti-exile poem finding its material and the source of its vitality in the local present that Pound (and Eliot) found inadequate" (21). *In the American Grain* (1925) was Williams's attempt to define a usable American past, and *Paterson* (1958) was the poem in which his ideas were applied.

Williams connected that past to the city: he depicted the land betrayed and the river polluted, all in the name of commerce and industry. Because language had also become polluted, speech fails the inhabitants. Man must turn inward, toward the land, and allow the imagination to recreate reality, to penetrate to the meaning of things and lift up the fallen world. The poet's function is not to read the symbolic meaning of nature but to create that meaning. But Williams approaches romantic poetry in his belief that the poet is the agent of change—that the poet speaks to and for a culture in a new and vital language. The poet creates the vision in his own imagination and then shows the reality of that vision in terms of the local, creating a mythology based on things ("no ideas but in things"). For Williams, "That is the poet's business. Not to talk in vague categories but to write particularly, as a physician works, upon a patient, upon the thing before him, in the particular to discover the universal" (*Autobiography*, 39).

He grounded that sense of the local in Paterson, New Jersey, which lies within the curve formed by the bending of the Passaic River and is bounded on the southeast by Garrett Mountain. The area was settled as early as 1679 by the Dutch. In 1791, Alexander Hamilton, then secretary of the treasury under President Washington, saw the industrial potential of the local falls and helped form the Society for Useful Manufactures (S.U.M.), which promoted Paterson as "the cradle of American industry." The city later became the center of silk and other kinds of manufacturing in the mills that lined and eventually polluted the river. The Colt revolver was manufactured in Paterson and, later, so were locomotives and submarines. The story of Paterson is thus inextricably connected with the rise of industry and the history of labor in America. In preparing for his long poem, Williams went to the historical as well as the physical roots of the city.

Williams anticipated *Paterson* in his earlier works, such as "The Wanderer" (1914). In *Kora in Hell,* he insisted that mythical giants are buried in the earth and that we must go through the soil to get to the timeless. Williams believed that all life emerged out of death, like Kora (Persephone), who emerges each year as new life from the barren ground; this was also the main theme of his poem *Spring and All* (1923), which connects this vegetative process with the Dionysus myth. We must come to terms with our Dionysian self—the dark, unknown region of our consciousness. *In the American Grain*—influenced by D. H. Lawrence's *Studies in Classic American Literature* (1923) and influencing in turn Crane's *The Bridge*—called for a return to our origins for historical renewal. *A Voyage to Pagany* (1928) is an extension of this thesis, his answer to Henry James's vision of Europe. A good deal of the argument is contrived. Williams, like many of his contemporaries, set up a dialectic between repression and freedom, embodied in the Puritan and the Indian. The Indian thus came to symbolize the liberty lost under Puritanism and to represent the spirit that must infuse all Americans, who must break free from the holds of the past.

Williams admired Joyce, who had similarly freed himself from the constraints of Anglo-Celtic culture: Joyce broke "with a culture older than England's when he goes into his greatest work. . . . It is to break the limitations, not to conform to the taste that his spirit runs" ("A Point for American Criticism," in *Selected Essays*, 88). His disruption was matched in America by Whitman: "Whitman. . . . For God's sake! He broke through the deadness of copied forms which keep shouting above everything that wants to get said today drowning out one man with the accumulated weight of a thousand voices in the past—re-establishing the tyrannies of the past" ("Against the Weather," in *Selected Essays*, 218).

To *Paterson* Williams brought a threefold purpose: (1) to create a new myth out of the history of an American city, (2) to reevaluate American history in the context of that myth, and (3) to show where America went wrong and when her cultural hopes were spoiled. Williams believed that there was no ideal to which we could return—no destiny waiting to be realized, no Edenic past or future waiting to be seized. However, he did explore a related theme that obsessed writers like Fitzgerald, Faulkner, and West—the belief that America had exhausted its possibilities, that Emersonian and Whitmanesque expectations had been compromised by industry, immigration, class differences, divisions of labor, and the end of the frontier. *Paterson* is a fallen version of Walt Whitman's world. But Whitman transcended time, and Williams engaged it. As Robert Lowell observes, *Paterson* is Whitman's America disorganized by industrial chaos ("Thomas, Bishop, and Williams"). To be redeemed, man must create new ideals, and the burden of such creation includes coming to terms with what is ugly as well as beautiful, with both death and the life force. One can find force, energy, drive in the modern urban world, but the urban experience also leads to repression; and what is driven underground must be brought to the surface through the release of pagan energies.

Paterson is made up of five books. In Book I, Williams confronts the physical city. He introduces its citizens, past and present, and then gives a history of the city, concentrating on deformities in nature—the dwarf, the gigantic fish. Life renews itself, but out of death: Mrs. Cummings falls into the river, and Sam Patch leaps to his death. Both deaths are generalized: failed language is a form of death. Book II takes place in a park. The poet climbs the cliff overlooking the city and walks through the park, cataloguing the people and things within it. In Book III, the heat of summer drives the poet within the walls of the library, the repository for the collected past that he rejects. Since the library contains records of the past, it exists at the expense of dreams and has the smell of death. The poet remembers catastrophic events in Paterson's history, like a tornado and fire. The fire is called a "beautiful thing" because it destroyed the previous library, the historical past, and thus allowed a new beginning; here Williams rejects Eliot's historical continuity, urban or otherwise. Book IV focuses on the elemental character of Paterson, describing what has happened to love in the modern world in a parody of the pastoral (the two primary characters are named Corydon and Phyllis). The poem moves on to the solarium, where a lecture is being given on atomic fission. Here the elements that make up the city (man-woman-park) are translated into chemical terms. The physicist is explaining how helium is changed to hydrogen when its atomic number is reduced. In this schema, the city is uranium, lacking stability and in constant flux; like uranium, like language, it must undergo change. When bombarded with slow neutrons, uranium undergoes rapid fission into smaller atoms, producing atomic energy; so the city is bombarded by historical events, out of which comes transforming energy and thus historical change. For Williams, metamorphosis is both a physical and literary matter.

Such metamorphoses move us away from the distinction that nature is given, the city man-made; Williams believes that the city is as alive as the things that constitute it. Its people, its park, its river, its landscape—like two giants, male and female—bring forth new life. Like everything else in the physical world, the city is subject to the forces of life and death, and out of death will come new life. Paterson the poet will die; the product of his imagination will live on. The last point is left unsaid in the poem, which is perhaps why Williams added Book V, which treats the subject of art and the imagination. It is the imagination that gives coherence to urban flux: it comes to terms with what constitutes the city, informs physical reality with language, and creates a new kind of being. Here the city, like the unicorn in this book, can go beyond its physical limits. Life is flux, which only art can arrest as it moves us toward permanence. The city has two realities: one, the imagination, sorts out urban chaos and gives meaning to the other, physical reality.

VII

In *Black Manhattan* (1930), James Weldon Johnson estimated the number of Negro migrants from the South to the North in the 1910s and 1920s at 1.5 million (33); in *Terrible Honesty* (1995), Ann Douglas puts the figure at 1.2 million (73). This shift in population was a shift in culture, away from the land and into the city. New York is many cities combined into one, and Harlem is both a part of and separate from New York. That is the impression we get from Ralph Ellison's *Invisible Man* (1952) and from an essay he wrote prior to the novel, "Harlem Is Nowhere" (1948), in which Harlem is presented as a metonym for urban alienation: "Overcrowded and exploited politically and economically, Harlem is the scene and symbol of the Negro's perpetual alienation in the land of his birth" (*Shadow and Act*, 297).

Ellison believes that blacks are more alienated in Harlem than in the South, where for generations they learned to survive with the help of religion, family, and a body of folklore. As modest as these cultural elements may be, they were of "inestimable psychological value" because they allowed an "almost mystical hope." When blacks lost a sense of a larger community, they lost "one of the bulwarks which men place between themselves and the constant threat of chaos" (*Shadow and Act*, 299). Harlem, in other words, is unmediated urban chaos, and its "process of chaotic change" transforms all within: "family disintegrates, . . . church splinters, . . . folk wisdom is discarded in the mistaken notion that it in no way applies to urban living." Diets change, speech hardens, clock time prevails, even jazz gives way to bebop. There is nothing to fall back on: religious institutions are "inadequate"; political institutions are "incomplete and opportunistic"; "one is nowhere," a "'displaced' [product] of American democracy" (300).

The last two-thirds of *Invisible Man* (roughly 400 pages) are set in Harlem. It is to Harlem that Ellison's unnamed narrator has come in the mistaken hope of redefining himself so he can once again return to his Eden, the college from which he has been expelled. But once in Harlem he is "nowhere"; he ends underground on a coal pile, from which he refuses to leave, his sense of commitment exhausted. No one is more emphatic than Ellison in seeing life in the city—or at least in Harlem— as dead-ended. *Invisible Man* depicts a search for identity; it follows a black journey into history from the agrarian South to the industrial North; and, most of all, it presents a study of power—its use and abuse.

The power plant that throbs on the college campus corresponds to the power plant that Lucius Brockway keeps going for Liberty Paints; in both cases what belongs to black America has been expropriated by white America, anticipating the coal pile—the potential "black power"—at the end of the novel. All of these forms of power—institutional and industrial—are directly or indirectly controlled by the white establishment.

As has been traditional since Tiresias, the narrator's blindness encourages inward sight: he better understands his own reality the more it is entangled with chaos, the more he exhausts the possibilities of history. Power functions collectively, whether it be the power of the college or that of Mr. Emerson (corporate America) or the Brotherhood (the Communist Party) or Ras the Exhorter (Black Nationalism). Each wants to organize and control the city and the nation for its own benefit. Each group become a re-presentation of the larger crowd, within which the individual is invisible. Personal destiny is sacrificed to collective destiny; the individual is important only when he can be used—as Tod Clifton in his death is used to energize the crowd into the riot (the Harlem riot of 1943) that ends the novel.

The riot becomes a way of both expressing and challenging institutional power. Both the Brotherhood and the Black Nationalists see the resulting urban chaos as benefiting them. Throughout the novel, there has been the suggestion that white power must be negated. At the Golden Day, the black vets, who have come to the bar from the insane asylum, are mostly professional people who have broken under urban stress. They are locked in place by a custodian whose name, Supercargo, reflects his function as a kind of superego, a form of white restraint. When Supercargo is knocked unconscious, the vets riot without inhibitions, prefiguring the larger disorder that follows. The power is present: it only has to be released—and then reorganized into social institutions that offer psychological protection against urban chaos (*Shadow and Act*, 299). But the task is too much for the unnamed narrator, who does not know where to begin, and who distrusts any organization that might control that power.

Two starkly divergent images of the black man emerge from Ellison's contemporaries. Saul Bellow's characters are unhappy in the modern megalopolis. Herzog feels the city intensify his sense of death; the crowds embody "trans-descendence," intelligence turned downward. Mr. Sammler is even unhappier in the city; he has escaped a mass grave in Poland only to be entombed in New York, which embodies for him "the collapse of civilization," mass suicide. "You could smell decay," the narrator insists (Bellow, 33). On the 72nd Street bus, Sammler sees a large, handsome, immaculately dressed black man (easily the brother of the king whom Henderson meets in Africa). Sammler watches in fascination as the black man picks pockets and purses. When the pickpocket realizes that Sammler is on to him, he follows Sammler to his apartment building, corners him in the empty lobby, and forces Sammler to look at his penis. Later Sammler thinks of this man "unbuttoning his puma-colored coat in puma silence to show himself. Was this the sort of fellow called by Goethe *eine Nature*? A primary force?" (257). The imagery here—the "puma coat" and "puma silence"—does suggest an animal force at work, only inverted and debased by the megalopolis. The great hunter-king has become a common pickpocket, embodying an inversion, the dark side of progress.

Robert Lowell's "For the Union Dead" (1960) provides another image. Lowell juxtaposes a number of urban images: the old Boston Aquarium closed and boarded; steam shovels (like dinosaurs) gouging a garage under Boston Common; the golden-domed statehouse, across from which stands St. Gaudens's statue of Colonel Shaw (a distant relative of Lowell), who led his Negro infantry into the Civil War battles in which half the regiment died, including Shaw. Their common grave is their real monument, not the statue nor what accompanies it in modern Boston—the urban ditch next to it or the Mosler Safe and the picture above it of "Hiroshima boiling," images of the city locked into money and destructive technology. Nor are they commemorated in the "faces of Negro school-children" on the television set, a reference to the antibusing movement that then plagued South Boston. The monument to Colonel Shaw and the TV screen are ironic commentaries on each other.[2] Nothing has changed; not even the city in its indifference to his-

---

2. Lowell's attack on the antibusing sentiments in South Boston perhaps reveals a certain antipathy to Irish Catholicism that runs through Boston fiction. One can find it in Holmes's *Elsie Venner* (1861), Howells's *Rise of Silas Lapham* (1885), Adams's *Education* (1907), and Eliot's depiction of Apeneck Sweeney, as well as in Lowell. Does Lowell attack one kind of prejudice (racial) in the name of another (class/religious), knowing that his assumptions are consistent with the largely liberal assumptions of his poem and its audience? Certainly no one vilified similar antibusing sentiments when they arose in Los Angeles soon after the Boston experience. I mention this not to rekindle an unhappy debate but to suggest how difficult it is to create a sense of community in the modern American city, a theme that imbues this book. There are no moral absolutes built into the city, only fraught tensions.

tory, past and present, where "a savage servility / slides by on grease" (*For the Union Dead*, 72).

In Bellow's writing, the black man embodies a failed primitive force in the modern city. In Lowell's, the black man embodies a failed social cause that connects Colonel Shaw and the schoolchildren, the monument with its mixed racial regiment allowing an ironic commentary on the present racial strife, as urban communities fragment into hostile groups. Bellow's sense of misdirected energy and Lowell's sense of misdirected resistance rest on different cultural assumptions; but like parallel tracks that seem to merge in the far distance, they reinforce and cancel each other out. Neither provides a redeeming sense of community: the black man is an outcast, precisely the image with which Ellison leaves us in *Invisible Man*.

When Ellison's narrator goes underground, the act reflects his existing isolation. He ventured beyond history, beyond urban possibility, because he could not find a community in which to ground the isolated self. Both white and black communities were given over to power that used rather than absorbed him, increasing his alienation. Perhaps new forms of historical commitment would eventually emerge. In the meantime, he would stay underground—in the manner of the underground man from Dostoyevsky to Richard Wright—defining himself against chaos. As he tells us, "In going underground, I whipped it all except the mind, the *mind*. And the mind that has conceived a plan of living must never lose sight of the chaos against which that pattern was conceived. That goes for societies as well as for individuals" (*Invisible Man*, 580–81). Ellison's conclusion remains true for every city novel. The city is always reorganizing itself out of previous forms of chaos, out of failed forms of power, and its commitment is always to renewed forms of power.

Commitment or hibernation, allegiance or anarchy, conformity or rebellion, community or isolation—these forms of order and chaos are at the very heart of city life. Defoe's H.F. sees the city as his only option; Balzac's Eugene Rastignac stays and fights, seemingly with more commitment than Dickens's Pip; Norris's Vandover, Dreiser's Hurstwood, and Dos Passos's Charley Anderson remain to the degenerative end. William Carlos Williams looks for the means to redeem the degenerating city. When one or another of these possibilities becomes unacceptable, there is always the possibility of disillusionment—as with Whitman and Crane; flight—as with Nick Carraway; insanity—as with Nathanael West's Tod Hackett; or hibernation—as with Ellison's Invisible Man.

The options are many, the winners few. Whether Bellow's lost energy or Lowell's lost cause, the difference hardly matters when there is no redeeming community. From Harlem as Nowhere to the Nowhere City: the move is from race to demography, from isolated community to urban sprawl. Since the city both offers and restricts possibility, the difference between the races may be of degree rather than kind. If everything comes down to urban possibility, then, in the words of Ellison's narrator, "Who knows but that, on the lower frequencies, I speak for you?" (*Invisible Man,* 581).

CHAPTER 15

Quest West

I

Both the rise of the British Empire and the settling of the American frontier gave life to ideologies that found form in narrative subgenres. The Sherlock Holmes detective novels accommodate those ideologies, as do the novels of imperial adventure and the western. The meaning of the frontier experience was codified in works such as Owen Wister's *The Virginian* (1904) and Jack Schaefer's *Shane* (1949), which helped create and extend the myth of the cowboy. (Wister's novel, which supplied the western formula, is the product of an eastern mentality brought West.) Both *The Virginian* and *Shane* concern the Johnson County War in Wyoming between the big ranch owners and the homesteaders. The ranchers accused the homesteaders of cattle rustling and brought in hired guns from Texas to keep vigilante order. When two homesteaders were hanged by the vigilante group, the homesteaders organized and "war" broke out, ending only when government troops were sent in. *The Virginian* depicts this battle from the point of view of the ranch owners, *Shane* from that of the homesteaders: the same narrative elements are used to express opposite political views. What these two works share is the belief that the land must be transformed through a new heroism: the Virginian (that is, Jeffersonian) idea of aristocracy and honor crosses the country to create in the West a new, natural aristocracy based on tests of courage and trial by ordeal. After his ordeal, the

Virginian remains on the land, marries, and becomes domesticated; Shane, always the loner, picks up and moves on, like Cooper's Natty Bumppo, staying one step ahead of domestication.

When this stereotype hits land's end on the West Coast, he will become Raymond Chandler's Marlowe (the name itself taken, as Chandler tells us, to suggest a modern knight). Chandler's hero is the hard-boiled detective endowed with the chivalric ideals of Wister's cowboy, now moved from the lawless range to the corrupted city. Like the cowboy, he is an outsider—lonely, chaste, motivated by personal ideals that are implicit moral comments on the degeneration of America. To be sure, the detective's urban story is cynical, his ideals tenuous, his accomplishments morally dubious—but all this reflects history as process, the eroding of expectations as Americans moved west; cultural values are at one with their literary expression.

Raymond Chandler's *The Big Sleep* (1939) begins and ends in the oil field owned by General Sternwood. As Marlowe looks out from the Sternwood mansion, he can see it in the distance:

On this lower level faint and far off I could just barely see some of the old wooden derricks of the oilfield from which the Sternwoods had made their money. Most of the field was public now, cleaned up and donated to the city by General Sternwood. But a little of it was still producing in groups of wells pumping five or six barrels a day. The Sternwoods, having moved up the hill, could no longer smell the stale sump water or the oil, but they could still look out of their front windows and see what had made them rich. If they wanted to. I didn't suppose they would want to. (*Big Sleep,* 18)

Chandler, who had worked for oil companies, connects the exploitation of the land and the moral recklessness that follows. Into this despoiled world comes Philip Marlowe, an urban knight who desires to be honorable despite the corruption around him, an avatar of the frontiersman and western cowboy transformed by the city. He follows a demanding code of honor, courage, and pride in a job well done (values also affirmed by Hemingway, as discussed below). In the tradition of the earlier detective (Dickens's Bucket and Conrad's Heat), he helps personalize the city; he cuts through its anonymity and assembles the pieces of the narrative's mystery.

Appropriately, the initial mystery involves the blackmailing of Carmen, General Sternwood's daughter, whose moral recklessness mirrors her father's capitalism—"appropriately," because blackmail involves the use of information for purposes of extortion, and extortion is simply a form of exploitation. General Sternwood's money, gained partly from exploiting others, leaves him vulnerable to being exploited; and Marlowe must make his way between legal and illegal realms, which turn out to be two faces of the same world. Just a few miles from the Sternwood mansion are found pornographic bookstores and illegal gambling—the world of the mob, whose motives, if not its methods, are substantially the same as those of Sternwood and his corporation.

In *The Big Sleep*, Carmen has murdered a man in the same oil field that made the family rich. Carmen killed Rusty Regan when he would not return her love, and she tries to kill Marlowe for the same reason and in the same place. Marlowe, however, refuses the Sternwood coin for his silence—the $15,000 that would make him complicit in murder and bring him into the center of the system. Marlowe prefers to remain on the edge of the city, prefers the urban "nastiness" (216) that he has made into a way of life. Chandler here pursues the meaning of the West as he shows the moral consequences of a state of mind tied to the industrial city, a state of mind inseparable from the desire to control people and the environment in the name of money. In Chandler's world next to the sea, the city has become a degenerative system. Rusty Regan dies and Marlowe is threatened in a symbolic landscape that is the source of both wealth and death—realities that go together in the post-Enlightenment city. Chandler extrapolates from a personal truth: the big sleep, which is at the heart of every life, is also at the heart of every city. His, too, is the naturalistic city in which a degenerative process is at work, though the novel lacks naturalistic commentary. His city, like its inhabitants, awaits death, the entropic force by which nature exercises its final dominance. Chandler takes us close to an existential urbanism: Marlowe realizes the futility of his task, realizes he is in an urban world too soiled to be renewed; but, like Camus's Sisyphus, he finds meaning in such futility.

II

The bridge between Wister's cowboy and Chandler's detective is Ernest Hemingway's hero, divested of knightly ideals. His tough guy or big game hunter would rather act than talk, is suspicious of abstractions and sentiment, tests values against his experience, takes pride in a job well done, believes in fair play, and puts friendship ahead of love—thus displaying many of the values of the West. Hemingway grew up reading westerns and superimposed this code on the battles of

World War I and the Spanish Civil War. As part of the ambulance corps in World War I, he first came to and was wounded in Italy. Hemingway spent almost a decade among the expatriate Americans in Europe, and he returned often in the next three decades as either a war correspondent or an observer. Three of his five novels are set in Europe; Paris and later Venice had a special meaning for him, as did Spain—especially its peasant people and its ritual of the bullfight.

Perhaps Spain's particular appeal was that it allowed him to locate meaning in a premodern world before the rise of the machine, which he was growing thoroughly to dislike, as he declares in *The Green Hills of Africa* (1935): "A continent ages. But the foreigner destroys, cuts down the trees, drains the water. . . . The earth gets tired of being exploited. A country wears out quickly unless man puts back in it all his residue and that of all the beasts. When he quits using beasts and uses machines, the earth defeats him quickly." Hemingway adds that those who now come to America "had come too late," concluding, "Now I would go somewhere else" (194). This was Hemingway's farewell to mainstream America, even though he did return to Ketchum, Idaho, the American rural West that he thought was different from urban America; and it is Hemingway's farewell to the twentieth century, because the places that remained untouched by urbanization were becoming fewer and fewer. Hemingway does not turn to old myths for the answer but instead creates a new mythology out of the fundamental. In *The Sun Also Rises* (1926), the only moments in which Jake finds peace occur when he is with a close friend, fishing the clear, cold streams of the Irati River in Spain, or when he has been washed clean of the fiesta by the sea of San Sebastian. These scenes contrast with those in a decadent Europe, especially in neon-lit Paris; one partakes of life, the other of death; one is connected with a dying order, the other with the elemental and primitive, embodied by Pedro Romero, for whom the final test of life against death takes place in the bullfighting arena. *For Whom the Bell Tolls* (1940) might seem to be Hemingway's one novel that cannot be considered in these elemental terms. But Hemingway believed that the Spanish Civil War, like the American Civil War, came at a pivotal moment in history, that it was a conflict between two opposed ways of life, and that Spain's agrarian nature was being threatened by the machine. This is why he sees the bombers as menacing, describing their savagery as something different from that of sharks—that is, as something outside of nature: "They move like no thing there has ever been. They move like mechanized doom" (*For Whom the Bell Tolls*, 235).

Across the River and into the Trees (1950), a novel Hemingway wrote while working concurrently on *The Old Man and the Sea* (1952) also contrasts two worlds, the city and the sea. As a city that sprang from the sea, Venice has confronted both nature and history and has participated in the cycles of life and death, victory and defeat. Colonel Cantwell loves the city, despite its proximity to where he was wounded in the war; and he has returned to Venice, where he will die, to complete a personal cycle. The colonel and the grand master share a kind of holy moment when they meet at the hotel: "contact was made between two old inhabitants of the Veneto . . . in their love of an old country, much fought over, and always triumphant in defeat, which they had both defended in their youth" (*Across the River,* 62). So too in *The Old Man and the Sea,* elemental forces are at work. Santiago alone confronts and inflicts death, refusing to give up when defeated and participating in an elemental urge that sends him deep into the sea (just as a more mysterious urge sends the leopard high into the Kilimanjaro).

For Hemingway, Africa provided an equivalent to the Wild West. In both he found expanses of untamed land outside the city. In Africa, Macomber becomes a man by testing himself against the final reality—death. Like Tarzan (Edgar Rice Burroughs, like Hemingway, was a midwesterner who moved West), Hemingway's heroes are but one step removed from an animality they transform by a personal aesthetic grounded in moral strength and self-generated honor. Such values can only originate and be tested outside of urban conformity. Hemingway's primal vision involves a natural aristocracy outside of culture and civilization—a journey back into history to a time before the city, beyond degeneration and decadence, to a realm of preculture. There one can be tested against the limits of the sea from which all life came and against the limits of the hunt, where the ritual of life and death is as natural as time.

Like Rudyard Kipling in *Captains Courageous* (1897) or Jack London in *The Sea Wolf* (1904), Hemingway aims in his narrative to get the protagonist outside of modern history, especially outside the mechanical order of the city, on a ship or on an island where a code of primitive values rules. Such a narrative maneuver allows Hemingway to contrast elemental and urban man. Another device involved locating a story in a moment of transition, like that of the Spanish Civil War, in which two ways of life—primitive and modern—were in conflict. A third approach was to examine one character in opposite cultures, as he did in *The Sun Also Rises* when he contrasts Jake in Paris and Jake in Burguete. Hemingway struggled to locate his preurban vision in idealized action and rituals that partake of the land and the sea, until finally he displaced the city (civilized life) with the extended arena (trial by combat).

Hemingway not only contrasted the primitive and civilized, but he depicted this world impressionistically. Impressionism, as we saw in chapter 5, dictated the move from naturalism to modernism—the treatment of detail driving the transition from an objective to a subjective realm. The distinction between descriptive detail and impressionistic detail is objectivity on the way to becoming subjectivity. Pater was the first to grasp this process, a lesson learned by Conrad, who influenced Stephen Crane, who in turn influenced Hemingway. Hemingway's is a naturalistic world seen through a Paterian prism, with the emphasis on a recording consciousness rather than on biology, heredity, or environment. For Jake Barnes, a world of force becomes personal, energized by an active critical intelligence. When Hemingway began writing *The Sun Also Rises,* he recorded in a notebook the world he was observing around him. It took almost fifty pages for Hemingway to move from this personal sphere into his story, creating Jake Barnes as a vehicle to convey his own impressions. Thus Jake expresses his likes and dislikes, his impatience with Paris, and his sense of relief in Burguete. Hemingway's aversion to the city is powerfully expressed through the vivid impressions of a viewer. When Jake describes Paris in the morning—the streets slick with water, the smell of roasting chestnuts, the scent of strong coffee from the cafe—that also captures an impression in a manner very close to impressionistic art, each detail illustrating an engaged subjectivity. Hemingway worked in primitive and elemental time grounded in the impressionistic. His city comes to life through such impressionistic detail; otherwise, he found the city wanting.

III

Ernest Hemingway was less concerned with endings and their significance than with the meaning of our origins: how primitive rituals involving life and earth could be preserved in an increasingly technological society. While he was indifferent to historical decline, F. Scott Fitzgerald rushed into it. *The Last Tycoon* opens with Monroe Stahr traveling east to west across the heavens. As the plane crosses the desert, Stahr looks down at the lights of Southern California in the distance and thinks how far he has come from his youth in the slums of New York.

He thinks also of America, a land that extends westward, stopped only by the sea.

As in many other Los Angeles novels, most of the action in *The Last Tycoon* is engendered by thoughts of progress. The seed of these thoughts, the idea of the West, was carried from Europe across the Atlantic and then across the continent. This movement—a by-product of the Enlightenment—went by a number of names: the frontier movement, Manifest Destiny, California Dreaming. Implicit in all its forms were the assumptions that natural rights took precedence over birthrights and that the land was there to be dominated, remade into cities like Los Angeles as monuments to progress. Los Angeles is perhaps the last major city to grow out of this notion. Crafted out of the desert, it could never have come into being without the technology that brings it water. In the late nineteenth century, two railroad lines met in Los Angeles, and the city became a resort for wealthy easterners who wanted to escape the winter. Later it attracted more ordinary folk from states like Indiana and Iowa, and later still it attracted the industries that made modern airfare and warfare possible, the precursors of Thomas Pynchon's Yoyodyne. Offering a perpetual present, Los Angeles defies its past. It seems to have been born full-blown into the modern world: a city without an origin and without a center—what Alison Lurie has titled the Nowhere City, 465 square miles of entangled and labyrinthine space. Los Angeles is a city that absorbs other cities—a city that absorbs consciousness. That Hollywood was among the first of the new industries to settle there coupled the dreamer to the dream.

The modern commercial city, which had its beginning in the eighteenth century, was transformed in the nineteenth century by the industrial revolution and underwent another transformation in the twentieth century. Los Angeles is the first city in the Western world to take its dimensions from the automobile—a fact that has determined its landscape and scale, which have overpowered a sense of human proportions. Probably no city in the Western world has a more negative image: one vast freeway system, enshrouded in smog, carrying thousands of dreamers to a kind of spiritual and physical dead end. In this world, we shift easily from a sense of promise to the grotesque, the violent, and the apocalyptic. Los Angeles, the supreme embodiment of the secular city, is built on the same geographic latitude as Jerusalem, the greatest Western holy city. The movement west was not without historical irony.

Fitzgerald may not have brought all of these ideas consciously to *The Last Tycoon,* but he sensed most of them. He depicted Los Angeles as located at an end point in time and "filling up with weary desperadoes" (*Last Tycoon,* 80). This image is consistent with his image of the grunion who throw themselves on the beach in an act that seems to promise something more than the death that results: "They came in twos and threes and platoons and companies, relentless and exalted and scornful, around the great bare feet of the intruders, as they had come before Sir Francis Drake had nailed his plaque to the boulder on the shore" (92). Something mysterious has also been pushing humanity west since Francis Drake and even before, something inseparable from the death that accompanies it. Thomas Pynchon was to rework these themes in *The Crying of Lot 49.*

In Fitzgerald's novel, Stahr, who embodies the process of moving westward, is himself a weary desperado. A man who has dominated a new industry, he is a former boy wonder who now finds his energy depleted. The labor leader Brimmer, a Communist, cannot believe that such a man is important in the system. But Brimmer sees only the shell of the man and fails to realize that Stahr is perhaps the last representative (as the title suggests) of inspired individualism (the basis for a theory of genius), soon to be replaced by the new corporatism and big unions. What Stahr brought with him was a dream born in Europe, transformed by Enlightenment values, and turned into the frontier movement. This dream was built on a personal sense of honor, a belief in the potential of self, and the desire to control through the power of will—romantic values fast becoming tenuous in a commercial/industrial, urban society. Fitzgerald came to believe that as the country's frontier moved west, it lured the dreamer toward ideals that were already dead. Gatsby played out this vision in the East, Monroe Stahr in the West. Fitzgerald set Stahr's story in "a lavish, romantic past that perhaps will not come again in our time" (*Last Tycoon,* 141).

Fitzgerald had experienced many of the emotions that he gave to Stahr. After early success, he too had come crashing down in the 1930s. The novel brilliantly depicts the need of a sick, tired man to start over, despite his loss of vitality. Stahr's love affair with Kathleen grows out of the need of the uprooted for roots, the need to arrest time and reverse defeat—a process that challenges individuality, of which he seems to be the end product. The frenzied drives through Los Angeles at night that take them to the Pacific Coast Highway form an axis between Stahr's home in Beverly Hills, where he is seldom found since he often sleeps at the studio, and the partly built home in Malibu, which is as unfinished as the grand design of his career. The rootlessness, the misplaced desire, the horror of standing still, the need for fulfillment that seems inseparable from movement, the sense of being incomplete in an unfinished home and in a city spawned between desert and sea—all of these feelings give an intensity to the story of Monroe Stahr that cannot be separated from the Los Angeles in which it takes place.

IV

Nathanael West's *The Day of the Locust* (1939) portrays Los Angeles as an urban hell. West begins with many of the themes that would inform *The Last Tycoon;* he shows Hollywood as the end of a dream in which the unfulfilled, restless self hopes for success and material gain. He concentrates not on what is glamorous in this pursuit but on shabby apartment houses, the loneliness of the displaced pilgrim, the burlesque that goes with grubbing a living, the misery of survival that is prelude to the dream. Aiming at a harsher portrait of Los Angeles than Fitzgerald's, West believes that beneath the false glamour of Hollywood (both the place and the industry) is a brutal violence waiting to erupt. In this version we edge toward apocalypse, as his satiric jeremiad shows us a process playing itself out destructively. Nature has given way to grotesqueries—to misplaced architecture that appears to result from an explosion in a time machine and houses that hang from hills like unnatural growths. It is a world where dwarfs unfold themselves out of rag piles in lonely corridors, where unwieldy hands jump uncontrolled at the end of wrists, and where meat and fruit become unnatural in the neon-lighted bins of grocery stores.

In *The Day of the Locust,* people come to Los Angeles to pursue their desires, or to retire, or to die. It is an end in itself—a world without a past, where buildings are raised and razed; a world where dreams can be warmed but not fulfilled by the sun. Part of what pushes people west is a sense of fantasy that often gives way to violence and death: no Los Angeles novel ends more violently. In West's world, youth and beauty have become commodities for sale in the market called Hollywood. Waiting to sell or buy leads to the terrible boredom that consumes many lives in this novel and explains the need to experience excitement, whether it be the morbid thrill of a funeral or the excitement of a movie premiere. Beneath the emptiness that neither ritual can relieve is a capacity for force and rage that seems atavistic, as if all restraint has given way here on the edge of the Pacific.

Tod Hackett is the moral voice of this narration, but Tod, who is himself capable of the lust and violence that he abhors in others, can never distance himself from the city of which he is a part. Hackett observes the pathos of this world: the superficiality of Faye Greener and her father's dream, as well as the violence of Earle Shoop, the first of the urban cowboys, whose very life seems to symbolize the natural giving way to the mechanical, the western range to the crowded city. Tod's observations start with the people whose motley clothes suggest the masquerade that is finally turned into an industry by Hollywood. He observes houses that seem transplanted from another planet and lonely apartment houses, the architectural equivalent of deracinated, lonely lives; the inhabitants live in separate rooms with no sense of family or community. Even those at the other end of the social scale are trapped in distorted lives: Claude Estee, the screenwriter, lives in a Los Angeles "southern mansion" with a plastic horse at the bottom of his swimming pool and watches pornographic movies as a main diversion.

Hollywood is one of the novel's sustaining metaphors. Not only is the place a dumping ground for dreams, but beneath the exterior of the film industry is something so thin that it collapses under the weight of life, transforming the heroic into the grotesque. The metaphor is literalized when the Waterloo set gives way during the filming of a movie about Napoleon—illusion collapsing and taking history with it. The Enlightenment ended with Napoleon and Waterloo, the hopes of which are now buried under Hollywood plywood and plaster. The violence of this scene is recapitulated three times in the novel—first when Faye and Earle dance, then at the cockfight that anticipates the fight between Earle and Miguel, and finally at the movie premiere when the characters seem to step into Tod's apocalyptic painting, *The Burning of Los Angeles,* an artwork prophetically ahead of history. The city's destiny, then, seems connected to a final destruction, as if we have come to the end of a process.

As we have seen, the city—of Defoe, Dickens, Balzac, Dostoyevsky, Conrad, Eliot, Fitzgerald, Williams, and Ellison—participates in its own undoing. Urban order is tenuous; chaos always lies just beneath its surface. Tod Hackett comes to learn that inextricably embedded in a frustrated, restless population is a force that can explode without direction—or can be organized and controlled politically, as West saw in 1939 when he looked to Europe, especially Germany. With prescience, he saw the modern city as an energy system that worked either toward its own destruction or toward totalitarian ends. In *The Day of the Locust,* he saw the thin separation between order and disorder, between the New Jerusalem and the Apocalypse. The Enlightenment city had offered new promise to eighteenth-century Europe, but the last of that hope vanished three centuries later on the outer edge of another continent.

PART 5

After *The Waste Land*

CHAPTER 16

From Myth to Mystery

I

Once the city became a system of signs, we needed a transcendental signifier (be it God, nature, history, or the rational mind) to hold the other signs in place. This assumption was challenged by Jacques Derrida, who argued that such abstractions became the foundations of unwarranted constructs, thus falsely privileging meaning from the outset. He questioned concepts such as "origins" and "destiny" on the grounds that they were unknowable, that meaning contained its own negation, and that language was unstable, in constant flux if not regression: here Western thought reaches its self-consuming dead end. In challenging both the mythic and the scientific conceptions of reality, Derrida turns reality into a system of dead signs to be deciphered as best we can. His disconnected and alienated objects cancel themselves out, as Pynchon's Oedipa Maas discovers.

Without a transcendental signifier, urban signs begin to float, and meaning gives way to mystery. Viewed from within a system as unstable as Derrida's system of language, the city loses claim to being "real." What we bring to the city is what we get back: the "echo" principle becomes the basis for our reality. The signs—failing to point toward a redeeming God (as they did for Robinson Crusoe), or a redeeming history (as they did for Hegel), or a redeeming nature (as they did for Wordsworth), or a redeeming art (as they did for Henry James)—

become self-referential. Having entered the postmodern world of urban signs, we find the problem of reading more complex. As free-floating signification eliminates meaning, interpretation becomes equivalent to paranoia, which is the end result of any self-enclosed system. We are left with a sense of a diminished humanity, of the anonymous and super-fluous, of human isolation and fragility, of anxiety and great nervous tension. Lacking transcendence, the city cannot go beyond what it consumes; the mind cannot go beyond itself.

The modern and the postmodern novel differ in their narrative modes: one—involving myth and symbolism, cyclical time, forms of Bergsonian consciousness—was undone by the other. Thomas Pynchon, John Barth, Robert Coover, Don DeLillo, and others systematically undo "the wasteland myth," the search for meaning in the historical past, and the belief in a subject—that is, a consciousness that centers meaning. This narrative shift was in keeping with and parallel to a philosophical and theoretical movement that collapsed consciousness into forms of structure (Saussure), discourse (Foucault), paradigm (Kuhn), systems (Bertalanffy), or grammar or rhetoric (Derrida, de Man).

Critics no longer argue about whether postmodernism is merely a realignment of modernism; I think most would agree that postmodernism creates a totally different kind of reality, whether we are talking about the city or the literary text. While modernism owed much to a theory of aesthetics, postmodernism takes its being from the linguistic-philosophical-anthropological paradigm displayed in Saussure's structural theory of language and applied by Lévi-Strauss to the reading of culture. Meaning is no longer in nature, manifested through revelation (Defoe) or through the unfolding of symbolism, whether cosmic (Coleridge) or evolutionary (Darwin): it is now understood as the structure the mind creates, so what is common between cultures is explained by shared consciousness and not by influence. Synchronic time replaces diachronic time; substance gives way to a system of signs and reality to relation. Meaning is "discovered" not in nature but in systems as vision is replaced by hermeneutics: objects (natural or social) become texts to be interpreted according to paradigms.

Moreover, postmodernism takes us away from the Newtonian universe, in which matter in motion is subject to predictable, mechanical laws of nature, to Max Planck's theory of discrete quanta of radiation. Niels Bohr's work on the discontinuous nature of energy in subatomic particles advanced Planck's theory and was advanced in turn by Werner Heisenberg and Kurt Gödel in their work on the uncertainty principle and probability theory. And Claude Shannon and Charles Sanders Peirce, who applied the principle of entropy to the way we process information, found within every principle of organization a principle of disorganization: information comes to us through static, noise, and redundancy. These scientific inquiries challenged what we know and how we know it. Probability and uncertainty replace determinate knowledge, as the world itself becomes both discontinuous and indeterminate: the complexity of the information we gain depends upon the complexity of the paradigms we produce. In this new interpretive context, the city becomes a very different realm of meaning.

Finally, postmodernism challenged the idea of the subject, the self as the source of independent consciousness. As we have seen, by challenging both Christian and Enlightenment assumptions Nietzsche was instrumental in fashioning the idea of modern consciousness. Modernism, I would argue, begins where Nietzsche left off—with human consciousness confronting an unmade universe, a universe without a creator. The quality of that consciousness may differ in James, Eliot, Woolf, Faulkner, and Hemingway, but their characters all define themselves and their world in terms of it. Postmodernism takes us one step further by asking what would happen if we postulate a universe without such subjectivity—a universe that is intelligible in terms of consciousness that is already collapsed into culture and thus inseparable from discourse, from the way we talk about it. No longer independent and in control, consciousness then comes into play as part of a system. Such consciousness is generated by and inseparable from a specific culture, held in place by that culture's institutions (that is, by power) and no longer personal. As a result, the city becomes a state of mind: it thinks us and not the other way around.

Thomas Pynchon is central to these cultural and literary changes: he systematically undercuts the mythic, historic, aesthetic, and moral elements of modernism, creating a series of "flattened" characters who lack subjectivity and find the past emptied of all but "stencilized" meaning. In his novels, the wasteland quest plays itself out in an entropic landscape. In both *V.* and *The Crying of Lot 49*, consciousness is lost in the indeterminate maze that becomes the postmodern city. In *V.* (1963), Pynchon undoes the myth of modernism by rewriting *The Waste Land*. Just as the questing knight goes in search of the Grail in Eliot's poem, so Herbert Stencil goes in search of the lost mother. But as he enters history, all he finds is what he brings to it—history becomes stencilized. What is lost turns out to be not ideal after all, myth itself collapses into history, and the mind is powerless to retrieve a lost past or to project an idealized future.

V. is a long, tangled novel with two plots that eventually converge like the letter V. In one, Herbert Stencil is in frenetic pursuit of the mysterious V, who we suspect to be and later learn is his mother. She appears in many guises, by turns a nineteen-year-old Yorkshire girl named Victoria Wren, a young temptress in Florence seducing Stencil's father, a lesbian in Paris where she is having an affair with a ballerina who dresses as a boy, "Veronica Manganese" in Malta, "Vera Meroving" in southwest Africa, and a "bad" priest in Malta where she dies in an air raid during World War II. As V moves through the novel she loses various body parts, becoming more a machine than a human being; after the air raid she is disassembled by a group of children who find her pinned under a roof beam in a demolished building. They pull off her wig, take out her glass eye (which has a clock for a pupil), detach her artificial leg, and finally kill her when they dig a star sapphire from her navel.

The story of V is told against the rise of a mechanical, urbanized world. She embodies the decline of woman from sex goddess to transvestite, from mother to manufactured object, from human to grotesque. As some critics have pointed out, she personifies what has happened to Henry Adams's Virgin in the age of the Dynamo, progressively devitalized in an era of urban sprawl and technology. Pynchon shares Adams's belief in entropy, the inevitable wearing down of the physical world and cultural systems, as well as the belief that Western man—with the megalopolis, technology, and the Dynamo all expanding, triumphing, and supporting a commercial/industrial system—is increasingly losing his own humanity. As the novel makes explicit, "A decadence...is a falling-away from what is human, and the further we fall the less human we become. Because we are less human, we foist off the humanity we have lost on inanimate objects and abstract theories" (*V.,* 380).

The city becomes an end in itself, its citizens mere relational parts. The second plot—the story of Benny Profane and the Whole Sick Crew—reinforces this theme. Without family, rootless, indifferent to all but creature comforts, Benny finds greatest pleasure in "yo-yoing": riding the subway up and down Manhattan, going nowhere, he displays mechanical energy as an end in itself, motion without direction. While the Stencil plot involves a search for a principle of harmony, the Profane plot recognizes the inevitability of chaos, the power of entropy to undo order and move toward death. Pynchon believes the machine age has pushed the Puritan fear of women (that is, of sex) to its final destructive conclusion, leading modern man "deeper into fetish-country" until the woman "becomes entirely and in reality...an inanimate object of desire" (386). Insofar as the journey into the past reveals no mythic or transcendent meaning—taking us only to the (stencilized) self with which we began—history becomes meaningless, a tenuous way of organizing meaning.

All of these themes—the power of entropy, the emptiness of myth and history, the mechanical limits of the city—are embodied in the lost city of Vheissu, a fantasy vision that owes much to Henry Adams's emphasis upon entropy. Carried to a doomsday conclusion, the second law of thermodynamics asserts that the universe will lose heat entropically until all matter and energy degrade to an ultimate state of uniformity. Pynchon's Vheissu, located near one of the poles and reached by ascending large mountains and then traveling through an elaborate network of caves, is frozen, motionless, barren, and lifeless. When Hugh Godolphin reaches it, he digs down several feet beneath the snow to find the corpse of a spider monkey buried in the ice. The monkey is the physical expression of the heat loss that occurs in the universe as we move from the tropics (the monkey) to the poles, from the primitive to the civilized, from the savage to the city, from life to death—dichotomies that run through Pynchon's major works. T. S. Eliot explored the precivilized to suggest that we might again make contact with a lost primitive energy that, when mythologized, could redeem the fallen city and be a source of new life, but Pynchon offers no mythic solution. His return to the primitive instead reveals a heat loss inseparable from our urbanized, industrialized existence and takes us to the frozen city and death. At some level of correspondence and meaning, Manhattan and Vheissu, like many other elements in this novel, converge, becoming perhaps the final V. Pynchon extends these themes in *The Crying of Lot 49* and *Gravity's Rainbow*.

II

Pynchon sees the modern city as the end of a historical process. Its origins could not be separated from the rise of Puritanism and, as we have seen, the new commercial class of the eighteenth century, which looked on the city as part of a profit system. As the new science and technology produced the machine, this city changed scale, as

Henry Adams saw, and the world of the Virgin, unified by the mythic imagination, was displaced by the Dynamo. Everything became subject to the laws of entropy and disunited because the principle of operation was discontinuous and indeterminate; the power of the Dynamo was limited only by its self-consumption on three levels: the mechanical or thermodynamic, ending in waste; the communicative, ending in silence; and the human, ending in decay and death.

In *The Crying of Lot 49* (1966), human entropy has created the army of outcasts who make up the Tristero—those who have been used up by capitalist society, their functions made obsolete, their presence rendered superfluous and unnecessary. The Tristero is a secret organization that came into being to counter Puritanism and capitalism. Like Max Weber and R. W. Tawney, Pynchon suggests that capitalism had its origins in Puritan thought and belief, finding evidence in a Puritan sect, the Scurvhamites, and in a Jacobean play, *The Courier's Tragedy,* a version of which may have been an attack on Puritanism. The play introduces the Trystero, a group that seems to have originated in the late Renaissance in response to the monopoly of the mails in the Low Countries held by the Thurn and Taxis families of Venice. After an internal dispute over the transfer of power, Hernando Joaquin de Tristero y Calavera became their new leader, "perhaps a madman, perhaps an honest rebel, according to some only a con artist" (*Lot 49,* 119). The Tristero became the antiestablishment, the disinherited; dressed in black (symbolic of night/death/exile), with their emblem the muted post horn, they began a systematic attack on the Thurn and Taxis mail routes. As Enlightenment capitalism spread west, the Tristero counterforce spread with it. Disguised on the American frontier in blackface as Indians, they preyed on the Pony Express and Wells Fargo couriers; when they reached the Pacific, "their empire [was] now toward silence, impersonation, opposition masquerading as allegiance" (130). The acronym W.A.S.T.E. (We Await Silent Tristero's Empire) suggests the idea of entropy; the Tristero are renewed by a negative entropy, the taking of human failures into their number, the derelicts of one kind or another that the System produces. They are certain that machines cannot forever produce waste byproducts; they also believe that the communication and information systems (including the mail) that sustain power can be undermined, leaving silence. Out of this entropic silence and waste will come the death of the System. In *Lot 49,* Pynchon substitutes scientific metaphors for mythic and religious ones: apocalypse gives way to entropy.

Oedipa Maas connects the city and the Tristero; she is the new detective in the urban labyrinth. As her name suggests, she is the daughter in the maze who must come to terms with the world of the Father and its Dynamo. Oedipa's task is to execute the legacy of Pierce Inverarity, who, a Howard Hughes figure, has helped develop the West. Through his understanding of the commercial system and his use of technology, Inverarity has imposed his control over the land, turning that control into complex holdings and a massive fortune. His legacy, Oedipa discovers, is America itself: "She had dedicated herself . . . to making sense of what Inverarity had left behind, never suspecting that the legacy was America. . . . [H]er love [for him remained] incommensurate with his need to possess, to alter the land, to bring new skylines, personal antagonisms, growth rates into being. 'Keep it bouncing,' he told her once, 'that's all the secret, keep it bouncing'" (134). Oedipa's task is not an easy one, not merely because of Inverarity's extensive holdings but because meaning in *Lot 49* functions like language, as a self-enclosed sign system. As Pynchon tells us, "Behind the hieroglyphic streets there would be either a transcendent meaning, or only the earth" (125–26). Unable to discover a transcendent meaning, Oedipa is left with the earth—or rather the mystery of the unreadable city. She is like Roland Barthes's prototypical postmodern figure, whom Barthes conceived as a new kind of Robinson Crusoe: "If I had to imagine a new Robinson Crusoe, I would not place him on a desert island but in a city of twelve million people [like Tokyo] where he could decipher neither speech nor writing: that, I think, would be the modern form of Defoe's tale" (Barthes, 122).

In her search for the meaning of the Tristero, Oedipa can find no totalizing perspective to explain the landscape of which she is a part: the mind can no longer decode the city. The signs fail to point toward a redeeming God, as they did for Robinson Crusoe, but become wholly self-referential, feeding into the suspicions with which she began or, worse, suggesting but not documenting the reality of Tristero, which moves her toward paranoia (the inevitable result of fear feeding on itself in a closed system). We have information (random data such as stock market quotations) without meaning (there is no context that allows for a principle of predictability—such as counting by twos, which allows one to know in advance the next number in a sequence). The more information she receives, the less meaning she has, and the more mysterious is her situation. When she visits Mr. Toth, Oedipa discovers that even history is unreliable: Toth has collapsed the stories told by his grandfather, who had ridden for the Pony Express, into the Porky Pig cartoons that he now watches on TV.[1] Oedipa thinks she can verify the meaning of the Tristero since their name is mentioned in *The Courier's Tragedy*. But when she goes back to earlier texts of the play, she discovers that there are a number of different editions, each contradicting the meaning of the other. Such is the fate of the postmodern detective.

As pure construct, the city exists for Oedipa to read. But once inside such a system, inside the labyrinth, she loses a centering consciousness and has no perspective outside it. She keeps getting her own feedback as she journeys self-absorbed to places with the significant names of Echo Court and San Narciso. Yet even the city as a state of mind has a physical reality with energy demands of its own. As unreal as such a city may seem, it exists to process the business of late capitalism and hence is as much an energy system as earlier cities, subject like them to the processes of waste and death.[2] Even in such a system, the search for the mythic and spiritual goes on, albeit unsuccessfully, as Oedipa, like the inhabitants of the first cities, journeys to the grave to see if she can communicate with Randy Driblette (whose spirit is perhaps contained in the jar of dandelion wine with which she returns). The funereal moment often appears in urban novels—Rastignac's journey to Père Lachaise cemetery, Leopold Bloom's visit to Glasnevin, Hurstwood's burial in Potter's Field, Nick Carraway's attendance at Gatsby's funeral: one's fate in the city often starts or ends with the grave.

While the individual in Pynchon's novel seems inseparable from a private fate, and while the chaos of the maze seems to prevail, Pynchon also suggests that much depends on that jar of dandelion wine. *Gravity's Rainbow* presents the conflict between the forces of life and the forces of death even more directly, identifying the latter with the Enlightenment mentality that has now conquered the West. His main concern is whether or not that mentality can suppress the mythic impulses—the desire, for example, of the living to communicate with the dead, of humans to believe in something beyond their physical limits and to trust

---

1. Pynchon thus discounts Toth, the god of the dead in ancient Egyptian religion, who possessed secret wisdom.

2. With its emphasis on constructed reality, postmodernism has never explained the independence of physical reality from the products of mind. Entropy is a physical law, not a cultural construct; its operation is the same in North America as in South Africa. If it did not operate universally, we would not have a different culture; we would have a different universe.

in a reality beyond mere sign systems—the impulses, that is, which were largely responsible for creating the city in the first place.

Once we lose transcendent meaning, our hold on the city is gone. All human values become tenuous; friendship and love hover over an abyss; Oedipa's husband is broken by drugs; her lover commits suicide; her analyst goes insane. At the end of the novel, she is left at the edge of the ocean, a rented car between her and the lifeless continent, holding a dead phone. She has come to land's end in the machine society, dependent on technological forms of communication that constantly fail her. What she gets back, as with a computer, is what she brings to it. All of Los Angeles has become an Echo Court, as the motel where she is staying is called. By the end of this novel, the world is breaking down into solipsism. When Oedipa tries to make contact with the man from the Inamorati Anonymous Association (a group that has given up all forms of love and human contact), he hangs up on her.

The angle of perception as well as the world perceived in *Lot 49* is different not just from the worlds of Hugo and Balzac, but also from those of Zola and Joyce, West and Fitzgerald. At the end of *Lot 49,* Oedipa goes to a stamp auction, hoping that she will find the all-significant clue that will reveal the meaning of the Tristero to her, but she experiences simply one more in a string of events that reflect only on each other. Substance has given way to signs, reality to relations: all Oedipa can do is create meaning rather than discover it—and in the urban maze that meaning is inseparable from the context in which she creates it.

Throughout modern history, the city has been an energy system that brings into being the fruits of Enlightenment commercialism and of industrial capitalism—at the same time that it feeds destructively off the natural world, leaving behind enormous waste. In its size and anonymity, the city allows the flowering of vividly personal sensitivities, which explains why one feels at once aroused by the city and submerged and powerless in its vastness (Grana, 70). There are always two cities at work: one visible, the other invisible; one of the surface, the other underground or hidden; one a realm of mastery and control, the other of mystery and turmoil. But the city itself has undergone radical change, as the capitalism that produced it has gone through a number of stages. By our time—the time of late capitalism—the money system has become so complex that it should be thought of as more a self-enclosed, self-energizing system than as anything material. That is to say, as the nature of capitalism changes, its mechanics change as well. Although capitalism and empiricism came into being simultaneously, they eventually lost their interdependence

The modern city established a new set of limits that marked the farthest point to which men and women could go and still remain human. A human imperative runs from the romantics through to the moderns and is transformed by postmodernism. As the postmodernists drain consciousness from both the subject and the urban world, the self is commodified along with other objects; what is human becomes virtually refined away, leaving us only a world of things and objects and the relations between them. This is the end of the liberal tradition and its trust in the individual. The modern city, which brought the individual into being, then destroyed individualism. The self that emerges from Defoe's city is collapsed into the maze of Pynchon's, and the old self is as different from the new as the simple mechanics of Defoe's commercial world are different from the complex mechanics of the world city. The world city exacts a high price, as the sense of individual freedom that emerges in Defoe gives way to totalism and repression in Pynchon.

III

Pynchon's *Gravity's Rainbow* (1973) is an excursion through postwar Europe and America, once again ending in Los Angeles where a film goes on even as a rocket is about to fall from the sky. The novel challenges the Enlightenment belief that reason can explain the universe and the workings of nature, as well as the idea that such explanations will allow us to come to terms with both a spiritual and a physical reality. Pynchon seems fascinated by the technical genius behind rocketry at the same time as he sees technology as part of a destructive process and questions the justification for technological control over nature. Indeed, the tools we invent take over and use us, leading to the destruction of the individual self: Slothrop, for example, as a child was conditioned by a derivative of Imipolex G to the extent that he no longer has control over his own body, despite some deconditioning. As a result, a strange coincidence exists between where the rockets fall and where Slothrop has his love affairs, only the effect comes before the cause: the rockets fall after his lovemaking.

Pynchon also sees the Enlightenment as responsible for nationalism: the belief that America has a special identity that is waiting to be realized in history. A similar sense of history and destiny in Germany led to Karl Popper's challenge of such a notion in *The Open Society*. Often it leads to imperialism—assuming the right to extend the nation beyond its physical borders, especially into undeveloped regions. Pynchon treats this theme in his handling of the Hereros and Squalidozzi. Like the Enlightenment itself, Pynchon's novel begins in Europe and ends in Los Angeles, the terminus of a cultural legacy. There we anticipate the end, the rocket about to fall from the sky onto the movie theater from which the people are emerging. For Pynchon, the Enlightenment legacy is a neurotic form of experience. Our desire to control nature, to work our will upon it, becomes inseparable from sadism and masochism, an idea that owes much to Norman O. Brown's belief that anality is connected with property and death. In fact, Brown is a constant source of reference, standing in the same relation to *Gravity's Rainbow* as Homer to *Ulysses:* a death wish seems to be built into the Enlightenment drive for wealth and power.

The Enlightenment also encouraged big business, a power system that eventually subsumed the idea of the nation-state—replacing it first with fascism and totalitarianism, then with the multinational corporation. This is the "Them" of the novel that seems to be pulling all the strings. It is depicted literally and metaphorically as an octopus, exercising control on both sides of the war. Pynchon also explores the ideology implicated in the Enlightenment, as science and politics are inseparable from culture, all part of the same reality into which our consciousness has been collapsed. Everything is on the same plane of existence—the theater and the rockets, the film and culture—and there is no difference between reading a novel and engaging the cultural reality that is outside the novel. Thus the workings of the rocket and the workings of the film industry are interconnected, and rocketry and film establish the two plots that make up the novel. They unfold together (we are back in the realm of *V.*); the rocketry plot dominates the whole novel, the movie plot the last half.

The rocketry plot opens with V-2 rockets falling on London in a way that duplicates Slothrop's lovemaking. Slothrop's desire to understand the meaning of these events leads him into the Zone, where he is watched by the White Visitation and Pointsman. The Zone involves the realm of Weissmann/Blicero and the mechanistic world they have created. The movie plot involves Pökler, who works for Blicero on Rocket 0000, the rocket that they hope will go beyond death. Instead, it falls on the theater, the final achievement of the mind relying on reason, science, and technology and controlling the environment. Once the process of destruction begins, we do not know where it will stop, as the ending of the novel suggests.

Gravity's Rainbow is a series of extended metaphors, thwarting any realistic reading. With its discontinuous plot, it cannot be read like one of Dickens's novels or even Joyce's *Ulysses;* it is the narrative opposite of Dreiser's *Sister Carrie,* with no causal connections between chapters, no unfolding, no chronology. The usual "identification" with characters is impossible, for they have been emptied of self and conditioned by culture; most do not have a past, or they have a past from which they cannot free themselves. The novel has an impersonal narrator, but this voice often gives way, generally without warning, to that of an individual character, so we do not always know who is speaking. The novel is thus intentionally difficult—it goes in and out of focus—and much of its complexity stems from the resulting narrative confusion.

Pynchon's world is vastly different from Joyce's. Joyce's prose is continuous (at least until *Finnegans Wake*), Pynchon's discontinuous; consciousness centers reality in Joyce but is collapsed into forms of culture in Pynchon—myth, history, self, consciousness are all one. The organic world of Joyce, where parts are related to the larger whole, becomes the paranoid world of Pynchon, where there is no center, no principle of unity, no way to connect parts to something greater. Myth gives way to mystery. The paranoid mind is not separate from culture; it is part of the new culture and is given physical form in the maze. Joyce's city is ultimately redeemable; Pynchon's is not.

IV

Pynchon and other postmodern novelists ask the same questions raised more directly by critics like Fredric Jameson and Jean Baudrillard. Jameson's 1984 essay "Postmodernism, or the Cultural Logic of Late Capitalism" covers many facets of what he calls postmodernism, but his main concern is the collapse of modernism into the postmodern, which caused a breakdown of categories and distinctions. Modernism, he argues, distinguished between high and low culture, believed in tradition (or the uses of the past), and believed in the vitality of language. Postmodernism, which finds the monumental past used up, engages "dead styles" or literature only as pastiche. The historical novel can no longer represent the past, Jameson tells us: we can no longer position ourselves in time in a way that gives authority to history or position ourselves in space in a way that will allow the meaning of a city to unfold.

All of this reflects the change from an industrial to an international money society locked into the present at the expense of the past—a society that exalts surface over depth and emphasizes space over time. The sublime is replaced by the banal: a Turner landscape gives way to a Warhol or Lichtenstein painting, and the architecture of Gropius or Corbusier to that of John Portman in his Hyatt Regency Hotels. Los Angeles becomes the city beyond knowing, as illustrated in the architectural trope of Portman's Bonaventure Hotel (see figures 9 and 10). The hotel is built out of four cylindrical towers that are connected by a similar tower in the middle. Jameson points out that once above the lobby, one enters the labyrinth, a Portman maze. One tower becomes indistinguishable from another, lacking any points of demarcation. Jameson extends this trope to include all of present-day Los Angeles. To move from the hotel to the city is to move within the same field of force—of space filled but not ordered. The mind, the powers of consciousness, ultimately fails us in this hyperspace.

In his construction of postmodernism, Baudrillard offers a radical departure. Abandoning Jameson's Marxism, he applies a semiotic system to an era of consumerism, advertising, and mass media. These new developments, he believes, have subverted the sense of difference that sustains the relation between sign and signification. As a result, we have no way of differentiating fantasy from reality—the two so interpenetrate that each is transformed—and we are left only the simulacrum, the product of repetition grounded in no original. Both theorists maintain that the subject and human consciousness have been seriously undercut, but they do so for very different reasons. Jameson sees late capitalism as a form of explosion, creating larger and larger concentric rings of conspiratorial activity that make it impossible for humans to decipher the world. Baudrillard, on the other hand, sees the era of consumerism as a giant implosion, the individual overwhelmed and overstimulated by a blitz of media and fashions, until nerve endings are naked and frayed, reality becomes surreal, and finally "hyperspace" is reached. Los Angeles has become the supreme embodiment of this imploded, hyperspace moment that conflates fantasy and reality. For Jameson the Bonaventure Hotel and the Gerhy house are the essence of postmodern Los Angeles, but Baudrillard claims Disneyland: "Disneyland is there to conceal the

Figures 9 and 10. The Bonaventure Hotel, downtown Los Angeles, inside and outside views. This building has become a visual symbol of postmodernism: it fills rather than orders space, creating the decentered maze that destroys memory and repetition, leaving the mind adrift in hyperspace. Photographs by Dan Soper. Courtesy of the Frances Loeb Library, Graduate School of Design, Harvard University.

fact that it is the 'real' country, all of the 'real' America, which is Disney-land.... Disneyland is presented as imaginary in order to make us believe that the rest is real, when in fact all of Los Angeles and the America surrounding it are no longer real, but of the order of the hyperreal and of simulation" (*Simulacra and Simulations,* 172).[3]

Despite their real dispute over the way the postmodern city works, Jameson and Baudrillard do share common ground: the hyperreal, after all, does intensify a sense of disorder and chaos, increasing the sense of anxiety and tension in the urban labyrinth. Thus the city, which came into being to accommodate a variety of human needs, may now be responsible for frustrating our attempts to meet those needs. Los Angeles, like all cities, is unreal for both critics. Jameson views it as a labyrinth with no center, beyond the grasp of the paranoid subject (though accessible to him via Marxist history, a contradiction never addressed). Baudrillard sees it as the source of contradictory stimuli, negating a predictable reality, the subject fraught in the hyperreal, as manufactured objects and experiences take on a reality of their own. Jameson spins us centrifugally out of Los Angeles, Baudrillard centripetally into it: in neither case is there a center the mind can hold.

V

Pynchon's concerns are shared by a number of his contemporaries, and he has helped create a postmodern discourse that determines how we conceptualize the literary city as imagined reality. For example, the same kind of urban discontinuity appears in the works of Don DeLillo, an author with an impressive narrative range; he has reinvented such major subgenres as the detective novel (*Running Dog,* 1978) and science fiction (*Ratner's Star,* 1976). DeLillo shows how reality has been turned into various narrative discourses, calling attention to the way we create such "reality" as well as revising major assumptions about the nature of American culture as depicted in fiction. In *White Noise* (1985) he takes up this problem of cultural reality, and in *Libra* (1988) he

3. Baudrillard believes signs lost their referential quality in stages: initially the sign reflects a basic reality (as in Defoe); then signs "mask" that reality (as in Conrad's Congo); then signs mask the absence of a basic reality (as in Beckett's use of Descartes); and finally signs bear no relation to reality (as in Disneyland).

applies it to an examination of a major historical event (President Kennedy's assassination). In these and other works, DeLillo deconstructs deconstruction: he moves beyond radical skepticism to show how the system of culture asserts itself to create meaning. While his novels make no special claim to a theory of the city, they do support the belief that the city is a self-sustaining system; moreover, reality involves a series of interconnecting loops that extend back to nature, where we are called back to what is biologically compelling.[4]

A novel that can serve as a commentary on both Pynchon and this study is Paul Auster's *Moon Palace* (1989). Auster is very good at suggesting the uncanny aspects of the city, the mystery of its interconnectedness. In going to work for Mr. Effing, the narrator leads Effing's son back to his lost father and in turn finds his own father; the "wilds" of Central Park lead to the wilds of the Utah desert; the streets of New York's Chinatown lead to the shores of the Pacific and to China beyond; the history of America is coextensive with the history of the city and leads to new frontiers, the Pacific rim and the moon. Once the country is compressed into urban space, coincidences abound and the city becomes the doorway into the mysteries of life, past and present. It is exactly this sense of mystery that Oedipa Maas is unable to ground.

Auster treats many of the same themes in *The New York Trilogy*. In *City of Glass* (1985), Quinn experiences the city as pure chance. A misdirected call involves him with the Stillman family. Peter Stillman, Sr., a professor of history, becomes obsessed with his theory of the Fall—seen as a fall not into sin but into the realm of Babel. In the Garden of Eden, words were not arbitrary signs but revealed the essence of things. If the human fall entails the fall of language, then human redemption involves recreating the language of Eden. Stillman believes that this task awaited America, the new world, with its wilderness. Hired to tail Stillman in his perambulations through the city, Quinn becomes like a character from Poe, following the man in the crowd. As Stillman walks through the city, he picks up all kinds of junk, which he then renames, trying to give each thing its essential meaning; his concern with urban junk connects him to Oedipa Maas in *Lot 49*. Each day of Stillman's travels seems to spell out a letter of the alphabet, which put together form the words THE TOWER OF BABEL. The urban journey is a hermeneutic circle. Like Oedipa, Quinn does not know if he has discovered truth or only made it up:

---

4. There is perhaps a connection, as some recent criticism has suggested (e.g., see Civello), between DeLillo's novels and the systems theory of Ludwig von Bertalanffy.

everything comes back to the products of his own mind. When Stillman disappears, Quinn feels that he lost something substantial—that he has defined himself through the urban chaos that Stillman brought into his life. Yet such chaos seems beyond redemption: Stillman commits suicide by jumping off the Brooklyn Bridge, Hart Crane's symbol of failed unity. The hope offered by the wilderness is not to be regained; we are left with the city, which, like a fallen language system, is all that we have. We can never go back to *essential* meaning, for the random connections we make in the city reveal the nature of the only reality we can know. We must define ourselves in terms of such randomness, in spite of its unpredictability and contradictions.

In *The Locked Room* (1986), the narrator's life is defined by random events when he agrees to edit and help publish the literary works of Fanshawe, at one time a friend, who has mysteriously disappeared. The task determines his life: he marries Fanshawe's wife, adopts his child, lives off his royalties. Fanshawe is a second self, discovered in the city. The narrator both identifies with and hates him, suggesting we often dislike in others what is most like ourselves. At the end the narrator speaks to Fanshawe through the door of a locked room. Whatever meaning Fanshawe can reveal is in a red notebook he gives the narrator. The city and language come together in the notebook, but the narrator refuses to read it, choosing to leave Fanshawe, like the city, a mystery.

Auster's novels rely on literary works, especially by Poe and Hawthorne, that precede them. His characters are defined most immediately by the randomness of the city, which is a realm of the unknown, its mystery always before them in uncanny ways. They then define themselves against a system of language that will not stay still. The relationship between Quinn and Stillman, or the narrator and Fanshawe, is not the relationship between Ulysses and Leopold Bloom. There is no fixed connection between Auster's characters and the past: the city can and does rewrite old stories, and meaning is now a matter of chance relations. As in Poe's story "The Man of the Crowd," Auster's city and the language it generates "cannot be read."

In *In the Country of Last Things* (1987), Auster perhaps uses the city most directly—here a futuristic city that has entropically exhausted itself. The inhabitants live either by reclaiming the dead (suggesting Dickens's *Our Mutual Friend*) or by salvaging waste objects (suggesting Pynchon's *Lot 49*). This city of the future combines the very worst elements of the historical city: at its center is some variation of brutal authority or harmful threat, at its margins the random search for junk on which life depends. Enlightenment expectations have been turned upside down: having depleted rather than controlled nature, the city has created a totally irrational kind of institututional power. Reason and restraint have given way to brute force and cunning: the force of authority, the cunning of the citizens. One has to be a keen reader of signs to survive in such a world, to know where to hunt for junk and when to avoid mindless authority. In this "City of Destruction," Auster has taken us from the early city, through the highly institutionalized and functional commercial/industrial city, to the other side of the postmodern entropic city. His vision takes us to the dead end.

Auster raises key questions: how far can the city take us into the unknown? How far can failed Enlightenment values take us beyond the conventional city, beyond ourselves, beyond our sense of the human? Auster depicts humans made over by the futuristic city, but Philip K. Dick goes a step further. His science fiction version of the uncanny takes us to the realm where urban technology finds humanity redundant, most notably in *Do Androids Dream of Electric Sheep?* (1968), the novel that Hollywood made into the movie *Blade Runner* (1986). In a Los Angeles of the future—a city ethnically diverse—cybernetics has pushed consciousness beyond human beings. Not only is consciousness inseparable from its context, it is also inseparable from the artificial intelligence that duplicates it. Dick uses this situation to ask the inevitable question: how does one differentiate the human from the nonhuman when their function is the same? Literary naturalism had to determine where the animal left off and the human began; cybernetics has to make the same distinction between human and machine. No longer does human essence separate us from the other beings in the environment. In a novel like William Gibson's *Neuromancer* (1984), humans simply are their environment, and where they begin and the city ends is no longer a meaningful question. The final challenge of the city is to the very idea of humanity.

Epilogue

Urban Paradigms: City Past, City Future

I

We have seen that the history of the city contains within it the history of Western civilization. Originally the city provided a way of organizing a community in relation to the land. A surplus of food allowed a diversity of labor, and writing was a prerequisite to commercial activity. Thus a fairly complex social structure was needed to bring the city into existence. And yet the early cities took their being from the agrarian communities that preceded them, and they kept many of the old gods in place, relying on vegetation myths for their worship and religious explanations. As the function of the city changed, so did its structure.

The most radical change began with the Enlightenment. Key here was the thinking of John Locke, who saw the wilderness as waste waiting to be reclaimed by a commercial/industrial process. His philosophy is grounded on two principles fundamental to urbanism—a belief in the individual and a belief in property: only through the work of the individual could the wilderness be turned into property. Enlightenment optimism rested firmly on a belief in progress, a trust in linear time to guarantee mechanical advancement. Emphasizing the power of reason and technology, Enlightenment thought treated the city as a way of controlling nature for the purpose of bringing wealth into being. Moreover, this was a city organized on the principle of natural rights rather than birthrights, so the individual could be called to it to pursue a higher sense of self, a personal destiny. The city is the end product of the evolution of capitalism—from commercialism, to mercantilism, to imperialism, to international capitalism and the multinational corporation.

The relationship between the city and its hinterland was symbiotic: the city was energized by its rural surroundings, and the hinterland supplied raw materials and a marketplace. It also became the basis for a mystical nationalism that allowed capital cities to turn into monuments to imperial and later to totalitarian power. Yet the imperial city was doomed to a process of self-destruction. Just as the capital city ate up the hinterland, making imperialism necessary, so it ate up its colonies. As the needs of the frontier became greater, including an extensive military, the cost to the capital city became prohibitive and the center began to weaken. When the imperial city was defeated by more robust enemies, the process of decline led to a national state of discontent, rife with individual frustration and ripe for a potential dictator intent on totalitarian powers.

The literary imagination chronicled the advantages and disadvantages of urban existence. The advantages of a material society had to be weighed against the cost in natural and human resources, and romanticism was the reaction against Enlightenment values. The romantics wanted an organic community that took its being from the land and that was consolidated through the working of myth, not pure reason. They reversed Locke's thinking: the wilderness was opportunity, which only became waste after the depredation of urbanism. One of the first poets to express this notion was William Blake (1757–1827), who in *Songs of Experience* (1794) maintained that the city encouraged luxury, allowing a radical departure from the natural state that led to decadence and waste. His "London" finds capitalism responsible for the dehumanized commercial city.

Naturalism also made inroads on Enlightenment assumptions. As a product of evolution, humanity was more a creation of environmental chance than the product of reasoned planning. Naturalism thus substituted causality for teleology: material forces rather than ends were written into nature. The naturalist city was a place of limits, a product of material activity and of mechanical forces, all working in a zero-sum way. The city produced only so much wealth; therefore if some were wealthy, others had to be poor. Adapting to the city involved the same rules as adapting to nature: some would succeed, others fail. Herbert Spencer believed in the survival of the fittest, especially as the city became more complex.

In its view of the city, modernism was another stage of romanticism. The modernist city was reconciled to myths of the land, involved a community of like selves, and kept alive a cyclical sense of time by juxtaposing the present against a more heroic past. The modernists—turning to aestheticism, religion, and politics—tried to ground the self within the city, but the result was often a sense of individualism either autistic or power hungry, paralleling the trials of the nation-state (which either collapsed upon itself or moved toward imperialism and later totalitarianism). As a result, modernism looked back toward what were considered simpler times. Both the romantics and the modernists held on to visions of the city that had already been discounted by the forces of industry. In Europe, Spengler's mystic nationalism had great influence between the wars; and in America, a Jeffersonian idea of democracy kept its allure from the beginning of the republic to the end of World War II. Given the political collapse of modernism in the twentieth century, one can understand the postmodernist search for alternative values.

Postmodernism provides a radical departure from earlier urban paradigms. For example, an existentialist like Jean-Paul Sartre, grounded in phenomenology, believes that consciousness (*pour soi*) brings the city (*en soi)* into being; Baudrillard, in contrast, believes that consciousness comes into being within the systems that produce it. Mass media informs urban reality. The postindustrial city also takes its meaning from the complex handling of international capital and from the multinational corporation. Urban activity becomes more abstract and "unreal" as power operates from hidden sources. Such a city is at once a physical reality and a state of mind: to read the city is to read an urbanized self, to know the city from within. Once we lose a transcendental signifier, the totalizing process is called into question and the city turns into a place of mystery: chance and the unexpected dominate, a romantic sense of the uncanny becomes exaggerated, and the city takes on the meaning of pure text, to be created by each individual and then read. The detective, no longer relying on Holmesian powers of induction, follows endless clues in a hermeneutic circle, which almost always leads back to self. But, as already suggested, this is no longer the Enlightenment self, calculating its endless possibilities, but a discontinuous self, fraught and overloaded with electronic stimuli—a self, if Roland Barthes is correct, that must read urban signs as if one is a Parisian in Tokyo.

The modern city is the world's dominant social structure. At the turn of the nineteenth century, only 14 percent of the global population lived in cities, and only eleven cities had a population of a million inhabitants.

Now there are four hundred cities with a population of at least a million and twenty with a population of over ten million. In the Western world, the city has taken two forms. In Europe, with remnants of the medieval city still at the center and industry at the margins, a provincial city like Angoulême would be familiar even now to Balzac. Industrial cities are usually located in river basins, expensive homes on the surrounding hills. In America, where industry grew up within the central city, the typical model is the doughnut: desolation at the center and energy moving to the sprawling margins and suburbs. Recently, such urban commentators as Paul Hawken, John Naisbitt, and Alvin Toffler have predicted that telecommunications will weaken the American city even further, as the workforce increasingly communicates from the edges by computer.[1] In *Crabgrass Frontier* (1985), Kenneth Jackson resists this prediction, arguing that metropolitan centers are the most complex creations of the human mind and will sustain their place of eminence as marketplaces of ideas. The city—a vortex, a power mechanism—is indeed a wonder. It brings together the forces of business, law, medicine, and education; it give us the glory of great universities, libraries, museums, theaters, restaurants, sports arenas, and parks. But these great benefits come with a price, and the literary imagination responds with both excitement and reservation—and more recently with a sense of fear of what awaits.

Recent data about the future city are disturbing. According to a 1996 report issued by the United Nations Population Fund (as reported in the *New York Times,* October 15, 1996), half the world's population will be living in urban areas by the year 2006. Of a global population of 6.6 billion, 3.3 billion will live in cities, and the biggest increase will be in developing countries, where the resources are already in short supply. By 2025, two out of every three inhabitants of poor countries will live in cities—4.4 billion people. Overpopulated cities will strain government services, be clotted by unemployed youth, and generate multiethnic tension. Future conflicts in the third world will begin in the cities. And as machines displace more workers in the industrial world, both in Europe and America, the main problem will be finding enough jobs to fuel a consumer society. Moreover, the futuristic city—that is, the future postmodern city—will require greater energy for its reduced industrial production, more central authority at the expense of personal freedom, more abstract and interconnected commercial activity. It will become

1. See John Naisbitt, *Global Paradox* (1994); John Naisbitt and Patricia Aburdene, *Megatrends 2000* (1991); and Alvin Toffler, *The Third Wave* (1981).

more difficult to read and to understand, especially at the margins of urban sprawl. Auster's "country of last things" may be here sooner than he predicted.

II

There have been several books that treat the literary city: Raymond Williams, Burton Pike, William Sharpe, and Hana Wirth-Nesher are authors of the most recent or important of such studies.[2] Most of these studies treat the city as a matter of dichotomy: country versus city, static city versus city of flux, or as private versus public space. Using a different strategy, I have defined the city in terms of its functions—as a commercial, industrial, or postindustrial entity. It is within these contexts that urban space is authentically defined and redefined, since the city is a changing rather than fixed realm. And as the physical city evolved, so did the way it was re-presented in literary terms, especially in the novel. Comic and romantic realism give us insights into the commercial city; naturalism and modernism into the industrial city; and postmodernism into the postindustrial city. The city and the literary text have had inseparable histories, and reading the city is only another kind of textual reading. Moreover, such readings concern intellectual or cultural history that has informed the city and contributed to the way it has been depicted by the literary imagination.

The city, at least until recently, has been thought mainly the by-product of male rather than female activity. But like men, women—Dreiser's Carrie, for example—have been called to the city in search of a larger self and—like Pynchon's Oedipa Maas—are now urban detective-observers. However, in the canonical literature of the West, the world of men and women usually has been split in two—compartmentalized into downtown and uptown, the realm of the boardroom and the realm of the salon—dividing material and artistic pursuits, where money is made and where it is spent.

In his essay on the genteel tradition, George Santayana (1863–1952) commented on the schizophrenic nature of American culture—a country, as he called it, with two mentalities: "The truth is that one half of the

---

2. Williams, *The Country and the City* (1973); Pike, *The Image of the City in Modern Literature* (1981); Sharpe, *Unreal Cities* (1990); and Wirth-Nesher, *City Codes* (1996).

American mind, that is not occupied intensely in practical affairs, has remained . . . slightly becalmed, while, alongside, in invention and industry and social organization the other half of the mind was leaping down a sort of Niagara Rapids." Santayana went on to declare that the American will inhabits the skyscraper and the American intellect inhabits the colonial mansion. "The one is the sphere of the American man; the other, at least predominantly, of the America woman. The one is all aggressive enterprise, the other is all genteel tradition" (Santayana, 39 – 40).

Santayana was, of course, describing what is now a lost world—the genteel realm of William Dean Howells, Henry James, Edith Wharton, and T. S. Eliot. In "The Love Song of J. Alfred Prufrock," Eliot takes us through the streets of a modern city (more than likely Boston) to the salon where the women (and the choice of gender is important) come and go, talking of Michelangelo. The division of gender roles, however, was not solely American. Charles Dickens had distinguished between the activities of the commercial city and the affairs of hearth and family. In *Great Expectations,* Wemmick divided his life into hermetic halves, living for portable property in the city and for the well-being of his aged father and his fiancée when he crossed the drawbridge that took him into the moated sanctuary of his home. It is true that modernist writers depicted the salon reaching into the realm of men. In *Buddenbrooks,* Thomas Mann showed how a typical bourgeois family (modeled on his own) weakened generation after generation; by the third generation, young Johann spends all his time with his mother in the salon, reading poetry and listening to music, unable to take over the business of his father, a hothouse plant so delicate that he will soon be carried away by death. The world of the salon was highly neurasthenic, as we know from the fate of Henry Adams's and T. S. Eliot's wives and from the stories of Bloomsbury. The recurrence of ill health suggests that urban life was far from being grounded in vital energy. A 1984 collection of essays on women writers and the city, edited by Susan Merrill Squier, reinforces this conclusion by concentrating on Virginia Woolf's city, where urban roles tend to bifurcate along gender lines.

With the passing of the salon, the division between men and women was refashioned rather than transformed. Women felt unfairly displaced in the city and wanted adjustment, sought an equal sense of urban place. Interestingly, many of these women spoke from an immigrant experience. In a wide-ranging essay ("Sister to Faust," in Squier), Blanche Gelfant examines feminist urban redress, focusing on such works as Mary Antin's *The Promised Land* (1912), Anzia Yezierska's *Hungry Hearts*

(1920), Betty Smith's *A Tree Grows in Brooklyn* (1943), Paule Marshall's *Brown Girl, Brownstones* (1959), and Dorothy Bryant's *Ella Price's Journal* (1972). The city was made and remade to accommodate capitalism, and capitalism was primarily a patriarchal system. Until recently gender roles were predefined in the city, a condition that seems to be changing. The feminist complaint today is not that women do not have a place in the city but that obstacles like the glass ceiling, perhaps a reminder of urban origins, impede the urban climb.

III

The City in Literature has examined some of the literary paradigms that have helped us conceptualize the city from its origins to postmodernism. In seeing the city as a product of the literary imagination, we are, of course, examining it as a text. But there are texts and texts. We can think of Newton's theory of gravity and Pynchon's *Gravity's Rainbow* as texts, but not of the same order: one (a theory of gravity) takes its meaning from physical reality, the other (Pynchon's novel) from language. Textualizing the city creates its own reality, becomes a way of seeing the city—but such textuality cannot substitute for the pavement and buildings, for the physical city. Before the city is a construct, literary or cultural, it is a physical reality with a dynamics of its own, even as that dynamics becomes difficult to assess. The most convincing constructs are those that confirm our sense of reality, validate experience, and suggest coherence in the face of chaos.

We have moved in this study from the centered, scriptable world of Enlightenment London to the discontinuous, decentered, unscriptable world of postmodern Los Angeles. But neither construct is "real," identical with the physical city. Abstracting from rather than grounding reality, each gives us a way of conceptualizing the city so that it can be retrieved in human terms, brought into intellectual focus, thus making possible an intellectual understanding of the city separate from its physical reality. Literary texts and cultural paradigms help us to focus and to arrest the flux of time. Ideologically charged, each construct carries an agenda—a way of preserving or transforming Enlightenment London or a way of relating Los Angeles to postmodernist mandates. Whether constructs depend upon economic history or sociobiology, they compete among themselves for dominance. Such intellectual systems determine the way we think of cities and complement the way urban power works politically and culturally. The loss of the modernist subject, for example, brings into being new forms of reality, both political and personal.

No matter how conceived, the city has played a large part in human destiny for almost five thousand years; it has created a historical rhythm of its own, even as its functions changed and its reality was reconstructed and transformed. Urban constructs must be continuously reexamined: they are, to be sure, artificial and diverse; but through them we interpret the past, test our sense of reality, and structure the future. And the city— for better or worse—is our future.

Bibliography

Ackroyd, Peter. *Notes for a New Culture: An Essay on Modernism.* London: Vision, 1976.

Adams, Henry. *The Education of Henry Adams.* 1907. Reprint, Boston: Houghton Mifflin, 1946.

Ahnebrink, Lars. *The Beginning of Naturalism in American Fiction: A Study of the Works of Hamlin Garland, Stephen Crane, and Frank Norris with Special Reference to Some European Influences, 1891–1903.* Cambridge, Mass.: Harvard University Press, 1950.

———. *Essays and Studies on American Language and Literature.* Uppsala, Sweden: A. B. Lundequistska Bokhandein, 1947.

Allen, Walter. *The Urgent West: The American Dream and Modern Man.* New York: Dutton, 1969.

Anderson, Chester G. *James Joyce and His World.* New York: Viking, 1968.

Anderson, Quentin. *The Imperial Self: An Essay in American Literary and Cultural History.* New York: Knopf, 1971.

Antoniades, Anthony C. *Epic Space: Toward the Roots of Western Architecture.* New York: Von Nostrand, 1992.

Asher, Kenneth. *T.S. Eliot and Ideology.* Cambridge: Cambridge University Press, 1995.

Auden, W. H. *City Without Walls.* New York: Random House, 1969.

———. *Look, Stranger!* London: Faber and Faber, 1936.

Austen, Jane. *Northanger Abbey.* 1818. Reprint, New York: Random House, 1992.

———. *Mansfield Park* (1814), edited by James Kinsley and John Lucas. New York: Oxford University Press, 1980.

Auster, Paul. *City of Glass.* New York: Viking, 1985.

———. *In the Country of Last Things.* New York: Viking, 1987.

———. *The Locked Room.* New York: Viking, 1986.

———. *Moon Palace.* New York: Viking, 1989.

Baguley, David. *Naturalistic Fiction: An Entropic Vision.* Cambridge: Cambridge University Press, 1990.

Balzac, Honoré de. *History of the Thirteen,* translated by Herbert J. Hunt. New York: Penguin Books, 1978.

——. *Lost Illusions,* translated by Herbert J. Hunt. New York: Penguin Books, 1971.

——. *Père Goriot,* translated by Henry Reed. New York: Signet Books, 1981.

——. *Splendors and Miseries of Courtesans.* Philadelphia: G. Barrie, 1895.

Baring-Gould, W. S. *Sherlock Holmes.* St. Albans, England: Panther Books, 1962

Baritz, Loren. *City on a Hill.* New York: John Wiley and Sons, 1964.

Barthes, Roland. *The Grain of the Voice: Interviews, 1962–1980,* translated by Linda Coverdale. New York: Hill and Wang, 1985.

Bataille, Georges. *Against Architecture,* translated by Betsy Wing. Cambridge, Mass.: MIT Press, 1989.

Baudelaire, Charles. *Les Fleurs du Mal,* translated by Alan Conder. London: Cassell, 1952.

——. *Intimate Journals,* translated by Christopher Isherwood. New York: Random House, 1930.

——. *Paris Spleen,* translated by Louise Varese. New York: New Directions, 1970.

Baudrillard, Jean. *Selected Writings,* edited by Mark Poster. Palo Alto: Stanford University Press, 1988.

——. *Simulacra and Simulations,* translated by Sheila Faria Glaser. Ann Arbor: University of Michigan Press, 1994. Originally published as *Simulacres et Simulation* (Paris: Galilée, 1981).

Becker, George J. *John Dos Passos.* New York: Frederick Ungar, 1974.

——. *Realism in Modern Literature.* New York: Frederick Ungar, 1980.

——, ed. *Documents of Modern Literary Realism.* Princeton: Princeton University Press, 1963.

Beckett, Samuel. *Malone Dies.* New York: Grove Press, 1956.

——. *Murphy.* New York: Grove Press, 1957.

——. *The Unnamable.* New York: Grove Press, 1958.

Beckford, William. *Vathek* (1786), edited by Roger Lonsdale. New York: Oxford University Press, 1983.

Beer, Gillian. *Darwin's Plots: Evolutionary Narrative in Darwin, George Eliot, and Nineteenth-Century Fiction.* London: Routledge and Kegan Paul, 1983.

Belkind, Allen, ed. *Dos Passos, the Critics, and the Writer's Intention.* Carbondale: Southern Illinois University Press, 1971.

Bell, Daniel. *The Coming of the Post-Industrial Society: A Venture in Social Forecasting.* New York: Basic Books, 1976.

——. "Crime as an American Life" (1933). In vol. 2 of *New Perspectives on the American Past,* edited by Stanley N. Katz and Stanley I. Kuttler. Boston: Little, Brown, 1972.

Bell, Michael Davitt. *The Problems of American Realism: Studies in the Cultural History of a Literary Idea.* Chicago: University of Chicago Press, 1993.

Bellamy, Edward. *Looking Backward, 2000–1887.* 1888. Reprint, Cambridge, Mass.: Harvard University Press, 1967

Bellow, Saul. *Mr. Sammler's Planet.* New York: Viking, 1970.

Benevolo, Leonardo. *The History of the City,* translated by Geoffrey Culverwell. Cambridge, Mass.: MIT Press, 1980.

Benjamin, Walter. *Charles Baudelaire: A Lyric Poet in the Era of High Capitalism,* translated by Harry Zohn. London: New Left Books, 1973.

Benstock, Bernard. "The Dead." In *James Joyce's "Dubliners,"* edited by Clive Hart. London: Faber and Faber, 1969.

Berard, Victor. *Les Phéniciens et l'Odyssée.* Paris: Arnold Colin, 1902–03.

Berger, Peter. *The Homeless Mind.* New York: Random House, 1973.

Bergson, Henri. *Creative Evolution,* translated by A. Mitchell. New York: Henry Holt, 1911. Originally published as *L'Evolution créatrice* (Paris: Felix Alcan, 1907).

Berman, Marshall. *All That Is Solid Melts into the Air: The Experience of Modernity.* New York: Simon and Schuster, 1982.

Bertalanffy, Ludwig von. *General Systems Theory: Foundations, Development, Applications.* New York: Braziller, 1968.

Bewley, Marius. "Melville and the Democratic Experience." In *Melville: A Collection of Critical Essays,* edited by Richard Chase. Englewood Cliffs, N.J.: Prentice-Hall, 1962.

Biencourt, Marius. *Une Influence du Naturalisme Français en Amerique.* Paris: Marcel Giard, 1933.

Birkett, Jennifer. *Sins of the Father: Decadence in France, 1870–1914.* New York: Quartet Books, 1986.

Blanchard, Marc Eli. *In Search of the City: Engels, Baudelaire, Rimbaud.* Stanford French and Italian Studies 37. Saratoga, Calif.: Anma Libri, 1985.

Boardman, John, Jasper Griffin, and Oswyn Murray, eds. *The Oxford History of the Roman World.* Oxford: Oxford University Press, 1991.

Bowen, Zack R. *"Ulysses."* In *A Companion to Joyce Studies,* edited by Zack R. Bowen and James F. Carens. Westport, Conn.: Greenwood Press, 1984.

Bowen, Zack R., and James F. Carens, eds. *A Companion to Joyce's Studies.* Westport, Conn.: Greenwood Press, 1984.

Bowersock, G. W., John Clive, and Stephen R. Graubard, eds. *Edward Gibbon and "The Decline and Fall of the Roman Empire."* Cambridge, Mass.: Harvard University Press, 1977.

Bradbury, Malcolm. "Cities of Modernity." In *Modernism: 1890–1930,* edited by Malcolm Bradbury and James McFarlane. Harmondsworth: Penguin, 1976.

———. "London, 1890–1920." In *Modernism: 1890–1930,* edited by Malcolm Bradbury and James McFarlane. Harmondsworth: Penguin, 1976.

Brand, Dana. *The Spectator in the City in Nineteenth-Century American Literature.* Cambridge: Cambridge University Press, 1991.

Brantlinger, Patrick. *Crusoe's Footprints: Cultural Studies in Britain and America.* New York: Routledge, 1990.

Braudel, Fernand. *Civilization and Capitalism, 15th–18th Centuries,* translated by Sian Reynolds. 3 vols. London: Collins, 1981–84. (Vol. 1, *The Structures of Everyday Life* [1981]; vol. 2, *The Wheels of Commerce* [1983]; vol. 3, *The Perspective of the World* [1984].)

Bremer, Sidney. *Urban Intersections: Meetings of Life and Literature in United States Cities.* Urbana: University of Illinois Press, 1992.

Breslin, James E. *William Carlos Williams: An American Artist.* New York: Oxford University Press, 1970.

Bridenbaugh, C. *Cities in the Wilderness: The First Century of Urban Life in America, 1625–1742.* New York: Roland Press, 1938.

Brontë, Charlotte. *Jane Eyre.* 1848. Reprint, New York: Signet, 1982.

Brontë, Emily. *Wuthering Heights* (1847), edited by William M. Sale, Jr. New York: W. W. Norton, 1963.

Brown, Frederick. *Zola: A Life.* New York: Farrar, Straus, and Giroux, 1995.

Brown, Homer O. "The Displaced Self in the Novels of Daniel Defoe." *ELH* 38 (1971): 562–90.

Buckley, Jerome. *Triumph of Time: A Study of the Victorian Concept of Time History, Progress, and Decadence.* Cambridge, Mass.: Harvard University Press, 1966.

Budgen, Frank. *James Joyce and the Making of Ulysses.* London: Grayson and Grayson, 1937.

Butler, Christopher. *After the Wake: An Essay on the Contemporary Avant-Garde.* Oxford: Clarendon Press, 1980.

Byrd, Max. *London Transformed: Images of the City in the Eighteenth Century.* New Haven: Yale University Press, 1978.

———, ed. *Daniel Defoe: A Collection of Critical Essays.* Englewood Cliffs, N.J.: Prentice-Hall, 1976.

Calinescu, Matei. *Faces of Modernity.* Bloomington: Indiana University Press, 1977.

Callow, Alexander B., ed. *American Urban History.* New York: Oxford University Press, 1973.

Canetti, Elias. *Crowds and Power,* translated by Carol Stewart. New York: Viking, 1962.

Cannadine, David. *Decline and Fall of British Aristocracy.* New Haven: Yale University Press, 1990.

Cather, Willa. *A Lost Lady.* New York: Knopf, 1922.

———. *My Ántonia.* 1918. Reprint, New York: Vintage, 1994.

———. *The Professor's House.* 1925. Reprint, New York: Vintage, 1953.

Carter, A. E. *The Idea of Decadence in French Literature.* Toronto: University of Toronto Press, 1958.

Carter, Margaret L., ed. *Dracula: The Vampire and the Critics.* Ann Arbor, Mich.: UMI Research Press, 1988.

Castells, Manuel. *The Urban Question: A Marxist Approach.* Cambridge, Mass.: MIT Press, 1977.

Chace, William. *The Political Identities of Ezra Pound and T. S. Eliot.* Stanford: Stanford University Press, 1973.

Chamberlin, Edward J., and Sander L. Gilman, eds. *Degeneration: The Dark Side of Progress.* New York: Columbia University Press, 1985.

Chandler, Raymond. *The Big Sleep.* 1939. Reprint, New York: Vintage, 1976.

Chapman, Joan, and Brian Chapman. *The Life and Times of Baron Haussmann: Paris in the Second Empire.* London: Weidenfeld and Nicolson, 1957.

Chase, Richard, ed. *Melville: A Collection of Critical Essays.* Englewood Cliffs, N.J.: Prentice-Hall, 1962.

Chevrel, Yves. *Le Naturalisme.* Paris: Presses universitaires de France, 1982.

Civello, Paul. *American Literary Naturalism and Its Twentieth-Century Transfor-mations: Frank Norris, Ernest Hemingway, Don DeLillo.* Athens: University of Georgia Press, 1994.

Clark, David R., ed. *Critical Essays on Hart Crane.* Boston: G. K. Hall, 1982

Clarke, Graham, ed. *The American City: Literary and Cultural Perspectives.* New York: St. Martin's Press, 1988.

Cohen, Morton. *Rider Haggard: His Life and Works.* London: Hutchinson, 1960.

Colley, Iain. *Dos Passos and the Fiction of Despair.* London: Macmillan, 1978.

Conarroe, Joel. *William Carlos Williams' Paterson: Language and Landscape.* Philadelphia: University of Pennsylvania Press, 1970.

Conrad, Joseph. *Heart of Darkness* (1902), edited by Robert Kimbrough. New York: W. W. Norton, 1988.

Corttrell, Leonard. *The Bride of Minos.* New York: Holt, Rinehart, Winston, 1953.

Cowan, Michael H. *City of the West: Emerson, America, and Urban Metaphor.* New Haven: Yale University Press, 1967.

Cowley, Malcolm. "John Dos Passos: The Poet of the World." In *Dos Passos, the Critics, and the Writer's Intention,* edited by Allen Belkind. Carbondale: Southern Illinois University Press, 1971.

Crane, Hart. *The Complete Poems.* Garden City, N.Y.: Doubleday Anchor Books, 1958.

Crawford, Robert. *The Savage and the City in the Work of T. S. Eliot.* Oxford: Clarendon Press, 1987.

Curtis, William J. *Le Corbusier: Ideas and Forms.* New York: Rizzoli, 1986.

Darwin, Charles. *Darwin: A Norton Critical Edition,* edited by Philip Appel-man. New York: W. W. Norton, 1979.

Davidson, Edward H. *Poe: A Critical Study.* Cambridge, Mass.: Harvard Uni-versity Press, 1966.

Davis, Mike. *City of Quartz.* New York: Vintage, 1992.

Day, Robert Adams, "Joyce's Waste Land and Eliot's Unknown God." In *Liter-ary Monographs,* edited by Eric Rothstein, vol. 4. Madison: University of Wisconsin Press, 1971.

Defoe, Daniel. *Augusta Triumphans: or, the Way to make London the most flour-ishing City in the Universe.* [London]: printed for J. Roberts in Warwick Lane, 1729.

———. *The Complete English Tradesman.* 2 vols. London: Printed for Charles Rivington, 1725–27.

———. *The History and Remarkable Life of Colonel Jack* (1722), edited by Samuel Holt Monk. New York: Oxford University Press, 1970.

———. *A Journal of the Plague Year.* 1722. Reprint, New York: Penguin Books, 1986.

———. *Moll Flanders* (1722), edited by Edward Kelly. New York: W. W. Norton, 1973.

———. *Robinson Crusoe* (1719), edited by Michael Shinagel. New York: W. W. Norton, 1975.

———. *Tour of Great Britain: A tour thro' the whole island of Great Britain.* 3 vols. 1724–27. Reprint, London: Frank Cass, 1968.

Detienne, Marcel. *Dionysus at Large,* translated by Mireille Muellner and Leonard Muellner. Cambridge, Mass.: Harvard University Press, 1989.

——. *Dionysus Slain,* translated by Arthur Goldhammer. Baltimore: Johns Hopkins University Press, 1979.

Deutsch, Helene. *A Psychoanalytic Study of the Myth of Dionysus and Apollo: Two Versions of the Son-Mother Relationship.* New York: International Universities Press, 1969.

Dickens, Charles. *Bleak House.* 1853. Reprint, New York: Penguin Books, 1976.

——. *Dombey and Son.* 1848. Reprint, New York: Penguin Books, 1970.

——. *Great Expectations.* 1860–61. Reprint, New York: Penguin Books, 1976.

——. *Little Dorrit.* 1857. Reprint, New York: Penguin Books, 1975.

——. *Oliver Twist.* 1837–39. Reprint, New York: Penguin Books, 1966.

——. *Our Mutual Friend.* 1864–65. Reprint, New York: Penguin Books, 1973.

Dillingham, William B. *Melville's Short Fiction, 1853–1856.* Athens: University of Georgia Press, 1977.

Donoghue, Denis. *Being Modern Together.* Atlanta: Scholars Press, 1991.

——. *The Old Moderns.* New York: Knopf, 1993.

——. *Walter Pater: Lover of Strange Souls,* New York: Knopf, 1995.

Dos Passos, John. *Manhattan Transfer.* 1925. Reprint, Boston: Houghton Mifflin, 1953.

——. *Midcentury.* Boston: Houghton Mifflin, 1961.

——. *U.S.A.* New York: Modern Library, 1937.

Dostoyevsky, Fyodor. *Notes from the Underground* (1864), translated by Constance Garnett. Garden City, N.Y.: Doubleday, 1960.

Douglas, Ann. *Terrible Honesty: Mongrel Manhattan in the 1920s.* New York: Farrar, Straus, and Giroux, 1995.

Doyle, Arthur Conan. *The Sign of Four.* 1890. Reprint, New York: Penguin Books, 1982.

——. *A Study in Scarlet.* 1887. Reprint, New York: Penguin Books, 1981.

——. *Thirty-seven Short Stories and a Complete Novel from "The Strand Magazine."* Secaucus, N.J.: Castle Books, 1980.

Doyle, Charles. *William Carlos Williams and the American Poem.* New York: St. Martin's Press, 1982.

Dreiser, Theodore. *A Book About Myself.* New York: Boni and Liveright, 1922.

——. *Sister Carrie* (1900), edited by Donald Pizer. New York: W. W. Norton, 1970.

Drinnon, Richard. *Facing West: The Metaphysics of Indian Hating and Empire Building.* Minneapolis: University of Minnesota Press, 1980.

Drucker, Peter. *Age of Discontinuity.* New York: Harper and Row, 1978.

Dumwald, Edward. *Thomas Jefferson, American Tourist.* Norman: University of Oklahoma Press, 1946.

Dyos, H. J., ed. *The Study of Urban History.* New York: St. Martin's Press, 1968.

Dyos, H. J., and Michael Wolff. *The Victorian City.* London: Routledge and Kegan Paul, 1973.

Earle, Peter. *The World of Defoe.* London: Weidenfeld and Nicolson; New York: Atheneum, 1976.

Ehrlich, Blake. *London on the Thames.* London: Cassell, 1966.

Eliot, T. S. *The Cocktail Party.* New York: Harcourt, Brace, 1950.

———. *Collected Poems, 1909–1962.* New York: Harcourt, Brace, and World, 1963.

———. *The Family Reunion.* New York: Harcourt, Brace, 1939.

———. "The Influence of Landscape upon the Poet." *Daedalus* 89 (1960): 420–22.

———. Introduction to *Intimate Journals,* by Charles Baudelaire, translated by Christopher Isherwood. New York: Random House, 1930.

———. *Selected Prose of T. S. Eliot,* edited by Frank Kermode. New York: Harcourt, Brace, Jovanovich, 1975.

———. *To Criticize the Critic and Other Writings.* London: Faber and Faber, 1965.

———. *The Waste Land: A Facsimile and Transcript of the Original Drafts,* edited by Valerie Eliot. New York: Harcourt, Brace, Jovanovich, 1971.

Ellis, Aytoun. *The Penny Universities: A History of the Coffee Houses.* London: Secker and Warburg, 1956.

Ellis, Kate F. *The Contested Castle.* Urbana: University of Illinois Press, 1989.

Ellison, Ralph. *Invisible Man.* 1952. Reprint, New York: Vintage, 1995.

———. *Shadow and Act.* New York: Random House, 1964.

Ellmann, Richard. *James Joyce.* New York: Oxford University Press, 1959.

———. *Ulysses on the Liffey.* London: Faber and Faber, 1952.

Ellul, Jacques. *The Meaning of the City,* translated by Dennis Pardee. Grand Rapids, Mich.: Eerdmans, 1970.

———. *The Technological Society,* translated by John Wilkinson. New York: Vintage, 1964.

Emerson, Ralph Waldo. *Selected Prose and Poetry,* edited by Reginald L. Cook. New York: Holt, Rinehart, and Winston, 1961.

Erasmus, Charles J. *In Search of the Common Good: Utopian Experiments Past and Future.* New York: Free Press, 1977.

Evans, Arthur. *The God of Ecstasy: Sex Roles and the Madness of Dionysus.* New York: St. Martin's Press, 1988.

Eyles, Allen. *Sherlock Holmes: A Centenary Celebration.* New York: Harper and Row, 1986.

Fairhall, James. *James Joyce and the Question of History.* New York: Cambridge University Press, 1993.

Fanger, Donald. *Dostoevsky and Romantic Realism.* Cambridge, Mass.: Harvard University Press, 1965.

Faulkner, William. *Go Down, Moses.* 1942. Reprint, New York: Modern Library, 1955.

———. *Sanctuary.* New York: Modern Library, 1932.

Fiedler, Leslie. "Mythicizing the City." In *Literature and the Urban Experience,* edited by Michael C. Jaye and Ann Chalmers Watts. New Brunswick, N.J.: Rutgers University Press, 1981.

Fish, Stanley. *Is There a Text in This Class? The Authority of Interpretive Communities.* Cambridge, Mass.: Harvard University Press, 1980.

Fisher, Philip. *Hard Facts.* New York: Oxford University Press, 1985.

Fitch, J. M. *Architecture and the Esthetics of Plenty.* New York: Columbia University Press, 1961.

Fitzgerald, F. Scott. "The Diamond as Big as the Ritz." In *The Stories of F. Scott Fitzgerald*. New York: Scribner, 1951.

——. *The Great Gatsby*. 1925. Reprint, New York: Scribner, 1957.

——. *The Last Tycoon*. New York: Scribner, 1941.

——. *Letters,* edited by Andrew Turnbull. New York: Scribner, 1963.

——. "My Lost City." In *The Crack-Up*. New York: New Directions, 1945.

——. *Tender Is the Night*. New York: Scribner, 1934.

——. "What I Think and Feel at 25." In *F. Scott Fitzgerald in His Own Time: A Miscellany,* edited by Matthew J. Bruccoli and Jackson Bryer. Kent, Ohio: Kent State University Press, 1971.

Folsom, James K., ed. *The Western: A Collection of Critical Essays*. Englewood Cliffs, N.J.: Prentice-Hall, 1979.

Fowler, Douglas. *A Reader's Guide to Gravity's Rainbow*. Ann Arbor, Mich.: Ardis, 1980

Frazer, James George. *The Golden Bough: A Study in Magic and Religion*. 1 vol. abridged ed. 1922. Reprint, New York: Macmillan, 1950.

Freud, Sigmund. *Group Psychology and the Analysis of the Ego,* translated by James Strachey. London: International Psychoanalytical Press, 1922.

Fried, Lewis. *Makers of the City*. Amherst: University of Massachusetts Press, 1990.

Fussell, Edwin. *American Literature and the American West*. Princeton: Princeton University Press, 1965.

Gans, Deborah. *The Le Corbusier Guide*. Princeton: Princeton Architectural Press, 1987.

Gelfant, Blanche. *The American City Novel*. Norman: University of Oklahoma Press, 1954.

——. "John Dos Passos: The Synoptic Novel." In *Dos Passos, the Critics, and the Writer's Intention,* edited by Allen Belkind. Carbondale: Southern Illinois University Press, 1971.

——. "Sister to Faust: The City's 'Hungry' Woman as Heroine." In *Women Writers and the City,* edited by Susan Merrill Squier. Knoxville: University of Tennessee Press, 1984.

Giddens, Anthony. *The Nation-State and Violence*. Berkeley: University of California Press, 1985.

Giedion, Sigfried. *Space, Time, and Architecture: The Growth of a New Tradition*. Rev. ed. Cambridge, Mass.: Harvard University Press, 1952.

Gill, Richard. *Happy Rural Seat: The English Country House and the Literary Imagination*. New Haven: Yale University Press, 1972

Girouard, Mark. *Life in the English Country House: A Social and Architectural History*. New Haven: Yale University Press, 1978.

——. *The Victorian Country House*. Oxford: Clarendon Press, 1971.

Glasheen, Adaline. *Third Census of "Finnegans Wake."* Berkeley: University of California Press, 1977.

Godwin, William. *Caleb Williams*. 1794. Reprint, New York: Holt, Rinehart, and Winston, 1963.

Goldsmith, Oliver. *The Vicar of Wakefield*. 1766. Reprint, Harmondsworth: Penguin, 1982.

Grana, Cesar. *Fact and Symbol: Essay in the Sociology of Art and Literature*. New York: Oxford University Press, 1971.

Gray, Robert. *A History of London*. London: Hutchinson, 1978.

Green, Martin. *Dreams of Adventure, Deeds of Empire*. London: Routledge and Kegan Paul, 1980.

Guerard, Albert. *The Triumph of the Novel: Dickens, Dostoevsky, Faulkner*. New York: Oxford University Press, 1976.

Haggard, Rider. *She, King Solomon's Mines, Allan Quatermain*. New York: Dover Publications, 1951.

Hall, Peter. *Cities of Tomorrow: An Intellectual History of Urban Planning and Design in the Twentieth Century*. Oxford: Basil Blackwell, 1988.

———. *The World Cities*. New York: McGraw-Hill, 1966.

Hall, Trevor H. "Thomas Stearns Eliot and Sherlock Holmes." In *Sherlock Holmes and His Creator*. London: Duckworth, 1978.

Hammond, J. R. *An Edgar Allan Poe Companion*. London: Macmillan, 1981.

Hammond, Mason. *The City in the Ancient World*. Cambridge, Mass.: Harvard University Press, 1972.

Harrington, Michael. *The Accidental Century*. New York: Macmillan, 1965.

Harrison, John. *The Reactionaries: A Study of the Anti-Democratic Intelligentsia*. New York: Schocken Books, 1967.

Harrison, Michael. *London Growing: The Development of a Metropolis*. London: Hutchinson, 1965.

———. *The World of Sherlock Holmes*. New York: E. P. Dutton, 1975.

Hart, Clive, ed. *James Joyce's "Dubliners."* London: Faber and Faber, 1969.

Harvey, David. *Consciousness and the Urban Experience: Studies in the History and Theory of Capitalist Urbanization*. Baltimore: Johns Hopkins University Press, 1985.

———. *The Urbanization of Capital*. Baltimore: Johns Hopkins University Press, 1985.

Hauser, Arnold. *The Social History of Art*. London: Routledge and Kegan Paul, 1951.

Hawthorne, Nathaniel. *The Blithedale Romance*. 1852. Reprint, New York: W. W. Norton, 1958.

Hazlitt, William. *Lectures on the English Poets*. London: J. Templeman, 1841.

Heilbroner, Robert L. *The Making of Economic Society*. Englewood Cliffs, N.J.: Prentice-Hall, 1962.

Hemingway, Ernest. *Across the River and into the Trees*. 1950. Reprint, New York: Dell, n.d.

———. *For Whom the Bell Tolls*. New York: Scribner, 1940.

———. *The Green Hills of Africa*. 1935. Reprint, New York: Permabooks, 1956.

Hemmings, F. W. J., ed. *The Age of Realism*. [Atlantic Highlands], N.J.: Humanities Press, 1974.

Hennessy, Brendan. *The Gothic Novel*. London: Longman, 1978.

Hesse, Hermann. *Blick ins Chaos*. Bern: Seldwyla, 1922.

Himmelfarb, Gertrude. *Darwin and the Darwinian Revolution*. New York: W. W. Norton, 1962.

Hicks, Granville. "The Politics of John Dos Passos." In *Dos Passos, the Critics, and the Writer's Intention,* edited by Allen Belkind. Carbondale: Southern Illinois University Press, 1971.

Hite, Molly. *Ideas of Order in the Novels of Thomas Pynchon.* Columbus: Ohio State University, 1983.

Hoffman, Daniel. *Poe, Poe, Poe, Poe, Poe, Poe, Poe.* New York: Doubleday, 1972.

Hook, Andrew, ed. *Dos Passos: A Collection of Critical Essays.* Englewood Cliffs, N.J.: Prentice-Hall, 1974.

Hooper, Finley. *Greek Realities: Life and Thought in Ancient Greece.* New York: Scribner, 1967.

Horton, Philip. *Hart Crane: The Life of an American Poet.* New York: W. W. Norton, 1937.

Howard, June. *Form and History in American Literary Naturalism.* Chapel Hill: University of North Carolina Press, 1985.

Hoyles, John. *The Literary Underground: Writers and the Totalitarian Experience, 1900–1950.* New York: St. Martin's Press, 1991.

Hugo, Victor. *Les Misérables,* translated by Norman Denny. New York: Penguin Books, 1976.

Huizinga, Johan. *The Waning of the Middle Ages: The Study of the Forms of Life, Thought, and Art in France and the Netherlands in the XIVth and XVth Centuries.* London: Edward Arnold, 1924.

Hunter, Allan. *Joseph Conrad and the Ethics of Darwinism: The Challenge of Science.* London: Croom Helm, 1983.

Huysmans, J. K. *Against the Grain (À Rebours).* 1884. Reprint, New York: Dover, 1969.

Hyams, Edward. *The Changing Face of England.* Harmondsworth: Penguin Books, 1974.

Hyslop, Lois, and Francis Hyslop, eds. and trans. *Baudelaire on Poe.* Bald Eagle, Pa.: Bald Eagle Press, 1952.

Jackson, Kenneth. *Crabgrass Frontier.* New York: Oxford University Press, 1985.

Jacobs, Jane. *The Economy of Cities.* New York: Random House, 1969.

Jameson, Fredric. "Postmodernism, or the Cultural Logic of Late Capitalism" (1984). In *Postmodernism, or, The Cultural Logic of Late Capitalism.* Durham, N.C.: Duke University Press, 1991.

Jaye, Michael C., and Ann Chalmers Watts, eds. *Literature and the Urban Experience.* New Brunswick, N.J.: Rutgers University Press, 1981.

Jefferson, Thomas. *Notes on the State of Virginia.* 1784–85. Reprint, Chapel Hill: University of North Carolina Press, 1964.

Johnson, James Weldon. *Black Manhattan.* 1930. Reprint, New York: Da Capa, 1991.

Jouve, Nicole Ward. *Baudelaire: A Fire to Conquer Darkness.* London: Macmillan, 1980.

Joyce, James. *The Critical Writings,* edited by Ellsworth Moran and Richard Ellmann. New York: Viking, 1959.

———. *A Portrait of the Artist as a Young Man.* 1916. Reprint, New York: Modern Library, 1944.

———. *Stephen Hero,* edited by Theodore Spencer. New York: New Directions, 1944.

———. *Ulysses.* 1922. Reprint, New York: Random House, 1961. [See also the edition by Hans Walter Gabler (New York: Vintage, 1986).]

Kain, Richard M. "Grace." In *James Joyce's "Dubliners,"* edited by Clive Hart. London: Faber and Faber, 1969.

Kaplan, Amy. *The Social Construction of American Realism.* Chicago: University of Chicago Press, 1988.

Kaplan, Charles. *Walt Whitman: A Life.* New York: Simon and Schuster, 1980.

Kenner, Hugh. *Ulysses.* London: Allen and Unwin, 1980.

———. "The Urban Apocalypse." In *Eliot in His Time,* edited by A. Walton Litz. Princeton: Princeton University Press, 1973.

Kiberd, Declan. *Inventing Ireland.* London: Jonathan Cape, 1995.

Kinkead-Weeks, Mark. "Defoe and Richardson—Novelists of the City." In vol. 4 of *History of Literature in the English Language, Dryden to Johnson,* edited by Roger Lonsdale. London: Sphere, 1971.

Knapp, Bettina L. *Emile Zola.* New York: Frederick Ungar, 1980.

Konvitz, Josef W. *The Urban Millennium: The City-Building Process from the Early Middle Ages to the Present.* Carbondale: Southern Illinois University Press, 1985.

Konvitz, Milton R. Introduction to *Emerson: A Collection of Critical Essays,* edited by Milton R. Konvitz and Stephen E. Whicher. Englewood Cliffs, N.J.: Prentice-Hall, 1962.

Konvitz, Milton R., and Stephen E. Whicher, eds. *Emerson: A Collection of Critical Essays.* Englewood Cliffs, N.J.: Prentice-Hall, 1962.

Kott, Jan. *The Eating of the Gods: An Interpretation of Greek Tragedy,* translated by Boleslaw Taborsky and Edward J. Czerwinski. London: Methuen, 1974.

Krampen, Martin. *Meaning in the Urban Environment.* London: Pion, 1979.

Landes, David S. *The Rise of Capitalism.* New York: Macmillan, 1969.

Lasch, Christopher. *The Culture of Narcissism: American Life in an Age of Diminishing Expectations.* New York: W. W. Norton, 1979.

Leatherdale, Clive. *The Origins of Dracula: The Background to Bram Stoker's Gothic Masterpiece.* London: William Kimber, 1987.

Le Bon, Gustave. *The Crowd: A Study of the Popular Mind.* 1896. Reprint, New York: Viking, 1960.

Le Corbusier. *The City of Tomorrow,* translated by Frederick Etchells. New York: Paysen and Clark, 1929.

———. *When Cathedrals Were White,* translated by Francis E. Hyslop, Jr. New York: Reynal and Hitchcock, 1947.

Lees, Andrew. *Cities Perceived: Urban Society in American and European Thought, 1820–1940.* New York: Columbia University Press, 1985.

Lehan, Richard. "The American Crusoe and the Idea of the West." In *Making America: The Society and Culture of the United States,* edited by Luther S. Luedtke. Chapel Hill: University of North Carolina Press, 1992.

———. "American Literary Naturalism: The French Connection." *Nineteenth-Century Fiction* 38 (1984): 529–57.

——. *A Dangerous Crossing: French Literary Existentialism and the Modern American Novel.* Carbondale: Southern Illinois University Press, 1973.

——. "Existentialism in Recent American Fiction: The Demonic Quest." *Texas Studies* 1 (1959): 181–202.

——. "F. Scott Fitzgerald and Romantic Destiny." *Twentieth Century Literature* 26 (1980): 137–56.

——. *F. Scott Fitzgerald and the Craft of Fiction.* Carbondale: Southern Illinois University Press, 1966.

——. *"The Great Gatsby": The Limits of Wonder.* Boston: G. K. Hall, 1990.

——. *Theodore Dreiser: His World and His Novels.* Carbondale: Southern Illinois University Press, 1969.

——. "Urban Signs and Urban Literature: Literary Form and Historical Process." *New Literary History* 18 (1986–87): 99–113.

Lethaby, W. R. *Architecture, Mysticism, and Myth.* New York: George Braziller, 1975.

Levin, Harry. *James Joyce: A Critical Introduction.* Norfolk, Conn.: New Directions, 1941.

Lewis, Matthew Gregory. *The Monk.* 1796. Reprint, New York: Oxford University Press, 1980.

Lewis, R. W. B. *The American Adam: Innocence, Tragedy, and Tradition in the Nineteenth Century.* Chicago: University of Chicago Press, 1955.

——. *The Poetry of Hart Crane: A Critical Study.* Princeton: Princeton University Press, 1972.

Lillywhite, Bryant. *London Coffee Houses.* London: Gallen and Unwin, 1963.

Lindsay, Jack. *The Monster City: Defoe's London, 1688–1730.* London: Hart Davis, 1978.

Litz, A. Walton. "Two Gallants." In *James Joyce's "Dubliners,"* edited by Clive Hart. London: Faber and Faber, 1969.

——, ed. *Eliot in His Time: Essays on the Occasion of the Fiftieth Anniversary of "The Waste Land."* Princeton: Princeton University Press, 1973.

Lopez, Robert S. "The Crossroads within the Wall." In *The Historian and the City,* edited by Oscar Handlin and John Burchard. Cambridge, Mass.: MIT Press, 1962.

Lowell, Robert. *For the Union Dead.* New York: Farrar, Straus, and Giroux, 1964.

——. "Thomas, Bishop, and Williams." *Sewanee Review* 55 (1947): 493–503.

Lynch, Kevin. *A Theory of the Good City.* 1970. Reprint, Cambridge, Mass.: MIT Press, 1981.

MacAndrew, Elizabeth. *The Gothic Tradition in Fiction.* New York: Columbia University Press, 1979.

Magalaner, Marvin, and Richard M. Kain. *Joyce: The Man, the Work, and the Reputation.* New York: New York University Press, 1956.

Mandel, Ernest. *Late Capitalism* (1975), translated by Jori DeBres. London: Verso, 1978.

Mannoni, Dominique O. *Prospero and Caliban.* New York: Frederick A. Praeger, 1964.

Manuel, Frank E. *Utopian Thought in the Western World.* 1966. Reprint, Cambridge, Mass.: Harvard University Press, 1979.

Martin, Ronald E. *American Literature and the Universe of Force*. Durham, N.C.: Duke University Press, 1981.

Martin, Timothy. *Joyce and Wagner: A Study of Influence*. Cambridge: Cambridge University Press, 1991.

Marx, Karl. *The Holy Family*. Moscow: Language Publication House, 1956.

Marx, Leo. *The Machine in the Garden: Technology and the Pastoral Idea in America*. New York: Oxford University Press, 1967.

Matthiessen, F. O. *The Achievement of T. S. Eliot*. New York: Oxford University Press, 1959.

——. *American Renaissance*. New York: Oxford University Press, 1941.

Maturin, Charles Robert. *Melmoth the Wanderer* (1820), edited by Douglas Grant. New York: Oxford University Press, 1989.

McGinty, Park. *Interpretation and Dionysus: Method in the Study of a God*. The Hague: Mouton, 1978.

McHale, Brian. *Constructing Post-Modernism*. New York: Routledge, 1992.

McKeon, Michael. *The Origins of the English Novel, 1600–1740*. Baltimore: Johns Hopkins University Press, 1987,

McLuhan, Marshall, "John Dos Passos: Technique vs. Sensibility." In *Dos Passos: A Collection of Critical Essays,* edited by Andrew Hook. Englewood Cliffs, N.J.: Prentice-Hall, 1974.

Melville, Herman. *The Confidence Man: His Masquerade* (1857), edited by Hershel Parker. New York: W. W. Norton, 1971.

——. *Omoo*. 1847. Reprint, New York: Doubleday, n.d.

——. *Pierre, or The Ambiguities*. 1852. Reprint, New York: Signet, 1964.

——. *Redburn*. 1849. Reprint, New York: Doubleday, 1957.

——. *Selected Tales and Poems,* edited by Richard Chase. New York: Rinehart, 1959.

——. "The Two Temples." In *Herman Melville*. New York: Library of America, 1984.

——. *Typee*. 1846. Reprint, New York: Grosset and Dunlap, n.d.

Merk, Frederick. *History of the Westward Movement*. New York: Knopf, 1978.

Michaels, Walter Benn. *The Gold Standard and the Logic of Naturalism*. Berkeley: University of California Press, 1987.

Mitchell, Lee Clark. *Determined Fictions: American Literary Naturalism*. New York: Columbia University Press, 1989.

Moody, A. David. *The Cambridge Companion to T. S. Eliot*. Cambridge: Cambridge University Press, 1994.

Moraze, Charles. *The Triumph of the Middle Classes*. London: Weidenfeld and Nicolson, 1957.

Moreland, Kim Ileen. *The Medievalist Impulse in American Literature: Twain, Adams, Fitzgerald, and Hemingway*. Charlottesville: University Press of Virginia, 1996.

Morris, William. *News from Nowhere*. 1891. Reprint, London: Routledge and Kegan Paul, 1970.

Mowry, George E., and Blaine A. Brownell. *The Urban Nation, 1920–1980*. New York: Hill and Wang, 1965.

Mumford, Lewis. *The City in History: Its Origins, Its Transformations, and Its Prospects.* New York: Harcourt, Brace, and World, 1961.

———. *The Culture of Cities.* New York: Harcourt, Brace, 1938.

Naisbitt, John. *Global Paradox.* New York: Morrow, 1994.

Naisbitt, John, and Patricia Aburdene. *Megatrends 2000.* New York: Avon, 1991.

Nelson, Brian, ed. *Naturalism in the European Novel: New Critical Perspectives.* New York: Berg European Studies/St. Martin's Press, 1992.

Nichols, Frederick D., and Ralph E. Griswold. *Thomas Jefferson: Landscape Architect.* Charlottesville: University Press of Virginia, 1978.

Nilsen, Helge Normann. *Hart Crane's Divided Vision: An Analysis of "The Bridge."* Oslo, Norway: Hougesund Bok & Offset, 1980.

Nordau, Max. *Degeneration* (1892). Translated 1895. Reprint, New York: H. Fertig, 1968.

Norris, Frank. "The Frontier Gone at Last." In *The Responsibilities of the Novelist.* New York: Doubleday, Doran, 1903.

———. *McTeague.* 1899. Reprint, New York: Rinehart, 1955.

———. *The Octopus.* 1901. Reprint, New York: New American Library, 1964.

———. *The Pit.* 1903. Reprint, New York: Grove Press, n.d.

———. *Vandover and the Brute.* 1914. Reprint, New York: Doubleday, Doran, 1928.

Norris, Margot. *The Decentered Universe of "Finnegans Wake": A Structuralist Analysis.* Baltimore: Johns Hopkins University Press, 1976.

Nye, Robert. *The Origins of Crowd Psychology: Gustave LeBon and the Crisis of Mass Democracy in the Third Republic.* Beverly Hills, Calif.: Sage, 1975.

O'Hanlon, Redmond. *Joseph Conrad and Charles Darwin: The Influence of Scientific Thought on Conrad's Fiction.* Edinburgh: Salamander Press, 1984.

Olsen, Donald. *The City as a Work of Art.* New Haven: Yale University Press, 1986.

Olson, Philip, ed. *America as a Mass Society.* New York: Free Press, 1963.

Oppenheim, A. Leo. *Ancient Mesopotamia: Portrait of a Dead Civilization.* Chicago: University of Chicago Press, 1964.

Orwell, George. *Nineteen Eighty-Four.* New York: New American Library, 1949.

Ousby, Ian. *Bloodhounds of Heaven: The Detective Novel in English Fiction from Godwin to Doyle.* Cambridge, Mass.: Harvard University Press, 1976.

Owen, E. J. *The City in the Greek and Roman World.* New York: Routledge, 1991.

Park, Robert Ezra, with Ernest W. Burgess and Roderick D. McKenzie. *The City.* Chicago: University of Chicago Press, 1925.

Pater, Walter. Preface and Conclusion to *The Renaissance.* In *Criticism: The Major Texts,* edited by W. J. Bate. New York: Harcourt, Brace, 1952.

Paul, Sherman. *Hart's Bridge.* Urbana: University of Illinois Press, 1972.

Payne, Robert. *The Triumph of the Greeks.* London: Hamish Hamilton, 1964.

Pearce, Richard, ed. *Critical Essays on Thomas Pynchon* Boston: G. K. Hall, 1981.

Pearce, Roy Harvey, ed. *Whitman: Critical Essays.* Englewood Cliffs, N.J.: Prentice-Hall, 1962.

Peck, Daniel. *Faces of Degeneration: A European Disorder, 1848–1919.* Cambridge: Cambridge University Press, 1989.

Perl, Jeffrey. *Skepticism and Modern Enmity.* Baltimore: Johns Hopkins University Press, 1989.

Phillipe, Charles-Louise. *Bubu of Montparnasse* (1901), translated by Alan Ross. Rev. ed. London: Weidenfeld and Nicolson, 1952.

Pike, Burton. *The Image of the City in Modern Literature.* Princeton: Princeton University Press, 1981.

Pirenne, Henri. *Economic and Social History of Medieval Europe.* New York: Harcourt, Brace, and World, 1937.

Pizer, Donald. *The Novels of Frank Norris.* Bloomington: Indiana University Press, 1966.

——. *Realism and Naturalism in Nineteenth-Century America.* Rev. ed. Carbondale: Southern Illinois University Press, 1984.

——. *The Theory and Practice of American Literary Naturalism: Selected Essays and Reviews.* Carbondale: Southern Illinois University Press, 1993.

——. *Twentieth-Century American Literary Naturalism: An Interpretation.* Carbondale: Southern Illinois University Press, 1982.

Poe, Edgar Allan. *Complete Works.* 10 vols. New York: Lamb Publishing, 1902.

——. *The Narrative of Arthur Gordon Pym.* 1838. Reprint, New York: Heritage Press, 1930.

——. *The Selected Poetry and Prose,* edited by T. O. Mabbott. New York: Modern Library, 1951.

——. *Tales and Poems,* edited by Philip Van Doren Stern. New York: Viking, 1945.

Poirier, Richard. *A World Elsewhere: The Place of Style in American Literature.* New York: Oxford University Press, 1966.

Polanyi, Karl. *The Great Transformation.* New York: Rinehart, 1944.

Pope, John C. "Prufrock and Raskolnikov Again: A Letter from Eliot." *American Literature* 18 (1947): 319–21.

Prendergast, Christopher. *Balzac: Fiction and Melodrama.* London: Edward Arnold, 1978.

——. *Paris and the Nineteenth Century.* Oxford: Blackwell, 1992.

Procopiou, Angelo. *Athens: City of the Gods, from Prehistory to 338.* New York: Stein and Day, 1964.

Punter, David. *A History of Gothic Fiction, 1765 to the Present.* London: Longmans, 1979.

Pynchon, Thomas. *The Crying of Lot 49.* 1966. Reprint, New York: Bantam Books, 1967.

——. *Gravity's Rainbow.* New York: Vintage, 1973.

——. *Slow Learner: Early Stories.* Boston: Little, Brown, 1984.

——. *V., a Novel.* 1963. Reprint, New York: Bantam, 1968.

Quinones, R. J. *Mapping Literary Modernism.* Princeton: Princeton University Press, 1985.

Radcliffe, Ann. *The Mysteries of Udolpho.* 1794. Reprint, New York: Oxford University Press, 1970.

Rancy, Catherine. *Fantastique et décadence en Angleterre, 1890–1914*. Paris: Editions du CNRS, 1982.

Reddaway, Thomas. *The Rebuilding of London after the Great Fire*. London: Jonathan Cape, 1940.

Reynolds, David S. *Walt Whitman's America*. New York: Knopf, 1995.

Rich, John, and Andrew Wallace, eds. *City and Country in the Ancient World*. New York: Routledge, 1991.

Richards, Thomas. *The Imperial Archive: Knowledge and the Fantasy of Empire*. London: Verso, 1993.

Richardson, Samuel. *Clarissa*. 1747–48. Reprint, Boston: Houghton Mifflin, 1962.

Richetti, John J. *Defoe's Narratives: Situations and Structures*. Oxford: Clarendon Press, 1975.

Ridley, Hugh. *Images of Imperial Rule*. New York: St. Martin's Press, 1983.

Rifkin, Jeremy. *Entropy: A New World View*. Rev. ed. New York: Bantam Books, 1989.

Risjord, Norman K. *Thomas Jefferson*. Madison, Wis.: Madison House, 1994.

Roby, Kinley E., ed. *Critical Essays on T. S. Eliot: The Sweeney Motif*. Boston: G. K. Hall, 1985.

Rodwin, Lloyd, ed. *The Future Metropolis*. New York: George Braziller, 1961.

Rosenberg, Samuel. *Naked Is the Best Disguise: The Death and Resurrection of Sherlock Holmes*. Indianapolis: Bobbs-Merrill, 1974.

Roszak, Theodore. *The Making of a Counter-Culture: Reflections on the Technocratic Society and Its Youthful Opposition*. New York: Doubleday, 1969.

Rude, George. *Hanoverian London, 1714–1808*. Berkeley: University of California Press, 1971.

Ryan, Judith. *The Vanishing Subject: Early Psychology and Literary Modernism*. Chicago: University of Chicago Press, 1991.

Saggs, H. W. F. *The Greatness That Was Babylon: A Sketch of the Ancient Civilization of the Tigris-Euphrates Valley*. New York: Hawthorn Books, 1962.

Said, Edward. *Joseph Conrad and the Fiction of Autobiography*. Cambridge, Mass.: Harvard University Press, 1966.

Santayana, George. *The Genteel Tradition*. 1913. Reprint, Cambridge, Mass.: Harvard University Press, 1967.

Schaefer, Jack. *Shane*. 1949. Reprint, New York: Bantam Books, 1983.

Schaub, Thomas H. *Pynchon: The Voice of Ambiguity*. Urbana: University of Illinois Press, 1981.

Schlesinger, Arthur M., Sr. *The Rise of the City, 1878–1898*. New York: Macmillan, 1933.

Schneider, Wolf. *Babylon Is Everywhere: The City as Man's Fate*. New York: McGraw-Hill, 1963.

Schorske, Carl. *Fin-de-Siècle Vienna: Politics and Culture*. New York: Knopf, 1980.

Schwarzbach, F. S. *Dickens and the City*. London: Athlone Press, 1979.

Scully, Stephen. *Homer and the Sacred City*. Ithaca: Cornell University Press, 1990.

Scully, Vincent J. *American Architecture and Urbanism.* New York: Praeger, 1969.

——. *The Rise of American Architecture.* New York: Praeger, 1970.

Sedgwick, Eve. *The Coherence of Gothic Conventions.* New York: Methuen, 1986.

Seidel, Michael. *Epic Geography: James Joyce's "Ulysses."* Princeton: Princeton University Press, 1976.

Sennett, Richard. *Classic Essays on Culture and Cities.* New York: Appleton, Century, Crofts, 1969.

——. *The Fall of Public Man.* New York: Knopf, 1977.

——. *The Uses of Disorder: Personal Identity and City Life.* New York: Knopf, 1970.

Sharpe, William. *Unreal Cities: Urban Figuration in Wordsworth, Baudelaire, Whitman, Eliot, and Williams.* Baltimore: Johns Hopkins University Press, 1990.

Sharpe, William, and Leonard Wallock, eds. *Visions of the Modern City: Essays in History, Art, Literature.* Baltimore: Johns Hopkins University Press, 1987.

Sherry, Norman. *Conrad's Western World.* Cambridge: Cambridge University Press, 1971.

Shirer, William L. *The Rise and Fall of the Third Reich.* New York: Fawcett Crest, 1960.

Silverman, Kenneth. *Edgar A. Poe: Mournful and Never-Ending Remembrance.* New York: Harper Collins, 1991.

Simmel, Georg. "The Metropolis and Mental Life." In *Individuality and Social Forms,* edited by Donald Levine. Chicago: University of Chicago Press, 1971.

——. *The Philosophy of Money* (1900), translated by Tom Bottomore and David Frisby. London: Routledge and Kegan Paul, 1978.

Sjoberg, Gideon. *The Preindustrial City, Past and Present.* Glencoe, Ill.: Free Press, 1960.

Skaff, William. *The Philosophy of T. S. Eliot: From Skepticism to a Surrealistic Poetic, 1909–1927.* Philadelphia: University of Pennsylvania Press, 1986.

Slade, Joseph W. *Thomas Pynchon.* New York: Warner, 1974.

Slochower, Harry S. *Literature and Philosophy Between Two World Wars.* New York: Citadel Press, 1964.

Slotkin, Richard. *The Fatal Environment: The Myth of the Frontier in the Age of Industrialization, 1800–1890.* New York: Atheneum, 1985.

——. *Gunfighter Nation: The Myth of the Frontier in Twentieth-Century America.* New York: Atheneum, 1992.

——. *Regeneration Through Violence: The Mythology of the American Frontier, 1660–1860.* Middletown, Conn.: Wesleyan University Press, 1973.

Smith, Michael. *The City and Social Theory.* New York: St. Martin's Press, 1979.

Snodgrass, Anthony. *Archaic Greece: The Age of Experiment.* Berkeley: University of California Press, 1980.

Spears, M. K. *Dionysus and the City.* New York: Oxford University Press, 1970.

Spencer, Herbert. *First Principles.* New York: D. Appleton, 1898.

Spengler, Oswald. *The Decline of the West* (1918–22), translated by Charles F. Atkinson. 2 vols. New York: Knopf, 1926–28.

Squier, Susan Merrill, ed. *Women Writers and the City.* Knoxville: University of Tennessee Press, 1984.

Stallybrass, Peter, and Allon White. *The Politics and Poetics of Transgression.* Ithaca: Cornell University Press, 1980.

Starr, Chester G. *The Ancient Romans.* New York: Oxford University Press, 1971.

Steiner, George. "The City under Attack." *Salmagundi,* no. 24 (1973): 3–18.

Stern, Fritz. *The Politics of Cultural Despair: A Study in the Rise of German Ideology.* Berkeley: University of California Press, 1961.

Stoker, Bram. *Dracula.* 1897. Reprint, New York: Oxford University Press, 1983.

Stoltzfus, Ben. "John Dos Passos and the French." In *Dos Passos, The Critics, and the Writer's Intention,* edited by Allen Belkind. Carbondale: Southern Illinois University Press, 1971.

Stone, Lawrence. *The Crisis of the Aristocracy, 1558–1641.* Oxford: Clarendon, 1965

Strout, Cushing. *The American Image of the Old World.* New York: Harper and Row, 1963.

Sue, Eugène. *The Mysteries of Paris.* London: G. Routledge, n.d.

Sultan, Stanley. *Eliot, Joyce, and Co.* New York: Oxford University Press, 1987.

Sypher, Wylie. *Loss of the Self in Modern Literature.* Westport, Conn.: Greenwood Press, 1979.

Tafuri, Manfredo. *Architecture and Utopia: Design and Capitalistic Development,* translated by Barbara Luigi La Penta. Cambridge, Mass.: MIT Press, 1976.

Tapscott, Stephen. *American Beauty: William Carlos Williams and the Modernist Whitman.* New York: Columbia University Press, 1984.

Tawney, R. H. *Religion and the Rise of Capitalism.* New York: Harcourt, Brace, 1926.

———. "The Rise of the Gentry, 1558–1640." *Economic Historical Review* 11 (1941): 1–38.

Taylor, George Rogers. *The Turner Thesis.* Boston: D. C. Heath, 1956.

Theal, Donald F. *The Medium in the Rear View Mirror: Understanding McLuhan.* Montreal: McGill-Queen's University Press, 1971.

Thornton, R. K. R. *The Decadent Dilemma.* London: E. Arnold, 1983.

Toffler, Alvin. *The Third Wave.* New York: Bantam Books, 1981.

Tompkins, Jane P. *West of Everything.* New York: Oxford University Press, 1992.

Toynbee, Arnold, ed. *Cities of Destiny.* London: Thames and Hudson, 1967.

Trachtenberg, Alan, ed. *Hart Crane: A Collection of Critical Essays.* Englewood Cliffs, N.J.: Prentice-Hall, 1982.

Trachtenberg, Alan, Peter Neill, and Peter C. Bunnell, eds. *The City: American Experience.* New York: Oxford University Press, 1977.

Trachtenberg, Stanley. *The Postmodern Movement.* Westport, Conn.: Greenwood Press, 1985.

Trotter, David. *Circulation: Defoe, Dickens, and the Economies of the Novel.* London: Macmillan, 1988.

Turner, Frederick Jackson. *The Frontier in American History.* New York: Henry Holt, 1920.

Twain, Mark. *The Complete Novels of Mark Twain,* edited by Charles Neider. 2 vols. Garden City, N.Y.: Doubleday, 1964.

——. *A Connecticut Yankee in King Arthur's Court.* 1889. Reprint, New York: Morrow, 1988.

——. "Notebooks." Twain Collection. Bancroft Library, University of California, Berkeley.

——. "Notes for a Social History of the United States from 1850 to 1900." Twain Collection. Bancroft Library, University of California, Berkeley.

Unterecker, John. *Voyager: A Life of Hart Crane.* New York: Farrar, Straus, and Giroux, 1969.

Vance, James E., Jr. *The Continuing City: Urban Morphology in Western Civilization.* Baltimore: Johns Hopkins University Press, 1990.

Varman, Devendra. *The Gothic Flame.* London: Arthur Baker, 1957.

Venturi, Robert, and Denise Scott Brown. *Learning from Las Vegas.* Cambridge, Mass.: MIT Press, 1977.

Vidler, Anthony. *The Architectural Uncanny: Essays in the Modern Unhomely.* Cambridge, Mass.: MIT Press, 1992.

Von Laue, Theodore H. *The Global City: Freedom, Power, and Necessity in the Age of World Revolutions.* Philadelphia: Lippincott, 1969.

Wade, Richard. *The Urban Frontier.* Cambridge, Mass.: Harvard University Press, 1959.

Walcutt, Charles Child. *American Literary Naturalism: A Divided Stream.*1956. Reprint, Westport, Conn.: Greenwood Press, 1973.

Walpole, Horace. *The Castle of Otranto* (1764), edited by W. S. Lewis. New York: Oxford University Press, 1982.

Walzl, Florence L. "The Liturgy of the Epiphany Season and the Epiphanies of Joyce." *PMLA* 80 (1965): 463–50.

Wasson, Richard. "The Politics of Dracula." *English Literature in Transition* 9, no. 1 (1966): 24–27.

Watt, Ian. *Conrad in the Nineteenth Century.* Berkeley: University of California Press, 1979.

——. *The Rise of the Novel: Studies in Defoe, Richardson, and Fielding.* Berkeley: University of California Press, 1957.

Weaver, Mike. *William Carlos Williams: The American Background.* Cambridge: Cambridge University Press, 1971.

Webb, Walter Prescott. *The Great Frontier.* Boston: Houghton Mifflin, 1952.

Weber, Max. *The City,* translated and edited by Don Martindale and Gertrude Neuwirth. New York: Free Press, 1968.

——. *The Protestant Ethic and the Spirit of Capitalism,* translated by Talcott Parsons. New York: Scribner, 1976.

Weimar, David R. *The City as Metaphor.* New York: Random House, 1966.

Wells, H. G. *The Complete Science Fiction Treasury.* New York: Avenel Books, 1978.

——. *The Invisible Man.* 1897. Reprint, London: Collins, 1953.

——. *The Island of Dr. Moreau.* 1896. Reprint, New York: Signet, 1988.

——. *The Mind at the End of Its Tether.* London: William Heinemann, 1945.

——. *The Time Machine.* 1895. Reprint, New York: Random House, 1931.

——. *When the Sleeper Wakes.* 1899. Reprint, London: Thomas Nelson and Sons, 1910.

Welsh, Alexander. *The City of Dickens.* Oxford: Clarendon Press, 1971.

Weston, Jessie. *From Ritual to Romance.* Cambridge: Cambridge University Press, 1920.

Whitman, Walt. *Complete Poetry and Collected Prose.* New York: Library of America, 1982.

——. *Leaves of Grass and Selected Prose,* edited by John Kouwenhoven. New York: Modern Library, 1950.

——. *Song of Myself,* edited by James E. Miller. New York: Dodd, Mead, 1964.

Wiener, Norbert. *The Human Use of Human Beings: Cybernetics and Society.* 1967. Reprint, New York: Avon Books, 1970.

Wilde, Oscar. "The Decay of Lying." In *Intentions.* New York: Dodd, Mead, 1894.

Williams, D. A., ed. *The Monster in the Mirror: Studies in Nineteenth-Century Realism.* New York: Oxford University Press, 1978.

Williams, Raymond. *The Country and the City.* New York: Oxford University Press, 1973.

Williams, William Carlos. *Autobiography.* New York: Random House, 1951.

——. *In the American Grain.* 1925. Reprint, New York: New Directions, 1956.

——. *Paterson.* 1958. Reprint, New York: New Directions, 1963.

——. *Selected Essays.* New York: New Directions, 1954.

——. *A Voyage to Pagany.* 1928. Reprint, New York: New Directions, 1970.

——. *The William Carlos Williams Reader,* edited by M. L. Rosenthal. New York: New Directions, 1962.

Wilt, Judith. *Ghosts of the Gothic.* Princeton: Princeton University Press, 1980.

Winks, Robin W. *The Myth of the American Frontier.* Leicester: Leicester University Press, 1971.

——, ed. *Detective Fiction: A Collection of Critical Essays.* Englewood Cliffs, N.J.: Prentice-Hall, 1980.

Wirth-Nesher, Hana. *City Codes: Reading the Modern Urban Novel.* Cambridge: Cambridge University Press, 1996.

Wister, Owen. *The Virginian.* 1902. Reprint, New York: Signet, 1979.

Wolf, John B. *France, 1840–1919.* New York: Harper and Row, 1963.

Wycherley, R. E. *How the Greeks Built Cities.* London: Macmillan, 1967.

Zola, Emile. *L'Assommoir,* translated by Leonard Tancock. New York: Penguin Books, 1970.

——. *La Bête Humaine,* translated by Louis Colman. New York: Julian Press, 1932.

——. *The Debacle (La Débâcle),* translated by Leonard Tancock. New York: Penguin Books, 1972.

——. *The Earth (La Terre),* translated by Douglas Parmee. New York: Penguin Books, 1980.

——. *Germinal,* translated by Leonard Tancock. Baltimore: Penguin Classics, 1954.

——. *Rougon-Macquart,* translated by Edward Vizetelly. 14 vols. London: Vizetelly, 1886.

Index

Absalom, Absalom! (Faulkner), 186
Across the River and into the Trees (Hemingway), 255
Adams, Henry: belief in entropy, 268, 269; Education, 127, 210, 248n; influences on, 77; nostalgia for Middle Ages/aristocracy, 210n; Virgin and Dynamo, 231, 270
Adventures of a Young Man (Dos Passos), 237
Aeschylus: Oresteia trilogy, 18
aestheticism, 74–75, 77, 105–6, 121, 148, 287. See also modernism, literary
After Strange Gods (Eliot), 189n, 220
alienation/helplessness: of blacks, 246, 249; in the mass society, 72; and Protestantism, 7
Al-Khadir, 116n
Allan Quatermain (Haggard), 93, 94
The American Scene (James), 189n
American vs. European cities, 167, 170, 288
Ames, Oakes, 188
Anderson, Chester, 116n
animality, 57, 63, 195
Annus Mirabilis (Dryden), 132
anthropology: Cambridge Ritualists, 136; magical, religious, and scientific stages of thought, 136; sacred grove of Nemi, 135–36; Victorian interest in, 92; views of the past, 136
Apollonian culture, 212, 216

archaeology, 79, 92, 111, 172
À Rebours (Huysmans), 126
L'Argent (Zola), 61, 62
aristocracy: in the American West, 251; as corrupt, 64–65, 67; the dandy, 75, 121; landed vs. moneyed, 36–39; Roman, 17, 18, 20–21
art: cubism, 78; destructiveness of, 150; impressionism, 77–79, 129; and inner reality, 80; vs. politics, 144; self as freedom of, 151. See also aestheticism
artist-flaneurs, 73, 74, 77. See also aestheticism
Artists' Plan, 53–54, 54, 73
L'Assommoir (Zola), 61, 63, 195, 219
atavism, 52
Athens, 17–18, 19–20
Atlantic cable, 183, 228
Au Bonheur des dames (Zola), 61, 62–63
Auden, W. H., 143, 145, 161; City Without Walls, 144; "In Memorial for the City," 144; Look Stranger! 144; "Paysage Moralisé," 144; Poems, 144; The Sea and the Mirror, 144; "Spain," 144
Augusta Triumphans (Defoe), 34
Augustine, Saint, 225; City of God, 6, 22–23, 131, 151
Augustus, 21
Austen, Jane, 37; Mansfield Park, 38–39; Northanger Abbey, 39

Compositor:	Impressions Book and Journal Services, Inc.
Text:	10/13 Galliard
Display:	Galliard
Printer and Binder:	Edwards Brothers, Inc.